ENCYCLOPEDIA OF THE MEXICAN AMERICAN CIVIL RIGHTS MOVEMENT

"Sal si Puedes" (Homage to César Chávez). Painting by Alfredo Arreguín. Photo by Rob Vinnedge. Reproduced with permission.

ENCYCLOPEDIA OF THE MEXICAN AMERICAN CIVIL RIGHTS MOVEMENT

**Matt S. Meier
and
Margo Gutiérrez**

Foreword by Antonia Hernández

GREENWOOD PRESS
Westport, Connecticut • London

Library of Congress Cataloging-in-Publication Data

Meier, Matt S.
  Encyclopedia of the Mexican American civil rights movement / Matt
S. Meier and Margo Gutiérrez ; foreword by Antonia Hernández.
    p. cm.
  Includes bibliographical references and index.
  ISBN 0–313–30425–4 (alk. paper)
    1. Mexican Americans—Civil rights—History—20th century
Encyclopedias. 2. Civil rights movements—United States—
History—20th century Encyclopedias. I. Gutiérrez, Margo.
II. Title.
  E184.M5M458 2000
  305.86872073'03—dc21   99–16143

British Library Cataloguing in Publication Data is available.

Library of Congress Catalog Card Number: 99–16143
ISBN: 0–313–30425–4

First published in 2000

Greenwood Press, 88 Post Road West, Westport, CT 06881
An imprint of Greenwood Publishing Group, Inc.
www.greenwood.com

Printed in the United States of America

The paper used in this book complies with the
Permanent Paper Standard issued by the National
Information Standards Organization (Z39.48–1984).

10 9 8 7 6 5 4 3 2 1

This book is dedicated to the memory of César Chávez, Ernesto Galarza, Gus García, Héctor Pérez García, Jovita Idar, Luisa Moreno, Graciela Oli-várez, Alonso Perales, George I. Sánchez, and the many other Mexican Americans, men and women, great and ordinary, living and dead, who fought and continue to fight resolutely for the civil rights of la raza.

Contents

Foreword

Documenting the history of Latinos in the United States has been very difficult because historians who have written the history of the United States have ignored the Latino Community. Until recently, we have been an invisible community. We have begun to emerge from obscurity as more Latinos take on the task of documenting our struggles and our many contributions to the American landscape.

The *Encyclopedia of the Mexican American Civil Rights Movement* serves as a rich source of up to date information on our people, their organizations, events, and issues shaping our community and society at large. As our community grows and becomes a larger presence in the American Landscape, the need to educate our children about our history also grows. It is very important for our children to know about the great men and women who came before us and fought a great struggle to insure that we as a community gain our rightful place in the American life. As we continue our struggle, organizations like Mexican American Legal Defense and Educational Fund (MALDEF) will continue protecting the interests of all Latinos, while serving as a role model for our young aspiring students who will be the leaders of tomorrow.

The *Encyclopedia* serves as a tool as we shape our future; knowing our past makes it possible to plan with great pride and dignity for a future not just for Latinos, but for all America.

Antonia Hernández
President and General Counsel
Mexican American Legal Defense and Educational Fund

Preface

In the growing body of literature on the Mexican American experience, there is a noticeable void on the subject of their struggle for civil rights in society and equality before the law. The authors hope that this work will fill that void. It is broadly conceived as a reference tool for those seeking basic information on the many aspects of the long Mexican American quest for civil rights and on the leading people involved, a story still told only in bits and pieces, a history much in need of intensive research and writing. In this single-volume reference work, concisely written entries offer a handy, up-to-date source of basic information on all aspects of that struggle. It includes the high points and low, succinct biographical sketches of its leaders, the histories of its organizations, legislation, and legal cases, accounts of its outstanding historical events, its failures and successes.

Some entries are obviously more important and central than others to the civil rights efforts of la raza and are, therefore, more detailed. The entries range in length from a concise paragraph to several pages. All are written in easily readable language and are followed by brief selected bibliographic suggestions for further reading. The suggested works are intended to provide a basis for additional details about the subject of each entry. They do not form a complete bibliography of the topic, nor do they include all the sources consulted. Theses, newspaper articles, and non–English language works have generally not been included, except in cases where they provide useful further information otherwise unavailable.

The reader is asked to note that the terms *Mexican American* and *Chicano* are used completely interchangeably. The broader but widely employed terms *raza* and *Mexicano* are also used in a cultural sense. Mexicano is used to refer to "mexicanos de este lado y del otro," that is, both Mexican Americans and non-U.S.-citizen Mexicans working and living in the United States. Persons of Mexican descent, citizens and sojourners alike, in

the past have frequently been, and today sometimes still are, lumped together as Mexican, especially in popular usage and particularly along the
border.

The terms *Tejano, Californio,* and *Nuevomexicano* are used to refer to
and to distinguish from Anglos the Mexican-descent persons of Texas, California, and New Mexico. The term *Anglo* is regularly employed to refer
to Americans of non–Mexican European descent. The four Spanish language words Mexicano, Tejano, Californio, and Nuevomexicano, are not
italicized but are capitalized in deference to English spelling practice. The
reader is asked to take note also that the broad terms *Latino* and *Hispanic*
(which may be applied to all persons of Spanish cultural background, not
only U.S Latinos) are sometimes used to refer to U.S. Latinos, usually because statistics are given in this wider category. The words *Latino* and
Hispanic are used interchangeably in this work.

The appendices include a chronology of the Mexican American civil
rights struggle, the Bill of Rights, the Fourteenth Amendment, Article IX
of the Treaty of Guadalupe Hidalgo (which guaranteed the civil rights of
the former Mexican citizens), a list of acronyms useful for identifying organizations in this work and elsewhere, and a brief Spanish-language pro-
nunciation guide. The detailed index provides easy access to further
information on the Mexican Americans' long battle for their civil rights.

In developing this encyclopedia the authors had the paramount satisfac-
tion and gratification of knowing that it would provide inquiring readers
with a useful tool for basic information and further research. The principal
frustration was the occasional difficulty in obtaining information, most of
which should have been readily available. A surprising number of queries
to organizations and individuals went unanswered; their positive responses
might have provided some entries with further valuable detail.

Acknowledgments

It is a truism that an undertaking such as this is the work of many hands. We wish to acknowledge the help of colleagues in our own universities, of librarians in the Southwest, and of others—especially Ann Beyer, Jesse Bernal, Gilberto Cárdenas, Martha Cotera, Steven Gelber, Ascensión Hernández, Ed Idar, Amanda Salinas, and Emilio Zamora.

Introduction

Mexican Americans, like many other Americans, have a long history of struggle for equality and civil rights. The Mexicano fight against discrimination and racism as manifested in Anglo political and societal institutions began in Texas at least a decade before the U.S.–Mexican War and the 1848 Treaty of Guadalupe Hidalgo. However, only in recent decades has the story of that striving begun to be included as a part of mainstream American history.

For convenience the history of the Mexican American struggle for civil rights may be divided into two broad time periods. The first stage, covering the century from the 1836 Texas revolt against the newly centralized Mexican government to the depression of the 1930s, was 100 years of limited regional, local, and individual efforts to assert and defend the rights guaranteed the new Americans by the Treaty of Guadalupe Hidalgo. The second period, characterized by extensive development of regional and national organizations as well as local groups and by a clarification and amplification of those rights, covers the remainder of the twentieth century.

During the first period the struggle began in Texas rather than in New Mexico or California for simple reasons, primarily having to do with geographic location, economic conditions, and the relative sizes of the Anglo and Mexicano populations. In the New Mexico region at the time of the Treaty of Guadalupe Hidalgo some 60,000 Nuevomexicanos, or Hispanos as most usually referred to themselves, formed a preponderant majority of the population and remained a numerical majority in the territory and state until the 1930s. Their elite leaders continued to participate extensively in community affairs, local politics, and territorial and state government. In California, by contrast, by 1850 some 8,000 Mexican Americans had become completely swamped by well over 100,000 gold rush in-migrants, mostly Anglo; as a result little organizational development took place there until the heavy influx of Mexican sojourners in the first two decades of the twentieth century.

In 1850 Texas had about 5,000 Mexicanos and a constantly increasing Anglo population in which Old South attitudes about race and ethnicity dominated. Persons of Mexican ancestry, whose number had increased to 71,000 by 1900, consistently suffered from overt prejudice, discrimination, and exploitation. Frequently the courts and law enforcement officers, especially the Texas Rangers, joined ranch owners in restricting or denying the basic civil rights of Mexicanos. Early Mexican American organizations, of a mutual aid nature, were small, local, and generally weak, with limited impact on the widespread and entrenched racist practices of the Anglo political and economic ruling class.

At the beginning of the twentieth century the Mexican American demographic picture began to change dramatically, largely a result of the Mexican revolution of 1910 and the labor demands of an American Southwest that was rapidly being integrated into the national economy. A continuing heavy population movement, largely of agricultural workers, from Mexico into Texas and increasing migration from both Mexico and Texas into California began to create a new set of demographic, economic, and social conditions.

By the end of the 1920s California, with 368,000 persons of Mexican descent, had become the state with the second largest population of Mexicanos. As the Mexicano presence became more highly visible in California, more virulent anti-Mexican attitudes began to develop as they had earlier in Texas. These discriminatory views, expressed in an increasing infringement and denial of civil rights, were given a boost by the Great Depression, which by the end of the 1920s had already begun to seriously reduce employment opportunities for Anglos and Mexicanos alike.

A second factor in arousing Mexican American concerns was the 1930s repatriation movement, in which the civil liberties of American citizens of Mexican descent as well as those of noncitizens were often ignored or violated. As a result, Mexican Americans began taking more serious steps to unite for their protection. Organizations like the League of United Latin American Citizens not only began discussing individual and community problems but also became the training grounds for a new, larger, and more aggressive young leadership. Texas and California became the vanguard of this revitalized Mexican American civil rights movement. In Arizona, New Mexico, and Colorado concerns for the civil rights of Mexican Americans continued to center on labor-related problems and had yet to become a "hot" issue.

World War II was a third factor leading to a more organized and institutionalized defense of Chicano civil rights. The war took place during a time characterized by the coming of age of second- and third-generation Mexican Americans, most of whom, unlike their parents, felt far more

American than Mexican despite the ethnic discrimination they commonly encountered. The war itself broke down some of the barriers to their acceptance into American society, and they harbored aspirations to participation in the American dream. Organized into groups like the American G.I. Forum and the Mexican American Political Association, the World War II generation began to demand the rights for which it had fought overseas, with a particular emphasis on political rights. For a variety of historical reasons—including greater facility with English, higher educational levels, a better understanding of the U.S. political system, and the advent of mass communication—Chicano veterans were able to organize much more widely and effectively than their predecessors. Out of their efforts arose numerous associations with new and aggressive emphases on civil rights.

Strongly influenced by the black civil rights leadership's successful use of confrontation and overt action, the post–World War II Mexican American organizing explosion peaked with the Chicano Movement of the late 1960s and early 1970s. Youthful activists, frustrated by the absence of fundamental change, challenged the system and sometimes even their own community elders. By the end of the 1960s César Chávez, Corky Gonzales, José Angel Gutiérrez, and Reies López Tijerina had become recognized as preeminent leaders in the Mexican American civil rights struggle. All four rose to national prominence and then declined in importance by the late 1970s. As a result of their inspirational leadership and the work of younger activists, important strides were made in gaining political, economic, and educational rights.

Yet, in spite of the efforts and successes of the "Big Four" and of hundreds of other important but less-known leaders, the struggle to achieve complete civil rights and full acceptance into American society remains incomplete. Notable gains have been made through legal battles and direct action; but today, at the beginning of the twenty-first century, many Mexican Americans still find their rights as American citizens often ignored, challenged, or violated. At a December 1997 Los Angeles symposium titled "Latino Civil Rights Crises" Antonia Hernández, president of the leading Chicano civil rights organization, the Mexican American Legal Defense and Educational Fund, and other speakers stressed the continuing need for Chicanos to become deeply involved politically, not to achieve greater civil rights compliance but just to stem the rollback of gains made in the past quarter of a century. The Mexican American search for equality and acceptance goes on. The battle for civil rights is a never-ending struggle.

DEFINITION

The first task, to define civil rights and their parameters, is not a simple one. To begin with, the list of civil rights has not been constant. Over the decades it has frequently been expanded as various natural and social rights have been given protection of the law. Additionally, there is no general agreement as to what rights are included, or should be included, under a definition of civil rights.

A basic definition of civil rights encompasses those rights guaranteed equally to all citizens by constitutional, federal, or state legislation. A similar but somewhat more complex definition includes those personal and property rights, political, economic, and human or natural, for the violation of which citizens may have recourse in the courts as a result of constitutional or statutory law. In this work a broad view of civil rights is followed.

The law, then, provides all citizens with guarantees for their civil rights. Noncitizens may not be guaranteed all the civil rights of citizens, but they may lay claim to natural or human rights, as can citizens. Natural rights are those that should be inherent to all persons as human beings. When these hard-won rights, many of which are immunities or restraints imposed on government, are buttressed by legislation, they are termed *civil liberties* by some authorities.

The term *social rights*, as used in this work, refers to those rights or privileges in social intercourse that are not guaranteed by constitutional or statutory provisions and for the violation of which there is no recourse in law. Both human and social rights may become civil rights through the passage of legislation.

Civil rights are concerned with political, economic, and social equality. The civil rights of primary concern to most Mexican Americans include the right to

property ownership and inheritance

the vote and political participation

equal protection under the law

equal access to education

equal employment opportunities

equal access to housing

equal treatment in public facilities

without discrimination or restriction because of race, ethnicity, skin color, national origin, gender, or creed.

A

ACOSTA, OSCAR ZETA, 1936–1974? As a result of his two autobiographical novels, *The Autobiography of a Brown Buffalo*, 1972, and *The Revolt of the Cockroach People*, 1973, Oscar Acosta became widely known in the early 1970s as one of the leading activist writers in the Chicano Movement. The 1974 Bantam Press edition of *The Revolt of the Cockroach People* made him one of the very early Chicano writers to be published by a mainstream press. In his writing he described his lifelong search for identity and gave voice to some of his serious concerns about Chicano civil rights.

Born in El Paso, Texas, Acosta grew up in Modesto, California. After completing service in the U.S. Air Force during the Korean conflict and earning a college degree in creative writing he took a newspaper job in San Francisco while he studied for the law. In 1966 he went to work for the East Oakland Legal Aid Society as a legal aid attorney but soon turned to political activism.

Acosta had a prominent role in the National Chicano Moratorium and was both outspoken and widely known for his court defense of a number of Chicano confrontational activists of the late 1960s, including Sal Castro, the Biltmore 7, the East Los Angeles 13, and various Brown Berets. Unconstrained in his criticism of racism and discrimination, he was described by people who knew him as also unstable, anarchic, and often out of control. Throughout his adult life he was apparently plagued by massive insecurities and feelings of inferiority that he assuaged by overindulgence in alcohol and drugs, leading to mental breakdown and nearly a decade of psychiatric therapy.

In 1971 Acosta gave up his practice of law and in the following year was the unsuccessful Raza Unida candidate for sheriff of Los Angeles County, endorsed by the Congress of Mexican American Unity. In 1974 he mysteriously disappeared. He is believed to have died or been killed in Mazatlán, Mexico.

See also BROWN BERETS; CONGRESS OF MEXICAN AMERICAN UNITY; MOVIMIENTO, EL; NATIONAL CHICANO MORATORIUM; RAZA UNIDA PARTY, LA.

FURTHER READING: Kawalczyk, Kimberly A. "Oscar Zeta Acosta: The Brown Buffalo and his Search for Identity." *Americas Review* 19:3–4 (1989) 199–209; *Chicano Literature: A Reference Guide*. Martínez, Julio A. and Francisco A. Lomeli, eds. Westport, Conn.: Greenwood Press, 1985; Stavans, Ilan. *Bandido: Oscar Zeta Acosta and the Chicano Experience*. New York: IconEditions, 1995.

ACUÑA, RODOLFO F., 1932– . Longtime activist Rudy Acuña has been involved in a wide variety of civil rights issues and concerns ranging from union organizing in the early 1950s; to the Rumford Fair Housing Act and the Delano farmworkers' strike in the 1960s; to bilingual education, opposition to the Bakke suit, and support for La Raza Unida Party in the 1970s; to police brutality cases in the 1980s. He has served as an expert witness for the American Civil Liberties Union in various civil rights cases and was the plaintiff in a suit against the Los Angeles police department for spying on his university classes. In 1995 he was awarded $326,000 by the U.S. District Court in a discrimination suit he had filed against the University of California four years earlier. He used most of the money to establish a foundation to combat discrimination against Latinos in employment. For the past decade he has expounded his civil rights views in a column he contributes to the *Los Angeles Herald Examiner*.

Acuña developed the very first course in Chicano history, which he taught at Mount St. Mary's College in Los Angeles in 1966. A few years later he founded the first Chicano studies department at San Fernando Valley State College, today California State University at Northridge. A pioneer Mexican American historian, he has written a dozen books on the Chicano experience, including a widely used general history of the Mexican American, *Occupied America: A History of Chicanos* (3rd edition, 1988). In his most recent work, *Sometimes There Is No Other Side: Chicanos and the Myth of Equality* (1998), he explores discrimination in the hiring of university faculty.

Acuña has been the recipient of numerous honors and awards for his pioneering community service in the field of civil rights, including the highly respected Liberty Hill award for his four decades of leadership as a community activist. At the beginning of 1998 Acuña received the prestigious Gustavus Myers Award, an annual prize for the best scholarship on intolerance in America. The Gustavus Myers Center for the Study of Bigotry and Human Rights in North America made the award for his 1996 book *Anything but Mexican: Chicanos in Contemporary Los Angeles*.

See also AMERICAN CIVIL LIBERTIES UNION; CHICANO STUDIES DEPARTMENTS; DISCRIMINATION.

FURTHER READING: Acuña, Rodolfo. *Anything but Mexican: Chicanos in Contemporary Los Angeles.* New York: Verso, 1996; Acuña, Rodolfo. *Sometimes There Is No Other Side: Chicanos and the Myth of Equality.* Notre Dame, Ind.: University of Notre Dame Press, 1998; *Acuña v. The Regents of the University of California et al.* Superior Court for Santa Barbara County, Case No. SB196297. U.S. District Court, Central District of California, Case No. CV93–1548HLH; Bortnick, Barry. "Rudy Acuña's Legal War . . ." *Santa Barbara News-Press,* 8 May 1998; Martínez, Julio A., ed. *Chicano Scholars and Writers: A Bio-Bibliographical Dictionary.* Metuchen, N.J.: Scarecrow Press, 1979. *Who's Who among Hispanic Americans, 1994–1995.* Detroit: Gale Research, 1994.

AFFIRMATIVE ACTION. The term *affirmative action* is commonly used to describe the use of race, gender, or ethnic identity as a substantial factor in selection, admission, hiring, and promotion. Central to the Great Society concept of President Lyndon Johnson, it encompassed a number of laws, regulations, programs, and practices having as their goal the redressing of past inequities and discrimination suffered by ethnic minorities and women in education, employment, and housing. At its heart was the Civil Rights Act of 1964. Its supporters view it as an adjustment rather than atonement. Opponents of affirmative action argue that it serves to perpetuate the very stereotypes it finds offensive.

Preferential treatment given to members of minority groups quickly led to charges of reverse discrimination that came to a first climax in the Bakke lawsuit. In 1978 the U.S. Supreme Court held that Alan Bakke, an Anglo, had been unfairly discriminated against when the University of California at Davis failed to admit him four years earlier. During the 1980s President Ronald Reagan's Republican administration added its powerful voice to a growing movement to completely do away with affirmative action practices in government agencies. By the mid-1990s affirmative action had been seriously weakened by court decisions and the actions of other governmental bodies as well as by a noticeable nationwide turnabout in popular attitude, partly the result of economic recession. In 1995 the University of California regents voted to abolish affirmative action preferences in determining student admissions. This action was followed by a decline in minority enrollment. In the wake of the demise of affirmative action practices, the economic and social gains of Mexican Americans and other minorities appear to be jeopardized.

A second climax came in November 1996 when California voters approved Proposition 209, which prohibited the use of race- and gender-based preferences in employment, contracts, and school admissions. Other preferences were not prohibited. The proposition was immediately challenged in the courts.

See also BAKKE SUIT; CIVIL RIGHTS ACT OF 1964; PROPOSITION 209.

FURTHER READING: Acuña, Rodolfo F. *Sometimes There Is No Other Side: Chicanos and the Myth of Equality.* Notre Dame, Ind.: University of Notre Dame Press, 1998; Chávez, Lydia. *The Color Bind: California's Battle to End Affirmative Action.* Berkeley: University of California Press, 1998; Eastland, Terry. *Ending Affirmative Action.* New York: Basic Books, 1996; García, F. Chris. "Latinos and the Affirmative Action Debate: Wedge or Coalition Issue?" In *Pursuing Power: Latinos and the Political System,* edited by F. Chris García. Notre Dame, Ind.: University of Notre Dame Press, 1997; Greene, Kathanne W. *Affirmative Action and Principles of Justice.* Westport, Conn.: Greenwood Press, 1990; Navarrette, Rubén, Jr. *A Darker Shade of Crimson: Odyssey of a Harvard Chicano.* New York: Bantam Books, 1993; Sowell, Thomas. *Preferential Policies: An International Perspective.* New York: William Morrow, 1990.

ALATORRE, RICHARD, 1943– . During his college years Richard Alatorre became deeply involved in student activism and after graduating as a sociology major continued his concerns for the poor and disenfranchised. With a master's degree in public administration, in 1967 he participated in the black civil rights movement as western regional director of the NAACP Legal Defense Fund.

Six years later active Democrat Alatorre won election to the California Assembly, where he served until 1986, becoming a close associate of the dynamic Assembly Speaker, Willie Brown. His continuing interest in the Chicano condition led him to resign in 1985 in order to run for a seat on the powerful city council of Los Angeles, the U.S. city with the largest Mexicano population. Strongly supported by the community and Latino businesspeople, he won a stunning upset victory, becoming the first Mexican American to serve on the council since Edward Roybal resigned in 1962, a quarter of a century earlier.

An active member of the National Association of Latino Elected and Appointed Officials, Alatorre has been honored with a number of awards for his contributions to the Chicano struggle for human rights and dignity. In 1980 he was named legislator of the year, and in the following year he received the Presidential Medallion Award from his alma mater, California State University at Los Angeles. Following that recognition, the Eagleton Institute of Politics at Rutgers University named him Outstanding State Legislator, and in 1988 the YMCA gave him its Human Dignity Award.

See also BLACK CIVIL RIGHTS INFLUENCE; NATIONAL ASSOCIATION OF LATINO ELECTED AND APPOINTED OFFICIALS; ROYBAL, EDWARD.

FURTHER READING: Fuentes, Dagoberto. "Stunning Victory for Alatorre." *Hispanic Business* 8, no. 2 (February 1986):12; *Who's Who among Hispanic Americans, 1994–1995.* Detroit: Gale Research, 1994.

ALBUQUERQUE WALKOUT, 1966. In late March 1966 fifty Mexican American delegates attending a federal Equal Employment Opportunity Commission (EEOC) hearing in Albuquerque, New Mexico, followed the lead of Albert Peña in walking out. Protesting that there were no Mexican American commissioners on the EEOC and that it was insensitive to minority needs and grievances, they demanded that President Lyndon Johnson host a White House conference on Mexican American problems. The leaders of the walkout also filed suit with the Civil Rights Commission, charging the EEOC with employment discrimination based on the fact that only 3 of its 150 staff members were Latinos.

In May President Johnson met with Chicano leaders, and they arranged for a conference to be held in El Paso. A number of prominent Chicano leaders, including Corky Gonzales, César Chávez, and Bert Corona, boycotted the meeting and met in El Paso's south barrio, where they organized their own rump conference to articulate raza problems.

The Albuquerque walkout was an extremely important milestone in the Chicano struggle for civil rights. Most historians have seen it and the subsequent rump session as marking the beginning of the Chicano Movement by supplying Mexican Americans with their first national forum.

See also CIVIL RIGHTS COMMISSION; MOVIMIENTO, EL; PEÑA, ALBERT, JR.

FURTHER READING: Meier, Matt S., and Feliciano Rivera. *Dictionary of Mexican American History.* Westport, Conn.: Greenwood Press, 1981; Pycior, Julie Leininger. *LBJ & Mexican Americans: The Paradox of Power.* Austin: University of Texas Press, 1997.

ALDRETE, CRIS[TÓBAL], 1924–1991. Cris Aldrete, the first member of his family to complete high school, used the G.I. Bill after World War II to enter the University of Texas. At the university he helped found the Alba club in 1946 to provide a center for Mexican American students and to break down their isolation. In 1949 his complaint against the segregation practices of Del Rio schools resulted in an early, if only partial, victory for desegregation. Having completed undergraduate studies, he obtained his law degree from the South Texas College of Law in 1951.

After law school Aldrete returned to his natal city, Del Rio, where he began to practice law and became active in the local American G.I. Forum (AGIF), especially in recruiting members and organizing new chapters. In 1956 as one of the AGIF lawyers representing convicted murderer Pete Hernández before the U.S. Supreme Court, he helped win a reversal of his conviction on the basis of civil rights denial. He also participated in Del Rio city government. After six years of service on the city council, in 1959 he was elected city attorney and two years later won election as Val Verde county attorney. In both positions he was deeply concerned with Chicano rights.

In 1965 Aldrete was appointed a regional director of the Office of Economic Opportunity's community action programs. During the following decade he acted as legislative assistant to Texas senator Lloyd Bentsen; and in 1977, when Jimmy Carter took over the presidency, he became co-chairman of the Southwest Border Regional Commission, an economic development agency. In the late 1980s he was executive director of the Texas Senate Hispanic Caucus. His death from cancer in 1991 ended the long and successful career of a charismatic and unassuming G.I. generation Tejano civil rights leader.

See also AMERICAN G.I. FORUM.

FURTHER READING: Pycior, Julie Leininger. *LBJ & Mexican Americans: The Paradox of Power*. Austin: University of Texas Press, 1997; San Miguel, Guadalupe, Jr. *"Let All of Them Take Heed": Mexican Americans and the Campaign for Educational Equality in Texas, 1910–1981*. Austin: University of Texas Press, 1987; Tyler, Ron, ed. *The New Handbook of Texas*. Vol 1. Austin: Texas State Historical Association, 1996.

ALIANZA FEDERAL DE PUEBLOS LIBRES. The Alianza, the Federal Alliance of Free Towns, founded by Reies López Tijerina in 1963 as the Alianza Federal de Mercedes (Grants), was at first primarily a Nuevomexicano land grantees' organization with headquarters in Albuquerque. Its ultimate goal was to regain lands awarded by the Spanish and Mexican governments to early settlers and to their townships (pueblos) and later lost for various reasons after the official U.S. takeover of the Southwest in 1848. Some authorities consider this dispossession of Mexican Americans as one of the earliest and most serious violation of their civil rights.

Boasting a membership estimated at several thousand during the mid-1960s, the Alianza moved between legal action and highly confrontational tactics. The latter aroused considerable public concern, which came to a climax as a result of the Tierra Amarilla courthouse raid by Alianza members in 1967.

The Alianza was deprived of Tijerina's leadership when he was sentenced to jail in 1970 and later paroled with the condition that he not hold any Alianza office for five years. These events, combined with the general decline of militancy in the Chicano Movement by the second half of the 1970s, changed both the nature and the tactics of the Alianza's leadership and led to considerable reduction in the organization's membership and activities. As a civil rights protest movement the Alianza slid into decline and then a state of dormancy.

See also MOVIMIENTO, EL; TIERRA AMARILLA; TIJERINA, REIES LÓPEZ.

FURTHER READING: Gardner, Richard. *¡Grito! Reies Tijerina and the New Mexico Land Grant War of 1967*. Indianapolis: Bobbs-Merrill, 1970; Jenkinson,

Michael. *Tijerina: Land Grant Conflict in New Mexico.* Albuquerque: Paisano Press, 1968; Knowlton, Clark S. "Violence in New Mexico: A Sociological Perspective." *California Law Review* 58 (October 1970):1054–1084; Swadesh, Frances L. "The Alianza Movement of New Mexico." In *Minorities and Politics*, edited by Henry J. Tobias and Charles E. Woodhouse. Albuquerque: University of New Mexico Press, 1969.

ALIANZA HISPANO-AMERICANA (AHA). Founded in 1894 in Arizona to defend Mexicanos' rights and to improve the quality of their lives, the Alianza was one of the earliest regional Mexican American organizations. Using Masonic lodges as models, it was initially mutualist in character and concerned itself primarily with providing death benefits for its members and with encouraging civic virtue and acculturation. During the 1920s its conservative middle-class leadership began to advocate the use of the ballot to rectify injustices and achieve civil rights. By the 1930s it had nearly 300 lodges scattered over the Southwest but mostly in Arizona; these provided its members with various social services and afforded some help to Mexicanos who encountered discrimination and denial of their civil liberties.

After World War II the Alianza began concerning itself more centrally with civil rights, educational inequities, and social justice. In the early 1950s it helped bring about an end to legal school segregation in Arizona; in 1955 it created a separate civil rights department headed by Ralph Guzmán. During the 1960 presidential election it was active in developing the Viva Kennedy clubs that helped bring about a Democratic victory. This stress on electoral politics and increased concern for civil rights issues supplied an example for young Chicanos who were about to set the movimiento into motion.

However, beginning in the late 1950s the Alianza became plagued with various internal problems. Bitter rivalries and charges of nepotism, financial mismanagement, and theft of Alianza funds finally led to the conviction of the president for embezzlement and to receivership for the Alianza. Despite financial and managerial reorganization, the Alianza continued to lose members to the more popular League of United Latin American Citizens and the American G.I. Forum. Efforts to attract new members from the World War II generation and movimiento Chicanos were unsuccessful.

See also AMERICAN G.I. FORUM; GUZMÁN, RALPH; LEAGUE OF UNITED LATIN AMERICAN CITIZENS.

FURTHER READING: Briegel, Kaye L. "Alianza Hispano-Americana, 1894–1965: A Mexican-American Fraternal Insurance Society." Ph.D. diss., University of Southern California, 1974; Gonzales, Sylvia Alicia. *Hispanic American Voluntary Organizations.* Westport, Conn.: Greenwood Press, 1985; Rosales, Francisco A. *Chicano!: The History of the Mexican American Civil Rights Movement.* Houston: Arte Público Press, 1996.

ALINSKY, SAUL, 1909–1972. Saul Alinsky is best known as the founder and head of the Industrial Areas Foundation (IAF), an aggressive community advocacy organization that teaches people how to organize and develop political power and effectiveness. After a college degree and graduate training in criminology Alinsky took a job working with juvenile delinquents. His work experiences led him to switch to community organizing, in which he was to spend the rest of his life.

In 1940 with support from Marshall Field III and Bishop Bernard Sheil of Chicago, Alinsky, a self-declared professional radical, created the IAF to train social activists in organizational skills and in the use of his often unorthodox tactics for empowering the powerless poor and defending their civil and community rights. Highly critical of what he called the "welfare colonialism" of federal anti-poverty programs, he and his followers helped many Chicano barrios in organizing to fight for their rights during the post–World War II era. His unique populist ideas and the IAF organizational structure inspired many Mexican American community civil rights groups, forming the basis for the Community Service Organization and United Neighborhood Organization. The success of his techniques brought him a national reputation and numerous disciples like Fred Ross, Sr., and Ernie Cortés, who helped spread Alinsky's ideas and carried on his work after his death.

See also COMMUNITY SERVICE ORGANIZATION; CORTÉS, ERNIE; ROSS, FRED, SR.; UNITED NEIGHBORHOOD ORGANIZATION.

FURTHER READING: Alinsky, Saul. *Reveille for Radicals.* Chicago: University of Chicago Press, 1947. 2nd ed. New York: Vintage Press, 1969; *Current Biography, 1968.* New York: H. W. Wilson Co., 1968; Finks, P. David. *The Radical Vision of Saul Alinsky.* New York: Paulist Press, 1984; Horwitt, Sanford D. *Let Them Call Me Rebel: Saul Alinsky, His Life and Legacy.* New York: Random House, 1989; Márquez, Benjamin. "The Industrial Areas Foundation and the Mexican-American Community in Texas: The Politics of Issue Mobilization." In *Pursuing Power: Latinos and the Political System,* edited by F. Chris García. Notre Dame, Ind.: University of Notre Dame Press, 1997.

ALURISTA (URISTA, ALBERTO B.), 1947– . Alberto Urista, commonly known simply as Alurista, was the preeminent poet of the Chicano Movement. One of the first Chicano poets to write bilingually, he used the medium of his poetry to arouse concern about Mexican American problems and the denial of their civil rights. No mere versifier, he took an active role in the civil rights movements as one of the founders of the Movimiento Estudiantil Chicano de Aztlán and also by helping develop the Plan Espiritual de Aztlán in 1969. He also was involved in establishing various community and student organizations.

An academician with a doctorate in Spanish literature, Alurista was also co-founder of the Chicano Studies department and the Chicano Studies

Center at San Diego State University in California. In addition to numerous articles on Chicano history, culture, and literature, Alurista has published nine collections of his poetry, some of them with distinct political overtones. He used his position as a leading Chicano writer and as editor of the literary magazine *Maize* to explore and further the cause of Chicano rights.

FURTHER READING: Alurista. *Z Eros/Alurista*. Tempe, Ariz.: Bilingual Press/ Editorial Bilingüe, 1995; Bruce-Novoa, Juan. *Chicano Authors: Inquiry by Interview*. Austin: University of Texas Press, 1980; Martínez, Julio A., and Francisco A. Lomelí, eds. *Chicano Literature: A Reference Guide*. Westport, Conn.: Greenwood Press, 1985.

AMERICAN CIVIL LIBERTIES UNION (ACLU). The American Civil Liberties Union was founded in 1920 by a group of social and political activists that included Norman Thomas, Roger Baldwin, and Jane Addams. Dedicated to protecting the civil liberties guaranteed to all citizens by the U.S. Constitution, in its early years the ACLU participated in pro-labor protests; but in recent decades it has concerned itself particularly with legal matters such as due process, equality before the law, and the right of freedom of opinion and expression. As a strictly nonpartisan organization defending all civil rights, it has frequently supported Mexican American organizations in legal suits concerning segregation and denial of the vote.

Because of its fundamental commitment to freedom of speech, the ACLU often defends highly controversial opinions and persons. It has defended the rights of American Nazis and communists, of Japanese American World War II internees, of Oliver North and John Scopes. As a result, it sometimes finds itself denounced by liberals as well as conservatives. Most important, it has greatly influenced the definition of civil liberties in the United States.

FURTHER READING: Chowder, Ken. "The ACLU Defends Everybody." *Smithsonian* 28, no. 10 (January 1998):86–97; Goldstein, Robert J. *Political Repression in Modern America: From 1870 to the Present*. Cambridge, Mass.: Schenkman Publishing Co., 1978; Walker, Samuel. *In Defense of American Liberties: A History of the ACLU*. New York: Oxford University Press, 1990.

AMERICAN COORDINATING COUNCIL OF POLITICAL EDUCATION (ACCPE). A nonpartisan political organization founded in Phoenix, Arizona, at the beginning of the 1960s, ACCPE was an early part of the movimiento's fight for political rights. It was heavily indebted to the ideas of the Political Association of Spanish-Speaking Peoples, from which it was an offshoot. It has conducted citizenship programs, organized registration drives, and supported Chicano candidates for public office. As its name might indicate, its goals were mainstream and inclusive. It even eschewed the word *Mexican* in its title although its membership was almost exclusively Mexican American.

With a sphere of influence largely limited to Arizona, ACCPE spread rapidly and achieved some political successes at the city level, electing Chicano candidates to town councils and school boards. Although it ultimately became active in 10 of Arizona's 14 counties, it was never able to translate its local success into victories at higher levels. Its failure to field winning candidates for county or state offices was perhaps attributable to the more politically partisan character of these positions.

See also POLITICAL ASSOCIATION OF SPANISH SPEAKING ORGANIZATIONS.

FURTHER READING: Castro, Tony. *Chicano Power: The Emergence of Mexican America.* New York: Saturday Review Press, 1967; Meier, Matt S., and Feliciano Rivera. *Dictionary of Mexican American History.* Westport, Conn.: Greenwood Press, 1981.

AMERICAN COUNCIL OF SPANISH-SPEAKING PEOPLE. The council was one of the first efforts by Mexican Americans to create an umbrella organization. It was established at the beginning of the 1950s at an El Paso convention of Chicano civil rights groups called by George I. Sánchez. With Sánchez as its first executive director and with financing from the Robert C. Marshall Trust Fund, it concentrated most of its efforts and its limited resources on school desegregation. In 1952 it joined the Alianza Hispano-Americana in filing suits against Arizona school districts that continued to practice segregation. With its $53,000 grant it was able to provide some legal assistance as well as leadership in discrimination and desegregation lawsuits during the first half of the 1950s. A little ahead of the general American civil rights movement, it was unable to obtain further funding for its activities. After expending the Marshall Foundation grant to promote civil rights it languished and finally expired in 1958.

See also ALIANZA HISPANO-AMERICANA; SÁNCHEZ, GEORGE I.

FURTHER READING: Acuña, Rodolfo. *Occupied America: A History of Chicanos.* 3rd ed. New York: Harper & Row, 1988; Tyler, Ron, ed. *The New Handbook of Texas.* Vol. 1. Austin: Texas State Historical Association, 1996.

AMERICAN G.I. FORUM (AGIF). Founded in Texas in the aftermath of World War II, largely through the efforts of Dr. Héctor Pérez García, the AGIF grew steadily to become one of the largest and most influential Mexican American civil rights organizations.

As a result of the 1949 Félix Longoria case in Texas some 40 existing Forum chapters, which had been loosely developed the year before, met in convention and formalized a more cohesive organizational structure. Veteran-oriented, from the beginning it was a successful fusing of American

(U.S.) identity with Chicano community roots. It concentrated its recruiting in the poorer sector of the community and developed a broad spectrum of interests with special emphasis on civil and social rights. It also strongly encouraged members to participate in the American political process.

During the 1950s the AGIF spread out from Texas, establishing chapters in the states of the Midwest and Southwest. It played a major role in various civil rights cases involving Mexican Americans. In Texas it took, and still takes, a significant part in all aspects of the fight against segregation, particularly segregation in the schools. In the pursuit of its goals it has been active at all levels of government in an officially nonpartisan position that often appears, however, to lean toward the Democratic Party. In the 1960 presidential elections several Forum leaders helped found Viva Kennedy clubs and nearly every AGIF chapter in the Southwest organized a club. Stressing political action and recourse to the courts to defend civil rights, the AGIF closely monitors state and federal legislative bills of particular interest to Chicanos. By providing its members with valuable services and immediate benefits it has been successful in maintaining its membership and thus remaining a powerful pressure group for Mexican American rights.

See also GARCÍA, HÉCTOR PÉREZ; KENNEDY, JOHN FITZGERALD; LONGORIA, FÉLIX; SEGREGATION.

FURTHER READING: Allsup, Carl. *The American G.I. Forum: Origins and Evolution*. Austin: Center for Mexican American Studies, University of Texas, 1982; "Civil Rights." *La Luz* 8, no. 6 (February–March, 1986):10–14; Parra, Ricardo, Victor Ríos, and Armando Gutiérrez. "Chicano Organizations in the Midwest: Past, Present, and Possibilities." *Aztlán* 7, no. 2 (Summer 1976):235–253; Pycior, Julie Leininger. *LBJ & Mexican Americans: The Paradox of Power*. Austin: University of Texas Press, 1997; Ramos, Henry A. J. *The American G.I. Forum: In Pursuit of the Dream, 1948–1983*. Houston: Arte Público Press, 1998; www.agif.org.

AMERICANS FOR DEMOCRATIC ACTION (ADA). A liberal, nonpartisan but basically Democratic, political organization, the ADA was founded in 1947. With Reinhold Niebuhr as its ideologue and one of its founders, it was motivated by opposition to communism and advocacy of domestic social legislation, especially in the areas of discrimination and education. In the 1948 presidential election it was instrumental in getting a strong civil rights stand written into the Democratic platform. The end of McCarthyism by the late 1950s, the 1960 election to the presidency of its favorite, John F. Kennedy, and the waning of communism as an issue in U.S. politics eventually brought about its decline in the next decade.

FURTHER READING: Diggins, John P. *The Proud Decades: America in War and Peace, 1941–1960*. New York: W. W. Norton & Co., 1988; Gillon, Steven M. *Politics and Vision: The ADA and American Liberalism, 1947–1985*. New York: Oxford University Press, 1987.

ANGUIANO, LUPE, 1929– . Guadalupe Anguiano has been a dedicated leader in both the civil rights and feminist movements. Serving the needs of the poor and voiceless has been a primary lifetime concern for her. Born in Colorado, she spent a decade and a half (1949–1964) as a teaching nun in the missionary sisters of Our Lady of Victory. Having become deeply aware of numerous Mexican American community problems, she requested secularization and left the order to become a lay social worker more directly and more intimately involved in Chicano rights.

Anguiano immersed herself in community work, becoming first a counselor in a California youth program and then coordinator of the Federal Poverty Program in Los Angeles. In 1966 she was appointed by President Lyndon Johnson to create a Mexican American unit within the Department of Health, Education, and Welfare (HEW), where she soon found herself chiefly monitoring affirmative action programs. Because of her own experience growing up, she strongly advocated bilingual education and helped write the Bilingual Education Act passed by Congress in 1968. She also used her position to encourage Chicanos, and especially Chicanas, to become personally involved in business and political affairs.

In 1967, somewhat disappointed by HEW limitations, Anguiano resigned to join the United Farm Workers (UFW) as an organizer. Soon she was tapped by César Chávez to head the grape boycott in Michigan. Although initially reluctant to undertake an aggressive leadership role, she learned from the experience that Chicanas could take an effective part in the movimiento and in the women's movement as well.

After a year with the UFW Anguiano returned to HEW as a civil rights specialist helping to implement the provisions of the Civil Rights Act of 1964 and then went to work in the Legal Defense and Education Department of the National Association for the Advancement of Colored People. Early in the 1970s she accepted from the National Conference of Catholic Bishops appointment as regional director in the Southwest. In 1977 she used her skills to co-found a feminist organization named National Women's Development, which she left two years later to create, with private funding, the National Women's Employment and Education Project. In the early 1990s she accepted appointment to the Division of Affirmative Recruitment in the U.S. Department of Personnel Management; here she continued her concern for civil rights.

See also BILINGUAL EDUCATION; CIVIL RIGHTS ACT OF 1964; UNITED FARM WORKERS.

FURTHER READING: Anguiano, Guadalupe. "Employment and Welfare Issues as They Affect Low Income Women." *Southwest Regional Office for the Spanish Speaking* (19 February 1976); Chacón, José A. *Hispanic Notables in the United States of North America.* Albuquerque: Saguaro Publishing, 1978; Newlon, Clarke. *Famous Mexican Americans.* New York: Dodd, Mead & Co., 1972; Pycior, Julie Leininger. *LBJ & Mexican Americans: The Paradox of Power.* Austin: University of Texas Press, 1997; Telgen, Diane, and Jim Kamp, eds. *Notable Hispanic American Women*. Detroit: Gale Research, 1993.

ARIZONA. After the Treaty of Guadalupe Hidalgo in 1848, Arizona remained largely isolated from the rest of the United States. Its inhabitants, most of whom lived in the southern half of the area, continued to be closely linked economically and socially to the adjoining Mexican state of Sonora. The new Americans, border Mexicanos who numbered over 1,000, remained more Mexican than American—largely a matter of isolation and familial, economic, and cultural ties with Sonora. Nevertheless, during the first decades of American control there were relatively high levels of interaction, including intermarriage, between Mexicano elites and Anglos. Although rights to lands granted by Spain and Mexico were guaranteed by the Treaty of Guadalupe Hidalgo and the Gadsden Purchase Treaty of 1853, in many instances the guarantees failed to protect Mexicano ownership. In the northeastern part of the territory Anglos, who came to own most of the land, generally controlled local government offices and politics.

Considerable cordiality between Anglos and elites continued, but good relations began to fade as the frontier receded during the 1880s and as Arizona became increasingly linked to the East Coast and the national economy. There began to arrive new Anglo settlers who viewed Mexicanos primarily as unskilled laborers. As the territorial population grew, preferential treatment was increasingly given to Anglos, while middle- and lower-class Mexicanos became objects of bias and discrimination. In Arizona's rapidly expanding mining areas segregated housing and dual pay scales were the norm, and acts of gratuitous violence against Mexicanos were commonplace except in the Tucson area. As discrimination became more deeply entrenched, segregation in schools, churches, and other public and semipublic areas increased. Mexicanos began turning to mutualist and other organizations for solace and some protection. To defend themselves, in 1894 they created one of the earliest Mexican American civil rights groups, the Alianza Hispano-Americana.

The period from the beginning of the new century to the 1930s was one of further adjustment for the Mexican American elite as they continued to lose political power. In 1901 the Arizona Rangers were created with the special objective of keeping the Mexicano labor force in subjugation. Copper mining and the statehood movement dominated Arizona's economic and political scene. Just before statehood was achieved in 1912, La Liga Protectora Latina was organized in Phoenix with the goal of defending Mexicano rights, particularly those of copper mine workers. The Liga protested civil rights abuses like Arizona's 1913 anti-alien land ownership law. It also concerned itself with education and lobbied for bilingual classes at the primary level.

The World War I demand for copper led to a new surge of immigration from Mexico, but when the postwar depression took place in the early 1920s, the rights of Mexican miners were completely ignored and they were sent packing or worse. Those who remained in the copper towns were harassed by the Ku Klux Klan, as were people of Mexican descent elsewhere. A decade later the "repatriation" of the 1930s evoked memories of similar earlier experiences. Thousands of miners and agricultural workers and their families, some of whom were American citizens, were urged, none too gently, across the border. In Tucson, where the elite retained some political power, urban Mexican Americans were less summarily treated by the Anglo establishment.

Except for the wartime demand for metals, especially copper, World War II had perhaps less impact on Arizona than on the rest of the Southwest. In the postwar period Arizona Mexicanos faced fewer legal barriers and less bigotry, but their struggle for civil rights was negatively affected by the continued heavy influx of Mexican agricultural labor and the nativism it engendered. Chicano leaders worked assiduously under the guidance of the Alianza Hispano-Americana to end school segregation. By the mid-1950s most Arizona schools were desegregated, helped by the Westminster victory in southern California in the late 1940s and the 1952 decision in the *Gonzales v. Sheely* case, which outlawed the segregation of Mexicano children in separate schools. In 1955 *Baca v. Winslow* forced the city of Winslow to end segregation in its public swimming pool.

The fight for equal opportunities and equal rights also went on in the workplace. Racist exclusion in many unions and stereotyping on the part of management continued to be the chief causes of discrimination in employment and promotion. However, by 1960 Chicanos had considerably improved their membership in unions, and a number of large employers had begun to abandon racist exclusionary policies. During the 1970s and 1980s labor union activities continued to be major issues for Arizona Chicano communities, especially in agriculture and mining. Chicanos, now appearing in the workforce in greater numbers, played a significant role in the Phelps-Dodge strike of the early 1980s.

In 1962 Arizona Chicanos, influenced by the success in Texas of the Political Association of Spanish-Speaking Organizations, whose hegemony they rejected, formed the American Coordinating Council of Political Education (ACCPE) to promote their political rights. After a jump start ACCPE membership leveled off, and it has remained strictly an Arizona organization. Efforts of ACCPE to increase Chicano political power through the vote has had only limited success.

The Chicano Movement came to Arizona largely from the California example. A Mexican American student association was founded at the University of Arizona in Tucson in 1967, and university and high school students carried the message of the movimiento to the community. Arizona Chicanos tended to be a bit more conservative than their California and

Texas counterparts, and some of the more aggressive student ideas took a while to germinate. Although Arizona State University at Tempe offered courses in Mexican American topics, it did not formally establish a Chicano studies program until 1992.

However, youthful leaders encouraged a new activism that laid stress on civil and political rights. In recent decades Arizona Mexican Americans have participated more widely and successfully in the state's political arena. Except for Tucsonenses, they evinced only limited interest in La Raza Unida Party in the early 1970s and less support for its candidates. They were nonetheless able to elect Chicanos to major positions at the city and county levels. Although still underrepresented in both local offices and the state legislature, by 1974 Spanish-surnamed individuals, who made up about 19 percent of Arizona's population, helped elect 11 representatives to the Arizona House of Representatives and made Raúl Castro the state's first and only Mexican American governor.

Over three fourths of Arizona Mexican Americans were born in the United States, and equal numbers are town or city dwellers. Despite advances, many still live in segregated, deteriorating, or dilapidated barrio housing. Generally they lag California and Texas Chicano populations in advancing their economic, social, and political rights.

See also AMERICAN COORDINATING COUNCIL OF POLITICAL EDUCATION; GONZALES ET AL. v. SHEELY ET AL; MOVIMIENTO, EL.

FURTHER READING: Crow, John E. *Mexican Americans in Contemporary Arizona: A Social and Demographic View.* San Francisco: R & E Research Associates, 1975; Getty, Harry T. *Interethnic Relationships in the Community of Tucson.* Reprint. New York: Arno Press, 1976; Mellinger, Phil. "The Men Have Organizers: Labor Conflict and Unionization in the Mexican Mining Towns of Arizona, 1900–1915." *Western Historical Quarterly* 23 (August 1992), 323–348; Officer, James E. *Arizona's Hispanic Perspective.* Phoenix: Arizona Academy, 1981; Officer, James E. *Hispanic Arizona, 1536–1856.* Tucson: University of Arizona Press, 1987; Sheridan, Thomas E. *Arizona: A History.* Tucson: University of Arizona Press, 1995; Sheridan, Thomas E. *Los Tucsonenses: The Mexican Community in Tucson, 1854–1941.* Tucson: University of Arizona Press, 1986.

ARREGUÍN, ALFREDO MENDOZA, 1935– . Alfredo Arreguín—painter, sculptor, and teacher—was born and grew up in the lovely colonial Mexican town of Morelia, the capital of the state of Michoacán. At age eight he was enrolled in the local Bellas Artes academy by his grandfather, which aroused his interest in art. Five years later he went to Mexico City to continue his education. While a university student, he often acted as a guide for *norteamericano* tourists in order to practice his English. One of these contacts led to a lasting friendship that brought him to Seattle where he subsequently enrolled at the University of Washington.

Since Arreguín had begun steps to become a U.S. citizen, he was drafted into the army in the late 1950s. After his service and discharge he returned to Seattle where he resumed his academic studies, supporting himself by working at various jobs. First an architecture major, he later switched to interior design and finally to fine arts. He received his B.A. in 1967 and his Master of Fine Arts two years later. Meanwhile he had begun to develop his distinctive, elaborately patterned, deeply layered painting style that featured broad vistas with calligraphically detailed flora and fauna of tropical Mexico. By the late 1970s his dense, kaleidoscopic, and, at times, surreal configurations with vibrantly colored monkeys, felines, and birds began to catch on. In 1979 he won the prestigious Palm of the People award at the International Festival of Painting at Cagnes-sur-Mer, France. Over the years Arreguín's painting style has evolved and matured. Some of his later paintings are less dense, and he sometimes has added pre-Columbian motifs, especially in the calligraphy. He also has added portraiture to his offerings, and his more recent paintings often incorporate ecological themes.

The popularity of Arreguín's works is attested to by numerous exhibitions, solo and group. In the 1980s and 1990s he had over three dozen solo exhibits and his paintings have been included in nearly 50 group exhibitions, in the United States, Japan, the former Soviet Union, Chile, and elsewhere abroad. On the occasion of the 450th anniversary of its founding, the Universidad de San Nicolás de Hidalgo in Morelia honored him in 1989 with a retrospective and the publication of a book on his life's work. In 1994 the National Museum of American Art acquired his large triptych "Sueño" as one of its most important acquisitions of the year. His paintings grace more than three dozen collections and adorn the covers of a dozen books of poetry, fiction and even history.

Arreguín has been the recipient of numerous other honors and awards. In 1980 and 1985 he was selected as a National Endowment for the Arts fellow and 4 years later he was commissioned to do the poster for the state of Washington's centennial celebration. In 1996 the National Academy of Sciences in Washington, D.C. presented a solo exhibition of his works. In 1997 he was selected to paint a commemorative poster for the 25th anniversary of the Centro de la Raza in Seattle—a portrait of Emiliano Zapata, and in the same year the government of Mexico gave him the highly prized OTHLI award for his community work among Mexican Americans.

FURTHER READING: Alcalá, Kathleen. "Deep Painting: An Interview with Alfredo Arreguín." *Raven Chronicles* 2:2 (Winter 1992):34–36; Arteaga, David. "Alfredo Arreguín: An Artist and his Work." *La Voz* (March 1985):17–19; Griswold del Castillo, Richard, Teresa McKenna, and Yvonne Yarbro-Bejarano. *Chicano Art: Resistance and Affirmation, 1965–1985*. Los Angeles: Wight Art Gallery, 1991; Chaplik, Dorothy. "Alfredo Arreguín." *Latin American Art* (Winter 1991):40–41; Gallagher, Tess. "Viva la Vida." Tacoma, Wash.: Tacoma Art Museum exhibition catalogue, 1992.

ASOCIACIÓN NACIONAL MÉXICO-AMERICANA (ANMA). ANMA, a leftist union of reform orientation, was founded in 1949 in Phoenix, Arizona, in order to protect the rights of Mexicano workers, particularly migrants, in the wake of a clash between police and Mexicano miners. Conceived as a militant national organization, it stressed unity based on class—the working class—as well as ethnicity. It fought against racism and exploitation and supported bilingual education while accepting that English was the public language for la raza's economic advancement. Strongly influenced by leftist ideology, it followed a popular front strategy throughout its short life.

Under the driving impetus of its president, Mine, Mill, and Smelter Workers organizer Alfredo Montoya, ANMA pursued a goal of civil rights for all Mexicano workers. It promoted a positive image of Mexicans and monitored the use of stereotypes in the media. It also called attention to the intimidation and frequent excessive use of force by police in dealing with Mexicanos. ANMA repeatedly condemned Attorney General Herbert Brownell's sweeping raids and indiscriminate expulsion of Mexicans from the United States during the infamous 1953 Operation Wetback. In the following year, despite its protests, ANMA was put on the attorney general's list of subversive organizations in the repressive climate of the McCarthy era. Its influence and potential were undermined by intense surveillance by the Federal Bureau of Investigation (which considered it subversive) and harassment from other governmental agencies. As a result it soon faded and by the late 1950s ceased to function.

See also OPERATION WETBACK.

FURTHER READING: Acuña, Rodolfo. *Occupied America: A History of Chicanos*. 3rd ed. New York: Harper & Row, 1988; García, Mario T. "Mexican American Labor and the Left: The Asociación Nacional México-Americana." In *The Chicano Struggle: Analyses of Past and Present Efforts*, edited by John A. García. Binghamton, N.Y.: Bilingual Press / Editorial Bilingüe, 1984; García, Mario T. *Mexican Americans: Leadership, Ideology, and Identity, 1930–1960*. New Haven, Conn.: Yale University Press, 1989; Urrutia, Liliana. "An Offspring of Discontent: The Asociación Nacional México-Americana, 1949–1954." *Aztlán* 15 (Spring 1984):177–184.

AUSTIN MARCH, 1966. Beginning on the Fourth of July 1966 several hundred agricultural workers in the south Texas melon strike at La Casita Farm spent two months walking nearly 300 miles from Rio Grande City on the Mexican border to the state capital. Led by Antonio Orendain, they proposed to present Governor John B. Connally with a list of demands, particularly the inclusion of farm workers in a proposed $1.25 per hour Texas minimum wage law. Connally refused to meet the marchers when they arrived on Labor Day, and agricultural workers were excluded from the minimum-wage legislation passed the following year.

Imported Mexican strikebreakers, Texas Ranger intimidation, and inadequate planning contributed to the failure of the march and strike. However, the march did bring the farmworkers' plight to public attention and may well have been a factor in a subsequent minor improvement in Texas agricultural wages. Furthermore, along with the strike from which it sprang, the march served as a catalyst in the civil rights movement in Texas.

A second march to Austin took place in mid-1977 when Antonio Orendain led a group of farmworkers to the state capital to request that Governor Dolph Briscoe support legislation to provide collective bargaining rights for workers in agriculture. Despite the thousands of signatures on their petition Briscoe refused to support their demand, and the Texas legislature failed to move a collective bargaining bill out of committee.

See also ORENDAIN, ANTONIO; TEXAS RANGERS.

FURTHER READING: García, Ignacio M. "The Many Battles of Antonio Orendain." *Nuestro* (November 1979):25–29; Procter, Ben H. "The Modern Texas Rangers: A Law Enforcement Dilemma in the Rio Grande Valley." In *The Mexican Americans: An Awakening Minority*, edited by Manuel P. Servín. Beverly Hills, Calif.: Glencoe Press, 1970; Rhinehart, Marilyn D., and Thomas H. Kreneck. "The Minimum Wage March of 1966: A Case Study in Mexican American Politics, Labor, and Identity." *The Houston Review* 91, no. 1 (1989):27–44.

AZTLÁN CONCEPT. Aztlán was the Mexica (Aztec) northern homeland from which, according to their traditions, they migrated southward to ultimately become conquerors of the central Mexican highlands. During the movimiento many Chicanos in their search for identity seized upon Aztlán as a symbolic name for the U.S. Southwest. The concept fitted in with the adoption of Mexican cultural symbols by movimiento leaders and their stress on cultural nationalism and the concept of indigenous roots.

Articulated in March 1969 at the first National Chicano Youth Liberation Conference in Denver, the Aztlán myth was central to Corky Gonzales's ideas about civil rights, self-determination, and ethnic nationalism. Later the concept was enshrined by Gonzales in the Plan Espiritual de Aztlán. For some activists it became the homeland to be reclaimed, at least metaphorically; for others it was a vaguely defined area of Chicano cultural formation and concentration in the U.S. Southwest.

See also GONZALES, CORKY; PLAN ESPIRITUAL DE AZTLÁN.

FURTHER READING: Anaya, Rudolfo A., and Francisco A. Lomelí, eds. *Aztlán: Essays on the Chicano Homeland*. Albuquerque: Academia / El Norte Publications, 1989. Muñoz, Carlos, Jr. *Youth, Identity, Power: The Chicano Movement*. New York: Verso, 1989; "El Plan Espiritual de Aztlán." *El Grito del Norte* 2 (1969).

B

BACA, POLLY B., 1941– . Motivated by the prejudice and discrimination she experienced as a child, Polly Baca became a political activist working for Chicano rights early in life. In high school she became involved in the Adlai Stevenson Young Democrats Club, and later at Colorado State University in Fort Collins she was the volunteer campus coordinator of the Viva Kennedy campaign in 1960.

After graduating from college Baca worked as public information officer in the Cabinet Committee on Opportunities for Spanish Speaking People during the Lyndon Johnson administration. In 1968 she served as deputy director of the Latino division in Robert Kennedy's brief bid for the Democratic presidential nomination. Following his assassination she joined the Southwest Council of La Raza as research director, a position she left two years later to accept the directorship of the Democratic National Committee's Office of Spanish-Speaking Affairs.

In 1974 Polly Baca sought and won a seat in the Colorado lower house and four years later was elected to the state senate. The first woman elected to that body, she was reelected in 1982 but was unsuccessful in a bid for election to the U.S. Senate four years later. During her years in the two Colorado legislative bodies she introduced and actively pushed a variety of bills, over 200 all told, many dealing with civil and social rights.

Baca's political success has been attributed to her extensive local and state civic involvement, combined with close ties to the national Democratic leadership. Among her civic activities, she has served on the boards of the Mexican American Legal Defense and Educational Fund, the National Chicano Planning Council, and the Latin American Research and Service Agency. In 1988 she was one of the initial group inducted into the National Hispanic Hall of Fame and in the following year was sent by the U.S.

Information Agency to the Far East to give a series of lectures on race and ethnicity in American life.

Retired from political office, Baca heads the consulting firm SierraBaca Systems and the Colorado Institute for Hispanic Education and Economic Empowerment. She also continues her activism in various political groups as part of her ongoing interest in Chicano civil rights. For her community activism and advancement of minority rights she has been the recipient of numerous awards, including an honorary LL.D. from Warburg College in 1989.

See also CHICANAS; MEXICAN AMERICAN LEGAL DEFENSE AND EDUCATIONAL FUND; NATIONAL COUNCIL OF LA RAZA.

FURTHER READING: Bonilla-Santiago, Gloria. *Breaking Ground and Barriers: Hispanic Women Developing Effective Leadership.* San Diego: Marin Publications, 1992; Chávez, Lucy. "Colorado's Polly Baca-Barragán, *Nuestro* 4, no. 2 (April 1980):18–19; Hardy, Gayle J., *American Women Civil Rights Activists.* Jefferson, N.C.: McFarland & Co., 1993; Mandel, Ruth B. *In the Running: The New Woman Candidate.* New Haven, Conn.: Tichnor & Fields, 1981; Telgen, Diane, and Jim Kamp, eds. *Notable Hispanic American Women.* Detroit: Gale Research, 1993; *Who's Who among Hispanic Americans, 1994–1995.* Detroit: Gale Research, 1994.

BÁEZ, JOAN CHANDOS, 1941– . Joan Báez has been a dedicated activist all of her adult life, working for human and civil rights as well as world peace. From the beginning of her musical career in the 1960s, she became directly and deeply involved in U.S. civil rights protests. Impelled by her Quaker background and youthful confidence, in 1962 she led a concert tour of Southern colleges, demanding integrated audiences. Although her role in the Mexican American civil rights movement has been limited, at times she lent her support to César Chávez and the United Farm Workers in their struggle for labor and human rights.

By the beginning of the 1970s Joan Báez had become a nationwide symbol of intensely earnest nonviolent protest, and soon she extended her concerns for rights worldwide. Toward the end of that decade she founded Humanitas International, a worldwide human rights organization. During the 1980s she met with such disparate rights leaders as Polish Solidarity chief Lech Walesa and the Dalai Lama. When she shut down Humanitas International at the beginning of the 1990s, she announced that its closing did not signify any lessening of her concern for human rights and world peace. In the second half of the 1990s she has continued her activities as a citizen deeply involved in issues of the day, especially those related to the peace and civil rights causes she strongly espouses.

FURTHER READING: Báez, Joan. *And a Voice to Sing With.* New York: Summit Books, 1987; Báez, Joan, and David Harris. *Coming Out.* New York: Pocket Books, 1971; *Current Biography, 1963.* New York: H. W. Wilson Co., 1963;

Telgen, Diane, and Jim Kamp, eds. ¡*Latinas! Women of Achievement*. Detroit: Visible Ink Press, 1996; Draper, Hal. *The New Student Revolt*. New York: Grove Press, 1965.

BAKKE SUIT, 1974–1978. In 1974 Allan Bakke, a 34-year-old Anglo, filed suit against the University of California (U.C.) after his application for admission to the medical school at U.C. Davis was rejected. He asserted that he was the victim of reverse discrimination because academically less qualified minority students had been admitted as the result of affirmative action policies. He argued that his Fourteenth Amendment rights to equal protection under the law were being violated. The California courts upheld Bakke's widely debated contention. The university then appealed the California Supreme Court's decision, and in June 1978 the U.S. Supreme Court, in a 5 to 4 decision based on the Civil Rights Act of 1964, upheld the lower courts' ruling. Bakke was admitted to the University of California medical school at Davis. He completed his medical training and went into private practice.

The *Bakke* decision marked the beginning of a general movement by the judiciary away from special considerations designed to increase equality of opportunity for minorities and to make adjustments for past and continuing unequal treatment.

See also CIVIL RIGHTS ACT OF 1964.

FURTHER READING: Acuña, Rodolfo F. *Sometimes There Is No Other Side: Chicanos and the Myth of Equality*. Notre Dame, Ind.: University of Notre Dame Press, 1998; Breiter, Toni. "Bakke and Morales: An Update." *Agenda* 7, no. 2 (March–April 1977):15; Burns, Haywood. "From Brown to Bakke and Back: Race, Law and Social Change in America." *Daedalus* 110, no. 2 (Spring 1981):219–231; Haro, Carlos M., ed. *The Bakke Decision: The Question of Chicano Access to Higher Education*. Los Angeles: Chicano Studies Center, University of California, 1976; Navarrette, Rubén, Jr. *A Darker Shade of Crimson: Odyssey of a Harvard Chicano*. New York: Bantam Books, 1993; *Regents of the University of California v. Bakke*. Supreme Court of the United States, 438 U.S. 265; Wilkinson, J. Harvie, III. *From Brown to Bakke: The Supreme Court and School Integration, 1954–1978*. New York: Oxford University Press, 1979.

BARAJAS, GLORIA, 1952– . Gloria Barajas began to develop her political skills in her Texas high school's Latin American Club and in the local Catholic Youth Organization. Her early jobs teaching and working for a local public housing authority brought forcibly to her attention the unmet needs in the Chicano community. From the beginning of her career in community and national affairs she has been active in political campaigns at local and state levels in Texas and Washington, D.C. In Washington she was a member of the D.C. Commission on Latino Community Development.

Later while a vice president of Congressional Education Associates, a Washington, D.C., consulting firm, Barajas helped establish the Washington chapter of the Mexican American Women's National Association (MANA) and was its first vice president for programming. In that position she developed and organized MANA's first leadership training workshop. Elected national president of MANA in 1986, she brought to the organization her extensive experience as a community and political activist. She developed a program of governmental involvement, focusing on the goal of more political positions for Chicanas. She also collaborated with other organizations to promote Chicana involvement in the electoral process as both campaigners and voters. After leaving the MANA presidency she became coordinator of the Women's Leadership Training Program in the Civil Rights Department of the National Education Association.

See also MANA: A NATIONAL LATINA ORGANIZATION.

FURTHER READING: Crocker, Elvira Valenzuela. *MANA: One Dream, Many Voices: A History of the Mexican American Women's National Association.* Washington, D.C.: MANA, 1991.

BERNAL, JOE J., 1927– . A San Antonio native, Joe Bernal was discharged from the armed services in 1946 after volunteer service in World War II. Using the G.I. Bill, he was able to attend college and complete a B.A. in sociology in 1950; four years later he earned an M.Ed. and in 1978 he received his doctorate. His B.A. degree enabled him to secure a position in the Texas public schools, where he taught for the next 13 years. His daily contact with young Chicanos and their problems convinced him that as a 1950s Texas reform Democrat, he could best contribute to solving raza problems by becoming a lawmaker.

In 1964 Bernal ran for the Texas House of Representatives and won. After his two-year term he then entered the race for a seat in the Texas Senate and was elected in a close race. His effective progressive leadership in the senate from 1967 to 1971 gave him a reputation as a militant reformer; however, his early opposition to the war in Vietnam disturbed many of his supporters. As a liberal Democrat espousing the rights of minorities and other disadvantaged groups, he had a special interest in education and was the author of the first Texas bilingual education act. As a legislator and social worker activist he was responsible for several bills on civil rights. In 1969 he received from the National Education Association its Human Rights Award for his outstanding contributions to the field of human relations.

In his concern for Chicano rights Bernal served on the Mexican American Legal Defense and Educational Fund board of directors and supported other raza organizations fighting for civil rights. He was active in the American G.I. Forum and a strong supporter of Mexican American Democrats of Texas. He also served on the San Antonio diocesan Commission for Mexican American Affairs and was involved in the Guadalupe Community Center in that city. He wrote on bilingual education and was the author, with Julian Samora and Albert Peña, of *Gunpowder Justice: A Reassessment of the Texas Rangers* (1979).

See also MEXICAN AMERICAN LEGAL DEFENSE AND EDUCATIONAL FUND; POLITICAL PARTICIPATION.

FURTHER READING: Bernal, Joe, Julian Samora, and Albert Peña. *Gunpowder Justice: A Reassessment of the Texas Rangers*. Notre Dame, Ind.: University of Notre Dame Press, 1979; Chacón, José A. *Hispanic Notables in the United States of North America*. Albuquerque: Saguaro Publishing, 1978; Joe J. Bernal Papers, 1942–1981. Benson Latin American Collection, General Libraries, University of Texas at Austin.

BILINGUAL EDUCATION. Bilingual education does not have a simple meaning; one of its persistent problems is that from inception it has meant different things to different people. Basically it refers to the teaching of students in two languages. The most widely accepted definition is a program to enable children with limited English-language skills to develop sufficient proficiency to benefit fully from education in that language. The program seemed to many Mexican Americans to improve educational opportunity for their children. Seen by many as a civil right of non-English-speaking children, it had the support of a majority of Americans and especially the leaders of nearly all Chicano political and social organizations.

Long practiced informally in the United States, the concept was officially recognized by the Bilingual Education Act of 1968. The act was further clarified and strengthened by amendments in 1974 and 1978. In the landmark case of *Lau v. Nichols* (1974) the U.S. Supreme Court ruled unanimously that failure to provide students instruction in their native languages violated the Civil Rights Act of 1964. As a result bilingual and bicultural education were institutionalized.

The rise of the Chicano Movement in the latter 1960s pushed demands for bilingual education as a civil right. However, from their beginnings in the 1960s bilingual programs aroused controversy, which persisted because of widely differing views of what comprised bilingual education and also because there was no consensus on how effective such education was in overcoming the educational disadvantages faced by minority students.

Since many Chicano activists viewed acculturation in the United States as a process whose purpose was to deprive them of their culture, they strongly supported bilingual education as a principal prop of biculturalism. Although support in the community has been less unequivocal, most Mexican Americans seem to favor continuing the programs. When bilingual education is interpreted as providing transitional help to Spanish-speaking children, support is even stronger. There is also a virtually unanimous belief in the importance of learning English. Obviously, support for bilingual education does not mean opposition to learning English.

When Richard Nixon took over the presidency in 1969, reaction to Lyndon Johnson's Great Society programs included a nativist, almost visceral attack on bilingual education. The Ronald Reagan administration (1981–1989) expanded this Republican opposition to the bilingual concept and did much in the 1980s to undermine the courts' previous decisions and earlier congressional legislation by reducing or terminating federal funding for various bilingual programs. In the 1990s the incomplete command of English by many Mexican American students and their inferior education continued to be reflected in lower scores on achievement tests. Further, the dropout rate of Chicano students remains intolerably high and college entrance levels remain low.

See also BILINGUALISM/BICULTURALISM; MOVIMIENTO, EL.

FURTHER READING: Cornejo, Ricardo J. "Bilingual Education: Some Reflections on Proposition 227." *Hispanic Outlook in Higher Education* 9, no. 3 (9 October 1998):27–32; Crawford, James. *Bilingual Education: History, Politics, Theory, and Practice.* 3rd ed. Los Angeles: Bilingual Educational Services, 1995; Donato, Rubén. *The Other Struggle for Equal Schools: Mexican Americans during the Civil Rights Era.* Albany: State University of New York Press, 1997; Fishman, Joshua A. *Language Loyalty in the United States.* New York: Humanities Press, 1966; González, Roseann Dueñas, Victoria E. Vásquez, and John Bichsel. "Language Rights and the Mexican Americans: Much Ado about Nothing." In *Community, Identity and Education.* Vol. 3: Perspectives in Mexican American Studies, edited by Juan R. García. Tucson: University of Arizona, Mexican American Studies & Research Center, 1992; Kloss, Heinz. *The American Bilingual Tradition.* Rowley, Mass.: Newbury House, 1977; Manuel, Herschel T. *Spanish-Speaking Children of the Southwest.* Austin: University of Texas Press, 1965; San Miguel, Guadalupe, Jr. "Conflict and Controversy in the Evolution of Bilingual Education in the United States—An Interpretation." In *The Mexican American Experience: An Interdisciplinary Anthology*, edited by Rodolfo O. de la Garza et al. Austin: University of Texas Press, 1985; Schmidt, Ronald J. "Language Education Policy and the Latino Quest for Empowerment: Exploring the Linkages." In *Latinos and Political Coalitions: Political Empowerment for the 1990s*, edited by Roberto E. Villarreal and Norma G. Hernández. Westport, Conn.: Greenwood Press, 1991; Turner, Paul R. *Bilingualism in the Southwest.* 2nd ed. Tucson: University of Arizona Press, 1982.

BILINGUALISM/BICULTURALISM. In the Mexican American context bilingualism is the ability to speak both English and Spanish fluently. Biculturalism describes the ability to function well in both Mexicano and Anglo societies. Truly bicultural persons have the ability to switch codes of personal and societal values and behavior as easily as the bilingual person switches languages.

After the Treaty of Guadalupe Hidalgo in 1848, conditions in the Southwest contributed to substantial economic and social interaction, including intermarriage between in-migrant Anglo males and daughters of the Mexican American elite. In much of the Southwest Spanish remained the widely used language of daily life while English quickly became the language of commerce. Early Anglo in-migrants adopted aspects of Mexican culture, while upper-class Mexican Americans accepted some Anglo ways. As a result, a degree of bilingualism and biculturalism developed within both groups. However, heavy Anglo in-migration and the drawing of the Southwest into the national economy and society by 1900 led to a considerable decline in this bilingual and bicultural pattern.

FURTHER READING: Fishman, Joshua A. *Language Loyalty in the United States*. New York: Humanities Press, 1966; Goodenough, Ward H. *Culture, Language and Society*. Reading, Mass.: Addison-Wesley, 1971; Sánchez, Rosaura. "Chicano Bilingualism." In *New Directions in Chicano Scholarship*, edited by Ricardo Romo and Raymund Paredes. Santa Barbara: University of California, Center for Chicano Studies, 1984; Skerry, Peter. *Mexican Americans: The Ambivalent Minority*. New York: Free Press, 1993.

BISBEE "DEPORTATIONS," 1917. In the midst of the World War I copper boom some 3,000 copper miners under Industrial Workers of the World leadership went on strike at Bisbee, Arizona, in late June 1917 demanding higher wages. Two weeks later the protesters, most of whom were Mexicanos, were rounded up by a force of over 2,000 men deputized by the local sheriff. Charged with various crimes but given a last chance to return to work, more than 1,000 obdurate strikers refused, were loaded into boxcars, and were taken across the state line into New Mexico, where they were abandoned in the desert and later rescued by federal troops. Although both state and federal charges were filed over this clear and extreme violation of civil rights, no one was convicted. Few of the deportees ever returned to Bisbee.

See also CIVIL RIGHTS ABUSE.

FURTHER READING: *Arizona: A State Guide*. Federal Writers Project, Arizona. New York: Hastings House, 1940; McWilliams, Carey. *North from Mexico: The Spanish-Speaking People of the United States*. Updated ed. Westport, Conn.: Praeger Publishers, 1990.

BISHOPS COMMITTEE FOR THE SPANISH SPEAKING. See SECRETARIAT FOR THE SPANISH SPEAKING.

BLACK BERETS. First established in Albuquerque, the Black Berets organization was an urban-based paramilitary youth group that arose in New Mexico and California during the Chicano movimiento. The Berets were based loosely on the contemporary Black Panther movement and took it upon themselves to be the aggressive shock troops of the movement for Chicano rights. They denounced police harassment, especially indiscriminate and excessive use of force, and both supported and spoke out for full equality for Chicanas. Strongly nationalistic, they set as their goals liberation through education and eventual self-determination.

The alienated, strident, and often anti-capitalist rhetoric of the Black Berets attracted support mostly from high school and college students. Their forceful entry into Governor Bruce King's Santa Fe office to air grievances ended in failure. Although they involved themselves in various worthy service projects in the community, they attracted only a limited following and later lost much of that to the more popular Brown Berets.

See also BROWN BERETS.

FURTHER READING: "Black Beret Organization." In *La Causa Política: A Chicano Politics Reader*, edited by F. Chris García. Notre Dame, Ind.: University of Notre Dame Press, 1974.

BLACK CIVIL RIGHTS INFLUENCE. The rise of the black civil rights movement in the 1950s aroused widespread interest in the role of race and ethnicity in American life and caused the country to become more aware of the conditions of minority groups, including Mexican Americans.

The Chicano civil rights movement borrowed heavily in ideas, tactics, and organizational structures from the African American struggle that had begun a decade earlier. Black Is Beautiful became Brown Is Beautiful. Black Power became Brown Power. Continuing black protest politics spurred on the development of Chicano activism; many early Mexican American civil rights leaders obtained their basic training by working for black organizations or modeled their activities on the black community's approach to racism and denial of civil rights. Vilma Martínez provides a good example of this transference.

See also ALATORRE, RICHARD; MARTÍNEZ, VILMA.

FURTHER READING: García, F. Chris, and Rodolfo O. de la Garza. *The Chicano Political Experience: Three Perspectives*. North Scituate, Mass.: Duxbury Press, 1977; Muñoz, Carlos, Jr. *Youth, Identity, Power: The Chicano Movement*. New York: Verso, 1989.

BLOODY CHRISTMAS, 1951. On Christmas Eve 1951 seven young Los Angeles Chicanos were arrested by the police and taken to the Lincoln Heights police station. There they were charged with interfering with the officers and with battery. While detained at the station they were brutally beaten by police during a Christmas Eve drinking party. Subsequently the Los Angeles grand jury indicted eight of the police officers for violating the

youths' civil rights. The resulting court trials led to conviction and prison terms for some of the officers; the rest were reprimanded and disciplined.
   See also CIVIL RIGHTS ABUSE.

FURTHER READING: Meier, Matt S., and Feliciano Rivera. *Dictionary of Mexican American History*. Westport, Conn.: Greenwood Press, 1981.

BOGARDUS, EMORY S., 1882–1973. After degrees from Northwestern University and the University of Chicago, in 1911 Emory Bogardus began his long teaching and administrative career at the University of Southern California. During a half century of diligent research and writing he investigated ethnic leadership, race relations, and immigration. As part of his active and productive academic career he published hundreds of articles and some 20 books dealing with race and immigration. His pioneering sociological studies of race relations and the problems of juveniles in Los Angeles created a basis for public perceptions and became the point of departure for further research by scholars. During World War I he headed the Los Angeles Social Service Commission, and in the 1920s he was a research director for the Pacific Coast Race Relations Survey.

FURTHER READING: Bogardus, Emory S. *The Mexican in the United States*. Reprint of 1934 edition, New York: Arno Press, 1970; *The Latino Encyclopedia*. Vol. 1. Chabrán Richard, and Rafael Chabrán, eds. New York: Marshall Cavendish, 1996; Meier, Matt S., and Feliciano Rivera. *Dictionary of Mexican American History*. Westport, Conn.: Greenwood Press, 1981.

BONILLA, TONY, 1936–   . Burly, outspoken Corpus Christi attorney Tony Bonilla was one of the leading figures in the development of Tejano civil rights consciousness. A co-founder of the Political Association of Spanish-Speaking Organizations, he made an equally important contribution to the rights struggle by his long service in the League of United Latin American Citizens (LULAC), which he helped jolt into greater action, particularly in the area of education. A very energetic member of the organization since the 1960s, he has held all local offices and was elected state director at the beginning of the 1970s. He also became deeply involved in the Texas political group Mexican American Democrats of which he was state chairman in the mid-1980s.
   After his law degree from the University of Houston in 1960, Bonilla entered the firm of Bonilla, Read, Bonilla, and Berlanga as a partner. He went into state politics immediately and four years later was elected to the Texas House of Representatives, where he represented his constituents until 1967. As a politician he was also active in the Corpus Christi Chamber of Commerce and was chosen chairman of its board of directors in 1973.
   In 1981 Bonilla was elected national president of LULAC, to which he brought the Bonilla brio or, as some viewed it, his firebrand rhetoric. Dur-

ing his two-year term as president he worked to bridge the chasm between blacks and Chicanos; he met with Jesse Jackson, Coretta King, and the black leaders of the Southern Christian Leadership Conference. Another important step he took was to expand LULAC's Washington, D.C., office, thereby enabling it to give testimony regularly before congressional committees on a wide variety of Chicano concerns, from education to law enforcement and immigration. To demonstrate LULAC's support for labor he also marched with farmworkers who were seeking recognition of their civil rights.

After stepping down as president of LULAC, in 1983 Bonilla was selected to chair the National Hispanic Leadership Conference, a Latino think tank. In 1983 he ran for mayor of Corpus Christi, and three years later he received the Cecil Burney Humanitarian Award from the Nueces County bar association.

See also LEAGUE OF UNITED LATIN AMERICAN CITIZENS.

FURTHER READING: Bonilla, Tony. "We Gave It Our Best Shot." *Latino* 54, no. 4 (May–June 1983):6; Cárdenas, Leo. "The Bonilla Years Come to an End." *Latino* 54, no. 4 (May–June 1983):8–9, 29; Kane, George. "The Entrepreneurial Professional." *Hispanic Business* (September 1983):36–37, 80; Salazar, Veronica. *Dedication Rewarded: Prominent Mexican Americans.* San Antonio: Mexican American Cultural Center, 1976; *Who's Who among Hispanic Americans, 1994–1995,* 3rd ed. Detroit: Gale Research, 1994.

BOYLE, EUGENE J., 1922– . The Reverend Eugene Boyle's principal civil rights contribution was his decades-long work for farm laborers, especially migrants. Deeply involved in the farmworker movement from the mid-1960s onward, he served as an organizer for César Chávez's United Farm Workers (UFW), becoming widely known as "César's Priest." As Chávez's trusted collaborator he coordinated boycotts, served as a mediator, and negotiated one of the UFW's first contracts. He also participated in the Sacramento march and during the next decade was jailed with Chávez at Fresno, California, in 1973.

Earlier Boyle acted as moderator of the San Francisco archdiocesan Catholic Interracial Council in 1964 and two years later founded and headed the diocesan Commission on Social Justice, in which he concerned himself with strategies for social action and their implementation. As pastor of San Francisco's inner-city Church of the Sacred Heart from 1968 to 1972, he became involved in community issues and was deeply concerned with empowering the poor to improve education, housing, and police-community relations. Feeling he could be of greater service to the poor in politics, in 1974 he ran for the state assembly and almost won.

As social action director for the diocese of San Jose from 1985 to 1994 Boyle continued his civil rights work and also served on the boards of various social justice organizations, many of which he had helped establish.

He was instrumental in shaping, in California at least, the Catholic Church's view of its role in social action and public policy. After a long and distinguished career in social action spanning from the 1965 Selma march with Dr. Martin Luther King, Jr., to the UFW boycotts of the 1990s, in 1996 he retired from his pastorate but not from fighting oppression and denial of civil rights. In February 1998 Boyle was honored with the Harry A. Fagan Roundtable Award for his "outstanding contribution to the development and promotion of Catholic social ministry."

See also CHURCHES; UNITED FARM WORKERS.

FURTHER READING: "Roundtable's 1998 Award to Father Eugene J. Boyle." *The Valley Catholic* 16, no. 5 (March 1998):1, 4; "Tribute to Father Boyle." *The Valley Catholic* 16, no. 6 (April 1998):2, 5.

BROWN BERETS, 1967–1972. The Brown Berets may be described as a confrontational organization of young Chicanos, founded in East Los Angeles by college student David Sánchez in late 1967, originally called Young Chicanos for Community Action. It created a free health clinic, protested educational inequities, and demanded an end to brutality and excessive use of force by police. One of the first highly militant Chicano groups, it had close ties to both the Mexican American community and high school students. It played a decisive role in organizing the student "blowouts" in 1968.

The Berets rapidly evolved into a paramilitary alert patrol patterned somewhat after the Black Panthers. Distinguished by uniforms of brown berets, army fatigues, and military boots, they alarmed most Anglos and some middle-class Mexican Americans. Holding that to be truly Chicano one had to be poor, undereducated, and a barrio dweller, the youthful members generally distrusted educated and intellectual Chicanos as well as Anglos, thereby isolating themselves. Yet, the Berets held a strong appeal for idealistic high school and college students and quickly spread throughout the Southwest, reaching a maximum membership of perhaps 4,000 in some 80 chapters, most in California and Texas.

In 1969 the Brown Berets took an important part in organizing the National Chicano Moratorium. Their seizure of Catalina Island as "Aztlán Libre" three years later probably lessened their support in the community. Police harassment, infiltration by agents provocateur, internal power struggles, and the leadership's inability to define clearly the group's purpose and goals led to a severe organizational crisis. As a result Sánchez disbanded the Brown Berets in late 1972.

See also BLACK BERETS; ORGANIZATIONS.

FURTHER READING: Castro, Tony. *Chicano Power: The Emergence of Mexican America.* New York: Saturday Review Press. 1974; Fields, Rona Marcia. "The Brown Berets: A Participant Observation Study of Social Action in the Schools of

Los Angeles." Ph.D. diss., University of Southern California, 1970; Marín, Christine. "Go Home, Chicanos: A Study of the Brown Berets in California and Arizona." In *An Awakened Minority: The Mexican American*, edited by Manuel P. Servín. Beverly Hills, Calif.: Glencoe Press, 1974; Sánchez, David. *Expedition through Aztlán*. La Puente, Calif.: Perspectiva Publications, 1978.

BROWN POWER. A part of the Chicano inheritance from the black civil rights movement was the slogan and concept of Brown Power, corresponding to Black Power among African Americans. Brown Power had different meanings for various groups within the Mexican American community, ranging from simply a buzzword to a strongly held concept of ethnic separateness and independence. In the last years of the 1960s and the early 1970s the term was used especially to characterize the movement by activists who called for full and immediate economic, political, and social equality for Chicanos in American society. Many youthful participants in the movement demanded the right of complete self-determination and the creation of a separate entity in the Southwest that some referred to as Aztlán. As a result of confrontation tactics and the greater sensitizing of Anglo society, many of the moderate goals of the Brown Power movement were achieved by the end of the 1970s.

See also AZTLÁN CONCEPT; BLACK CIVIL RIGHTS INFLUENCE; STUDENT ACTIVISM.

FURTHER READING: Acuña, Rodolfo. *Occupied America: A History of Chicanos*, 3rd ed. New York: Harper & Row, 1988; Rosales, Francisco A. *Chicano!: The History of the Mexican American Civil Rights Movement*. Houston: Arte Público Press, 1996.

BROWN v. BOARD OF EDUCATION OF TOPEKA, KANSAS, 1954, 1955. Following precedent set by the lower federal courts in the *Méndez* case (1945, 1947), in 1954 the U.S. Supreme Court in a unanimous vote held that segregation in the public schools was a violation of the Fourteenth Amendment rights of minority students. The court further asserted that the separate but equal concept of its 1896 *Plessy v. Ferguson* decision inevitably resulted in unequal treatment of minorities. In public education, it said, separate but equal facilities based on race were inherently unequal and indefensible. In the following year it ordered schools to desegregate with due speed. The court's decision in the *Brown* case had only limited immediate effect but later became an extremely important precedent in advancing Chicano civil rights.

See also MÉNDEZ ET AL. v. WESTMINSTER SCHOOL DISTRICT; PLESSY v. FERGUSON.

FURTHER READING: Acuña, Rodolfo. *Occupied America: A History of Chicanos*, 3rd ed. New York: Harper & Row, 1988; Burns, Haywood. "From Brown to Bakke and Back: Race, Law and Social Change in America. *Daedalus* 110, No. 2

(Spring 1981):219–231; Coles, Robert. *Uprooted Children*. Pittsburgh: University of Pittsburgh Press, 1969; *Report of Pupils in Texas Public Schools Having Spanish Surnames*. Austin: Texas Education Agency, 1957; Wilkinson, J. Harvie, III. *From Brown to Bakke: The Supreme Court and School Integration, 1954–1978*. New York: Oxford University Press, 1979.

BURCIAGA, JOSÉ ANTONIO, 1940–1996. José Antonio Burciaga made his principal contributions to the advancement of Chicano civil rights through his writing and his murals. Born in El Paso, Texas, he served in the military during the Korean conflict and then completed his college degree at the University of Texas at El Paso.

Going to work in Washington, D.C., as a graphic artist for the Central Intelligence Agency, Burciaga began to participate in the movimiento and met and married Cecilia Preciado. When she was hired by Stanford University, the couple moved to California. After a decade there working in journalism, in 1985 Burciaga became a Stanford resident fellow as an artist, writer, and poet.

Burciaga used his position and skills to call attention to the denial of civil rights to Mexican Americans. His murals depicted the raza experience in American society; his essays and poetry focused on political and social issues of discrimination and racism. Through humorous satire, which often had a biting edge, he illuminated the Chicano experience in Anglo society with an aim at demanding social justice and cultural freedom. Burciaga was the recipient of numerous awards. He died of cancer at age 56 after a two-year fight against the disease.

FURTHER READING: García, Nasario. "Interview with José Antonio Burciaga." *Hispania* 68, No. 4 (December 1985):821–825; "Latino Artist, Activist Succumbs to Cancer." *San Jose Mercury News*, 8 October 1996, 1B, 4B; Lomelí, Francisco, and Carl R. Shirley, eds. *Dictionary of Literary Biography, Chicano Writers*. Vol. 82. Detroit: Gale Research, 1992. *Who's Who among Hispanic Americans, 1994–1995*. Detroit: Gale Research, 1994.

C

CABEZA DE BACA, EZEQUIEL, 1864–1917. Political leader and newspaper editor and owner Ezequiel Cabeza de Baca was the first Mexican American to be elected governor of New Mexico. His family status and press affiliations naturally led him into politics, where he became a powerful voice for la raza in northeastern New Mexico. As a member of a prominent family he used his excellent education to advance the civil rights of all Nuevomexicanos. As a politician and as a newspaperman he spoke out for their rights, especially in the areas of land grants and education. In 1890 he was one of the founders of El Partido del Pueblo Unido, a populist movement that attracted many Nuevomexicanos who had become disillusioned with the Republican and Democratic parties.

In 1910 Cabeza de Baca opposed ratification of early versions of the proposed state constitution for New Mexico as being insufficiently protective of raza rights. When New Mexico became the forty-seventh state in 1912, he ran on the Democratic slate and was elected its first lieutenant governor, which position he used to support educational reforms. In the following election he was the unanimous Democratic choice as candidate for the governorship and won the election. He died a few weeks after his inauguration after a long bout with pernicious anemia.

See also NEW MEXICO.

FURTHER READING: Beck, Warren A. *New Mexico: A History of Four Centuries.* Norman: University of Oklahoma Press, 1962; Vigil, Maurilio E. *The Hispanics of New Mexico: Essays on History and Culture.* Bristol, Ind.: Wyndham Hall Press, 1984; Vigil, Maurilio E. *Los Patrones: Profiles of Hispanic Political Leaders in New Mexico History.* Washington, D.C.: University Press of America, 1980.

CABINET COMMITTEE ON OPPORTUNITIES FOR SPANISH
SPEAKING PEOPLE (CCOSSP). The CCOSSP was a government agency
established in 1969 during the administration of Lyndon Johnson to replace
the earlier Inter-Agency Committee on Mexican American Affairs
(IACMAA). It broadened the scope of the IACMAA to include all U.S.
Latinos and continued to pursue its goals of aiding them through government programs and federal appointments. Its first chairman, Martín Castillo, who had been deputy director of the Civil Rights Commission,
achieved the major accomplishments of the agency's five-year life.

The CCOSSP was considerably politicized during the less supportive administration of President Richard Nixon, who succeeded Johnson. Castillo
was replaced by Henry Ramírez, who proved a somewhat lackluster leader
but did secure appointment of a number of Mexican Americans to federal
positions despite Nixon's personal lack of enthusiasm (revealed in his tapes)
for ethnic diversity in government employment. When the agency's term
expired during Gerald Ford's administration, it was not renewed.

FURTHER READING: "Cabinet Committee on the Spanish Speaking: Its Information and Its History." *La Luz* 1, no. 1 (1972):18–19; de la Isla, José. "The
Politics of Reelection: Se habla español." *Aztlán* 7, No. 3 (Fall 1976):427–451.

CADENA, CARLOS, 1915– . Judge Carlos Cadena has devoted a lifetime
to the use of the law to end discrimination and bigotry and thereby to
enable Mexican Americans to lead more dignified and rewarding lives. His
outstanding academic career as a student at the University of Texas at
Austin and its law school led to employment as assistant San Antonio city
attorney in 1941. After service in World War II he returned to his position
as assistant city attorney and also taught at St. Mary's University Law
School. Several years in private practice followed, and in 1954 Cadena
became the San Antonio city attorney. Eleven years later he was appointed
judge of the Texas Fourth Court of Civil Appeals by Governor John Connally.

As a lawyer Cadena helped obtain court decisions mandating an end to
school segregation, the exclusion of Mexican Americans from jury panels,
and restrictive property covenants. He was deeply involved in several prominent Mexican American civil rights cases, the most important of which
was *Hernández v. Texas*, a major civil rights victory argued before the U.S.
Supreme Court in 1954. The recipient of various honors, Cadena was appointed chief justice of the Texas Fourth Court of Civil Appeals in 1977.
He retired from the bench in 1990.

See also HERNÁNDEZ v. THE STATE OF TEXAS.

FURTHER READING: García, Mario T. *Mexican Americans: Leadership, Ideology, and Identity, 1930–1960.* New Haven, Conn.: Yale University Press, 1989;

Salazar, Veronica. *Dedication Rewarded: Prominent Mexican Americans*. Vol. 2. San Antonio: Mexican American Cultural Center, 1981.

CALDERÓN, ANTONIO, 1933– . After serving in the army during 1955–1956, Antonio Calderón returned to San Antonio, where he started his civil service career as an employee at Fort Sam Houston and soon became seriously involved in civil rights concerns. In the mid-1960s, through Representative Joe Bernal, he helped bring about Texas legislation basing public assistance on residence rather than citizenship, thereby helping elderly Mexicanos, many of whom had been taxpayers in the state for decades without becoming U.S. citizens. Encouraged by this success and pursuing long-range goals of social rights, Calderón and several friends founded an organization they named Involvement of Mexican Americans in Gainful Endeavors (IMAGE). Under Calderón's leadership IMAGE sought to improve the quality of life for Mexican Americans, especially the young. Concerned with the high dropout rate among Chicano students, he also created the Youth Entrepreneurship Program to motivate and tutor high school students.

In 1968 Calderón was in the forefront of the drive to erase the poor media image of Mexican Americans, campaigning against "Frito Bandito" advertising and similar stereotyping of Latinos in the media. Because of his concern about the adverse effects of stereotyping, he also established IMAGE Productions, Inc., an entertainment agency to showcase talented Latinos like Joe Kapp, José Feliciano, and the Lennon Sisters.

See also BERNAL, JOE; INVOLVEMENT OF MEXICAN AMERICANS IN GAINFUL ENDEAVORS; STEREOTYPING.

FURTHER READING: Chacón, José. *Hispanic Notables in the United States of North America*. Albuquerque, N.M.: Saguaro Publishing, 1978.

CALIFORNIA. Civil rights problems began early for Mexican Americans in California. The rapid and heavy influx of Anglo miners and settlers quickly reduced the Californios to a small, nearly powerless minority. The state's Foreign Miners License Law of 1850 and the federal Land Act of 1851, passed by the U.S. Congress, greatly accelerated the violating of their rights, as did extensive Anglo squatter activity during the decade. The extent of social banditry in the state was a measure of the deteriorating position of Californios and of their loss of civil rights. By the end of the century most had become almost completely disfranchised and relegated to low economic status.

Beginning early in the twentieth century California became the destination of a flood tide of workers from the Southwest and refugees fleeing Mexico as a result of the Mexican revolution of 1910. During the 1920s this influx was further enlarged by rapid economic development, especially in agriculture—the factories in the fields of Carey McWilliams. The Spanish-speaking population increase led to more overt and stronger anti-Mexican attitudes in the state, especially as the economy began to falter toward the end of the decade. The heavy Mexican immigration of the 1920s was terminated by the Great Depression that followed the 1929 stock market crash and sent roughly a million Mexicanos southward across the border. In 1931 more than 50,000 Mexicanos were shipped out of Los Angeles alone. This "repatriation," which resulted from the scapegoating of minorities, involved considerable violation of civil rights, particularly of those, a majority of them children, who were U.S. citizens by birth.

By the late 1930s a large first- and second-generation Mexican American population in California began to speak out more forthrightly about its concern for its citizen rights. The civil rights violations in the Sleepy Lagoon case and the "Zoot Suit" riots of the 1940s helped spur extensive organizational development at the end of World War II. The creation of the Mexican American Political Association at the end of the next decade initiated a new stage in civil rights activism. In the 1960s the advent of the Chicano Movement, in which California played a cutting-edge role, marked a decisive further step in the demand for equality and full rights as citizens. César Chávez's leadership in the unionization of farmworkers in the Central Valley initiated a renewed push for their human and civil rights, as did the establishment of the California Rural Legal Assistance in 1966.

Although the movimiento had slowed down by the end of the 1970s, the advances and spirit it had engendered continued to animate the struggle for Mexican American rights in California. Symbolic of the advances made, in 1980 President Jimmy Carter appointed as U.S. ambassador to Mexico professor Julian Nava of California, the first Mexican American to be appointed to such an important diplomatic post. In 1996 Cruz Bustamante's selection as the first Chicano speaker of the California state house was further evidence and recognition of Mexican American political activism and potential. Three years later he took the oath of office as lieutenant governor, the first Mexican American to hold that position in a century and a quarter.

On the negative side, in 1986 a successful ballot initiative amended the state constitution to make English California's official language. Moreover, in 1994 Governor Pete Wilson, using a race-baiting anti-immigrant strategy, won reelection by more than a million votes despite overwhelming opposition and turnout by Asians and Latinos. Exit polls in the 1996 election indicated that the latter voted at about a 50 percent rate, up from 30 percent in 1990. Despite the increased participation by Chicano voters, two years later Proposition 227, which aimed at ending bilingual education, easily passed.

See also CHÁVEZ, CÉSAR; SLEEPY LAGOON; ZOOT SUIT RIOTS.

FURTHER READING: Acuña, Rodolfo F. *Anything but Mexican: Chicanos in Contemporary Los Angeles.* New York: Verso, 1996. Almanza, Arturo S. *Mexican-Americans and Civil Rights.* Los Angeles: County Commission on Human Relations, 1964; California. Mexican Fact-Finding Committee. *Mexicans in California: Report* . . . Reprint, San Francisco: R & E Research Associates, 1970; Camarillo, Albert. *Chicanos in California: A History of Mexican Americans in California.* San Francisco: Boyd & Fraser, 1984; McWilliams, Carey. *Southern California Country.* New York: Duell, Sloan & Pierce, 1946; Menchaca, Martha. *The Mexican Outsiders: A Community History of Marginalization and Discrimination in California.* Austin: University of Texas Press, 1995; Pitt, Leonard M. *The Decline of the Californios: A Social History of the Spanish-Speaking Californians, 1846–1890.* Berkeley: University of California Press, 1966; Romo, Ricardo. *East Los Angeles: History of a Barrio.* Austin: University of Texas Press, 1983; U.S. Commission on Civil Rights. *Political Participation of Mexican Americans in California.* Washington, D.C.: U.S. Government Printing Office, 1971; Wollenberg, Charles. *Ethnic Conflict in California History.* Los Angeles: Timmon-Brown, 1970.

CALIFORNIA RURAL LEGAL ASSISTANCE (CRLA). The CRLA was established in 1966 as a nonprofit organization with a grant from the Office of Economic Opportunity. It set as its task the advancement of civil rights by providing free legal service to poverty-level clients, with emphasis on class-action suits that would benefit larger numbers of people. A majority of the persons it served were Mexican Americans. Its activities aroused the vocal opposition of many conservative Californians and especially of Governor Ronald Reagan, who tried to emasculate it. The CRLA included a task force to ascertain the needs for law services to defend civil rights in housing, education, and employment. Its headquarters in San Francisco oversaw the work of 160 employees who were handling over 13,000 cases annually in the 1980s.

See also CALIFORNIA.

FURTHER READING: Bennett, Richard, and Cruz Reynoso. "California Rural Legal Assistance: The Survival of a Poverty Law Practice." *Chicano Law Review* 1 (1972):1–79; Trillin, Calvin. "U.S. Letter: McFarland." *New Yorker* 43 (4 November 1967):173–181.

CAMPA, ARTHUR LEÓN, 1905–1978. Dr. Arthur Campa, outstanding authority on the folklore of the Southwest, took a moderate stance in the Chicano civil rights movement. Before World War II he was active in and briefly head of the leftist Congreso de los Pueblos de Habla Española; after the war he strongly supported the civil and social rights efforts of the more moderate American G.I. Forum and the League of United Latin American Citizens. However, he remained less active politically than many of his peers in academia.

See also CONGRESO DE LOS PUEBLOS DE HABLA ESPAÑOLA.

FURTHER READING: Campa, Arthur L. "Colorado's Youth Looks to the Skies." Denver: Colorado Department of Education, 1949; García, Mario T. *Mexican Americans: Leadership, Ideology, and Identity, 1930–1960.* New Haven, Conn.: Yale University Press. 1989; Sonnichsen, Philip. "Arthur León Campa." *La Luz* 7, no. 12 (December 1978):20, 26.

CANALES, J[OSÉ] T[OMÁS], 1877–1976. Prominent south Texas jurist and politician J. T. Canales of Brownsville was also an active defender of Mexicano civil rights. Although a member of the Anglo political machine in south Texas through his marriage to an Anglo, he was also a close friend of lawyer-activist Alonso Perales and aggressively defended the civil rights of Mexicanos. During the border unrest attendant on the 1910 Mexican revolution he spoke out sharply against the violent treatment of Mexicanos by Texas Rangers and became widely known for filing formal charges against them in January 1918 over their brutal actions and use of excessive force. As a result of his initiative a long investigation of the charges ensued and the Ranger force was eventually reduced to five companies.

In the 1920s J. T., as he was known, played an influential role in the developing Mexican American civil rights movement. Active first in the Latin American Citizens League (LACL), in 1929 he was one of the founders of the League of United Latin American Citizens (LULAC), which grew out of the LACL. He had a leading part in writing the first LULAC constitution and occupied a number of important positions in the organization, including the presidency in 1932 and 1933. At the end of the 1930s he led the revision of LULAC's constitution to conform to its expansion into a national group.

Canales, a progressive but at times somewhat maverick politico, took an active part in south Texas politics throughout the first half of the twentieth century. After serving several terms in the Texas legislature during the late teen years, Canales formed a local political party in the 1930s but later returned to the Democratic fold. Greatly interested in education and irrigation rights, he also favored broad humanitarian reforms like prohibition and suffrage for women. As an octogenarian he supported Lyndon Johnson's political career in the 1960s.

Canales was a prolific writer of articles, pamphlets, and books; he is best known as the author of a two-volume historical work, *Bits of Texas History in the Melting Pot*, published at Brownsville between 1950 and 1957.

See also TEXAS RANGERS.

FURTHER READING: Anders, Evan. *Boss Rule in South Texas.* Austin: University of Texas Press, 1982; Canales, José T. *Bits of Texas History in the Melting Pot.* 2 vols. Brownsville, Tex.: 1950–1957; Canales, José T. *Juan N. Cortina Presents His Motion for a New Trial.* San Antonio, Tex.: Artes Gráficas, 1951; Pycior, Julie Leininger. *LBJ & Mexican Americans: The Paradox of Power.* Austin: University of Texas Press, 1997; Tyler, Ron, ed. *The New Handbook of Texas*. Vol. 1. Austin: Texas State Historical Association, 1996.

CASTRO, SAL(VADOR) M., 1933–   . Sal Castro, American-born son of undocumented immigrant parents, accompanied them in their repatriation to Mexico in the 1930s and later came back to the United States. After returning to the United States he served in the Korean conflict. Educated in California, he became active in the Democratic Party during his college years and later took part in the Mexican American Political Association. After college he obtained a position teaching at a Los Angeles high school. As a teacher Castro came to the conclusion that Mexican American students needed to take steps for their own educational rights. The concept of the student walkout was his approach to solving the problem.

Castro leaped into the media spotlight in March 1968 when some 5,000 Los Angeles high school students walked out of the classroom. Active in picketing, sit-ins, demonstrations, and demands, he quickly became the symbol as well as the leader of the walkout. Along with 12 others he was indicted in June by a Los Angeles grand jury on charges of felonious conspiracy. He was convicted. Two years later on appeal the charges were found unconstitutional and dropped, but Castro was barred from teaching for five years and continued to be harassed.

See also MEXICAN AMERICAN POLITICAL ASSOCIATION; STUDENT ACTIVISM.

FURTHER READING: Muñoz, Carlos, Jr. *Youth, Identity, Power: The Chicano Movement*. New York: Verso, 1990; Palacios, Arturo, ed. *Mexican American Directory*. Washington, D.C.: Executive Systems Corp., 1969.

CENTRO DE ACCIÓN SOCIAL AUTÓNOMA (CASA). CASA was founded in late 1968, largely through the efforts of Bert Corona, as an organization with goals of Chicano political awareness and international solidarity. From its beginning ideological purity and party discipline were important matters to its leftist leadership. CASA became deeply involved with the problems of undocumented immigration and other working-class concerns. With a membership made up mostly of workers plus some students and professionals, it developed close ties to the Mexican American community and provided militant leaders for organizing Mexicano workers and developing political activists.

Structural weaknesses of CASA and unresolved differences between bitterly opposed cliques and factions in the organization caused repeated conflicts that erupted in divisive accusations and denunciations. In 1972 these internal problems led to splits that restructuring and reorganization in the following years failed to heal. CASA ceased to exist as an organization, but some local chapters continued to function and their leaders remained active in the community. During the few years of its existence CASA had some successes. In the long run it was more important for developing aggressive leaders for other organizations that followed.

See also CORONA, BERT; ORGANIZATIONS.

FURTHER READING: García, Mario T. *Memories of Chicano History: The Life and Narrative of Bert Corona.* Berkeley: University of California Press, 1994; Gómez-Quiñones, Juan. *Chicano Politics: Reality and Promise, 1940–1990.* Albuquerque: University of New Mexico Press, 1990.

CHÁVEZ, CÉSAR ESTRADA, 1927–1993. Although often characterized as a labor or farmworker leader, César Chávez was really much more than that; to a considerable degree he converted the Mexican American farmworkers' struggle for better conditions into a civil rights movement. A great admirer of Mohandas Gandhi and Martin Luther King, Jr., whose ideas he studied and followed, he derived the charisma of his leadership from his personal moral probity and a deep concern for the rights of others, as well as from his strong commitment to nonviolence. He was the closest thing to a civil rights leader like Martin Luther King, Jr., that the Chicano movimiento produced.

Having served in World War II, César Chávez returned home to migrant agricultural work and joined an early union. Years later, during the summer of 1952, he became acquainted with Fred Ross, Sr., a Saul Alinsky disciple who was organizing for the Community Service Organization (CSO) in southern California. Chávez soon joined the CSO as an unpaid volunteer, working in voter registration. By 1958 he had become a director in the CSO, but he resigned from the organization four years later to devote his time and energies to working for farm laborers' rights, a cause he believed in deeply.

With the help of his wife and a few devoted followers Chávez created the National Farm Workers Association, which later became the United Farm Workers (UFW). In 1965 he took the union into the Delano grape strike. By presenting the workers' problems in the context of the civil rights movement, he quickly converted the strike (La Huelga) from a labor dispute to a civil rights crusade—La Causa (The Cause). In April 1966 he led a march to the state capital, Sacramento, to demand justice and full civil rights for farmworkers. Throughout the five difficult years of the strike he strongly stressed its moral basis, endured jail sentences, and went on fasts, thereby constantly reinforcing its character as a civil rights movement. His long fight for the rights of laborers in harvest agriculture brought the wretched treatment they suffered vividly to the attention of all Americans.

When the country began a conservative swing in the 1980s, Chávez remained a world-recognized Mexican American leader and a national metaphor for humaneness and agricultural workers' rights. During the latter 1970s there was talk of Chávez as a candidate for a Nobel Prize. In November 1990 the president of Mexico awarded him the Aguila Azteca, the highest honor the Mexican government can confer on a foreigner. A year after his unexpected death in 1993, César Chávez was awarded the Presidential Medal of Freedom by President Bill Clinton for his leadership in the Chicano rights movement.

See also DELANO GRAPE STRIKE; HUERTA, DOLORES; ROSS, FRED, JR.; UNITED FARM WORKERS.

FURTHER READING: Day, Mark. *Forty Acres: César Chávez and the Farm Workers.* New York: Praeger, 1971; Ferriss, Susan, and Ricardo Sandoval. *The Fight in the Fields: César Chávez and the Farmworkers Movement.* Troy, N.Y.: Harcourt Brace, 1997; Goodwin, David. *César Chávez: Hope for the People.* New York: Fawcett Columbine, 1991; Griswold del Castillo, Richard, and Richard García. *César Chávez: A Triumph of Spirit.* Norman: University of Oklahoma Press, 1995; Hammerback, John C., and Richard J. Jensen. *The Rhetorical Career of César Chávez.* College Station: Texas A & M University Press, 1998; Levy, Jacques E. *César Chávez: Autobiography of La Causa.* New York: W. W. Norton & Co., 1974; Ross, Fred, Sr. *Conquering Goliath: César Chávez at the Beginning.* Keene, Calif.: United Farm Workers, 1989; Vizzard, James L. "The Extraordinary César Chávez." *Progressive* 30 (July 1966):16–20.

CHÁVEZ, DENNIS (DIONISIO), 1888–1962. Dennis Chávez, U.S. senator from New Mexico from 1935 to 1962, was a strong advocate of civil rights throughout his political life. He saw his role in the U.S. Senate as advancing New Mexican interests. During World War II he introduced and strongly supported an equal rights amendment to the Constitution. In the postwar years Chávez did some of his best work. He exerted forceful leadership in writing and pushing a bill to establish a permanent Federal Fair Employment Practices Commission; he also worked quietly to improve the lot of Native Americans. An individualist and at times paradoxical politician, in 1960 he voted to send a civil rights bill back to committee, thereby effectively killing it.

Dennis Chávez was a grade school dropout, but he continued his education by his voracious reading of history. Through an intense attraction to Thomas Jefferson he developed an early interest in politics and the law. After earning his law degree through night classes, at the ripe age of 32 he set up practice in Albuquerque in 1920 and quickly entered the state's political arena. Ten years later he was elected to the U.S. House of Representatives. Appointed to the U.S. Senate in 1935 upon the death of New Mexico's Senator Bronson Cutting, he was easily elected in the following year and thereafter was regularly returned to the Senate until his death.

In the U.S. Senate Chávez worked without respite and consistently supported the rights of his Nuevomexicano constituents. His most important contribution, especially to the Hispanos of his state, was his advocacy of and support for civil rights and education. In 1953 he first introduced legislation to provide them with equal opportunity for employment. At the same time he was one of a handful who dared denounce the infamous Senator Joseph McCarthy for riding roughshod over constitutional and civil rights. Posthumously he was selected by the New Mexico Historical Society for the honor of representing the state in the Statuary Hall of the Capitol in Washington, D.C.

See also NEW MEXICO; POLITICAL PARTICIPATION.

FURTHER READING: *Current Biography, 1946*. New York: H. W. Wilson Co., 1947; Keleher, William A. *Memoirs: 1892–1969: A New Mexico Item*. Santa Fe, N.M.: Rydal Press, 1969; Luján, Roy. "Dennis Chávez and the Roosevelt Era, 1933–1945." Ph.D. diss., University of New Mexico, 1987; Perrigo, Lynn I. *Hispanos: Historic Leaders in New Mexico*. Santa Fe, N.M.: Sunstone Press, 1985; Popejoy, Tom. "Dennis Chávez." In *Hall of Fame Essays*, edited by Victor Westphall. Albuquerque: Historical Society of New Mexico, 1963.

CHÁVEZ, LINDA, 1947– . Jolted by racism and discrimination in her high school years, Linda Chávez became an active member of both the Congress of Racial Equality and the National Association for the Advancement of Colored People. However, as a student on the University of Colorado's Boulder campus she was never attracted to the confrontational tactics and often radical rhetoric of the Chicano Movement during its early days in the late 1960s.

As a doctoral student at the University of California at Los Angeles in 1970, Linda Chávez was persuaded to teach a class in Chicano literature. Reluctant to accept the validity of Chicano literature as a college subject and frequently hectored by campus militants, she left the university two years later and joined her husband, Christopher Gersten, in Washington, D.C. After a year and a half there as a political staffer she became a lobbyist for the National Education Association and in 1975 accepted the position of assistant director of legislation for the more conservative American Federation of Teachers (AFT).

In 1977 Chávez was appointed director of research for the AFT and editor of its influential quarterly, *American Educator*. During her six-year editorship she wrote a series of powerful articles on the need to teach traditional values in the public schools. Her conservative views attracted favorable attention in the Ronald Reagan administration, and in August 1983 she was offered appointment as staff director of the U.S. Commission on Civil Rights.

As director of the commission, the first woman to hold that position, Chávez helped President Ronald Reagan for the next two years in his drive to cripple the commission. She vehemently denied the efficacy of affirmative action and opposed using a quota system to balance racial and gender discrimination. In 1985 her appointment to the powerful position of director of the White House Office of Public Liaison made her the highest-ranking woman in the Reagan administration. Less than a year later she resigned to run for the U.S. Senate from Maryland. Despite President Reagan's support in an aggressive and acrimonious campaign against her liberal Democratic opponent, she lost the election.

In 1987 Linda Chávez was named president of U.S. English, a national right-wing anti-immigrant organization. Although in general agreement with U.S. English's tenets, she resigned a year later in protest against public anti-Latino and anti-Catholic statements by founder John Tanton. She then accepted an appointment as senior fellow with the Manhattan Institute for Policy Research, a conservative Washington-based think tank. In 1991 she published her forthright and deeply conservative views on ethnic political involvement, affirmative action, and multiculturalism in her book *Out of the Barrio: Toward a New Politics of Hispanic Assimilation*. Four years later she founded the Center for Equal Opportunity, which provides legal support for efforts to fight challenges to California's Proposition 209 and Proposition 227.

Linda Chávez continues to expound her views in a weekly syndicated column published in 50 newspapers and in articles for *Fortune* and other conservative journals. An articulate, forceful speaker, she is also a frequent guest on National Public Radio and Cable News Network.

See also AFFIRMATIVE ACTION; CHICANAS; ENGLISH ONLY.

FURTHER READING: Barrett, Paul M. "Linda Chávez and the Exploitation of Ethnic Identity." *Washington Monthly* 17 (June 1985):25–29; Chávez, Linda. *Out of the Barrio: Toward a New Politics of Hispanic Assimilation*. New York: Basic Books, 1991; Hernández, Macarena. "Conservative and Hispanic, Linda Chávez Carves Out Leadership Niche." *New York Times*, 19 August 1998, A26; Saavedra-Vela, Pilar. "Linda Chávez: Commentary by a Political Professional." *Agenda* 7, no. 5 (September/October 1977); Telgen, Diane, and Jim Kamp, eds. *Notable Hispanic American Women*. Detroit: Gale Research, 1993.

CHICANAS. As a group within the Mexican American community Chicanas have been at a considerable disadvantage. Gender-based discrimination and low societal expectations have served to keep them on the lowest rungs of the political, economic, educational, and social ladders. Until the post–World War II period civil rights activities by Chicanas, with a handful of notable exceptions, most in radical organizations, were limited to distinctly secondary roles in support of their husbands or other males.

There were, of course, outstanding early activists like Lucía González Parsons and María Hernández and later Josefina Fierro de Bright, Luisa Moreno, and Emma Tenayuca, as well as others less widely known. Clearly many civil rights organizations like the Congreso de Los Pueblos de Habla Española, Asociación Nacional México-Americana, Orden Caballeros de América, El Comité Mexicano Contra el Racismo, and Liga Pro-Defensa Escolar (in San Antonio) owed much to the early activism of Chicanas.

They provided much of the drive as well as behind-the-scenes support in various community organizations.

During World War II more Chicanas took on heavier responsibilities as wage-earners, heads of families, and community leaders. In the postwar movimiento they made up much of the organizational backbone for the new civil rights–oriented groups that developed. Women like Julia Luna Mount and Grace Montañez were important in the expansion of the Mexican American Political Association in the 1960s and early 1970s. Dolores Huerta made herself a highly valued lieutenant of César Chávez in organizing the United Farm Workers. Chicanas played significant supportive roles in the development of the Mexican American Youth Organization (MAYO), doing much of the vital daily routine work. Tejanas Juanita Bustamante and Alma Canales played a critically important part in MAYO and La Raza Unida Party.

After the war many Chicanas for the first time became acutely aware that a majority of their male cohorts considered them fit only for less important work: this despite their active participation throughout the Southwest in educational reforms and their activity in fighting for labor rights. This new awareness led them to raise their voices in demands for gender equality as well as full civil rights. They established a variety of Chicana organizations whose broad goals were to advance the cause of equal treatment and rights for all.

During the decade of the 1970s middle-class Chicana groups showed great organizational vigor. In 1970 the Comisión Femenil Nacional Mexicana was organized, and four years later the Mexican American Women's National Association (MANA), was founded in Washington, D.C. In 1976 the Chicana Forum was established, followed in the next year by the National Network of Hispanic Women. In terms of membership MANA and the League of United Latin American Citizens' women's subsidiary, Mujeres en Acción, have remained the most influential Chicana groups. One measure of the Chicana movement's success was that at the beginning of the 1990s Latinas represented nearly 25 percent of all raza elected officials.

See also HERNÁNDEZ, MARÍA; HUERTA, DOLORES; IDAR, JOVITA; MANA: A NATIONAL LATINA ORGANIZATION; MORENO, LUISA.

FURTHER READING: Alarcón, Norma, et al. *Chicana Critical Issues*. Berkeley, Calif.: Third Woman Press, 1993; *Chicanas and Chicanos in Contemporary Society*. Edited by Roberto M. de Anda. Boston: Allyn & Bacon, 1996; *Chicanas/Chicanos at the Crossroads*. Edited by David R. Maciel and Isidro D. Ortiz. Tucson: University of Arizona Press, 1996; Cotera, Martha P. *Diosa y hembra: The History and Heritage of Chicanas in the U.S.* Austin, Tex.: Information Systems Development, 1976; García, Alma M., ed. *Chicana Feminist Thought: The Basic Historical Writings*. New York: Routledge, 1997; García, Juan R., ed. *Perspectives in Mexican American Studies: Mexican American Women Changing Images*. Tucson: University of Arizona, Mexican American Studies and Research Center, 1995; *Latina Issues: Fragments of Historia (ella) Herstory*. Edited by Antoinette Sedillo López. New York: Garland Publishing, 1995; Mirandé, Alfredo, and Evangelina Enríquez. *La Chicana: The Mexican-American Woman*. Chicago: University of Chicago Press, 1979; Mora, Magdalena, and Adelaida R. Del Castillo, eds. *Mexican Women in the United States: Struggles, Past and Present*. Los Angeles: Chicano Studies Research Center, University of California, 1980; *Las Mujeres: Mexican American/ Chicana Women*. Windsor, Calif.: National Women's History Project, 1991; Navarro, Armando. *Mexican American Youth Organization: Avant-Garde of the Chicano Movement in Texas*. Austin: University of Texas Press, 1995; Pardo, Mary S. *Mexican American Women Activists: Identity and Resistance in Two Los Angeles Communities*. Philadelphia: Temple University Press, 1998; Ruiz, Vicki L. *From Out of the Shadows: Mexican Women in Twentieth-Century America*. New York: Oxford University Press, 1998; Segura, Denise A., and Beatriz M. Pesquera. "Chicana Feminisms: Their Political Context and Contemporary Expressions." In *The Latino Studies Reader: Culture, Economy, and Society*, edited by Antonia Darder and Rodolfo D. Torres. Malden, Mass.: Blackwell Publishers, 1998; Sosa Riddell, Adaljiza. "Chicanas and el Movimiento." *Aztlán* 5, nos. 1 & 2 (Spring and Fall 1974):155–165; Vidal, Mirta. *Chicanas Speak Out: Women, New Voices of La Raza*. New York: Pathfinder Press, 1971.

CHICANO LITERATURE. In the century and a half since the Treaty of Guadalupe Hidalgo Mexican American authors have written in many literary forms on a wide variety of topics. Most of their themes, especially in the second half of the twentieth century when Chicano literature came of age, derive directly from the experience of growing up Chicano in Anglo society. For many of them an embittering aspect of that experience has been racism and segregation—denials of their civil rights. In this connection the black civil rights movement of the mid-1960s changed forever the way Chicanos viewed themselves and their relationship to Anglo society. They demanded their rightful economic and political place in the United States and refused to accept anything less than first-class citizenship.

Many Chicano writers saw literature as a natural way to articulate their feelings about racism and civil rights as well as to explicate their search for roots and identity. In their writings some sought their identity through a cultural nationalism that stressed feelings of pride in and loyalty to Mexican culture. By its very nature the Chicano Movement, with its goals of self-definition, self-realization, and human rights, tended to speak out against repression and denial. It is not surprising, therefore, that these topics loomed large in Mexican American writing as authors channeled feelings of resentment and resistance to ethnic discrimination into literary outlets. Works like Raymond Barrio's *The Plum Plum Pickers* (1969) decried the ill-treatment and suffering of migrant Mexican workers; five years later Miguel Méndez called attention to social injustice and human rights abuses at the border and in the workplace in his *Peregrinos de Aztlán. The*

Revolt of the Cockroach People (1973) by Oscar Z. Acosta and even works as neutral as José Antonio Villarreal's *Pocho* (1959) and Tomás Rivera's *. . . y no se lo tragó la tierra* (1971) presented further implicit evidence of the denial of civil rights to Mexican Americans. In *Zoot Suit* Luis Valdez resuscitated the memory of a popular hysteria against young Chicanos and a gross miscarriage of justice during World War II.

Chicano writers used short stories as well as the novel to delineate both the lack of civil rights and the struggle to obtain them. Sandra Cisneros, the first Chicana to be published by a mainstream press, provided a feminine perspective to the Chicano experience with her presentation of strong-willed women fighting the denial of their rights by Chicano males as well as by Anglo society. In his semi-autobiographical sketches of migrant life Francisco Jiménez limned the negative experiences of migrant children both in the fields and in the education system.

Even poetry served to carry the message of the Mexican American civil rights movement. Corky Gonzales's *I Am Joaquín*, which so strongly influenced the movimiento, was a powerful evocation of an Indian past but also expressed clearly the repressed anger at racism and discrimination that characterized much of Chicano literature of the 1970s. Among the poets were outstanding Chicanas who took the discussion of denial of rights a step farther. For example, Bernice Zamora crafted poems that illustrated the inferior position to which Chicanas were condemned in Mexican American as well as Anglo society.

Lastly, Chicano journals like *El Grito, Caracol*, and *Aztlán*, as well as others, many of them short-lived, spread the message of the civil rights struggle and provided Mexican American writers with a forum in which they could expound on their societal concerns, make their readers aware of widespread repression, and condemn victimization, discrimination, and racism.

See also ACOSTA, OSCAR ZETA; MOVIMIENTO, EL.

FURTHER READING: Jiménez, Francisco, ed. *The Identification and Analysis of Chicano Literature*. New York: Bilingual Press, 1979; Lomelí, Francisco A., ed. *Handbook of Hispanic Cultures in the United States: Literature and Art*. Houston: Arte Público Press, 1993; Rendón, Armando B. *Chicano Manifesto*. New York: Macmillan, 1971; Shirley, Carl R., and Paula W. Shirley. *Understanding Chicano Literature*. Columbia, S.C.: University of South Carolina Press, 1988. Tatum, Charles. *Mexican American Literature*. Orlando, Fla.: Harcourt Brace Jovanovich, 1990.

CHICANO STUDIES DEPARTMENTS. Civil rights unrest among Mexican Americans in the 1960s was perhaps the most important single factor in the emergence of Chicano studies departments and programs in various U.S. universities, particularly in the Southwest. These departments usually encompassed the study of Chicano history, sociology, psychology, and folklore. Also called Chicano studies centers and sometimes ethnic studies departments or programs (especially in smaller universities and colleges), these agencies were both the result of the civil rights ferment among Mexican Americans and an important factor in the further demand for those rights.

Because of the nature of the gestation of these departments, they developed goals that differed in some particulars from those of traditional university departments. They tended to be more activist politically and to become closely involved in the Chicano community and its problems. As a result of the research and publishing that they fostered, a greater awareness of past and current denial of social justice and civil rights was developed and many students and faculty became more deeply concerned with bringing about change for la raza.

See also EDUCATION; STUDENT ACTIVISM.

FURTHER READING: Acuña, Rodolfo F. *Sometimes There Is No Other Side: Chicanos and the Myth of Equality.* Notre Dame, Ind.: University of Notre Dame Press, 1998; Cordova, Teresa, ed. *Chicano Studies: Critical Connection between Research and Community.* Albuquerque: National Association for Chicano Studies, 1992. Muñoz, Carlos, Jr. *Youth, Identity, Power: The Chicano Movement.* New York: Verso, 1989. *El Plan de Santa Barbara.* Santa Barbara, Calif.: La Causa Publications, 1969.

CHURCHES. The churches, Catholic and Protestant, have played a significant role in the ongoing Mexican American search for civil rights and social justice. During most of the nineteenth century Catholic and Protestant clergy, for somewhat differing reasons, worked to incorporate Mexicanos into American society. Until the beginning of the twentieth century both groups looked at Mexicanos primarily from a missionary perspective. There is little evidence of any special concern for raza social and civil rights. Only the last two decades of that century showed faint beginnings of an awareness of Mexicanos' serious and unmet temporal needs.

In their evangelizing efforts in the Southwest, Protestant and Catholic clergy alike faced conditions of vast distances, an inadequate financial base, and limited church organizational development and support. The rural reality of small scattered and often isolated settlements in most of the Southwest tended to obscure the need for protecting civil rights. With the burgeoning of the U.S. industrial revolution at the approach of the twentieth century, however, church leaders increasingly recognized their followers' need for social justice and began to see this as an important part of pastoral stewardship. This awareness was a leading factor in the incipient development of the social gospel movement at this time in the Southwest.

At the beginning of the twentieth century the modern civil rights movement had a slow start among Chicanos possibly because of their rural demographic distribution and the paucity of Catholic priests, most of whom showed little concern about social justice issues. The Catholic Church, to which most Mexican Americans belonged, lagged behind the Protestant denominations in moving to active social Christianity with its emphasis on the temporal welfare of the poor. However, *Rerum Novarum*, the 1891 encyclical of Pope Leo XIII, did assert the rights of workers and decades later began to influence the thinking of a handful of more progressive American Catholic bishops. Nevertheless, there is no evidence that the pope's ideas were applied directly to day-by-day conditions existing among Mexicano workers.

A 1920 survey in Los Angeles with its large Mexicano population showed that Catholics and Protestants alike had established only a scant handful of social services centers. Moreover, until the 1960s the churches provided little or no support or assistance directly aimed at obtaining civil rights. The civil rights violations inherent in the great "repatriation" movement of 1929–1936 brought only limited response from the churches. However, a few Catholic bishops like Robert Lucey and Francis Furey did begin to concern themselves about the ill-treatment of their exploited parishioners.

After World War II social action for its own sake began to attract a larger number of church leaders. In 1945, under Lucey's leadership, the Bishops Committee for the Spanish Speaking was organized and began developing various rights-oriented social services including citizenship classes and voter registration drives. The creation of the Catholic Youth Organization made available to young Chicanos organizational and leadership training as well as an ideology of social service. In farming areas the National Catholic Rural Life Conference began to provide support for the social justice aspirations of agricultural workers.

However, budget constrictions and lack of enthusiasm for social Christianity on the part of many older clerics limited the success of Catholic and Protestant efforts. On the Protestant side the interdenominational Migrant Ministry, founded in the 1920s with support from the National Council of Churches, did excellent work but often encountered apathy or downright hostility among local ministers, particularly those of the more conservative denominations. Nevertheless, attitudes were changing, if slowly. In the early 1960s Vatican II led to greater focus in the Catholic Church on the plight of the poor; in the United States that meant especially Mexicanos. Rome pushed the Catholic movement of greater concern for human rights; some local clergymen, seeking to alleviate their parishioners' economic problems, began devoting attention to the temporal as well as spiritual needs of minorities.

The various Protestant denominations have had a significant influence in the Chicano's post–World War II struggle for civil rights. With funding from the National Council of Churches, many Protestant clerics began taking up the civil rights concerns of Chicanos. In 1964 the Presbyterian

Church sponsored a conference in Phoenix titled "The Role of the Church in the Civil Rights of the Spanish Speaking." Episcopalian, Presbyterian, and Methodist leaders gave evidence of considerable political skills in the quest for social justice and civil rights and also showed increasing sensitivity to aspects of Mexican Christianity, like devotion to the Virgin of Guadalupe. Fundamentalist ministers, usually heading relatively small congregations and often operating out of storefronts, placed less emphasis on civil and human rights. However, they were highly successful in attracting converts, perhaps because they offered a more effective religious experience, often in Spanish. Some ministers were Mexican Americans who had additional leadership roles within the community. Reies López Tijerina would be an outstanding example.

The occasion of the Delano grape strike in the second half of the 1960s witnessed a widespread outpouring of church support, both Protestant and Catholic. The Migrant Ministry, which had turned more and more toward union organizing as a way to achieve greater civil rights for workers, played an important role in the strike. In the end its successful conclusion was directly attributable to the ad hoc Catholic Bishops Committee on Farm Labor.

The Mexican American civil rights movement of the 1960s and 1970s hastened the sensitization of the churches to the continuing marginalized and exploited conditions of Mexicanos throughout the Southwest. The civil rights vision of the overwhelming majority of younger Protestant and Catholic clergy played an important role in the gains in recent years by Mexicano agricultural workers. In many cities the churches have been strong supporters of local rights organizations like Communities Organized for Public Service and the United Neighborhood Organization. A 1984 pastoral statement by U.S. bishops titled "Catholic Social Teaching and the United States Economy" pledged a forthright commitment to social and economic justice. In Washington, D.C., the Secretariat for the Spanish Speaking, successor to the Bishops Committee, worked to improve social conditions, to put an end to discriminatory practices, and to extend civil rights to both immigrant and American workers.

See also BOYLE, EUGENE J.; FLORES, PATRICK; LUCEY, ROBERT E.; SECRETARIAT FOR THE SPANISH SPEAKING.

FURTHER READING: "Bishops Support César Chávez." *America* 122, no. 21 (30 May 1970):574; *Church Views of the Mexican American*. Reprint, New York: Arno Press, 1974; Dolan, Jay P., and Gilberto M. Hinojosa. *Mexican Americans and the Catholic Church, 1900–1965*. Notre Dame, Ind.: University of Notre Dame Press, 1994; Hartmire, Wayne C. "The Church and the Emerging Farm Workers Movement. A Case Study." National Farm Workers Ministry, 1967; Hurtado, Juan. *An Attitudinal Study of Social Distances between the Mexican American and the Church*. San Antonio: Mexican American Cultural Center, 1975; Kostyu, Frank A. *Shadow in the Valley: The Story of One Man's Struggle for Justice*. Garden City,

N.Y.: Doubleday Co., 1970; Lucey, Robert E. "The Spanish Speaking of the Southwest and the West." *Report on the Conference of Leaders.* Washington, D.C.: National Catholic Welfare Conference, 1943; Meier, Matt S. "The Established Churches and the Quest for Social Justice by Chicanos in America at the Turn of the Century." In *Transactions of the Conference Group for Social and Administrative History,* Vol. 5. Oshkosh, Wisc.: 1974; Meier, Matt S. "Mexican-Americans in the Southwest." In *Catholics in America,* edited by Robert Trisco. Washington, D.C.: Committee for the Bicentennial, National Conference of Catholic Bishops, 1976; Privett, Stephen A. "Planting Seeds: National Committee for the Spanish Speaking." *Living Light* 30 (1994):3–16; "Protestants and Mexicans." In *The Mexican American People: The Nation's Second Largest Minority,* edited by Leo Grebler, Joan W. Moore, and Ralph C. Guzmán. New York: Free Press, 1970; Sandoval, Moisés, ed. *Fronteras: A History of the Latin American Church in the U.S.A. since 1513.* San Antonio: Mexican American Cultural Center, 1983; Walsh, Albeus. "The Work of the Catholic Bishops' Committee for the Spanish Speaking in the United States." Master's thesis, University of Texas at Austin, 1952.

CISNEROS, HENRY GABRIEL, 1947–   . Moderate to conservative in many respects, in public office Henry Cisneros has always shown deep liberal concerns about social issues like civil rights. As secretary of the Department of Housing and Urban Development (HUD) in the first Clinton administration (1993–1997), he ordered the reversal of federal policies that he characterized as promoting and abetting racial segregation in housing. He has labeled racism with its rejection of the civil liberties of minorities as a malignancy at the heart of big-city problems.

Strongly influenced toward public service by his father, who rose from migrant farmworker to a colonel in the U.S. Army, and his journalist maternal grandfather, in fall 1964 Cisneros enrolled in Texas A & M University at College Station. After earning an A.B. degree in city planning, an M.A. in urban and regional planning, a White House fellowship, a Ford Foundation grant that took him to Harvard, and a second M.A., this one in public administration, in 1974 he earned a Ph.D. in public administration at George Washington University.

Only months after his return to San Antonio from Washington, D.C., Cisneros plunged into local politics and was elected to the city council, the youngest councillor in the city's history. Six years later, in 1981, by an overwhelming vote he became San Antonio's first Mexican American mayor since the early 1840s and was easily reelected for three subsequent terms. Viewing politics as a way "to change things," as mayor he worked with a local civil rights advocacy group, Communities Organized for Public Service, to advance the political power of Mexican Americans and brought the Anglo and Mexicano communities closer together.

Cisneros's meteoric political rise made him one of the top contenders for the Democratic vice presidential nomination in 1984. Nine years later he accepted appointment to President Bill Clinton's first cabinet, where he tried to bring about change by focusing on racial issues to enable HUD to better serve the minority poor. Because of problems in his personal life, at the end of Clinton's first term he resigned from HUD and left politics. In January 1997 he became president and chief operating officer of Miami-based Univisión Communications, which dominates U.S. Spanish-language television.

FURTHER READING: Chavira, Richard, and Charlie Ericksen. "An American Political Phenomenon Called Cisneros." *La Luz* 19, no. 6 (August-September 1981):26–27; *Current Biography Yearbook 1987*. New York: H. W. Wilson Co., 1987; Diehl, Kemper, and Jan Jarboe. *Cisneros: Portrait of a New American*. San Antonio: Corona Publishing Co., 1985; Lehman, Nicholas. "First Hispanic." *Esquire* 102, no. 6 (December 1984):480–486.

CISNEROS v. CORPUS CHRISTI INDEPENDENT SCHOOL DISTRICT, 1970.

Cisneros v. Corpus Christi Independent School District was an important early step in the slow advancement of the Mexican American school desegregation struggle. In this case the federal district court, following the decision of the U.S. Supreme Court in the 1956 *Hernández v. Texas* case, held that Mexican Americans, although white, were an identifiable ethnic minority, comparable to Italian Americans. The federal judge ruled that in public education Mexican Americans were therefore entitled to the protections already guaranteed to blacks in the 1954 landmark case of *Brown v. Board of Education*. This recognition of Mexican Americans as a distinguishable ethnic minority helped deter school districts from avoiding court-ordered desegregation through the expedient of integrating Chicano students with black students and by means of the maneuver maintaining all-Anglo schools.

See also BROWN v. BOARD OF EDUCATION; EDUCATION.

FURTHER READING: Salinas, Guadalupe. "Mexican-Americans and the Desegregation of Schools in the Southwest." In *Voices: Readings from El Grito, 1967–1973*, 2nd ed., edited by Octavio I. Romano-V. Berkeley, Calif.: Quinto Sol Publications, 1973; San Miguel, Guadalupe, Jr. *"Let All of Them Take Heed": Mexican Americans and the Campaign for Educational Equality in Texas, 1910–1981*. Austin: University of Texas Press, 1987.

CITIZENSHIP.

Until the World War II era the Mexicano attitude toward U.S. citizenship was often tinged with apathy. A number of factors account for this lack of interest: the unresponsiveness of the system to Mexican American citizens; the widespread Anglo belief that Mexicans were inferior and therefore not citizenry material; the widespread exclusion, by law and custom, of Mexican Americans from the political process; the scarcity in the Southwest, where most Mexicanos lived, of institutions promoting naturalization; the Anglo attitude in the Southwest that persons of Mexican descent were Mexicans no matter where they were born, what their political status, or where their allegiance might lie. Minimal educational, economic, and social status (generally associated with low naturalization levels), limited proficiency in English, migrant-work lifestyles, and not uncommon lack of official documentation—all influenced the low levels of naturalization. This unconcern about citizenship was often encouraged among immigrants as well as sojourners by the local Mexican consul, who understandably tried to maintain their identification with Mexico.

The 1930 census indicated that only 5.5 percent of Mexican-born adults had become naturalized compared to 49.7 percent of all foreign-born. The explanation of this discrepancy lies in a number of factors in addition to those listed above. Most important were the recency of heavy Mexican immigration in the 1920s; a long history of border crossing for seasonal employment dating back to the late 1800s; and the widely held belief or dream of many that their stay in the United States was to be temporary, that they were sojourners only, not immigrants.

The relatively low levels of naturalization reduced the potential political power of Mexican-descent persons and made defense of their civil rights additionally difficult. Fully one third of Mexicanos were not citizens and were therefore ineligible to vote. Only in the post–World War II period did levels of naturalization show a marked increase. In 1996 alone an unprecedented 255,000 Mexicans became American citizens—a historical record for any group in a single year.

See also VOTING.

FURTHER READING: González, Isabel. *Step-Children of a Nation: The Status of Mexican-Americans*. New York: American Committee for the Protection of the Foreign Born, 1947. Reprinted in *The Mexican American and the Law*. New York: Arno Press, 1974; Grebler, Leo. "The Naturalization of Mexican Immigrants in the U.S." *International Migration Review* 1 (Fall 1966):17–32; Grebler, Leo, Joan W. Moore, and Ralph C. Guzmán, eds. *The Mexican American People: The Nation's Second Largest Minority*. New York: Free Press, 1970; McNamara, Patrick. *Mexican Americans in Los Angeles County: A Study in Acculturation*. San Francisco: R & E Research Associates, 1975.

CIVIL RIGHTS ABUSE. From the 1850s to the present there have been numerous instances of notorious abuse of Mexican Americans' civil rights. Among the more outrageous were the U.S. Land Act of 1851, which was used to despoil many Californios of their lands; the 1855 California anti-vagrancy law, which singled out persons "commonly known as Greasers"; the Texas Cart War of 1857, in which Mexicano teamsters were assaulted for months and some even murdered by Anglo competitors before federal government interposition ended the attacks; the overzealous pursuit and often killing of alleged Mexican bandits by the Texas Rangers; the California Sleepy Lagoon case and the Zoot Suit riots in 1943; the ejection of World War II Medal of Honor winner Sergeant Macario García from the

Oasis Cafe near Houston when he insisted on service and his subsequent arrest on charges of assault; the refusal of a Texas restaurant to serve José Mendoza López, another Congressional Medal winner, just after he had returned from an army-sponsored goodwill tour of Mexico; the Bloody Christmas case of 1951, in which seven Los Angeles youths were brutally beaten in jail by police officers; the Félix Longoria case (1948), which showed that even in death Mexican Americans did not escape discrimination and denial of rights.

To these blatant specific incidents was added much long-term over-policing of the barrio and other harrying and hounding, as in the prohibition in many schools until the 1970s against speaking Spanish, even on the playground. Mexicanos in Texas, especially in rural Texas, learned to avoid the Texas Rangers when they were on the prowl. For urban Chicanos brutality and the excessive use of force by police became a top civil rights issue. With little understanding of Mexicano culture, the overwhelmingly Anglo police force entertained stereotypes of Mexicanos that encouraged abuse. The 1960s civil rights movement and legislation, which focused on blacks, gave other minority groups like Mexican Americans only limited attention and amelioration.

Too often Mexican Americans settled for less than their full civil rights because of concern for their jobs and the safety of their families. However, increasingly more have become convinced that achieving their goals depends on a persistent push for full civil rights and greater political involvement. In the post–World War II era they made continuing land and labor abuses prime initial targets of the Mexican American civil rights movement. As they became more aware of the potential power residing in ethnic consciousness and solidarity, they expanded the number of concerns in politics and education and have adopted more direct and aggressive tactics.

See also BLOODY CHRISTMAS, CIVIL RIGHTS ACTS; CIVIL RIGHTS LEGISLATION, HISTORY OF.

FURTHER READING: Almanza, Arturo S. *Mexican-Americans and Civil Rights*. Los Angeles: County Commission on Human Relations, 1964; Balderrama, Francisco E. *Decade of Betrayal: Mexican Repatriation in the 1930s*. Albuquerque: University of New Mexico Press, 1995; Burma, John H. "The Civil Rights Situation of Mexican Americans and Spanish Americans." In *Race Relations: Problems and Theory*, edited by J. Masouka and P. Valien. Chapel Hill: University of North Carolina Press, 1961; Camarillo, Alberto, and Pedro Castillo, eds. *Furia y muerte: los bandidos chicanos*. Los Angeles: Chicano Studies Center, University of California, 1973; "Civil Rights." *La Luz* 8, no. 6 (February-March 1980):10–14, 41, 43; Diamond, Robert A., and Arlene Allgood, eds. *Civil Rights Progress Report, 1970*. Washington, D.C.: Congressional Quarterly, 1971; Endore, S. Guy. *Justice for Salcido*. Los Angeles: Civil Rights Congress of Los Angeles, 1948. Reprinted by Arno Press in *The Mexican-American and the Law*, 1974; McWilliams, Carey. *North from Mexico: The Spanish-Speaking People of the United States*. Updated ed. Westport, Conn.: Praeger Publishers, 1990; Mirandé, Alfredo. *Gringo Justice*. Notre Dame, Ind.: University of Notre Dame Press, 1987; Rodríguez, Roberto. *Justice: A Question of Race*. Tempe, Ariz.: Bilingual Review Press, 1997.

CIVIL RIGHTS ACT OF 1957. The first congressional civil rights legislation since the post–Civil War era, the 1957 Civil Rights Act was passed by Congress and signed by President Dwight D. Eisenhower despite his earlier reservations about its possible social impact. Its most important provision was the creation of the Civil Rights Commission, mandated to investigate and report on compliance with the Fourteenth Amendment provision prohibiting the denial or abridgement of the rights of all citizens. Most important to the problems of the times, it specifically forbade interference with the process of voting and provided streamlined procedures for requesting protection of the federal government at the polls. To this end it established within the Justice Department the Civil Rights Division, which could obtain court injunctions against interference with citizens' right to vote. It was the first important step in the twentieth century to broader, more active federal government support of civil rights.

See also CIVIL RIGHTS COMMISSION; CIVIL RIGHTS DIVISION, JUSTICE DEPARTMENT.

FURTHER READING: Anderson, John W. *Eisenhower, Brownell, and the Congress*. Birmingham: University of Alabama Press, 1964; Bardolph, Richard, ed. *The Civil Rights Record*. New York: Thomas Y. Crowell Co., 1970; *Revolution in Civil Rights, 1945–1968*. 4th ed. Washington, D.C.: Congressional Quarterly, 1968.

CIVIL RIGHTS ACT OF 1960. The 1960 act strengthened the powers of the Civil Rights Commission created in the 1957 Civil Rights Act by expanding the role of the federal government in the electoral process. It gave federal courts the power to appoint referees to hear claims of exclusion from voter registration and also made the use of threats or force to interfere with or to obstruct court orders (in civil rights cases) a federal offense. The law proved difficult to enforce.

See also CIVIL RIGHTS LEGISLATION, HISTORY OF.

FURTHER READING: Berman, Daniel M. *A Bill Becomes a Law: Congress Enacts Civil Rights Legislation*. New York: Macmillan, 1966; Bardolph, Richard, ed. *The Civil Rights Record*. New York: Thomas Y. Crowell Co., 1970; *Revolution in Civil Rights, 1945–1968*. 4th ed. Washington, D.C.: Congressional Quarterly, 1968.

CIVIL RIGHTS ACT OF 1964. The 1964 Civil Rights Act was proposed by President John F. Kennedy but passed after his assassination and after a lengthy filibuster by opponents. By the act Congress greatly extended the scope of the federal government in guaranteeing all citizens' rights. Like its

1957 predecessor it was primarily concerned with African Americans but also helped Mexican Americans.

One of this comprehensive document's most important provisions was the creation of the federal Equal Employment Opportunity Commission; in addition, the new law prohibited discrimination in employment because of sex or race. It also provided for equality of treatment in theaters, hotels, restaurants, and other places of public accommodation. Finally, it prohibited discrimination in activities that involved the use of federal funds and empowered the U.S. attorney general to bring suit on behalf of individuals in order to hasten school desegregation, in which there was much foot-dragging. The U.S. Supreme Court promptly upheld the constitutionality of the law's far-reaching scope.

See also CIVIL RIGHTS LEGISLATION, HISTORY OF.

FURTHER READING: Bardolph, Richard, ed. *The Civil Rights Record*. New York: Thomas Y. Crowell Co., 1970; Graham, Hugh Davis. *The Civil Rights Era, 1960–1972*. New York: Oxford University Press, 1990; Moore, Joan, and Harry Pachón. *Hispanics in the United States*. Englewood Cliffs, N.J.: Prentice-Hall, 1985.

CIVIL RIGHTS ACT OF 1968. The 1968 Civil Rights Act centered on housing. It made available the power of the federal government to protect the rights of all citizens, particularly minorities, by prohibiting discrimination in housing based on race or ethnicity. It also reflected the times by concerning itself with rioting, in response to which it made various acts in fomenting unrest federal offenses. Lastly, it extended the accepted judicial rights of U.S. citizens to Amerindians being tried in tribal courts.

See also CIVIL RIGHTS LEGISLATION, HISTORY OF; HOUSING.

FURTHER READING: Bardolph, Richard, ed. *The Civil Rights Record*. New York: Thomas Y. Crowell Co., 1970; "New Accent on Civil Rights: The Mexican American." *Civil Rights Digest* 2, no. 1 (Winter 1969):16–23.

CIVIL RIGHTS COMMISSION. The commission is a nonpartisan, independent federal board of six commissioners appointed by the U.S. president and confirmed by the Senate, with broad powers to collect information on abuses of civil rights, to investigate grievances, and to evaluate federal legislation and policies, and their enforcement. First established by President Harry Truman, it was later incorporated into the Civil Rights Act of 1957 by Congress.

The commission acts as a clearinghouse for civil rights information and complaints through seven regional offices. Although without enforcement powers, through its annual reports it has been able to influence considerably the attitude of federal agencies toward civil rights. A majority of its recommendations have been implemented; its greatest achievement was the Voting Rights Act of 1965.

Often critical of federal agencies' dawdling and presidential inaction, in 1970 the commission pointed out to the Richard M. Nixon administration the need to provide better protection for the civil rights of Mexican Americans in the Southwest. It noted that despite recent improvements, the administration of justice to Mexican Americans left much to be desired. In its 1970 report, *Mexican Americans and the Administration of Justice in the Southwest*, it highlighted numerous problems, including serious underrepresentation on juries, underrepresentation in employment, widespread police misconduct, official interference with organizational efforts, and inadequacy of local remedies for these problems. The commission later reported that Chicano children were unfairly treated in schools and penalized for language and cultural differences—treatment that contributed to ethnic isolation. In late 1972 half of the commissioners, including its well-known chairman, President Theodore Hesburgh of Notre Dame University, resigned in protest against the Nixon administration's notable lack of enthusiasm in enforcing civil rights legislation.

See also CIVIL RIGHTS ACT OF 1957; HESBURGH, THEODORE.

FURTHER READING: Burke, Joan M. *Civil Rights: A Current Guide to People, Organizations, and Events*, 2nd ed. New York: R. R. Bowker, 1974; Castro, Tony. *Chicano Power: The Emergence of Mexican America*. New York: Saturday Review Press, 1974; U.S. Commission on Civil Rights. *The Mexican American*. Washington, D.C.: U.S. Government Printing Office, 1968; U.S. Commission on Civil Rights. *Mexican Americans and the Administration of Justice in the Southwest*. Washington, D.C.: U.S. Government Printing Office, 1970.

CIVIL RIGHTS DIVISION, JUSTICE DEPARTMENT. Established in 1957 as a result of the civil rights act of that year, the agency was given the task of enforcing civil rights legislation and executive orders against discrimination. Through its field offices in various states it has carried out this mandate by monitoring discrimination and denial of rights in voting, education, housing, employment, public facilities, and federally funded programs. In the early 1970s it initiated a drive in the courts to force southern school districts to comply with court-mandated desegregation. Later it filed and prosecuted several hundred court cases against school districts and city fire and police departments for practices discriminating against minorities in hiring and promotion. The division also concerns itself with the civil rights of inmates in mental hospitals, prisons, and juvenile centers.

See also CIVIL RIGHTS ACT OF 1957; CIVIL RIGHTS LEGISLATION, HISTORY OF.

FURTHER READING: Burke, Joan M. *Civil Rights: A Current Guide to the People, Organizations, and Events*. New York: R. R. Bowker, 1974.

CIVIL RIGHTS LEGISLATION, HISTORY OF. Historically the earliest protection of the rights of citizens was embodied in the first ten amendments to the U.S. Constitution, frequently referred to as the Bill of Rights, ratified in 1791 (see Appendix B). They were aimed solely at restraining the federal government, a matter of considerable concern to the founding fathers, who had experienced arbitrary government by the British crown and who viewed state and local governments as the natural defenders of citizen rights. Most states subsequently adopted legislation similar to the first ten amendments to protect their citizens from arbitrary state government action.

In 1848 the rights of the new Mexican American nationals were guaranteed in Article IX of the Treaty of Guadalupe Hidalgo (see Appendix D), which specified that until they were admitted to full citizenship in the United States (at the discretion of Congress) with its attendant rights, they were to enjoy their property and liberty. The term *civil rights*, used in the draft of the treaty, was dropped from Article IX of the treaty as signed and ratified by the two countries.

Widespread use of the term *civil rights* came into use after the Civil War (1861–1865) in the process of distinguishing between those rights of the former slaves that were deemed natural and those that were guaranteed by recently enacted laws. From the Civil War until the end of the nineteenth century, nearly all civil rights legislation related only to ex-slaves. The Fourteenth Amendment (see Appendix C), ratified in 1868, added greater specificity to the protection of citizens' civil rights and included the important phrase "equal protection of the laws."

The dramatic expansion of civil rights came in the 1950s and 1960s with the post–World War II resurgent demands of greater equality for all Americans. Using the Fourteenth Amendment guarantee of "equal protection of the laws" to all citizens, the courts ruled vigorously and broadly against discrimination and denial of civil rights. However, only in the second half of the twentieth century did federal and state governments begin to consider the problem of violation of civil rights by groups and individuals, a concern voiced by the English philosopher John Locke over 200 years earlier.

The protection of civil rights has been advanced, therefore, by federal and state constitutions, federal and state legislation, and, as importantly, by decisions of the courts, especially the U.S. Supreme Court. Court decisions took the lead—along with urbanization, education, the post–World War II civil rights movement, Chicano activism, and aggressive new leadership—in reducing discrimination and advancing the cause of civil rights for all Mexican Americans.

See also CIVIL RIGHTS ABUSE; CIVIL RIGHTS ACTS.

FURTHER READING: Castro, Tony. *Chicano Power: The Emergence of Mexican America.* New York: Saturday Review Press, 1970; Gómez-Quiñones, Juan. *Roots of Chicano Politics, 1600–1940.* Albuquerque: University of New Mexico Press, 1994.

COLORADO. During the Spanish and Mexican periods Colorado was the sparsely settled far northern frontier of the New Mexico–Arizona region with fewer than 1,000 Mexicans, mostly subsistence farmers and ranchers. Coal and silver mining development in the latter 1800s brought into Colorado large numbers of European miners and Anglo American settlers, rapidly changing the area's demographics. A few elite Mexican Americans like Casimiro Barela, "The Perpetual Senator," were able to continue participating in territorial and state politics. In 1875 Barela, the only Hispano delegate to the state constitutional convention, was able to include some protection for the civil rights of Spanish-speaking Coloradans in the Constitution. A Mexican American majority in the southern part of the state made possible limited control of local political offices there.

At the turn of the century the development of the sugar beet industry led to large-scale agriculture and a resultant influx of Mexicanos from adjacent New Mexico and Texas to work in the beet fields. Soon the growers were recruiting workers from northern Mexico, aided by the 1910 revolution, which uprooted thousands of agricultural laborers there. During the 1920s American Federation of Labor organizer C. N. Idar was working diligently to unionize Colorado beet workers. The depression of the following decade probably affected Colorado Chicanos less than those in the more highly developed areas of California, Texas, and the industrial Midwest.

In the post–World War II era a second heavy Anglo influx greatly reduced the number of towns and counties in which Chicano majorities still held political power. To retain influence in state and local politics Colorado Mexican Americans began to organize. However, not until the rise of Corky Gonzales in the 1960s did they begin to take a significant political role and begin to play an important part in the Chicano civil rights movement. Gonzales organized Chicano youths, railed against police brutality, supported high school walkouts, demanded educational reforms, and led a strongly nationalist movement. In 1970 Crusade for Justice leaders ran Albert Garrule for governor on a Raza Unida Party (LRUP) ticket. He garnered less than 2 percent of the vote. Four years later the Colorado LRUP withdrew from the national organization.

See also GONZALES, CORKY; LÓPEZ, LINO; LUDLOW MASSACRE.

FURTHER READING: Campa, Arthur L. *Hispanic Culture in the Southwest.* Norman: University of Oklahoma Press, 1979; Deutsch, Sarah. *No Separate Refuge: Culture, Class, and Gender on an Anglo-Hispanic Frontier in the American Southwest, 1880–1940.* New York: Oxford University Press, 1987; *Status of Spanish-Surnamed Citizens in Colorado.* Denver: Colorado Commission on Spanish-Surnamed Citizens, 1967.

COMISIÓN HONORÍFICA MEXICANA. Initially the commission was a civil rights organization for Mexican citizens. In the 1920–1921 depression anti-Mexicano rioting, part of a general anti-foreign and anti-black movement, caused Mexican consuls to become involved with the violation of the civil rights of Mexican citizens in the United States. Established first in Texas by the Mexican consulate and then in California, the commissions were made up of local volunteers who provided Mexican nationals with emergency assistance until they could obtain help from the nearest Mexican consul, who might be 100 or more miles away.

Although the commissions' early objectives stressed loyalty of Mexicans to the *patria* (homeland), in the aftermath of World War II they were broadened to include concerns of the Chicano community, especially civil liberties, educational opportunity, and economic and social betterment.

FURTHER READING: Balderrama, Francisco E. *In Defense of La Raza: The Los Angeles Mexican Consulate and the Mexican Community, 1929–1936.* Tucson: University of Arizona Press, 1982.

COMMUNIST PARTY. During the 1930s and 1940s the Communist Party played an important role as a radical reformist element within labor and ethnic minority struggles for civil rights. Mexican Americans who were deeply troubled by denial of civil rights saw the party as the only organization trying to do something about their concerns. Chicanos were attracted to the party more by the willingness of militant Communists to speak out for Mexicano rights than by Marxist ideology or revolutionary radicalism. As a result of this attraction some Mexicano civil rights activists became party members or sympathizers. Some of them were prominent in organizations like the Asociación Nacional México-Americana and the Congreso de Los Pueblos de Habla Española; some, who were Mexican nationals, were later deported under the 1952 McCarran-Walter Act.

See also SAGER, MANUELA SOLÍS; TENAYUCA, EMMA.

FURTHER READING: García, Mario T. *Mexican Americans: Leadership, Ideology, and Identity, 1930–1960.* New Haven, Conn.: Yale University Press, 1989.

COMMUNITIES ORGANIZED FOR PUBLIC SERVICE (COPS). Founded in San Antonio in 1974 by Ernie Cortés, some lay Catholics, and several young priests, COPS is a nonpartisan community service group based on Catholic Church parishes. Like the Community Service Organization, it was greatly influenced by the community-organizing ideas of Saul Alinsky, especially his persuasive confrontation tactics. Ernesto Cortés, Jr., who trained at the Industrial Areas Foundation (IAF) in Chicago, was COPS chief architect, with support from San Antonio's bishop, Francis Furey.

COPS, like other IAF-inspired groups, is completely self-sufficient. It has helped develop the political clout of the San Antonio Mexican American community by politicizing it and by voter registration and get-out-the-vote campaigns. COPS is nonpartisan. Its policy has been to support its friends in local government, for example, Henry Cisneros, and to withhold its support from their opponents, regardless of party affiliation. It has worked closely with other community organizing and political-empowering groups. The growth of COPS in the 1980s enabled it to achieve statewide as well as local reforms. The strength and success of COPS has been the result of its energetic and able leaders, many of them Chicanas, of wide support from a large civil service population in San Antonio, and of the endorsement and help of local Catholic clergy under the leadership of bishops Francis Furey and Patrick Flores.

See also ALINSKY, SAUL; CHURCHES; CORTÉS, ERNIE.

FURTHER READING: García, F. Chris, and Rodolfo O. de la Garza. *The Chicano Political Experience: Three Perspectives*. North Scituate, Mass.: Duxbury Press, 1977; Sekul, Joseph D. "Communities Organized for Public Service: Citizen Power and Public Policy in San Antonio." In *Latinos and the Political System*, edited by F. Chris García. Notre Dame, Ind.: University of Notre Dame Press, 1988; Skerry, Peter. *Mexican Americans: The Ambivalent Minority*. New York: Free Press, 1993.

COMMUNITY SERVICE ORGANIZATION (CSO). The CSO is a broad-based nonpartisan, nonpolitical organization without citizenship or language qualifications. It seeks to make Mexicanos aware of their civic responsibilities and rights, strongly encourages political participation, and aims at integration. It promotes English-language, citizenship, voter registration, and get-out-the-vote programs.

Under the leadership of Fred Ross, Sr., a Saul Alinsky disciple, the CSO was first founded in the Los Angeles area during fall 1947 in part to support the candidacy of Edward Roybal for a seat on the city council. After its success in electing Roybal it turned to broader community issues of civil rights and citizenship.

To solidify its long-term support in the community the CSO, under the leadership of World War II veterans, adopted some mutualist goals. It soon spread elsewhere within the state and outside, especially in Arizona. However, during the late 1960s it suffered a decline in membership because of the more confrontational mood of the decade and competition from new, more aggressive Chicano organizations. In the early 1970s it expanded its mutual benefit programs to include a buyers club and a consumers complaint center. When the Chicano Movement subsided in the late 1970s, the CSO regained some of its lost membership and again began to enjoy wider community support.

The CSO has been particularly notable as the training ground for Fred Ross, Sr., César Chávez, Dolores Huerta, Antonio Orendain, and other leaders in the Chicano civil rights struggle.

See also ROSS, FRED, SR.

FURTHER READING: García, F. Chris. *La Causa Política*. Notre Dame, Ind.: University of Notre Dame Press, 1974; Guzmán, Ralph. "Politics and Policies of the Mexican-American Community." In *California Politics and Policies*, edited by Eugene Dvorin and Arthur Misner. Palo Alto, Calif.: Addison-Wesley, 1966; Ross, Fred W., Sr. *Community Organization in Mexican-American Communities*. Los Angeles: American Council on Race Relations, 1947.

COMPEÁN, MARIO C., 1940– . After his early life in a San Antonio barrio and in the migrant agricultural stream, Mario Compeán entered St. Mary's University, where he met and became a co-worker and friend of José Angel Gutiérrez. In 1967 with Gutiérrez and other students he helped found the Mexican American Youth Organization (MAYO). During the following two years he became deeply involved in student activism and electoral politics. In April 1969 he ran for mayor of San Antonio on the Committee for Barrio Betterment ticket and lost, but the votes he garnered nearly forced a runoff election between the two leading candidates.

After serving as vice chair of MAYO, in 1969 Compeán replaced Gutiérrez as state chair and then in 1970 became one of the founders and leaders of La Raza Unida Party (LRUP) in Texas. Two years later he was named state chair of LRUP at the party's first convention. After Ramsey Muñiz's loss as the LRUP candidate for governor in 1972, a bitter rivalry developed between the two men. In 1978 Compeán ran for governor of Texas but suffered a devastating defeat, garnering less than 2 percent of votes cast. This catastrophic loss was ascribed to his failure to develop a grassroots base in the community, resulting in a lack of enthusiasm for his candidacy on the part of many Mexican Americans. There was also the fact that LRUP had nearly disintegrated by 1978 in the midst of a growing conservative trend in the United States.

In the 1980s Compeán headed the Chicano studies program at the University of Wisconsin in Madison and in the mid-1990s held a position as policy researcher for the Minnesota Spanish-Speaking Affairs Council while working on a doctorate in education.

See also MEXICAN AMERICAN YOUTH ORGANIZATION; RAZA UNIDA PARTY, LA.

FURTHER READING: García, Ignacio M. *United We Win: The Rise and Fall of La Raza Unida Party*. Tucson: University of Arizona, MASRC, 1989; "LRUP Leaders Today." *Hispanic* (April 1989):46; Navarro, Armando. *Mexican American Youth Organization: Avant-Garde of the Chicano Movement in Texas*. Austin: University of Texas Press, 1995; Rosales, Francisco A. *Chicano!: The History of the Mexican American Civil Rights Movement*. Houston: Arte Público Press, 1996.

CONGRESO DE LOS PUEBLOS DE HABLA ESPAÑOLA. Founded in 1938 by Luisa Moreno, Josefina Fierro de Bright, Bert Corona, and other community and union leaders, the leftist Congreso was one of the early Mexican American organizations with specific civil rights goals. It was planned as a national umbrella organization, and its first convention, originally scheduled for Albuquerque but moved to Los Angeles because of conservative opposition in New Mexico, attracted Latinos from all over the United States. The Congreso and many of its leaders became intensely involved in union organizing as well as in protesting widespread race and ethnic discrimination.

The Congreso's forthright and often radical stance and its militancy focused government attention on its activities, and some of its leading members were investigated and harassed by the Federal Bureau of Investigation. Because of its left-leaning leadership and its strong positions on concerns like union organizing, discrimination, police brutality, and vigilantism, it was often labeled a Communist organization in the press, although there was no documentary evidence for the charge.

The Congreso provided Mexicanos with counseling services for immigration and naturalization questions and protested a number of southern California cases of excessive use of force by the police. Deploring the segregation of Chicano students in Los Angeles schools, the Congreso worked to improve the substandard facilities and education they were experiencing. It also concerned itself with employment discrimination in defense industries at the end of the 1930s. After the United States entered World War II, Congreso leaders continued to demand and work for civil and human rights reforms despite early wartime pressures to "all pull together."

As a result of developments during World War II, including a liberal-radical split in its leadership, the Congreso virtually ceased to function by the end of 1942, although individual leaders continued their activism, as, for example, did Fierro de Bright in the Sleepy Lagoon Defense Committee. Hopes for a revival of the Congreso after the war were dashed by McCarthyism and the deportation of Moreno and Fierro in the early 1950s. The Congreso, always a relatively small movement with limited finances and a close-knit, exclusionary leadership clique, expired. Although short-lived, the Congreso inspired many community activists and had a valuable incubating and leadership role in the Chicano struggle for civil rights.

See also CORONA, BERT; FIERRO DE BRIGHT, JOSEFINA; MORENO, LUISA; ORGANIZATIONS.

FURTHER READING: Acuña, Rodolfo. *Occupied America: A History of Chicanos.* 3rd ed. New York: Harper & Row, 1988; Camarillo, Albert. *Chicanos in California.* San Francisco: Boyd & Fraser, 1984; García, F. Chris. *La Causa Política.* Notre Dame, Ind.: University of Notre Dame Press, 1974; García, Mario T. *Memories of Chicano History: The Life and Narrative of Bert Corona.* Berkeley: University of California Press, 1994; García, Mario T. *Mexican Americans: Leadership, Ideology, and Identity, 1930–1960.* New Haven, Conn.: Yale University Press, 1989.

CONGRESS OF MEXICAN AMERICAN UNITY (CMAU). The CMAU, part of efforts to create an umbrella organization for Chicano rights, was formally established in 1968 to represent over 200 groups in the Los Angeles area. It served as a funnel for a variety of community concerns, especially related to civil rights. Among its early successes it counted the election of historian Julian Nava to the Los Angeles Board of Education. In fall 1970 it had an important part in the National Chicano Moratorium march in East Los Angeles. Although it supplied an important forum for discussion of civil rights concerns of southern California Chicanos in its early years, it declined as the movimiento slowed in the latter 1970s. It later dissolved largely because of the intransigence of its youthful leaders and their often hardline radical stance in the face of a nationwide conservative trend.

See also NATIONAL CHICANO MORATORIUM; ORGANIZATIONS.

FURTHER READING: "C.M.A.U. (Congress of Mexican-American Unity)." Los Angeles: *La Causa*, 28 February 1970.

CONGRESSIONAL HISPANIC CAUCUS (CHC). Formally established in December 1976 by Latino members of the U.S. House of Representatives, especially Mexican American Edward Roybal of California, the CHC aimed at developing national policies that would reflect Latino concerns. Its principal role is to monitor legislative action, but it is also concerned with policies and practices in the executive branch and the judiciary. Most of its activity takes place, of course, within the House of Representatives, where it strongly opposes all legislation it considers inimical to Latinos and especially to their citizen rights. It also aims to enlarge and strengthen the role of Latinos at all governmental levels. Since its inception the Caucus has dealt with issues of immigration and bilingual education as well as various other civil liberties concerns such as housing discrimination and police brutality.

Although small in membership, the CHC has had an impact, especially in congressional committees where it has been able to position newly elected Latino members. During the Carter administration (1977–1981), the CHC, representing interests of a variety of Latino organizations, met regularly with the president to discuss issues of concern, especially in political representation and education. More recently, it has been regularly consulted by the Clinton administration.

See also ORGANIZATIONS; ROYBAL, EDWARD R.

FURTHER READING: Yzaguirre, Raúl. "The Hispanic Congressional Caucus: A New Sign of Unity." *Avance* (1978).

CORONA, BERT N., 1918–   . All of his life Bert Corona has been a dynamic community leader and union organizer who has pioneered in all areas of social, economic, and educational reform. His firm dedication to social change has made him, above all else, an activist in politics and labor.

Over the years he was important in the genesis and evolution of a number of civil rights–oriented organizations, including the Asociación Nacional México-Americana, the Congreso de Los Pueblos de Habla Española, and the Community Service Organization. He held high offices in these groups.

Consistently taking the initiative to bring about the betterment of Mexican Americans in American society, Corona was one of the principal founders of the Mexican American Political Association (MAPA) in 1959. As an officer in California MAPA he participated in various civil rights coordinating councils and worked on campaigns to achieve greater civil rights for minorities. He was deeply involved in California Democratic politics and helped Edward Roybal win his first election to the U.S. House of Representatives. He also took an active part in the 1960 Viva Kennedy committees and the Viva "Pat" Brown movement two years later, and he was co-chair of the national Viva Johnson campaign. In 1967 he was appointed to the U.S. Civil Rights Commission by President Lyndon Johnson.

An untiring foe of ethnic discrimination and social injustice, Corona influenced the Chicano Movement but distanced himself from those members who advocated a strong nationalism. During the 1960s, 1970s, and 1980s he repeatedly spoke out forthrightly for the human and civil rights of immigrants, particularly of undocumented sojourners. Through his leadership in La Hermandad Mexicana Nacional he led a fight to protect the rights of undocumented workers. In 1981 he opposed the Simpson-Mazzoli immigration bill, parts of which he found disquieting.

Corona's outspoken opposition to discrimination and his clearly articulated defense of civil and human rights over the years illustrate the outstanding importance of his leadership in the Chicano civil rights struggle. Although often accused of being a radical and sometimes of being a communist, Bert Corona was and is in reality a fairly moderate social reformer. He deserves great credit for his many contributions to the promotion of civil and social rights for Chicanos.

See also CONGRESO DE LOS PUEBLOS DE HABLA ESPAÑOLA; MEXICAN AMERICAN POLITICAL ASSOCIATION; ORGANIZATIONS.

FURTHER READING: Corona, Bert N. *Bert Corona Speaks on La Raza Unida Party and the "Illegal Alien" Scare*. New York: Pathfinder Press, 1972; García, Mario T. *Memories of Chicano History: The Life and Narrative of Bert Corona*. Berkeley: University of California Press, 1994; Hammerback John C., "An Interview with Bert Corona." *Western Journal of Speech Communication* 44, no. 3 (Summer 1980):214–220; Larralde, Carlos. *Mexican American Movements and Leaders*. Los Alamitos, Calif.: Hwong Publishing Co., 1976; Muñoz, Carlos, Jr. *Youth, Identity, Power: The Chicano Movement*. New York: Verso, 1989.

CORTÉS, ERNIE (ERNESTO, JR.), 1943–   . Best known as one of the principal founders of Communities Organized for Public Service (COPS) in

San Antonio, Ernie Cortés is a firm believer in and a zealous practitioner of Saul Alinsky's ideas for helping minority communities achieve self-sufficiency and political power by working for their own civil and social rights.

As a college student in the 1960s Cortés became emotionally caught up first in the black civil rights movement and then by César Chávez's charismatic leadership in the fight for farmworkers' rights. While still a graduate student in economics at the University of Texas during the second half of the 1960s he began his civil rights career by organizing support for Texas farmworkers in their struggle to gain union recognition. Through his work in the United Farm Workers he became aware of Saul Alinsky's ideas for teaching powerless groups how to organize in order to increase their political power.

Cortés spent nearly three years with Alinsky's Industrial Areas Foundation (IAF) of Chicago, where he worked with midwestern Chicano groups. In 1974 he returned to his native San Antonio and began putting IAF ideas into practice there, developing COPS by organizing Mexican Americans in local, parish-oriented groups. Supported by local Catholic Church officials, COPS was able to achieve considerable success. Cortés then moved on to East Los Angeles, where in 1975, with help from auxiliary bishop Juan Arzube and other clergy, he created a similar organization that he called the United Neighborhood Organization (UNO). Less involved in electoral politics than COPS because of Los Angeles's large, nonvotable undocumented population, UNO proved less effective, although it had some successes.

In 1987 Cortés was appointed supervisor of all IAF-affiliated organizations in Texas. Now the southwest regional director for the Industrial Areas Foundation, he oversees two dozen affiliated organizations, most of which he founded. His importance as a civil rights organizer is indicated by the fact that in the mid-1980s over half of all IAF-inspired groups in the United States were the result of his founding efforts. In 1998 he was still working on a renewed effort to organize communities in southern California.

Cortés has been awarded many honors. In 1990 he was the recipient of a McArthur Foundation fellowship ("the genius grant"), and in January 1998 he received a $250,000 Heinz Award for leadership in public policy. In 1998 he was the Martin Luther King, Jr. visiting professor at the Massachusetts Institute of Technology.

See also ALINSKY, SAUL; COMMUNITIES ORGANIZED FOR PUBLIC SERVICE; UNITED NEIGHBORHOOD ORGANIZATION.

FURTHER READING: Cortés, Ernesto, Jr. "Changing the Locus of Political Decision Making." *Christianity and Crisis* 47, no. 1 (February 1987):18–22; Northcott, Kaye. "To Agitate the Dispossessed." *Southern Exposure* 13, no. 4 (July-August 1985):16–23; Rogers, Mary Beth. *Cold Anger: A Story of Faith and Power Politics*. Denton: University of North Texas Press, 1990.

CORTINA, JUAN NEPOMUCENO, 1824–1892. In the middle of the nineteenth century Juan "Cheno" Cortina became a concern to officials on both sides of the U.S.–Mexican border as the leader of a Tejano rights movement. Having become a U.S. national by the Treaty of Guadalupe Hidalgo in 1848, Cortina, member of a prominent border family, turned to direct action to secure protection for Tejanos whose property rights were being attacked and denied them. As they lost their lands, he saw their civil rights becoming endangered. In order to protect them he suggested the creation of a buffer republic between Mexico and the United States, which would be controlled by Tejanos.

As the result of an incident in 1859, Cortina became the leader of a growing movement of forcible resistance to the routine Anglo ignoring of Mexicano rights in the Texas border region. In September he led a raid on Brownsville and proclaimed a buffer Republic of the Rio Grande. The episode marked the beginning of Cortina's active career as a border bandit-reformer-revolutionary. From a family rancho in Cameron County, Texas, he issued a statement outlining his goals and affirming his determination to defend the rights of his fellow Tejanos. His outspoken aggressive leadership for Mexicano rights soon attracted a large following even after he moved his headquarters across the Rio Grande to Matamoros.

After the Civil War, in which his sympathies lay with the North, he helped the great Mexican leader Benito Juárez expel the occupying French forces from Mexico. His subsequent petition to be allowed to return to his Texas ranch holdings was rejected by the state legislature. In 1875, several years after Juárez's death, he was arrested and jailed by Mexican authorities who feared his continuing leadership in a border separatist movement. He was ultimately allowed out of his Mexico City prison on parole. When he died in Mexico City in 1892, his earlier career as a defender of civil rights was long forgotten and his last wish, to be buried in Texas, was denied. His adult life in the second half of the 1800s in many ways mirrored the turbulent conditions of the times on the Southwest border.

FURTHER READING: Canales, José T., ed. *Juan N. Cortina Presents His Motion for a New Trial*. San Antonio: Artes Gráficas, 1951; Castillo, Pedro, and Albert Camarillo, eds. *Furia y muerte: los bandidos Chicanos*. Los Angeles: Chicano Studies Center, University of California, 1973. Cortina, Juan N. "The Death of Martyrs." In *Aztlán: An Anthology of Mexican American Literature*, edited by Luis Valdez and Stan Steiner. New York: Alfred A. Knopf, 1972; Goldfinch, Charles W. *Juan Cortina, 1824–1892: A Reappraisal*. Brownsville, Tex.: Bishop's Print Shop, 1950; Larralde, Carlos. *Mexican American Movements and Leaders*. Los Alamitos, Calif.: Hwong Publishing Co., 1976; Thompson, Jerry D. *Juan Cortina and the Texas-Mexico Frontier, 1859–1877*. El Paso: Texas Western Press, 1994; Thompson, Jerry D., ed. *Fifty Miles and a Fight: Major Samuel Peter Heintzelman's Journal of Texas and the Cortina War*. Austin: Texas State Historical Association, 1998.

COTERA, MARTHA P., 1938– . A youthful immigrant from Mexico, Martha Cotera received her education at today's University of Texas at El Paso and Antioch College in Ohio. After college she went to work as a university librarian, first at El Paso and then at Austin, where in 1964 she became director of documents in the Texas State Library. Radicalized and activated by the discrimination she encountered in Austin, she became deeply involved in the Chicano Movement. In 1969 Cotera and her husband helped organize the Crystal City, Texas, high school walkout protest against denial of student rights. After Crystal City she became an enthusiastic participant in the La Raza Unida Party (LRUP), which she helped establish. In 1972 she ran for the state board of education as the LRUP candidate.

Much of Cotera's activism has been in the field of education. In 1970 she was one of the founders of Jacinto Treviño College (which later became Juárez-Lincoln University), where she taught for five years. In 1973 she helped establish the Texas Women's Political Caucus and in the following year founded the Chicana Research and Learning Center in Austin. Then she organized a publishing company named Information Systems Development. In 1980 she was a co-founder of Mexican American Business and Professional Women, another effort to politicize Chicanas, also in Austin. For the past quarter century she has organized training sessions and conducted workshops to inform Mexican Americans of their rights and to increase Chicanas' awareness of gender inequality. Although she has been very active in women's causes, Cotera does not consider herself a feminist. She continues to be active in voter registration drives and political campaigns and currently teaches courses in Mexican American history at Austin Community College.

Martha Cotera is the author of numerous works, most having to do with education and women's rights. She has received a number of prestigious awards.

See also CHICANAS; CRYSTAL CITY; MOVIMIENTO, EL; RAZA UNIDA PARTY, LA.

FURTHER READING: Cotera, Martha P. *Diosa y Hembra: The History and Heritage of Chicanas in the U.S.*. Austin: Information Systems Development, 1976; *Las Mujeres: Mexican American / Chicana Women*. Windsor, Calif.: National Women's History Project, 1991; Telgen, Diane, and Jim Kamp, eds. *Notable Hispanic American Women*. Detroit: Gale Research, 1993.

COUNCIL OF MEXICAN AMERICAN AFFAIRS (CMAA). Established in Los Angeles in 1953, the CMAA was one of the earlier efforts by Mexican Americans to create an umbrella organization for Mexican American community groups working to better the lot of la raza. Although the council started with over 40 member organizations interested in leadership development, the CMAA's middle-class orientation limited its ability to attract working-class Chicanos. CMAA efforts to coordinate the work of the various groups withered for feebleness of community support and insufficient finances to carry out the council's objectives.

In 1963 the CMAA was reorganized by new leaders with their own set of ideas for helping the community. The new CMAA saw itself as an elitist high-level political and social pressure group working for all Mexican Americans, a concept that ran counter to grassroots community attitudes.

See also ORGANIZATIONS.

FURTHER READING: Tirado, Miguel David. "Mexican American Community Political Organization." In *La Causa Política*, edited by F. Chris García. Notre Dame, Ind.: University of Notre Dame Press, 1974.

COURT OF PRIVATE LAND CLAIMS, 1891–1904. The Court of Private Land Claims was established by the U.S. Congress in early 1891 to address the problem of validating Spanish and Mexican land grant titles in New Mexico, Colorado, and Arizona. (The land ownership issue had already been dealt with in California and Texas.) Because of political pressures and the urgent need to end ambiguity in land ownership, the 52nd U.S. Congress created a court of five judges to adjudicate the validity of about 300 claims to some 35 million acres. The court's verdicts were appealable only directly to the U.S. Supreme Court. Loss of documents and other records prevented about two-thirds of the claimants from satisfying the court and establishing their rights. The court ruled that claims to more than 32 million acres were invalid.

See also LAND ACT OF 1851.

FURTHER READING: Bradfute, Richard W. *The Court of Private Land Claims: The Adjudication of Spanish and Mexican Land Titles, 1891–1904.* Albuquerque: University of New Mexico Press, 1975; Cortés, Carlos, ed. *Spanish and Mexican Land Grants.* Reprint, New York: Arno Press, 1974; Ebright, Malcolm. "The Embudo Grant: A Case Study of Justice and the Court of Private Land Claims." *Journal of the West* 19, no. 3 (July 1980):74–85; Knowlton, Clark S. "Causes of Land Loss among the Spanish Americans in Northern New Mexico." In *The Chicanos: Life and Struggles of the Mexican Minority in the United States,* edited by Gilberto López y Rivas. New York: Monthly Review Press, 1973.

COURTS. The experience of Mexican Americans with U.S. courts and the U.S. system of justice began with the Treaty of Guadalupe Hidalgo in 1848. They quickly discovered that the courts belonged to the Anglos. Despite the treaty's guarantees of civil rights, Mexican Americans soon found themselves excluded from juries and in some instances denied the right to testify in court because of their ethnic identity. An 1856 Texas law prohibiting the use of Spanish in courts was widely enforced except in border areas. The Land Act of 1851 and the 1891 Court of Private Land Claims were seen as Anglo devices to abrogate land grantees' civil rights, and the courts generally gave them little hope for impartial justice. In addition, courts and juries often applied rules of justice more stringently to Mexicanos, usually victimizing them thereby. As a result, in the nineteenth century the courts were little used by most Mexican Americans, with the exception of Nuevomexicanos.

The rise of the Mexican American generation in the twentieth century and its creation of organizations with specific civil rights goals led to more widespread use of the courts. Following the example of the black leadership, Chicanos saw how the courts might be used as an alternative or addition to confrontation tactics in order to obtain and defend civil rights. The creation of California Rural Legal Assistance in 1966 and the Mexican American Legal Defense and Educational Fund two years later illustrate and exemplify this trend. Court victories in various school segregation cases confirmed the usefulness and potential of the legal approach to achieving civil rights.

However, the expectations of many Chicanos were dimmed in 1978 when the U.S. Supreme Court upheld the California courts' ruling in the *Bakke* case that the use of racial quotas as a factor in university admissions was discriminatory and therefore unconstitutional. In recent years the courts, although more conservative in their rulings, continue to be one of a variety of approaches to achieving greater civil rights for Chicanos.

See also CALIFORNIA RURAL LEGAL ASSISTANCE; COURT OF PRIVATE LAND CLAIMS; LAND ACT OF 1851.

FURTHER READING: Cortés, Carlos. *The Mexican-American and the Law*. New York: Arno Press, 1974; Cortner, Richard. *The Supreme Court and Civil Liberties Policy*. Palo Alto, Calif.: Mayfield Publishing Co., 1975; de la Garza, Rodolfo O. et al., eds. *The Mexican American Experience: An Interdisciplinary Anthology*. Austin: University of Texas Press, 1985; Mirandé, Alfredo. *Gringo Justice*. Notre Dame, Ind.: University of Notre Dame Press, 1987; Morales, Armando. "Justice and the Mexican American." *El Grito* 1, no. 4 (Summer 1968):42–48.

CRYSTAL CITY, TEXAS. Crystal City first became a beacon in the Mexican American civil rights struggle in 1963 when a Mexican American political revolt elected its slate of councillors, thereby abruptly ending decades of complete Anglo control. Progress in reducing discrimination and advancing civil rights was quickly undermined, however, by widespread intimidation from the city's powerful Anglo minority. The elected Mexican Americans immediately lost their jobs, and two years later the Anglo ruling clique was able to regain political control of the town.

In 1969 a second revolt, growing out of discrimination in the high school, led to broad educational changes and the organization of the Raza Unida Party (LRUP) by José Angel Gutiérrez, a native of Crystal. Chicanos now gained control of the school system and city government and introduced many innovative programs in both. These efforts were denigrated by Texas governor Dolph Briscoe, who created an atmosphere of alarm among many Anglos by dubbing Crystal City "little Cuba." An exodus of businesses and finance from the town resulted. After a decade Chicano control ended because of well-financed Anglo political and economic opposition, fratricidal Chicano rivalries, and the sharp decline of LRUP.

Crystal City became the vanguard of the Chicano movimiento in Texas principally because of its early able leadership and organization; it ultimately failed because of factionalism and lack of economic power, as well as Anglo opposition.

See also GUTIÉRREZ, JOSÉ ANGEL; RAZA UNIDA PARTY, LA.

FURTHER READING: Hirsch, Herbert, and Armando Gutiérrez. *Learning to Be Militant: Ethnic Identity and the Development of Political Militance in the Chicano Community*. San Francisco: R & E Research Associates, 1977; Miller, Michael V., and James D. Preston. "Vertical Ties and the Redistribution of Power in Crystal City." *Social Science Quarterly* 53, no. 4 (March 1973):772–784; Navarro, Armando. *The Cristal Experiment: A Chicano Struggle for Community Control*. Madison: University of Wisconsin Press, 1998; Shockley, John S. *Chicano Revolt in a Texas Town*. Notre Dame, Ind.: University of Notre Dame Press, 1974; Trillin, Calvin. "U.S. Journal: Crystal City, Texas." *New Yorker* 47 (17 April 1972):102–107.

CURSILLO DE CRISTIANDAD MOVEMENT. Originally a Catholic religious concept started in Spain, the Cursillo movement came to the Southwest via Mexico after World War II. It stresses self-reform and personal responsibility with an emphasis on community involvement. As a result of these ideas and the cooperative atmosphere in the religious retreats that it conducts, the movement has developed social action and civil rights components and provided leadership training. In parts of the Southwest, especially in isolated rural areas, it has played an important role in alleviating some problems of Mexican American communities. The Cursillo concepts appear to be distantly related to liberation theology, a movement that surged in the 1970s with an emphasis on *comunidades de base* (base communities).

See also FLORES, PATRICK.

FURTHER READING: Marcoux, Marcene. *Cursillo: Anatomy of a Movement, the Experience of Spiritual Renewal*. New York: Lambeth Press, 1982; Rodríguez, Edmundo. "The Hispanic Community and Church Movements: Schools of Leadership." In *Hispanic Catholic Culture in the U.S.: Issues and Concerns*, edited by Jay P. Dolan and Allan Figueroa Deck. Notre Dame, Ind.: University of Notre Dame Press, 1994.

D

DELANO GRAPE STRIKE, 1965–1970. Central to the California farm laborers' struggle for their civil and human rights was the Delano grape strike. In 1965, on Mexican independence day, September 16, César Chávez led his fledgling union into what was to be a five-year struggle for the right of workers to organize and have the union recognized as their bargaining agent. The strikers also demanded an increase in wages. Through Chávez's inspired leadership the strike was converted into a moral crusade that sought and obtained support from numerous civil rights and religious groups. Following a policy of nonviolence despite imported strikebreakers and various provocations, the Delano strikers faced up to giant companies like Schenley Industries and the Di Giorgio Corporation.

The intrusion into the strike of the Teamsters Union, favored by most of the growers, caused Chávez to take his union into the AFL-CIO as the United Farm Workers Organizing Committee. By 1967 most wine-grape growers had agreed to field elections to determine union representation, but table-grape growers held out until mid-1970 when, with an assist from the Catholic Bishops Committee on Farm Labor, the last of the growers, led by John Giumarra, Sr., signed three-year contracts with the union.

Chávez's casting the strike in the mold of a struggle for the rights of farmworkers undoubtedly helps explain both its widespread support and its eventual, though temporary, success.

See also CHÁVEZ, CÉSAR; HUERTA, DOLORES; ROSS, FRED, SR.; SACRAMENTO MARCH.

FURTHER READING: Castro, Tony. *Chicano Power: The Emergence of Mexican America.* New York: Saturday Review Press, 1974; Day, Mark. *Forty Acres: César Chávez and the Farm Workers.* New York: Praeger Publishers, 1971; Dunne, John Gregory. *Delano.* New York: Farrar, Straus & Giroux, 1971; Kushner, Sam. *The Long Road to Delano.* New York: International Publishers, 1975; Levy, Jacques E.

César Chávez: Autobiography of La Causa. New York: W. W. Norton & Co., 1975.

DELGADO ET AL. v. BASTROP INDEPENDENT SCHOOL DISTRICT

ET AL. 1948. Minerva Delgado and other parents in four central Texas communities brought suit against the school district in Bastrop County, alleging violations of their children's civil rights and asking for damages. The class-action suit was filed by the League of United Latin American Citizens in the federal district court at Austin as a part of its post–World War II program of protesting violations of Mexican Americans' civil rights. The plaintiffs argued that segregation of Mexicano children in separate schools was both arbitrary and discriminatory and violated the Fourteenth Amendment to the U.S. Constitution. They also pointed out that the practice persisted despite the Texas attorney general's opinion that it was illegal.

In June 1948 Judge Ben H. Rice, Jr., held for the plaintiffs after they dropped their request for damages. Judge Rice did allow for the possible segregation, in the first grade only, of children who did not speak English, but he also stipulated that their classrooms could not be on a separate campus. The decree of the court was followed in the same month by a policy statement from the state superintendent of public instruction, L. A. Woods, with instructions to local school boards to end segregation of Mexicano students. In May 1950 the Texas State Board of Education reiterated this policy statement. Most school districts circumvented the judge's ruling, the superintendent's instructions, and the board of education's policy statement by concocting various evasive schemes. For the next 10 years LULAC and the American G.I. Forum continued the fight for compliance.

See also AMERICAN G.I. FORUM; COURTS; LEAGUE OF UNITED LATIN AMERICAN CITIZENS.

FURTHER READING: Allsup, Carl. "Education Is Our Freedom: The American G.I. Forum and the Mexican American School Segregation in Texas, 1948–1957." *Aztlán* 8 (1977):27–50; Carter, Thomas P. *Mexican Americans in School: A History of Educational Neglect.* New York: College Entrance Examinations Board, 1970; Sánchez, George I. *Concerning Segregation of Spanish-Speaking Children in the Public Schools.* Austin: University of Texas, 1951; San Miguel, Guadalupe, Jr. *"Let All of Them Take Heed": Mexican Americans and the Campaign for Educational Equality in Texas, 1910–1981.* Austin: University of Texas Press, 1987.

DISCRIMINATION.

Discrimination against Mexican Americans existed even before the 1836 Texas revolt against Mexico, its admission to the United States, and the Treaty of Guadalupe Hidalgo in 1848. Based on skin color, ethnic culture, and low economic position assigned to Mexicanos by American society, discrimination has resulted in the denial of civil and social rights in the political arena, employment, housing, and education. Segregated schools for Mexican American children continued to be the norm until long after World War II.

Mexican American veterans returning from World War II found that their fight to save the world for democracy had not won them equality of treatment in their own country. The Longoria case in Texas in 1948 was only the most notorious of many denials of civil and social rights—in this instance, even beyond this life. Many Texas town cemeteries still maintained a segregated section for Mexicanos.

Chicano family migration to the cities in the postwar years disrupted existing patterns and helped create Anglo angst and resentment, aggravated segregation, and led to further discrimination. As a result, Chicanos created organizations to fight for their civil rights. Their efforts were hindered by the large number of recent immigrants and sojourners, who historically have had a lesser involvement in the local culture of resistance and struggle. Restrictive housing covenants, as well as low incomes, have helped keep Mexican Americans in the barrio. They still find it difficult to obtain the better, higher-paying jobs, and decision-making managerial positions often remain beyond their reach.

However, the increased size of the Mexican American middle class and the accompanying growth of its consumer market have served to moderate Anglo attitudes. Today discrimination against Mexican Americans tends to be covert rather than overt, de facto rather than de jure. Much of it is historical and institutional and therefore difficult to extirpate. The long fight for equality, while achieving improvements in the past several decades, still goes on.

See also CIVIL RIGHTS ABUSE; HOUSING; SEGREGATION; STEREOTYPING.

FURTHER READING: McWilliams, Carey. *North from Mexico: The Spanish-Speaking People of the United States*. Updated ed. Westport, Conn.: Praeger Publishers, 1990; Nava, Julian. *¡Viva La Raza!: Readings on Mexican Americans*. New York: D. Van Nostrand Co., 1973; Rodríguez, Roberto. *Justice: A Question of Race*. Tempe, Ariz.: Bilingual Press, 1997; Rosales, Francisco A. *Chicano! The History of the Mexican American Civil Rights Movement*. Houston: Arte Público Press, 1996; Rose, Arnold, ed. *Race Prejudice and Discrimination*. New York: Alfred A. Knopf, 1951.

DISTRICT ELECTIONS. One important aspect of the movement for overcoming discrimination against Mexican Americans and improving their civil rights was the drive to replace at-large elections with district elections. Beginning in the early 1960s with help from the Mexican American Legal Defense and Educational Fund, the campaign accelerated rapidly after the Voting Rights Act of 1965. In local elections the change not only led to greater minority voter turnout but also increased the number of Mexican American candidates seeking office and being elected to city councils and school boards. This experience serving in local government then provided hands-on training valuable in campaigns for higher political office. The normal neighborhood orientation of those elected by districts also led to a more equitable distribution of public employment and other benefits available from city government and the education system.

See also VOTING RIGHTS ACT OF 1965.

FURTHER READING: Baird, Frank L., ed. *Mexican Americans: Political Power, Influence, or Resource.* Lubbock: Texas Tech Press, 1977; Polinard, J. L. et al. *Electoral Structure and Urban Policy.* Armonk, N.Y.: M. E. Sharpe, 1994.

E

EAST LOS ANGELES COMMUNITY UNION, THE (TELACU).
TELACU, a part of the Johnson administration's Great Society program, was originally conceived in 1968 as an anti-poverty effort concerned with community economic development in order to provide financial support for social programs. Although it was primarily involved with jobs, housing, and other basic economic goals, it also became involved in civil rights politics and was able to secure political appointments for some of the community leaders it developed. At least indirectly, therefore, it has aided in the struggle for Mexican American civil rights.

A widely trumpeted 1982 charge of misuse or embezzlement of $47 million ultimately led merely to a federal court ordering TELACU to repay a $1 million agricultural grant the judge considered misused.

See also ORGANIZATIONS.

FURTHER READING: Chávez, John R. *Eastside Landmark: A History of the East Los Angeles Community Union, 1968–1993*. Stanford, Calif.: Stanford University Press, 1998; Guernica, Antonio J. "TELACU: Community Change through Economic Power." *Agenda* 7, no. 6 (November-December 1977):14–16; "TELACU: America's Leading Model in Massive Community Economic Development." *La Luz* 9, no. 3 (March 1981):7–9; Weyr, Thomas. *Hispanic U.S.A.: Breaking the Melting Pot*. New York: Harper & Row, 1988; www.telacu.com.

EDUCATION. There is an almost unanimous consensus among Mexican Americans that education holds a promise of a way out of poverty and is therefore among their most important civil rights. Early in the twentieth century they began the fight against the "separate Mexican school" policy generally in effect throughout the Southwest. Despite their long struggle to end discrimination in school systems, de facto segregation began to be terminated only after World War II. Even then, racist testing procedures and language difficulties caused some Chicano students to continue to be placed in classes for the mentally retarded simply because they understood little or no English.

The continuing struggle to reform the American educational system to provide a better and more meaningful school experience for Chicano children was at the heart of the Chicano Movement in the 1960s and 1970s. Some progress has been made. The Civil Rights Act of 1964 ultimately initiated widespread desegregation in school districts, and the 1974 decision by the U.S. Supreme Court in *Lau v. Nichols* marked the beginning of the bilingual education movement throughout the United States.

Since World War II civic organizations like the American G.I. Forum and the League of United Latin American Citizens have increasingly concerned themselves with Mexican American educational issues. Working through these and other groups, Chicanos have sought, and obtained, redress of grievances concerning the education of their children. Programs like Upward Bound have helped to reduce the educational problems of Mexican American families, as has the sensitizing of teachers to stereotyping.

Between 1984 and 1995 Latino college enrollment doubled, but the original base was abysmally low. By 1995 the percentage of high school graduates had crept up from about 50 percent to 58.6 percent. However, a 1997 study indicated that despite the gains made, today high schools in California are graduating fewer Chicano students eligible to enter college than they were a few years ago. Less than 12 percent of California Latino graduates are able to qualify to enroll in the state universities, and under 4 percent qualify for the University of California system.

The plight of migrant workers' children continues to be especially bleak. Typically they are two grades or more behind their age groups and have little hope of ever catching up. They are hampered by many barriers: poverty, language, single-parent families, poor health, lack of mentors, and all that poverty implicates. Their excessive dropout rate remains totally unacceptable in a society that views education as a civil right as well as the best route to upward mobility.

At a symposium in Los Angeles in December 1997 the president of the Mexican American Legal Defense and Educational Fund, Antonia Hernández, was quoted as saying, "To me, the most important civil right for Latinos, bar none, is education." In the June 1998 election Californians voted to disband bilingual education programs.

See also CIVIL RIGHTS ACT OF 1964; VARIOUS COURT CASES.

FURTHER READING: Carter, Thomas P. and Roberto Segura. *Mexican Americans in the Public Schools: A History of Neglect*. Princeton, N.J.: College Entrance Examination Board, 1979; *Education and the Mexican American*. Reprint, New York: Arno Press, 1974; Fraga, Luis Ricardo, Kenneth J. Meier, and Robert E. England. "Hispanic Americans and Educational Policy Limits to Equal Access." In *Pursuing Power: Latinos and the Political System*, edited by F. Chris García. Notre

Dame, Ind.: University of Notre Dame Press, 1997; Navarrette, Rubén, Jr. *A Darker Shade of Crimson: Odyssey of a Harvard Chicano.* New York: Bantam Books, 1993; Pérez, Bertha. "Dropouts: The Need for a Latino Community Response." In *Latinos and Political Coalitions,* edited by Roberto E. Villarreal and Norma G. Hernández. Westport, Conn.: Greenwood Press, 1991; Romo, Harriet D., and Toni Falbro. *Latino High School Graduation: Defying the Odds.* Austin: University of Texas Press, 1995; Sánchez, George I. "Concerning Segregation of Spanish-Speaking Children in the Public Schools." Austin: University of Texas Inter-American Education Occasional Papers 9, 1951; Valencia, Richard R., ed. *Chicano School Failure and Success: Research and Policy Agendas for the 1990s,* London: Falmer Press, 1991.

ELIZONDO, VIRGILIO P., 1935– . Virgilio Elizondo, son of Mexican immigrant parents, was nearly a grade school dropout because of language difficulties, but he was turned around by a caring teacher. He went on to complete high school and college and to become a Catholic priest. As a result of the 1960s liberation theology and the Medellin (Colombia) conference of Latin American bishops, which he attended, he became convinced that social justice was an integral part of the Gospel message. With the strong support of Archbishop Robert Lucey, in 1972 he established the Mexican American Cultural Center in San Antonio as a community-centered agency to sensitize, train, and develop social activist nuns, clergy, and laypersons to work with Chicanos. He remained director and guiding spirit of the center until 1983, when he was named rector of San Antonio's cathedral.

The author of numerous articles and nine books primarily concerned with Chicanos and the Catholic Church, Elizondo has often spoken out in defense of Mexicanos' right to their folk Catholicism. He was also active during the early years of the Padres Asociados para Derechos Religiosos, Educativos, y Sociales, the raza priests' association founded in 1968, which had as one of its goals making the Chicano poor aware that they have the power to defend their civil rights and to bring about social change for themselves and their children.

See also LUCEY, ROBERT E.

FURTHER READING: Maeroff, Gene I., ed. *Sources of Inspiration: Fifteen Modern Religious Leaders.* Kansas City: Sheed & Ward, 1992; Martínez, Julio A. *Chicano Scholars and Writers: A Bio-Bibliographic Directory.* Metuchen, N.J.: Scarecrow Press, 1979; Zapor, Patricia. "His Roots Are San Antonio, but His World Is the Globe."*Migration World Magazine* 24, no. 5 (September-October 1996):43–44.

ENGLISH ONLY MOVEMENT. Energized by a rising tide of xenophobia in the country, the English Only movement arose in the late 1970s to defend American society from what its advocates viewed as a threat from heavy immigration, principally Mexican. Through Senator S. I. Hayakawa of California, a well known specialist in linguistics, the group was able to get legislation introduced into the U.S. Congress to make English the official language of the United States. Although the movement found little support in Congress, at state and local levels it was much more successful. By the 1990s half of the states, and even some municipalities, had passed resolutions or legislation designating English as their sole official language. Rallying xenophobic sentiments at the local level, English Only advocates in Narcross, Georgia, even got an ordinance in the late 1990s mandating that all commercial signs must be 75 percent English, as determined by local authorities.

Early in January 1999 the U.S. Supreme Court refused to review Arizona's English Only law, which the state Supreme Court had by unanimous vote struck down the previous April. Also in January Utah's House of Representatives for the fourth time turned down English Only legislation after an emotional debate. While English Only laws have had very limited effect, the possibility exists that such nativist legislation could mandate the use of English in a number of citizen-government interactions such as court cases and various government services such as driver-testing, as well as in printed forms and information.

In the early 1980s Hayakawa helped found and became the honorary chairman of Washington-based lobbying and informational U.S. English. Well financed, the English Only and U.S. English people, who had ties to anti-immigration groups, attacked bilingual education programs and advocated a written English-proficiency test for citizenship. Opposition to Mexican immigration and to the use of Spanish seemed to form the real heart of their shrill "defense" of English. To counter the English Only offensive, Mexican American activists and others formed the English Plus Information Clearinghouse, which supports mastery of English along with retention of Spanish. A majority of Mexican Americans accept that the United States should have only one public language—English.

See also BILINGUAL EDUCATION; CHÁVEZ, LINDA.

FURTHER READING: Baron, Dennis. *The English-Only Question: An Official Language for Americans?* New Haven, Conn.: Yale University Press, 1990; Piatt, Bill. *Only English? Law and Language Policy in the United States.* Albuquerque: University of New Mexico Press, 1990; Schmidt, Ronald, Sr. "Latinos and Language Policy: The Politics of Culture." In *Pursuing Power: Latinos and the Political System,* edited by F. Chris García. Notre Dame, Ind.: University of Notre Dame Press, 1997; Tatalovich, Raymond. *Nativism Reborn? The Official English Language Movement and the American States.* Lexington: University Press of Kentucky, 1995; Vigil, Maurilio. *Hispanics in American Politics: The Search for Political Power.* Lanham, Md.: University Press of America, 1987.

EQUAL EDUCATIONAL OPPORTUNITY ACT, 1974. Public Law 93–380, the Equal Educational Opportunity Act, passed by the U.S. Congress in 1974, amended the Elementary and Secondary Education Act of 1965. It made a policy declaration about equal educational opportunities and prohibited the denial of such opportunity.

The act created the Office of Bilingual Education within the U.S. Office of Education and provided financial assistance for bilingual education programs. It expanded existing bilingual programs and included programs for the education of adults as well as children.

FURTHER READING: Avila, Joaquín G. "Equal Education Opportunities for Language Minority Children (Symposium: Educational Equality Thirty Years after Brown v. Board of Education)." University of Colorado Law Review 55, no. 4 (Summer 1984):559–569; "Public Law 93–380: Educational Amendments of 1974." Congressional Information Service Annual. Part 1. Washington, D.C.: Congressional Information Service, 1975; Thomas, Stephen B. "Legal Update—The Fifth Circuit and Education." Texas Tech Journal of Education 9, no. 2 (Spring 1982):133–139.

EQUAL EMPLOYMENT OPPORTUNITY ACT, 1972. The Equal Employment Opportunity Act gave the Equal Employment Opportunity Commission (EEOC), created as a result of the 1964 Civil Rights Act, the power to file suit against violators of equal employment standards. The act helped primarily urban Chicanos, since agricultural workers were exempt from the EEOC job discrimination guidelines. In the 1980s the EEOC shifted its focus from class-action suits on behalf of large groups of workers to individual legal actions.

FURTHER READING: Downing, Paul M. The Equal Employment Opportunity Act of 1972: Legislative History. Washington, D.C.: Library of Congress Research Service, 1977.

ESCOBAR, ELEUTERIO, JR., 1894–1970. Civil rights activist Eleuterio Escobar's lifetime concern was equality of opportunity for all Mexican Americans, particularly in education. As a firsthand observer of the dire poverty and abysmal conditions in south Texas, he very early came to the conclusion that education was a key to improving life for la raza. After service in World War I he returned to entrepreneurial activity in San Antonio and soon joined the Knights of America, which he later represented at the founding of the League of United Latin American Citizens (LULAC) in 1929. Early in the next decade, with Alonso Perales and others, he began organizing Mexican Americans for political activity. Although the Association of Independent Voters, of which he was a founder and first president, soon collapsed over policy differences, it did set the stage for further Mexican American participation in Texas electoral politics.

As head of a LULAC committee concerned with the gross inferiority of educational facilities for Mexican American children in San Antonio, Escobar tried in vain to move the school board to ameliorative action; instead he was eased out of his committee chairmanship. However, he was quickly offered the presidency of the new Liga Pro-Defensa Escolar, which at its peak spoke for some 70 community groups. After much hard work and politicking under Escobar's leadership in the late 1930s, the Liga succeeded in expanding and improving westside (Mexican American) educational facilities. Then came World War II, and the school campaign went dormant.

In 1947 Escobar was elected president of a revived and revitalized Liga representing some 30 community organizations and supported by 50 more, all of which demanded an end to dangerously substandard westside school facilities for Chicano children. As a result of his leadership and drive, part of a $9.3 million school bond issue was used to carry out a majority of the Liga's forceful recommendations. Although Escobar was unable to achieve fully his goals for educational equality, he was able to force the school board to action and at the same time to demonstrate to the community what could be achieved by organized action. In 1958 Escobar was honored for his leadership by having a new high school named after him.

See also LEAGUE OF UNITED LATIN AMERICAN CITIZENS; ORGANIZATIONS.

FURTHER READING: García, Mario T. *Mexican Americans: Leadership, Ideology, and Identity, 1930–1960.* New Haven, Conn.: Yale University Press, 1989.

ESPARZA, CARLOS, 1828–1885. After the 1848 Treaty of Guadalupe Hidalgo it was not unusual for border Mexicanos to move readily from a Mexican to an American point of view. Carlos Esparza was one of these, a border rancher like Juan N. Cortina whom he supported in the latter's struggle for Tejano civil rights, but also a literary figure and poet. After the Civil War he made an unsuccessful effort to defend the lands and rights of Mexicanos in the Texas political arena. In the last decade of his life political cynicism replaced his earlier idealism and he despaired of a democratic society. He believed that education was ultimately the only way to improve the lot of la raza, but he also recognized that it was a luxury that few border Mexicanos enjoyed.

FURTHER READING: Larralde, Carlos. *Carlos Esparza: A Chicano Chronicle.* San Francisco: R & E Research Associates, 1977.

F

FAIR EMPLOYMENT PRACTICES COMMITTEE (FEPC). The FEPC was created in the Office of Production Management by presidential order of Franklin D. Roosevelt in 1941 just before the United States entered World War II. The agency was given the task of ferreting out employment discrimination in companies having government contracts and of taking steps to eliminate it. Texas historian Dr. Carlos Castañeda was appointed special assistant to the committee by President Roosevelt to monitor the civil rights concerns of Mexican Americans.

The agency had considerable success in protecting the rights of Chicanos in terms of equal treatment in hiring and promotion. At the end of the war Congress rejected President Harry Truman's recommendation to establish the agency on a permanent basis and it was allowed to expire. However, in 1964 the U.S. Congress created the Equal Employment Opportunity Commission, with essentially the same powers to bring an end to discrimination in employment, pay, and promotion, and with the power to bring suit against offenders in the federal courts. Various states also established fair employment practices agencies in emulation of the federal example.

See also EQUAL EMPLOYMENT OPPORTUNITY ACT.

FURTHER READING: Daniel, Clete. *Chicano Workers and the Politics of Fairness: The FEPC in the Southwest, 1941–1945.* Austin: University of Texas Press, 1991; *Sí, se puede.* Sacramento, Calif.: Fair Employment Practices Commission, Government Publications Section, 1964.

FARM LABOR ORGANIZING COMMITTEE (FLOC). Developed in the late 1960s, FLOC was the brainchild of Baldemar Velásquez, assisted by his father and a small circle of fellow farmworkers. It was envisioned as an agency to combat discrimination, poor working conditions, and the wretched standard of living endured by farmworkers.

Over the years FLOC has become a leading force in midwestern farm labor affairs. With deep convictions about social justice, the organization's leaders have consistently maintained a close association with harvest field workers and a high level of commitment to their welfare. One of FLOC's characteristics has been its reliance on outside groups—civic organizations, churches, and unions—to help it achieve its objectives. In turn, FLOC has publicly supported civil rights groups and other allies like César Chávez's United Farm Workers union, with which it has cooperated closely.

See also ORGANIZATIONS; VELÁSQUEZ, BALDEMAR.

FURTHER READING: Barger, W. K., and Ernesto M. Reza. *The Farm Labor Movement in the Midwest*. Austin: University of Texas Press, 1994.

FIERRO DE BRIGHT, JOSEFINA, 1920–   . Josefina Fierro came by her radicalism honestly. The daughter of refugees from the 1910 revolution in Mexico, she accompanied her mother, a staunch supporter of the Mexican prerevolutionary socialist leader Ricardo Flores Magón, to Los Angeles, California. She began her struggle for equal rights early in life. Married to Hollywood screenwriter and Communist Party (CP) member John Bright while she was still a teenager, she quickly moved into the Hollywood leftist community. Although probably never a CP member, she was undoubtedly a leftist; and though not self-consciously feminist, she fought for equal rights for women.

At age 18, while a student at the University of California at Los Angeles, she helped Luisa Moreno found the Congreso de Los Pueblos de Habla Española (Congress of Spanish-Speaking People), which quickly became one of the leading organizations defending Mexicano civil rights and advocating a broad range of reforms. She was secretary of the Congreso and remained one of its chief leaders until its demise in the mid-1940s as a result of its World War II stand. During the war she was one of the leaders in organizing the Sleepy Lagoon Defense Committee.

In 1951 Fierro was unsuccessful in her run for Congress as part of a serious effort by the Asociación Nacional México-Americana. She was accused of being a subversive during the McCarthyite red scare at midcentury. As a result, she voluntarily left the United States for Mexico in the 1950s.

See also ASOCIACIÓN NACIONAL MÉXICO-AMERICANA; CONGRESO DE LOS PUEBLOS DE HABLA ESPAÑOLA; SLEEPY LAGOON.

FURTHER READING: García, Mario T. *Memories of Chicano History: The Life and Narrative of Bert Corona*. Berkeley: University of California Press, 1994. García, Mario T. *Mexican Americans: Leadership, Ideology, and Identity, 1930–1960*. New Haven, Conn.: Yale University Press, 1989.

FLORES, PATRICK, 1929–   . On Cinco de Mayo 1970 Patrick Fernández Flores became the first Mexican American and second U.S. Latino to be appointed a bishop in the Roman Catholic Church. As a parish priest he had been deeply concerned with the needs of his impoverished Chicano parishioners for jobs, housing, and education. As bishop of El Paso (1977) and then archbishop of San Antonio (1979) he continued to be intensely active in support of the rights of his enlarged flock.

Born into an illiterate Texas sharecropper family, Flores experienced only a sporadic education until he decided to study for the priesthood. He graduated from high school at age 20 and seven years later was ordained. Never forgetting his humble roots and strongly influenced by the charismatic Cursillo movement among Mexican Americans in the Southwest, he introduced their attitudes into his services. He soon became widely known in Texas as the *mariachi* pastor.

While still a parish priest Flores strongly backed César Chávez in his struggle for farmworkers' rights, was a supporter of the Chicano Movement, and helped found and gave continuing support to Communities Organized for Public Service. As bishop and archbishop he has not hesitated to speak out for raza rights and against their abuse by local and federal agencies as well as by companies. He was chair of the Texas Advisory Committee to the U.S. Civil Rights Commission and a founder and national chair of PADRES, a Mexican American priests' rights group. He has been profoundly concerned with immigrants' problems and at times even with Mexicanos accused of crimes. Better educational opportunities for Mexican American youths has been his particular concern. Many of his ideas and programs derived from his acquaintance with Saul Alinsky's Industrial Areas Foundation, in which he was a director.

See also CHURCHES; COMMUNITIES ORGANIZED FOR PUBLIC SERVICE.

FURTHER READING: *American Catholic Who's Who, 1980–1981.* Vol. 23. Washington, D.C.: N.C. News Service, 1980; Cook, Joy. "Bishop Patrick Flores: The Barrio Bishop." *La Luz* 1, no. 4 (August 1972):19–21; McMurtrey, Martin. *Mariachi Bishop: The Life Story of Patrick Flores.* San Antonio: Corona Publishing, 1985.

FORD FOUNDATION. Established in 1938, the Ford Foundation has concentrated its concerns in the areas of education, economic opportunity, and democratic government. One of its early grants to a Chicano project was to fund the Mexican American Study Project at the University of California at Los Angeles, which resulted in the encyclopedic *The Mexican-American People: The Nation's Second Largest Minority*, published in 1970.

During the 1960s the foundation, advised by consultant Herman Gallegos, also began funding Chicano advocacy groups and supported activists all over the Southwest. In 1968 it provided $2.2 million as seed money to organize and develop the Mexican American Legal Defense and Educational Fund, and in the 1970s it financed the formation of the National Chicano Council on Higher Education. It also made grants to local organizations like the Mexican American Youth Organization in Texas and regional groups such as the Southwest Council of La Raza, which later became the National Council.

See also MEXICAN AMERICAN LEGAL DEFENSE AND EDUCATIONAL FUND; MEXICAN AMERICAN YOUTH ORGANIZATION.

FURTHER READING: Acuña, Rodolfo. *Occupied America: A History of Chicanos*. 3rd ed. New York: Harper & Row, 1988; Nielson, Waldemar. *The Big Foundations*. New York: Columbia University Press, 1972.

FOREIGN MINERS LICENSE TAX LAW. Enacted by the California legislature in 1850, the Foreign Miners License Tax Law imposed a $20 monthly fee on all foreign miners, which designation included Californios and other former Mexicans recently made U.S. nationals by the Treaty of Guadalupe Hidalgo. The legislation was clearly a violation of the civil rights of these Mexican Americans and was replaced in the following year with a more limited law aimed primarily at Chinese miners.

FURTHER READING: Coy, Owen C. *Gold Days*, Los Angeles: Powell Publishing Co., 1929; Hart, James D. *A Companion to California*. New York: Oxford University Press, 1978.

G

GADSDEN PURCHASE TREATY, 1853–1854. In the wake of the Treaty of Guadalupe Hidalgo railroad tycoon James Gadsden, the U.S. minister to Mexico, was instructed by the secretary of state to buy for a future transcontinental railway route as much of northern Mexico as its president, Antonio López de Santa Anna, would sell. Politically weak, needing finances, and pressured by the presence of U.S. troops sent to the border "to preserve order," Santa Anna agreed to the proposed sale, and the treaty was ratified by the U.S. Congress at the end of June 1854. By treaty with Mexico the United States purchased a 29 million acre triangle of land in southern Arizona and New Mexico for $10 million.

The Gadsden Treaty caused some hundreds of Mexicans who had moved across the 1848 Guadalupe Hidalgo Treaty border in order to remain in Mexican territory to be thrust back into the United States. The terms of the Gadsden Treaty were less protective of property rights and land claims than were the articles of the Treaty of Guadalupe Hidalgo.

See also ARIZONA.

FURTHER READING: Garber, Paul N. *The Gadsden Treaty*. Philadelphia: University of Pennsylvania Press, 1923; Meier, Matt S., and Feliciano Rivera. *Dictionary of Mexican American History*. Westport, Conn.: Greenwood Press, 1981; Rippy, J. Fred. "The Boundary of New Mexico and the Gadsden Treaty." *Hispanic American Historical Review* 4 (November 1921):715–742.

GALARZA, ERNESTO, 1905–1984. Because of a lifetime devoted to fighting for the rights of others, in 1979 Ernesto Galarza became the first Mexican American to be suggested for a Nobel Prize. His life's work centered on his fight in post–World War II for agricultural workers' rights through union organizing. Perhaps his most important contribution to the Mexican American civil rights movement was in gaining allies for its broader cause.

Pushed to the United States during Mexico's great revolution of 1910 as a child, Galarza excelled in school, ultimately earning his doctorate from Columbia University in New York. After research positions in the Foreign Policy Association and at the Pan American Union (PAU) in Washington, D.C., at the beginning of the 1940s he was promoted to director of the PAU's new Division of Labor and Social Information. This appointment resulted in a lifelong focus on the rights of Latino workers, particularly in agriculture.

When his policy recommendations to the PAU were ignored, Galarza resigned in 1947 to undertake the organizing of California agricultural workers. In the face of state "right to work" legislation, he spent the next dozen years trying to unionize farm laborers, most of them Mexicanos. Leaving the agricultural labor scene in 1959, during the next decade Galarza took on a variety of jobs related to urban workers and their civil rights. He served on the board of the Mexican American Legal Defense and Educational Fund and also became involved in the developing Chicano movement. Increasingly recognized as a leading Mexican American intellectual, he added education to his interests, writing books about labor and union problems and teaching at Harvard, Notre Dame, and several California state universities. In spite of poor health during the last decade of his life, until shortly before his death he was a frequent and active participant in conferences and workshops devoted to workers and their rights.

See also LEADERSHIP.

FURTHER READING: Chabrán, Richard. "Activism and Intellectual Struggle in the Life of Ernesto Galarza (1905–1984)." *Hispanic Journal of Behavioral Sciences* 7, no. 2 (June 1985):135–152; Galarza, Ernesto. *Spiders in the House and Workers in the Field*. Notre Dame, Ind.: University of Notre Dame Press, 1970; Guilbault, Rose del Castillo. "Scholar, Labor Leader, Poet, Hero." *San Francisco Chronicle: This World*, 23 September 1990, 3–4; London, Joan, and Henry Anderson. "Man of Fire: Ernesto Galarza." In *Chicano: The Evolution of a People*, edited by Renato Rosaldo, Robert Calvert, and Gustav Seligmann. Minneapolis: Winston Press, 1973.

GALLEGOS, HERMAN E., 1930–   . Veteran civil rights leader and community organizer Herman Gallegos sees his activist work in the creation and development of the Community Service Organization (CSO) in the 1950s as his most important contribution to the Mexican American civil rights movement. In that activity he helped make possible a training ground for future civil rights leaders. But he also advanced the movement by becoming, in the early 1970s, one of the first Mexican Americans elected to serve on the board of directors of a private corporation.

Born in the Colorado mining town of Aguilar, Gallegos received his education in two California state colleges (1948–1952) and the University of California at Berkeley (1955–1958). After graduating from San Jose State in 1952, he took employment with Santa Clara County and at the same time worked with Saul Alinsky organizing a local CSO. From 1958 to 1960 he was national president of the CSO and then served on the California Fair Employment Practices Commission. In the mid-1960s he became a consultant to the Ford Foundation and, with Ernesto Galarza and Julian Samora, helped it become seriously involved in providing financial support for the Chicano civil rights movement. In 1968 with a Ford grant he helped establish, and from 1968 to 1970 was the first executive director of, the Southwest Council of La Raza (now the National Council).

In 1967 Gallegos strongly advocated a White House conference on Mexican American problems. When President Johnson organized a conference in El Paso instead, a disappointed Gallegos was among the community leaders who absented themselves and then met in a rump session. In the early 1970s he accepted a teaching appointment at San Jose State and subsequently turned his attention more to the private sector while continuing his concerns for civil rights.

Firmly committed to issues of justice and equity, Gallegos has served on the board of various leading foundations, including the Rockefeller Foundation and the Rosenberg Foundation. He has been a trustee of the University of San Francisco and of the University of California at San Francisco as well as a board member of various corporate organizations. In addition, he was a founder and chief executive officer of several business firms, including the Human Resources Corporation in San Francisco, a management firm. He is now a private consultant. He continues to be involved with the issues of housing and the homeless. He firmly believes that the private sector can help la raza achieve its goals, but also that the government has a responsibility to protect civil rights.

Gallegos has received various honors for his active participation in the work of numerous service organizations. Among his published writings is "U.S. Foundations and Minority Group Interests" (1975), a seminal study profiling philanthropic support for minority causes.

See also FORD FOUNDATION; MEXICAN AMERICAN POLITICAL ASSOCIATION; NATIONAL COUNCIL OF LA RAZA.

FURTHER READING: Gallegos, Herman E. "Equity and Diversity: Hispanics in the Nonprofit World." Berkeley: University of California, The Bancroft Library, Regional Oral History Office, 1989; Gallegos, Herman E. "Hispanics Need a Strategy for the 90s." *Hispanic Business* (February 1985):10; Gallegos, Herman E., and Michael O'Neil, eds. *Hispanics and the Nonprofit Sector.* New York: Foundation Center, 1991; "People." *La Luz* (March-April 1975):5.

GALLUP INCIDENT, 1935. In the early 1930s the leftist National Miners Union (NMU) began organizing the mostly Mexicano coal miners near Gallup, New Mexico. Union recognition and an end to racial discrimination were the two main objectives of the miners. When a local landowner tried to force the miners to buy, at highly inflated prices, the houses they were renting, the union organized the miners' resistance. As miners were evicted from their houses, feelings ran high, and in one clash during the evictions a sheriff was shot and killed. Over 100 Mexicano workers, most of them NMU officials, were arrested, 10 were indicted for murder, and 3 were convicted. About 100 mine workers who were Mexican nationals were deported, and the union was destroyed.

See also CIVIL RIGHTS ABUSE.

FURTHER READING: Rubinstein, Harry R. "The Great Gallup Coal Strike of 1933." *Southwest Economy & Society* 3, no. 2 (Winter 1977/78):33–53.

GARCÍA, GUS (GUSTAVO) C., 1915–1964. Gus García's single most important contribution to the defense of civil rights was his work as chief counsel in the landmark U.S. Supreme Court case of *Hernández v. The State of Texas*. A brilliant scholar and outstanding lawyer, after graduation from the University of Texas law school in 1938 he became San Antonio assistant city attorney, then Bexar County assistant attorney, and later legal advisor to the League of United Latin American Citizens (LULAC). During World War II he served in the Judge Advocate Corps.

Upon his return to San Antonio from the army García immediately became active in politics, working with the American G.I. Forum, LULAC, and other Mexican American civic groups, especially in the area of education reform. In the 1948 case of *Delgado et al. v. Bastrop Independent School District et al.* he led the team of attorneys who succeeded in bringing an end to the de jure segregation of Mexican American school children in Texas. He was also involved in the Longoria incident and *Hernández v. State of Texas*. In 1956 he persuaded the Supreme Court to a rare unanimous decision by his eloquence in the *Hernández* case, arguing successfully that the exclusion of Mexican Americans from the jury violated Hernández's Fourteenth Amendment rights.

Because of his civil rights work for Mexicanos, García was frequently reviled by the Anglo legal establishment in Texas and yet was underappreciated in the Chicano community. Bitterly disappointed and disillusioned by the treatment he received, he destroyed his career and ultimately his life through alcoholism.

See also COURTS; HERNÁNDEZ v. DRISCOLL; HERNÁNDEZ v. THE STATE OF TEXAS.

FURTHER READING: Chacón, José A. *Hispanic Notables in the United States of North America*. Albuquerque: Saguaro Publishing Co., 1978; García, Arnold, Jr. "A Tough Competitor Speaks from the Grave." *Austin American-Statesman*, 21 September 1997; García, Mario T. *Mexican Americans: Leadership, Ideology, and Identity, 1930–1960*. New Haven, Conn.: Yale University Press, 1989; Reyna, Abel

A., Jr. "Gus García." *La Luz* 4, no. 2 (May 1975):38; Tyler, Ron, ed. *The New Handbook of Texas*. Vol. 3. Austin: Texas State Historical Association, 1996.

GARCÍA, HÉCTOR PÉREZ, 1914–1996. During his lifetime Dr. Héctor García was honored by numerous groups for his outstanding civil rights leadership. Because of his work for civil rights over the years, he was one of the first U.S. Latinos given the Presidential Medal of Freedom, awarded to him in 1984 by President Ronald Reagan. Five years later the Texas Senate passed a formal resolution recognizing his life's work for civil and human rights. These were only two of numerous high honors, appointments, and awards this civic-minded Mexican immigrant received in a lifetime of service that began with his youthful decision to become a physician.

After completing his A.B., in 1935 Héctor García entered the University of Texas School of Medicine because of parental and older-sibling influence, completed his M.D. degree four years later, and then did a two-year internship at Creighton University in Nebraska because of discrimination in Texas. He volunteered in World War II, serving in the infantry, the engineers, and lastly in the Medical Corps as a combat surgeon. After his release from the army he returned to Texas to practice family medicine in Corpus Christi and soon contracted with the Veterans Administration (VA) to provide medical care for veterans. He quickly became aware that Mexican American veterans were being subjected to discrimination by the VA and often were denied their basic rights.

The refusal of the Three Rivers, Texas, mortuary to handle the reburial of World War II casualty Félix Longoria created a protest in which Dr. García took a leading part. To do something more lasting about the denial of rights to Mexican American veterans, he then organized a meeting of Mexican American ex-service personnel, out of which the American G.I. Forum (AGIF) emerged in March 1948. During the 1950s Dr. García traveled throughout Texas helping to organize voter registration drives. Despite threats and physical harassment, he continued the activism and devotion to civil rights that he had shown earlier through his participation in the League of United Latin American Citizens.

Inevitably drawn into the political arena by his concerns, he became very active in Democratic politics and was named national coordinator of the Viva Kennedy clubs in the 1960 presidential election. During the postelection period he led efforts to create a nationwide Mexican American civil rights organization. The less-than-national Political Association of Spanish-Speaking Organizations that resulted elected him its first president.

García played a major role in the *Hernández* case and in the Félix Longoria dispute. As a result of his deep commitment to the struggle for civil rights and his devotion to community affairs as well as to the Democratic Party, in 1968 he was appointed to the U.S. Commission on Civil Rights by President Lyndon Johnson and in the following year received an honorific civil rights award from the National Association for the Advancement of Colored People.

Along with intense involvement in numerous civil rights activities, Dr. García continued his medical practice well into his seventies. After suffering from cancer for more than a decade, he died in July 1996 at age 82 from congestive heart failure and pneumonia.

See also AMERICAN G.I. FORUM; LEADERSHIP; LONGORIA, FÉLIX.

FURTHER READING: Allsup, Carl. *The American G.I. Forum: Origins and Evolution.* Austin: University of Texas, Center for Mexican American Studies, 1982; Ávila, Alex. "Freedom Fighter." *Hispanic* (January–February 1996):18; Chacón, José. *Hispanic Notables in the United States of North America.* Albuquerque: Saguaro Publishing, 1978; "Héctor Pérez García Dies: Led Hispanic Rights Group." *New York Times,* 29 July 1996; "President Honors G.I. Forum Founder." *Nuestro* 8, no. 4 (May 1984):27–31; Pycior, Julie Leininger. *LBJ & Mexican Americans: The Paradox of Power.* Austin: University of Texas Press, 1997; Ramos, Henry A. J. *The American G.I. Forum: In Pursuit of the Dream, 1948–1983.* Houston: Arte Público Press, 1998.

GARCÍA (MACARIO) INCIDENT. Sergeant Macario García, a World War II veteran and Congressional Medal of Honor recipient, was denied service in a small-town Texas restaurant and arrested for assault when he protested the refusal to serve him. The Houston council of the League of United Latin American Citizens established a defense committee for García.

See also CIVIL RIGHTS ABUSE.

FURTHER READING: Perales, Alonso. *Are We Good Neighbors?* Reprint, New York: Arno Press, 1974.

GARZA, CATARINO ERASMO, 1859–1895. As a young man border Mexicano Catarino Garza turned his interests toward journalism partly as an effort to counter stereotyping of Mexicanos by the Anglo press in Texas. During the 1880s he edited ephemeral and peripatetic Spanish-language newspapers in Brownsville, Eagle Pass, Corpus Christi, and San Antonio, using them to spread his liberal political ideas, his enthusiasm for mutualista societies, and his attacks on the mistreatment and lynching of Mexicanos in Texas. His caustic editorials sharply criticizing the not infrequent ruthless actions of the Texas Rangers made him the object of that organization's anger and resulted in his arrest. They also served to make him a preeminent leader in the late nineteenth-century Mexican American struggle for civil rights as well as a leading figure among exiles who wanted to overthrow President Porfirio Díaz in Mexico.

More revolutionary than social critic, toward the end of the 1880s Garza began using his leadership position among Mexicanos to organize a border guerrilla band to bring about the overthrow of Díaz. In 1890 and 1891 he led a series of three attacks across the border; the third raid ended in a crushing defeat and the dispersal of his forces. Continued unrelenting harassment from the U.S. Army and a long manhunt by the Texas Rangers soon turned him into a folk hero for many in south Texas. He persisted in his border guerrilla activities until 1893, when he left the United States with a handful of associates. A committed revolutionary, he then joined the struggle for Cuban independence from Spain and shortly afterward the fight for Panamanian independence from Colombia. He was killed in 1895 during the latter effort.

See also CORTINA, JUAN N.; TEXAS RANGERS.

FURTHER READING: Cuthbertson, Gilbert M. "Catarino E. Garza and the Garza War." *Texana* 13, no. 4 (1975):335–348; Garza, Catarino E. "La lógica de los hechos, o sean observaciones sobre las circunstancias de los mexicanos en Texas desde el año 1877 hasta 1889," Tomo I. Corpus Christi, ca. 1890. Ms. in Benson Latin American Collection, General Libraries, University of Texas at Austin; Larralde, Carlos. *Mexican American: Movements and Leaders.* Los Alamitos, Calif.: Hwong Publishing Co., 1976; Thompson, Jerry. *A Wild and Vivid Land: An Illustrated History of the South Texas Border.* Austin: Texas State Historical Association, 1997; Young, Elliott G. "Twilight at the Texas-Mexico Border: Catarino Garza and Identity at the Crossroads." Ph.D. diss., University of Texas at Austin, 1997.

GARZA, KIKA (ELIGIO) DE LA, 1927–   . Although an active participant in the Congressional Hispanic Caucus and a longtime member of the League of United Latin American Citizens, Kika de la Garza has consistently taken conservative political positions. In both Texas and Washington, D.C., he often opposed civil rights bills, thereby upsetting many of his Mexican American constituents.

Born in Mercedes, Texas, de la Garza served in the Korean conflict as well as in the last days of World War II. After attending college and earning a law degree in 1952, he started a law practice and a political career. He served 12 years in the Texas legislature, where he showed little enthusiasm for civil rights legislation. In 1964 he was elected to the United States House of Representatives, to which he was consistently reelected as a conservative southern Democrat. In 1978 he was honored with the Aguila Azteca award by the Mexican government.

FURTHER READING: Ehrenhalt, Alan, ed. *Politics in America.* Washington, D.C.: Congressional Quarterly, 1983; Ralph Nader Congress Project. *Eligio de la Garza, Democratic Representative from Texas.* Washington, D.C.: Grossman Publishers, 1972.

GARZA, REYNALDO G., 1915–   . Reynaldo Garza became the first Mexican American, after Harold Medina back in the 1940s, to be appointed judge of a federal district court, chief judge of a federal judicial district, and in 1979 a judge in the U.S. Court of Appeals. Although he personally experienced little discrimination growing up, he early became aware of the existence of racism and the denial of civil rights to la raza. The influence of a liberal family helped shape his views on human rights and social issues. While still a student at the University of Texas, he attempted to make Austin's Anglo leaders aware of and sensitive to segregation and other infringements of Mexicanos' civil rights. After receiving his law degree he returned to Brownsville to use his training to bring legal aid to Mexican Americans. In 1940 he joined the League of United Latin American Citizens and within the year was elected the Brownsville chapter president, a position he used to promote equal treatment of Mexican Americans.

His career interrupted by World War II, after four years in the service Garza returned to Brownsville, resumed his civic activities, and reentered local politics. A decade later he was appointed to the Texas Good Neighbor Commission and in 1961 became the second Mexican American on a federal bench, the U.S. District Court. During the Vietnam War he supported the civil rights of students suspended for distributing anti-war leaflets. In the 1970s he presided over numerous cases arising out of the Civil Rights Act of 1964.

Although Garza's position on civil rights in labor cases was fairly conservative, in the 1972 *Medrano v. Allee* suit he came down strongly on the side of the union and against the Texas Rangers. In 1979 he was appointed by President Jimmy Carter to the Fifth Circuit Court of Appeals, where he continued his forthright opposition to school segregation. As a judge he ruled in 1983 that at-large voting districts and other election practices essentially discriminated against Chicano voters.

See also COURTS; TEXAS GOOD NEIGHBOR COMMISSION.

FURTHER READING: Fisch, Louise Ann. *All Rise: Reynaldo G. Garza, the First Mexican American Federal Judge.* College Station: Texas A&M University Press, 1996.

GERRYMANDERING. The practice of creating the boundaries of an electoral district so as to benefit a particular political group. Typically at the time of redistricting after each decennial census the political party in power tries to set voting district boundaries to maintain or improve its electoral position.

Gerrymandering has often been used to weaken the voting strength of opposition parties and minority groups, including Mexican Americans. It has therefore resulted in minority political underrepresentation, so it constitutes a restriction or denial of citizens' rights. Since 1970 the Voting Rights Act of that year forbids the altering of district boundaries if the change would negatively affect a minority's voting strength. Nevertheless, Chicanos remain underrepresented in terms of political power.

FURTHER READING: *Concise Dictionary of American History.* New York: Charles Scribner's Sons, 1962; Foner, Eric, and John A. Garrity, eds. *The Reader's Companion to American History.* Boston: Houghton Mifflin, 1991; Griffith, Elmer Cummings. *Rise and Development of the Gerrymander.* Reprint, New York: Arno Press, 1974; Regalado, James A., and Gloria Martínez. "Reapportionment and Coalition Building." In *Latinos and Political Coalitions: Political Empowerment for the 1990s,* edited by Roberto E. Villarreal and Norma G. Hernández. Westport, Conn.: Greenwood Press, 1991.

GÓMEZ-QUIÑONES, JUAN, 1940– . Juan Gómez-Quiñones has been a political activist since his student days in the early 1960s at the University of California at Los Angeles. He was a co-founder of the United Mexican American Students (UMAS) and also helped develop a number of educational groups and community organizations. A historian with special interests in Chicano political movements, he has served on the boards of Los Angeles Urban Coalition and the Mexican American Legal Defense and Educational Fund.

In 1970 Gómez-Quiñones founded the preeminent Chicano journal *Aztlán* at UCLA's Chicano Studies Research Center and was its first editor. From 1975 to 1985 he served as director of the research center. He is the author of several books and numerous journal articles dealing especially with labor organizing and the student movement in which he was an active participant.

See also STUDENT ACTIVISM; STUDENT ORGANIZATIONS.

FURTHER READING: Gómez-Quiñones, Juan. *Mexican Students Por La Raza: The Chicano Student Movement in Southern California, 1967–1977.* Santa Barbara, Calif.: Editorial La Causa, 1978.

GONZALES, CORKY (RODOLFO), 1928– . For most urban Mexican Americans Corky Gonzales was the most important Chicano civil rights advocate of the 1960s. In addition to his activities as a civic leader, political reformer, and Chicano nationalist, he became widely known for his 1967 epic poem, *I Am Joaquín,* which inspired thousands of youthful Chicanos to demand their full civil rights.

Rodolfo Gonzales moved from a career as a prize-winning young boxer to active participation in Democratic politics, becoming Colorado coordinator for the successful "Viva Kennedy" campaign in the 1960 presidential election. After involvement in various local social services agencies he concentrated his attention on the problems of Colorado Mexican Americans. A former member of the American G.I. Forum, in the second half of the 1960s he organized La Cruzada para la Justicia (The Crusade for Justice) to fight for Chicano economic and political equality as well as civil rights. During the decade 1968 to 1978 the Crusade was an important organization throughout the Southwest.

As part of his crusade for Chicano liberation Gonzales led several hundred Mexican Americans in the 1968 Poor Peoples March to Washington, D.C. There, as the strongest advocate of Chicano nationalist ideology, he issued the Plan del Barrio, a series of demands for Chicano rights. In the following year he called for a conference at Denver to discuss concerns of young Mexican Americans. Under his sponsorship some 1,500 youthful delegates attending this Chicano Youth Liberation Conference drew up the Plan Espiritual de Aztlán, which stressed self-determination and ethnic nationalism. The conference also called for the creation of a Chicano political party. After the conference Gonzales continued to express his concerns about the problems of young Chicanos, sharply criticizing their education, supporting student walkouts, protesting police brutality, and defending the civil rights of those arrested in demonstrations.

To raise Mexican American consciousness and to advance his political ideas Corky Gonzales formed the (Colorado) Raza Unida Party (LRUP) in 1970. Meanwhile, he had begun to move from Chicano nationalism to concepts of class struggle and internationalism. Two years later at the first national LRUP convention in El Paso, called in an effort to develop greater political unity, he lost an intense leadership battle to the more politically pragmatic José Angel Gutiérrez, the Texas LRUP leader.

As the Chicano Movement ebbed in the second half of the 1970s, Gonzales's leadership declined further; he remained head of the greatly weakened Crusade, now largely limited to Colorado. In October 1987 a severe automobile injury left him with a long and difficult recovery. In the mid-1990s a visibly aging Corky Gonzales still spoke out for civil rights, albeit less passionately than earlier.

See also COLORADO; KENNEDY, JOHN FITZGERALD; LEADERSHIP; MOVIMIENTO, EL.

FURTHER READING: Castro, Tony. *Chicano Power: The Emergence of Mexican America*. New York: Saturday Review Press, 1974; Hammerback, John C., Richard J. Jensen, and José Angel Gutiérrez. *A War of Words: Chicano Protest in the 1960s and 1970s*. Westport, Conn.: Greenwood Press, 1985; Larralde, Carlos. *Mexican American: Movements and Leaders*. Los Alamitos, Calif.: Hwong Publishing Co., 1976; Marín, Christine. *A Spokesman for the Mexican American Movement: Rodolfo "Corky" Gonzales and the Fight for Chicano Liberation, 1966–1972*. San Francisco: R&E Research Associates, 1977; Pycior, Julie Leininger. *LBJ & Mexican Americans: The Paradox of Power*. Austin: University of Texas Press, 1997.

GONZALES, M[ANUEL] C., 1900–1986. Manuel C. Gonzales, known throughout his adult life simply as M. C., got an early taste for the law by working as a teenage clerk for a district judge in a southeast Texas border county, as a chief clerk in the state capital, and later as a secretary in an Austin law firm. After the American entrance into World War I he received appointment as an interpreter for the military attaché in Madrid and later

in Paris although he was not yet 20. Upon his return to the United States
he studied law, passed the bar, and went to work for the district attorney
of Bexar County.

M. C. began his long career in civil rights while still a teenager. He played
a dynamic part in creating La Liga Protectora Mexicana before his eigh-
teenth birthday and helped organize other local associations in the 1920s.
At the end of that decade he was secretary of the convention that created
the League of United Latin American Citizens (LULAC), and in 1931 he
was elected president of the organization. He remained active in LULAC
for the rest of his long life.

Gonzales also took a vital role in all aspects of Mexicano affairs, being
widely acknowledged in Texas as one of la raza's principal leaders. During
the 1930s he worked constantly for the San Antonio Mexicano community,
filing class-action petitions against segregation in the schools and organizing protests against unpopular school board decisions. He was a strong
supporter of the "Better Government" group in its campaign against machine politics in San Antonio.

In his newspaper, *El Luchador*, his constant themes were that Mexican
Americans should fight for their rights and that they should unite as citizens
to do so. In his many published writings M. C. stressed American patri-
otism as well as Mexican culture and heritage, the obligations of citizenship
as well as its rights. When he died in 1986, he left an extensive legacy of
vigorous civil rights defense that was acknowledged throughout the Southwest.

See also LEAGUE OF UNITED LATIN AMERICAN CITIZENS; LIGA
PROTECTORA MEXICANA.

FURTHER READING: Garcia, Richard A. *Rise of the Mexican American Middle
Class, San Antonio Texas, 1929–1941.* College Station: Texas A&M University
Press, 1991; Salazar, Veronica. *Dedication Rewarded: Prominent Mexican Ameri-
cans.* San Antonio: Mexican American Cultural Center, 1976; Tyler, Ron, ed. *The
New Handbook of Texas.* Vol. 3. Austin: Texas State Historical Association, 1996.

GONZALES, SYLVIA ALICIA, 1943–   . After university studies that cul-
minated in a doctorate in education from the University of Massachusetts,
Sylvia Gonzales began her professional career in 1968 as an analyst for the
U.S. Commission on Civil Rights in Washington. She later left the com-
mission and in 1974 accepted a position as assistant professor in Mexican
American studies at California State University in San Jose. Active in the
Mexican American Women's National Association (MANA), in 1977 she
was a delegate at the International Women's Year Conference in Houston,
Texas.

Gonzales's concerns tend to be more feminist than purely civil rights.
Primarily known for her publications, she has written about feminist issues
and has especially devoted herself to the political empowerment of Chica-

nas. In 1971 she edited *Women in Action* for the U.S. Civil Service Commission. She has decried the divisiveness and factionalism that she perceives among Latinas and sees the need for changes both within the community and in the larger society to improve conditions for Chicanas. These can be achieved only by group consciousness and cooperation, she believes.

See also CHICANAS; MANA: A NATIONAL LATINA ORGANIZATION.

FURTHER READING: Fisher, Dexter, ed., *The Third Woman: Minority Women Writers of the United States*. Boston: Houghton Mifflin, 1977; Gonzales, Sylvia. "The Latina Feminist: Where We've Been, Where We're Going. *Nuestro* (August/ September 1981):45–47; Telgen, Diane, and Jim Kamp, eds. *Notable Hispanic American Women*. Detroit: Gale Research, 1993.

GONZÁLES ET AL. v. SHEELY ET AL., 1951. At the beginning of the 1950s Porfirio Gonzales and other petitioners filed suit against Arizona elementary public school authorities for segregating their children. They argued that the schools, under cover of state legislation, were denying their children their constitutional rights. In March 1951 the U.S. District Court ruled in their favor, holding that the practice of placing Mexican American children in separate school buildings with inferior facilities violated their constitutional rights and was therefore discriminatory and illegal.

See also ARIZONA; COURTS.

FURTHER READING: *Gonzales et al. v. Sheely et al*. Civ. No. 1473. 96 F Supp. 1004. United States District Court D Arizona, March 26, 1951.

GONZÁLEZ, HENRY BARBOSA, 1916– . During his more than 35 years of service in the U.S. House of Representatives and 5 years before that in the Texas legislature, Henry B. González has consistently supported and advanced the interests of the poor and powerless. The economic and civil rights of his constituents have always been his primary concern.

Like many Mexican Americans of his age group Henry González was born in the United States of parents who had recently fled the Mexican revolution of 1910. After graduation from St. Mary's University in San Antonio, with his law degree he worked at a variety of jobs; then during World War II he served in an armed forces intelligence unit. In the immediate postwar era he worked as a juvenile probation officer until the end of the 1940s.

In 1953 González was elected to the San Antonio city council, where he soon became involved in civil rights issues, particularly segregation. Three years later he was elected to a four-year term in the Texas Senate. The first Mexican American to serve in that body since the mid-1800s, he quickly proved himself a champion of minority civil rights and a vigorous foe of racist legislation. In the late 1950s González attracted national attention by leading the longest filibuster in Texas Senate history in order to defeat a group of racist bills.

By his election to the U.S. House of Representatives, in 1961 Henry González became the first Tejano in history to hold a national office. Since then, he was regularly reelected to the House, where he continued to demonstrate his concern for the rights of the poor and disadvantaged. He sponsored and supported many bills to protect minority rights and expand opportunities, including abolition of the poll tax, basic adult education, educational benefits for Vietnam veterans, workforce training, and a conservation corps for youths.

Fiercely independent and staunchly supporting what he believes to be right, González opposed the strident anti-gringo rhetoric of the youthful Chicano members of the Mexican American Youth Organization in Texas. In 1976 this moderately liberal Democrat was one of the founders of the Congressional Hispanic Caucus. At the end of 1998 he retired from the House of Representatives for reasons of health.

See also CONGRESSIONAL HISPANIC CAUCUS; LEADERSHIP.

FURTHER READING: Castro, Tony. *Chicano Power: The Emergence of Mexican America*. New York: Saturday Review Press, 1974; Conroy, Ed. "Give 'em Hell, Henry." *Mother Jones* 16, no. 4 (July–August 1991):12; Ehrenhalt, Alan, ed. *Politics in America*. Washington, D.C.: Congressional Quarterly, 1983; "Profile of a Public Man." *Nuestro* 2, no. 13 (March 1983):13–19, 50; Rodríguez, Eugene. *Henry B. González: A Political Profile*. New York: Arno Press, 1976; Sloane, Todd A. *González of Texas: A Congressman for the People*. Evanston, Ill. John Gordon Burke Publisher, 1996; Vigil, Maurilio E. *Hispanics in Congress: A Historical and Political Survey*. Lanham, N.Y.: University Press of America, 1996.

GONZÁLEZ, PEDRO J., 1895–1995. After fighting in the revolutionary army of Pancho Villa, then crossing into the United States in 1923, and working as a dockhand in Los Angeles, Pedro González became the leader of a musical group named Los Madrugadores. He was one of the first Spanish-language radio announcers in the Los Angeles area. His extremely popular early morning radio show featured cherished Mexican ballads, and he spoke out boldly against discrimination, human rights violations, and the mass deportation of Mexicanos in the early 1930s.

González's outspokenness led to harassment and finally to his conviction for rape on a trumped-up charge in 1934. His teenage accuser later admitted her charges were completely false, and after serving 6 years of a 50-year sentence he was released from San Quentin and deported as an undesirable alien. González renewed his musical career in radio across the border in Tijuana and again spoke out plainly against injustice and denial of civil liberties.

After three decades in exile González was allowed to return to the United States in 1971, and in his declining years he continued to fight for Mexican

American equality. By the time of his death at age 99, he had received numerous honors as a warrior in the struggle for social justice and civil rights. The TV documentary *Ballad of an Unsung Hero* (1983) and the subsequent film *Break of Dawn* recounted the story of this true folk hero.

See also CIVIL RIGHTS ABUSES; DISCRIMINATION.

FURTHER READING: Parlee, Lorena M. "Ballad of an Unsung Hero." *Nuestro* 8, no. 10 (December 1984):22–24.

GONZÁLEZ DE ARROYO BUCKLEY, ESTHER, 1948– . A lifelong Laredo, Texas, resident and precocious student, Esther González was only 15 when she was chosen valedictorian of her graduating high school class. Having completed an undergraduate degree in mathematics and graduate work at Southwestern Medical School in Dallas, she suspended her studies in 1970 and returned to Laredo with her husband, Elmer Buckley. After several years as a housewife and teacher she became deeply involved in the county Republican Women's Club, where she quickly earned a reputation as a sharp, hard-working political aspirant. Her political activities led to the chair of the Webb County Republican organization. Governor Bill Clements appointed her to the Texas Teachers Professional Practices and Ethics Commission, through which she subsequently met President Ronald Reagan.

When President Reagan gutted the national Commission on Civil Rights in mid-1983 by ousting three commissioners who disagreed strongly with his soft position on civil rights, Buckley was one of his appointees to the new commission created by Congress in December. Her appointment was denounced in some quarters as solely political, since she had no experience with civil rights issues, disapproved the proposed Equal Rights Amendment to the Constitution, had denounced busing as a brutal inconvenience, and sought solutions other than quotas and affirmative action to level the playing field for minorities.

See also AFFIRMATIVE ACTION; CIVIL RIGHTS COMMISSION; TEXAS.

FURTHER READING: "MALDEF Fights for Rights Commission." *MALDEF* 12, no. 2 (Fall/Winter 1983); Worthington, Rogers. "An 'Unknown' Enters Rights Arena." *Chicago Tribune* Section 1, 20 December 1983).

GORRAS BLANCAS, 1889–1895. Las Gorras Blancas (The White Caps) was organized in New Mexico in the late 1880s by Juan José Herrera and others in response to encroachment on pueblo lands, especially by railroads and Anglo cattlemen. One of the first secret organizations created to defend Nuevomexicano rights, it hoped to halt and roll back the private takeover of pueblo grant lands. Especially in San Miguel County, the fencing-in of common lands previously available to all for grazing aroused great concern among Nuevomexicano sheep herders and led to the destruction of miles of fencing and thousands of railroad ties.

The aggressive actions of the masked Gorras Blancas antagonized many elite Nuevomexicanos as well as most Anglos, but the organization had extensive popular support and soon claimed a membership of 1,500. In November 1889 indictments of alleged members of the group led to an outpouring of support for the jailed suspects.

In 1890 the Gorras entered the political arena in support of the newly organized People's Party, El Partido del Pueblo Unido. The nomination of one of the more radical Gorras Blancas members for the territorial legislature led to an organizational crisis and split. Many of the moderate members withheld their electoral support. While the Gorras had stemmed the tide of land grabbing in 1889 and 1890, internal dissent and the turn to politics brought an end to its effectiveness. By the mid-1890s its political arm, the People's Party, had faded away and it had lost popular support.

See also ORGANIZATIONS.

FURTHER READING: Martínez, Félix. "Las Gorras Blancas." In *Foreigners in Their Native Land: Historical Roots of the Mexican American*, edited by David J. Weber. Albuquerque: University of New Mexico Press, 1973; Schlesinger, Andrew B. "Las Gorras Blancas, 1889–1891." *Journal of Mexican American History* 1 (Spring 1971):87–143.

GUADALUPE HIDALGO, TREATY OF, 1848. The Treaty of Guadalupe Hidalgo brought the United States–Mexico War to an end in February 1848. It provided that the approximately 80,000 Mexicans living in the area acquired by the U.S. through the treaty had the choice of remaining Mexican citizens or of becoming nationals, and eventually citizens, of the United States. Whichever choice they made, their property rights were guaranteed by the treaty. Those who opted to become U.S. nationals were to enjoy "all the rights of citizens of the United States according to the principles of the Constitution" (see Appendix D). The rights guaranteed by the treaty, particularly in the matter of land ownership, were later often violated and ignored by "reinterpretation" of the treaty's intent.

See also CIVIL RIGHTS LEGISLATION, HISTORY OF; GADSDEN PURCHASE TREATY; IN RE RICARDO RODRÍGUEZ; LAND GRANTS.

FURTHER READING: Conmy, Peter T. *A Centennial Evaluation of the Treaty of Guadalupe Hidalgo. 1848–1948.* Oakland, Calif.: Oakland Public Library, 1948; Griswold del Castillo, Richard. *The Treaty of Guadalupe Hidalgo: A Legacy of Conflict.* Norman: University of Oklahoma Press, 1990; Klein, Julius. *The Making of the Treaty of Guadalupe Hidalgo, February 2, 1848.* Berkeley: University of California, 1905; Miller, Hunter, ed. *Treaties and Other International Acts of the United States of America.* Vol. 5. Washington, D.C.: U.S. Government Printing Office, 1937.

GUTIÉRREZ, JOSÉ ANGEL, 1944–   . Of the principal Mexican American civil rights leaders at the end of the 1960s, José Angel Gutiérrez unquestionably showed the greatest promise. Son of a Crystal City, Texas,
physician, he was a highly motivated and studious youth who did well
academically. After earning a B.S. in political science in 1966, he obtained
a master's degree at St. Mary's University in San Antonio and a decade
later completed the requirements for a doctorate in political science at the
University of Texas at Austin. Toward the end of the 1980s he earned a
second doctorate, in law, at the University of Houston.

While at St. Mary's University Gutiérrez was one of the five leaders who
formed the Mexican American Youth Organization and was elected its first
president. After his master's degree in political science and some practical
experience as a research investigator for the Mexican American Legal Defense and Educational Fund, he returned to Crystal City to put into practice
his ideas for organizing Mexican Americans in order to achieve civil rights
and economic betterment. A 1969 high school walkout over racist discrimination provided an opportunity that Gutiérrez used to organize a political
power base, La Raza Unida Party (LRUP).

On a LRUP ticket Gutiérrez and two additional raza candidates were
elected to the school board, and in 1970 two Chicanos won seats on the
city council. As a result Mexican Americans of Crystal City achieved some
immediate political power and were able to institute bilingual and bicultural programs in the schools. Although Gutiérrez favored a focus on local
issues, success in Crystal City created pressure to take La Raza Unida national. At the 1972 LRUP convention in El Paso he won a clear but divisive
leadership victory over Corky Gonzales, but he lost the battle to keep LRUP
local. In the 1972 elections the party made a poor showing, but two years
later Gutiérrez won a judgeship in Zavala County. As a judge he soon
found himself involved in a power struggle with the Anglo court establishment; after a long feud with the Texas judicial commission Gutiérrez
handed in his resignation in 1981.

After teaching at two Oregon colleges José Angel Gutiérrez returned to
Texas in 1986 to resume his civil rights work as the director of the Greater
Dallas Legal and Community Development Foundation. Having obtained
his J.D. (doctor of law) in 1988, he became an administrative law judge
for the city of Dallas. Five years later Gutiérrez entered the race for the
U.S. Senate as a Democrat. Despite an energetic campaign he was unable
to convince Texas voters that he was the best of two dozen candidates.
Unfortunately for him, many persons, both Mexican American and Anglo,
perceived him as an extremist rather than as the rhetorical radical and
political pragmatist he always was. He still operates a legal aid center as
part of his continuing fight for Mexican American civil rights.

See also CRYSTAL CITY; LEADERSHIP; MEXICAN AMERICAN
YOUTH ORGANIZATION; RAZA UNIDA PARTY, LA.

FURTHER READING: Castro, Tony. *Chicano Power: The Emergence of Mexican America*. New York: Saturday Review Press, 1974; García, Ignacio. *United We Win: The Rise and Fall of La Raza Unida Party*. Tucson: MASRC, University of Arizona, 1989; Gutiérrez, José Angel. *The Making of a Chicano Militant: Lessons from Cristal*. Madison: University of Wisconsin Press, 1998; Gutiérrez, José Angel. *La Raza and Revolution*. San Francisco: R & E Research Associates, 1972; Gutiérrez, José Angel. "Toward a Theory of Community Organization in a Mexican American Community in South Texas." Ph.D. diss., University of Texas at Austin, 1976; Hammerback, John C., Richard J. Jensen, and José Angel Gutiérrez. *A War of Words: Chicano Protest in the 1960s and 1970s*. Westport, Conn.: Greenwood Press, 1985; Muñoz, Carlos, Jr. *Youth, Identity, Power: The Chicano Movement*. New York: Verso, 1990; Shockley, John S. *Chicano Revolt in a Texas Town*. Notre Dame, Ind.: University of Notre Dame Press, 1974.

GUZMÁN, RALPH C., 1924–1985. During the early years of the Chicano Movement Ralph Guzmán played an influential role in the struggle for civil liberties. In 1955 he was named director of the Alianza Hispano-Americana's newly founded civil rights department, and he soon became well known for his skill in developing community support organizations. With an academic background in political science, he was one of the founders of the Community Service Organization in the Los Angeles area, along with Fred Ross, Sr. and others.

Even before he obtained his doctorate, Guzmán began a long and successful academic career. He was appointed a director in the Mexican American Study Project at the University of California at Los Angeles and helped develop *The Mexican American People: The Nation's Second Largest Minority* (1970), an outstanding resource book that documented the prevalence of racist discrimination. Meanwhile, in the Department of Politics and Community Studies at the University of California at Santa Cruz, he had already begun educating an entire generation of students in the varied problems of racism, discrimination, and denial of civil rights in the United States. In addition to teaching and performing important State Department service, he was a highly respected and widely employed consultant as well as a prolific author who published extensively on various facets of racism and civil rights.

See also COMMUNITY SERVICE ORGANIZATION.

FURTHER READING: Acuña, Rodolfo. *Occupied America: A History of Chicanos*. 3rd ed. New York: Harper & Row, 1988; Guzmán, Ralph C. *The Political Socialization of the Mexican American People*. New York: Arno Press, 1976; "In Memoriam." *U.C. Mexus News* 16 (Winter 1986):6; "Ralph C. Guzmán." *Political Science* 29, no. 1 (Winter 1986).

H

HEAD START. Project Head Start was a facet of President Lyndon B. Johnson's War on Poverty program, initiated in 1964. In part, Head Start grew out of a preschool English-language program called The Little School of the 400, which was begun in 1957 by the League of United Latin American Citizens. At first under the Office of Economic Opportunity, in 1966 Head Start was transferred to the Department of Health, Education, and Welfare.

Head Start programs were developed to meet perceived community needs and to actively involve parents in the educational process. It was hoped that providing compensatory educational training to children of poor families would enable more of them to achieve their full potential. Most observers regarded Head Start as an excellent effort to redress injustices in American society by providing an initial boost on the ladder of upward mobility and by encouraging full self-realization in underprivileged families.

See also JOHNSON, LYNDON BAINES; LEAGUE OF UNITED LATIN AMERICAN CITIZENS.

FURTHER READING: Currie, Janet, and Thomas Duncan. *Does Head Start Help Hispanic Children?* Cambridge, Mass: National Bureau of Economic Research, 1996; Ziegler, Edward. *Head Start: The Inside Story of America's Most Successful Educational Project.* New York: Basic Books, 1992.

HERNÁNDEZ, ALFRED J., 1917– . Judge Alfred Hernández was one of the principal leaders of the rump caucus that followed the walkout of 50 Mexican American delegates attending the March 1966 Equal Employment Opportunity Commission meeting in Albuquerque. President of the League of United Latin American Citizens (LULAC) at the time, Hernández pointed out the lack of Mexican American representation on the commission and the government's indifference to la raza as the chief reasons for the rump caucus.

Three months later at the annual LULAC convention he advocated a policy of greater militancy. In July he was one of the organizers of the 400-mile march to Austin and in the following April took an important part in a "Brown Power" conference in Sacramento, California. Later that year he testified before the U.S. Civil Rights Commission on abuses of migrant workers' rights.

In the 1970s Judge Hernández left the bench and returned to private practice.

See also LEAGUE OF UNITED LATIN AMERICAN CITIZENS.

FURTHER READING: Chacón, José A. *Hispanic Notables in the United States of North America*. Albuquerque: Saguaro Press, 1978.

HERNÁNDEZ, ANTONIA, 1948– . Influenced by immigrant parents who believed strongly in public service, Antonia Hernández participated in several Chicano organizations as a college student and served on an admissions committee of the University of California at Los Angeles law school. She also worked as a clerk in the California Legal Rural Assistance program. After receiving her law doctorate in 1974 she went to work as an attorney in the East Los Angeles Center for Law and Justice and a year later became directing attorney for the Legal Aid Foundation. In 1978 she accepted a staff position on the U.S. Senate Judiciary Committee in Washington, D.C., where she devoted her time and energies for the next three years to human rights issues, especially in the area of immigration.

When the Democratic Party lost its U.S. Senate majority in 1981, Hernández lost her job and took a position as an attorney in the Washington office of the Mexican American Legal Defense and Educational Fund (MALDEF). She played an important role in the defeat of the 1982 Simpson-Mazzoli bill, which would have instituted the use of ID cards to certify U.S. citizenship. Later as employment litigation director in MALDEF's Los Angeles office she promoted affirmative action and greater federal employment opportunities for Latinos. In 1985 she became the president of MALDEF. As that agency's highly visible president and general counsel she sought to increase cooperation between civil rights organizations. During her term as president she particularly highlighted such civil rights concerns as at-large elections, redistricting, voting rights, equal educational opportunities, discrimination in employment, and immigrant rights.

Under Hernández's leadership MALDEF sharply opposed employer sanctions provisions in the Immigration Reform and Control Act of 1986. Arguing that the sanctions would lead to more extensive discrimination against U.S. Latinos, she persuaded the 1990 Leadership Conference on Civil Rights to support their repeal. Because of her extensive community involvement she was appointed to the Rebuild Los Angeles commission by Mayor Tom Bradley after the 1992 rioting there.

See also MEXICAN AMERICAN LEGAL DEFENSE AND EDUCATIONAL FUND.

FURTHER READING: Groller, Ingrid. "Law in the Family." *Parents' Magazine*, (March 1985):96; Gross, Lisa L. "Antonia Hernández: MALDEF's Legal Eagle." *Hispanic* (December 1990):16–18. Hernández, Antonia. "Affirmative Action Services Close Brush with Bush." *Hispanic Business* (February 1992):10; Shaw, Katherine. "Antonia Hernández." *Vista* (October 1985):16; Telgen, Diane, and Jim Kamp, eds. *¡Latinas! Women of Achievement*. Detroit: Visible Ink Press, 1996.

HERNÁNDEZ, MARÍA LATIGO, 1896–1986. Throughout her 90 years María Hernández lived the life of activism that she advocated for all Mexican Americans. She participated in nearly all the important raza civil rights struggles in Texas during the twentieth century. While still a teenager she began organizing workers to fight for their rights. Well into her seventies she remained the active community leader and eloquent voice for civil rights.

Born in Mexico and crossing into Texas during Mexico's revolution of 1910, as a young woman Hernández became a collaborator of civil rights activist Alonso Perales in San Antonio. With him and her equally activist husband Pedro she helped organize several early civil rights groups, culminating in the League of United Latin American Citizens (LULAC) at the end of the 1920s. She stressed voter registration and voting and viewed political activism as a citizen's duty toward the community.

Always a strong advocate of women's rights, in 1932 Hernández became the first female radio announcer in San Antonio, promoting LULAC and its objectives. In the mid-1930s she was one of the founders of the Liga Pro-Defensa Escolar, which lucidly articulated Mexican American educational needs in Texas. She spoke out publicly for workers' rights in the 1938 San Antonio pecan shellers' strike despite widespread opposition from the city and church leaders.

An untiring fighter on the cutting edge of the rights struggle, Hernández continued to make speeches, lead marches, and organize protests in support of educational reform and civil rights for Chicanos during World War II and after. As part of her effort to promote cultural awareness among young Mexican Americans, she insisted on making her speeches only in Spanish. Despite her advanced years she took an active part in the Chicano Movement of the late 1960s and was an important figure in and a strong supporter of La Raza Unida Party in Texas during the following decade. She and her husband Pedro traveled throughout the state making speeches in support of its candidates in the 1972 election. She died of pneumonia in January 1986.

See also CHICANAS; LEADERSHIP; PERALES, ALONSO.

FURTHER READING: Cotera, Martha. *Profile of the Mexican American Woman.* Austin: National Educational Laboratory, 1976; Hammerback, John, Richard J. Jensen, and José Angel Gutiérrez. *A War of Words: Chicano Protest in the 1960s and 1970s.* Westport, Conn.: Greenwood Press, 1985; *Las Mujeres: Mexican American / Chicana Women.* Windsor, Calif.: National Women's History Project, 1991.

HERNÁNDEZ v. DRISCOLL CONSOLIDATED INDEPENDENT SCHOOL DISTRICT, 1957.

In 1955 the American G.I. Forum (AGIF) and the League of United Latin American Citizens filed suit in the federal district court accusing the Driscoll school district of ethnic discrimination. Attorney Gus García, representing the AGIF, argued that the placement of Mexican American children in separate classes in the first and second grades by the Driscoll Consolidated Independent School District was a violation of their Fourteenth Amendment rights. School officials of the southwest Texas town argued that the segregation was based on language deficiencies rather than ethnicity, although they admitted that no formal language tests had been given the students. They were unable to explain why one Mexican American child who spoke no Spanish, only English, was included in the segregated class.

The court ruled, in January 1957, that the district's "separate grouping" of Mexican American children was not based on the students' tested individual capacities and was therefore arbitrary and unreasonably discriminatory. It further ordered an end to the practice and issued an injunction against grouping based on ethnic ancestry.

Despite the court's ruling in favor of the Mexican American position, local school officials had little difficulty in finding subterfuges and delaying tactics to enable them to continue de facto segregation. Mexican Americans found it necessary to continue their long struggle for educational equality.

See also COURTS; EDUCATION.

FURTHER READING: San Miguel, Guadalupe, Jr. *"Let All of Them Take Heed":* *Mexican Americans and the Campaign for Educational Equality in Texas, 1910–1981.* Austin: University of Texas Press, 1987.

HERNÁNDEZ v. THE STATE OF TEXAS, 1956.

In a unanimous decision the U.S. Supreme Court under Chief Justice Earl Warren set aside the murder conviction of farmworker Pete Hernández of Texas, declaring that he had not received a fair trial because no Mexican Americans served on the jury. In this landmark civil rights case the court held that the exclusion of Mexican Americans from juries in Texas violated the equal protection clause of the Fourteenth Amendment to the U.S. Constitution. A momentous aspect of the court's decision was its recognition, for the first time, that Mexican Americans formed a distinguishable ethnic group within the "white" classification and suffered from discriminatory practices as a result. The case was argued before the Supreme Court for the American G.I. Forum and the League of United Latin American Citizens by five attorneys headed by Gus García and Carlos Cadena.

See also CIVIL RIGHTS ABUSE.

FURTHER READING: García, Mario T. *Mexican Americans: Leadership, Ideology, and Identity, 1930–1960*. New Haven, Conn.: Yale University Press, 1989; "Gus García." *La Luz* 4, no. 2 (May 1975):38; Pycior, Julie Leininger. *LBJ & Mexican Americans: The Paradox of Power*. Austin: University of Texas Press, 1997.

HESBURGH, THEODORE M., 1917– . President of the University of Notre Dame for 35 years (1952–1987), Theodore Hesburgh was appointed to the U.S. Civil Rights Commission upon its creation in 1957 during Dwight D. Eisenhower's administration and served until 1972. Particularly as commission chairman from 1969 to 1972, he had a great impact on the civil rights movement because he viewed the commission's role as being that of a national conscience. In 1972 he publicly criticized President Richard M. Nixon for his lack of concern about civil rights and especially his failure to foster implementation of the 1954 Supreme Court decision on school desegregation. As a result he was forced by Nixon to resign from the commission.

See also CIVIL RIGHTS COMMISSION.

FURTHER READING: Ames, Charlotte A. *Theodore M. Hesburgh, a Bio-Bibliography*. Westport, Conn.: Greenwood Press, 1989; Hesburgh, Theodore M. *God, Country, Notre Dame*. New York: Doubleday, 1990; Lungren, John C. *Hesburgh of Notre Dame*. Kansas City, Mo.: Sheed & Ward, 1987.

HIGH SCHOOL WALKOUTS, 1968. See STUDENT WALKOUTS.

HISPANIC CAUCUS. See CONGRESSIONAL HISPANIC CAUCUS.

HOPWOOD v. STATE OF TEXAS, 1992–1996. In 1992 Anglos Cheryl Hopwood and others filed suit against the state of Texas alleging discrimination in the admissions policy of the University of Texas law school. Four years later, in March 1996, the Fifth U.S. Circuit Court of Appeals ruled that the law school's admission policy, which gave preferences to Mexican and African Americans, constituted reverse discrimination. Judge Jerry E. Smith, an appointee of President Ronald Reagan, said the policy violated the Fourteenth Amendment rights by denying the equal protection guarantee of the Constitution to the plaintiffs.

The *Hopwood* decision resulted in the dismantling of racially based recruitment policies, admission programs, scholarships, and financial aid packages and led to a significant decrease in minority enrollment at the university. It was appealed to the Fifth Circuit Court by the University of

Texas. In 1998 the Mexican American Legal Defense and Educational Fund and the National Association for the Advancement of Colored People joined in that appeal, asking to be named intervenors in the case.

See also AFFIRMATIVE ACTION; BAKKE SUIT.

FURTHER READING: Eastland Terry. "Perspective on Affirmative Action. . . ." *Los Angeles Times*, 22 March 1996, Metro 9B; Gwynne, S. C. "Undoing Diversity: A Bombshell Court Ruling Curtails Affirmative Action." *Time*, 1 April 1996, 54; "Two Groups Seek Court Status to Defend Minority Interests in Hopwood Case." *Dallas Morning News*, 9 June 1998, 13A.

HOUSING. Decent housing available to all without discrimination has long been a Mexican American civil rights goal. Prejudice against la raza in housing, although less severe than against blacks, is an obvious aspect of urban segregation. The housing available in the barrio, as well as in rural areas, has typically been both substandard and overcrowded.

Historically most towns of the Southwest had well-defined barrios to which Mexicanos were largely restricted by economic status and real estate covenants. Because of racial discrimination and low incomes, only dilapidated tenements and the least desirable housing have been available to Mexicanos in the large urban centers of Texas and California. In these cities housing segregation has increased rather than decreased for many Mexicanos. As late as the 1960s real estate boards were penalizing agents for ignoring restrictive housing covenants by selling to Chicanos. Housing segregation is also a considerable factor in school segregation.

Housing conditions in New Mexico, Colorado, and Arizona have generally been somewhat better for Mexican Americans. The differing levels of home ownership in the southwestern states may be partly related to percentages of recent immigrants in the Mexicano population of the various states. Housing available to Mexicanos has improved noticeably in the past half century, but not relative to the upgrading of housing among Anglos. Since World War II higher levels of family income have enabled Mexican Americans to obtain better rental housing and achieve increased home ownership. However, income is only one factor in home ownership levels, which remain lowest in California and Texas. Some banks have been accused of setting higher standards for housing loans to Chicanos.

Substandard barrio housing is often accompanied by poor quality in urban services: unpaved or deteriorating streets, lack of sidewalks, inadequate or nonexistent street lighting, ill-provided garbage collection and poor public transportation, and absence of parks and playgrounds. Disruption of communities by urban renewal or the building of new freeways cutting them off from the heart of the city has continued despite protests and sit-ins by Mexican Americans. The focused efforts of Henry Cisneros as secretary of Housing and Urban Development (1993–1996) to end racial discrimination in housing appears to have had only limited success.

See also CISNEROS, HENRY; CIVIL RIGHTS ABUSE; SEGREGA-TION.

FURTHER READING: Cubillos, Herminia L. "Fair Housing and Latinos." In *Land Grants, Housing, and Political Power*, edited by Antoinette Sedillo López. New York: Garland Publishing, 1995; Dolbeare, Cushing N. *The Hispanic Housing Crisis.* Washington, D.C.: National Council of La Raza, 1988; Guzmán, Ralph. "The Hands of Esau: Words Change, Practices Remain in Racial Covenants." *Frontier* 7, no. 8 (June 1956):7, 16; "Housing Conditions" and "Residential Segregation." In *The Mexican American People*, edited by Leo Grebler, Joan W. Moore, and Ralph Guzmán. New York: Free Press, 1970; Moore, Joan W., and Frank G. Mittelbach. *Residential Segregation in the Urban Southwest.* Los Angeles: University of California, 1966.

HUERTA, DOLORES, 1930–   . Dolores Fernández Huerta began her life-time of promoting Chicano civil rights during the 1950s by registering and organizing voters for the Community Service Organization (CSO) in Stock-ton, California. She later moved to the position of director of the Los Angeles CSO. Having been politicized by the tide of post–World War II Chicano activism, she became disillusioned with the CSO after a few years and early in the 1960s accepted César Chávez's invitation to help him fight for farmworkers' rights. She began her new career by recruiting members for the union he was creating and later in the decade took an important part in the famous Delano grape strike, developing into a multitalented labor leader and Chávez's most valuable associate.

Huerta used her skills as a dynamic speaker and aggressive negotiator to improve the civil rights of Mexicano agricultural workers. Always a prag-matic organizer, she persuaded her listeners to become active participants in the fight for their rights. She also developed into a highly adept contract negotiator, effective lobbyist, and cagey union strategist. She was a com-bative second-in-command to Chávez in shaping the United Farm Workers (UFW). In the late 1970s she headed the UFW's political arm, the Citizen-ship Participation Day Department. In 1988 she participated in a peaceful San Francisco demonstration against federal policies and was seriously in-jured as a result of excessive use of force by police. She was later awarded damages for the assault.

In the 1990s Huerta gradually and quietly resumed her work in the UFW, concerning herself primarily with issues like immigration reform, pesticide abuse, and general farm labor health conditions. Tightly focused in her ideas of social justice and equality, she has become an important symbol in the Mexican American workers' struggle for their rights, especially since César Chávez's death in 1993. The UFW remains the arena of her lifelong campaign for Mexican American civil rights.

See also CHICANAS; LEADERSHIP; UNITED FARM WORKERS.

FURTHER READING: Bonilla-Santiago, Gloria. *Breaking Ground and Barriers: Hispanic Women Developing Effective Leadership*. San Diego: Marín Publications, 1992; Coburn, Judith. "Dolores Huerta: La Pasionaria of the Farmworkers." *Ms* (November 1976):11–16; Garcia, Richard A. "Dolores Huerta: Woman, Organizer, and Symbol." *California History* 72, no. 1 (Spring 1993):56–71; Jensen, Joan M., ed. *With These Hands: Women Working the Land*. New York: McGraw-Hill 1981; Rose, Margaret. "Traditional and Nontraditional Patterns of Female Activism in the United Farm Workers of America, 1962 to 1980." *Frontiers* 11, no. 1 (1990): 26–32; Telgen, Diane, and Jim Kamp, eds. *¡Latinas! Women of Achievement*. Detroit: Visible Ink Press, 1996.

HUMAN RIGHTS. Natural or human rights are those that are conceived as belonging inherently to all persons as human beings. When buttressed by legislation, these "inalienable" rights, many of which are immunities or restraints imposed on government after long struggles, are sometimes distinguished from civil rights by the name civil liberties. Noncitizens, of course, have human rights but not all civil rights.

The term *social rights*, also used, should perhaps be limited to those rights in social intercourse that are not guaranteed by legal statute or constitutional provision and for the violation of which there is no recourse in law. Both human rights and social rights may be converted into civil rights through the passage of legislation.

See also SOCIAL RIGHTS.

I

IDAR, CLEMENTE NICASIO, 1893–1934. Son of pioneering civil rights journalist Nicasio Idar, Clemente Idar grew up in a home where concerns of Mexicanos were the frequent topics of intense discussion. Following closely in his father's footsteps, he became a civil rights activist as well as a labor union organizer for the AFL. In his labor union activities he demonstrated his civil rights concerns by consistently arguing for an end to ethnic discrimination and racism within the union. In the early 1920s he played a leading role in the founding of the Order of Sons of America. Although less directly involved in the League of United Latin American Citizens (1929), shortly after its founding he was named honorary president of a San Antonio chapter. He regularly promoted the inclusion of Chicanas in the new civil rights organizations.

See also IDAR, NICASIO; LEAGUE OF UNITED LATIN AMERICAN CITIZENS.

FURTHER READING: Tyler, Ron, ed. *The New Handbook of Texas.* Vol. 3. Austin: Texas State Historical Association, 1996; Zamora, Emilio. *The World of the Mexican Worker in Texas.* College Station: Texas A&M University Press, 1993.

IDAR, EDUARDO, 1887–1947. Like his father Nicasio, Eduardo Idar was both a journalist and a civil rights activist. Strongly committed to the development of greater unity among Mexican Americans in order to further their fight for justice, he participated in the family advocacy of the Primer Congreso Mexicanista in 1911. He was active in the founding of the League of United Latin American Citizens in 1929, taking an important part in writing its constitution and other organizational documents. He later became president of the Laredo council. Like the rest of his family he was a strong advocate of women's rights.

See also PRIMER CONGRESO MEXICANISTA, EL.

FURTHER READING: Limón, José E. "El Primer Congreso Mexicanista de 1911: A Precursor to Contemporary Chicanismo." *Aztlán* 5, nos. 1 & 2 (Spring and Fall 1974):85–117; Tyler, Ron, ed. *The New Handbook of Texas*. Vol. 3. Austin: Texas State Historical Association, 1996.

IDAR, ED, JR., 1920–   . Ed Idar was one of thousands of World War II veterans who were able to achieve a university education through the G.I. Bill. Even before earning his law degree from the University of Texas at Austin in 1956, he had long been active in the American G.I. Forum. Five years earlier he had succeeded Dr. Héctor Pérez García as state chair, and from 1958 to 1966 he held the important position of executive secretary. As state chair and executive secretary he organized the raising of funds to prosecute several Texas school segregation cases and to take the landmark civil rights case of Pete Hernández to the Supreme Court and ultimate victory.

At the beginning of the 1960s Idar was deeply involved in the formation of the Political Association of Spanish-Speaking Organizations, but resigned as executive secretary in 1962. Early in the next decade he served as associate counsel for the Mexican American Legal Defense and Educational Fund (MALDEF). As a MALDEF attorney in the case *White v. Regester*, he successfully argued for single-member legislative districts in the 1972 redistricting by the Texas House of Representatives and in the following year successfully argued the case before the U.S. Supreme Court on appeal.

Among Ed Idar's lifelong goals of assuring Mexican Americans equal rights and opportunities he includes improving educational opportunities, broadening economic opportunity, and increasing political opportunity— all in order to enable them to become arbiters of their own destinies. To these ends he has supported poll tax drives, school segregation suits, better conditions for migrant workers, and other efforts to improve the lives of Mexican Americans.

See also AMERICAN G.I. FORUM; MEXICAN AMERICAN LEGAL DEFENSE AND EDUCATIONAL FUND.

FURTHER READING: Chacón, José A. *Hispanic Notables in the United States of North America*. Albuquerque, N.M.: Saguaro Publishing Co., 1978; Pycior, Julie Leininger. *LBJ & Mexican Americans: The Paradox of Power*. Austin: University of Texas Press, 1997; Salazar, Veronica. *Dedication Rewarded: Prominent Mexican Americans*. San Antonio: Mexican American Cultural Center, 1976.

IDAR, JOVITA, 1885–1946. For most of her life Tejana journalist Jovita Idar followed in the activist footsteps of her father, Nicasio Idar. Through impassioned articles she wrote for her father's paper, *El Progreso*, she became deeply involved in fighting the denial of civil rights and educational opportunities to Mexicanos as well as in promoting feminist causes.

In 1911 Jovita Idar participated in the Primer Congreso Mexicanista and led in the founding of La Liga Femenil Mexicanista—perhaps her most important single contribution to the early rights movement. During Mexico's 1910 revolution she helped found La Cruz Blanca to nurse the wounded and care for the homeless along the border. On one occasion in 1914 she defied the Texas Rangers who came to close down *El Progreso*. She remained active in the many concerns of the border Tejano communities until her death.

See also CHICANAS; ORGANIZATIONS; PRIMER CONGRESO MEXICANISTA, EL.

FURTHER READING: Berson, Robin Kadison. *Marching to a Different Drummer: Unrecognized Heroes of American History*. Westport, Conn.: Greenwood Press, 1994; Tyler, Ron, ed. *The New Handbook of Texas*. Vol. 3. Austin: Texas State Historical Association, 1996.

IDAR, NICASIO, 1855–1914. An early civil rights leader primarily through his editorial and publishing activities, Nicasio Idar was also a Laredo city marshal and justice of the peace as well as a community activist. At the beginning of the twentieth century, in a climate of escalating oppression of Mexicanos in Texas, he undertook a campaign of sharply criticizing this trend. He advocated education, organization, and solidarity as the solution to many problems of Mexicanos in Texas and converted his weekly paper, *La Crónica*, into a clarion voice for rights and justice.

In 1910 Idar began a series of articles in his weekly, condemning specific instances of mistreatment and discrimination as well as the widespread racial hatred of and contempt for Mexicanos. His zeal in fighting for Mexicano civil rights and his active leadership in their defense led him to call for a convention of Tejano leaders. His persistence resulted in the assembling of El Primer Congreso Mexicanista at Laredo on September 14, 1911, and the organizing of La Gran Liga de Beneficencia y Protección. Several of his children followed in his activist footsteps.

See also LEADERSHIP; PRIMER CONGRESO MEXICANISTA, EL.

FURTHER READING: Limón, José E. "El Primer Congreso Mexicanista de 1911: A Precursor to Contemporary Chicanismo." *Aztlán* 5, nos. 1 & 2 (Spring and Fall 1974):85–117; Tyler, Ron, ed. *The New Handbook of Texas*. Vol. 3. Austin: Texas State Historical Association, 1996.

IMMIGRATION REFORM AND CONTROL ACT, 1986. The Immigration Reform and Control Act of 1986 came out of years-long reform efforts. It had three principal goals: to reduce undocumented immigration by greater control of the border, to reduce jobs available to undocumenteds by imposing sanctions on their employers, and to provide an amnesty program. It also included efforts at curtailing employer abuses of workers' rights. Mexican Americans were divided in their reaction to the law.

Clearly the law was most successful in its effort to reduce the size of the undocumented alien population through its amnesty program. By the end of the decade nearly 3 million aliens had applied for amnesty; about two thirds were Mexicans. There is less evidence that the law seriously reduced the number of employers who are willing, even anxious, to hire undocumented workers. Lastly, the expanded Border Patrol and increased border controls have not appreciably deterred those who still envision the United States as El Norte, the land of opportunity.

FURTHER READING: Bean, Frank D., Barry Edmondston, and Jeffry S. Passel, eds. *Undocumented Migration to the United States: IRCA and the Experience of the 1980s*. Washington, D.C.: Urban Institute Press, 1990; Meier, Matt S., and Feliciano Rivera. *Mexican Americans / American Mexicans: From Conquistadors to Chicanos*. New York: Hill & Wang, 1993.

IN RE RICARDO RODRÍGUEZ, 1897. Ricardo Rodríguez, a 10-year resident of San Antonio, Texas, filed a request in the federal court for final approval of his application for citizenship in order that he might vote. His application moved into the judicial system the issue of citizenship for Mexican immigrants, under heavy attack from Anglo politicians toward the end of the nineteenth century. A determined and highly vocal Anglo opposition argued that Mexicans were not eligible because they were neither black nor white. The case aroused strong and widespread interest among Mexicanos in Texas.

Early in May 1897 federal district judge Thomas Maxey, citing the Fourteenth Amendment and the Treaty of Guadalupe Hidalgo, held that Rodríguez had the right to obtain citizenship and to vote. He further pointed out that neither race nor skin color was a legal determinant in citizenship. His benchmark ruling discouraged and hindered, but did not end, Texas attempts to use the courts to deny Mexican Americans their civil rights.

See also CIVIL RIGHTS ABUSE; COURTS; TEXAS.

FURTHER READING: De León, Arnoldo. *In Re Ricardo Rodríguez: An Attempt at Chicano Disenfranchisement in San Antonio, 1896–1897*. San Antonio: Caravel Press, 1979; Padilla, Fernando. "Early Chicano Legal Recognition: 1846–1897." *Journal of Popular Culture* 13, no. 3 (Spring 1979):564–574.

INCORPORATED MEXICAN AMERICAN GOVERNMENT EMPLOYEES (IMAGE). National IMAGE, Inc., as it is also called, is an organization formally created in 1972 by a group of Mexican American federal government employees who banded together to counter discrimination against the Spanish-speaking, particularly in government hiring. IMAGE soon expanded its scope to welcome in its fold all Latino employees at all levels of government. It sought, and seeks, equality and expanded opportunity for U.S. Latinos in hiring at federal, state, and local levels as well as career advancement for those already employed. It is also concerned with achieving equal treatment for Latinos in all aspects of public service, and local chapters sponsor workshops on affirmative action, voting rights, voter registration, and citizenship.

National IMAGE goes beyond merely fighting existing discrimination in hiring by actively recruiting and training Latinos for federal jobs. It puts on an annual women's training conference, and local chapters regularly conduct job fairs. Its Washington, D.C., office maintains a Latino talent bank, and its more than 120 chapters in 40 states publicize information about available positions and encourage qualified candidates to apply for them.

To avoid confusion with Involvement of Mexican Americans in Gainful Endeavors (IMAGE), the Texas-based youth-oriented group, it is often referred to as National IMAGE.

See also ORGANIZATIONS.

FURTHER READING: "Civil Rights: National Image Inc.: The Concern for Equality." *La Luz* (February–March 1980):12; Córdova, José. "IMAGE Is No Mirage; It's Here to Stay." *La Luz* (September 1972):36–37; Gonzales, Sylvia A. *Hispanic American Voluntary Organizations*. Westport, Conn.: Greenwood Press, 1985; Treviso, Rubén. "National IMAGE." *Caminos* (September 1982):37–38.

INDUSTRIAL AREAS FOUNDATION. See ALINSKY, SAUL.

INVOLVEMENT OF MEXICAN AMERICANS IN GAINFUL ENDEAVORS (IMAGE). Founded by Tejano Antonio Calderón, IMAGE has as its goal the economic, political, educational, and social advancement of Mexican Americans. The San Antonio–based society concerns itself primarily with Chicano youths. Not to be confused with Incorporated Mexican American Government Employees (IMAGE), sometimes referred to as National IMAGE, Inc. to distinguish the two organizations.

FURTHER READING: Chacón, José. *Hispanic Notables in the United States of North America*. Albuquerque: Saguaro Publishing, 1978.

J

JOHNSON, LYNDON BAINES, 1908–1973. As president from 1963 to 1969, Lyndon Johnson of Texas built on the groundwork of John F. Kennedy in the area of civil rights. Partly because of Kennedy's assassination he was able to use his persuasive skills to prod Congress into enacting the comprehensive 1964 Civil Rights Act and the equally important 1965 Voting Rights Act, both benchmarks for Chicanos in the struggle for their rights as Americans. His anti-poverty programs for social and economic betterment were important in expanding Mexican American political awareness and involvement, which had been sparked originally by the Kennedy election campaign in 1960. The programs provided Mexican Americans, especially those in lower-income brackets, with valuable hands-on experience for participation in civic affairs and politics.

Johnson never forgot his early experience teaching Mexican American children in Cotulla, Texas, and "his" Mexicans in the G.I. Forum and the League of United Latin American Citizens reciprocated with their firm political support. However, his relationship with la raza was often contentious as well as strong. Early in his national career he responded favorably to grower interests in deference to his Anglo Texan supporters and refused to support the concept of a federal fair employment practices commission. Later his failure to appreciate the depths of frustration felt by leaders of the Mexican American generation and the desire for a voice in their own governance sometimes created serious tensions. In 1966 all 50 Chicano representatives at an Equal Employment Opportunity conference in Albuquerque walked out when the demands they presented to the president were simply ignored. The following year in El Paso Johnson's White House conference on Mexican American problems was boycotted by most community leaders who then met in a rump session.

Strong raza support for Johnson's domestic programs, referred to as the

Great Society, was offset by disapproval of his involving the country more deeply in the Vietnam struggle, in which Chicano casualties were disproportionately high. In part because of mounting opposition to his Vietnam policy, opposition in which raza youths took a prominent part, at the end of his presidential term in 1969 he retired to his Texas ranch on the Pedernales River.

See also AFFIRMATIVE ACTION; CIVIL RIGHTS ACT OF 1964; VOTING RIGHTS ACT, 1965.

FURTHER READING: Caro, Robert A. *The Years of Lyndon Johnson.* New York: Knopf, 1990; Dallek, Robert. *Lone Star Rising: Lyndon Johnson and His Times.* New York: Oxford University Press, 1991; Goodwin, Doris Kearns. *Lyndon Johnson and the American Dream.* New York: New American Library, 1977; Pycior, Julie Leininger. *LBJ & Mexican Americans: The Paradox of Power.* Austin: University of Texas Press, 1997; White, Theodore S. *The Professional: Lyndon B. Johnson.* Boston: Houghton Mifflin, 1964.

K

KENNEDY, JOHN FITZGERALD, 1917–1963. John Kennedy's most important contribution to the Mexican American civil rights movement was possibly his running for the presidency in 1960. His candidacy mobilized many Mexican Americans who, up to that time, had not taken part in elections or in political organizational development. The electoral campaign marked the definite entrance of middle-class raza leaders into national politics.

The Viva Kennedy clubs, organized in every Mexican American community, swept across the Southwest and played a key role in his victory and in postelection political organizing among Chicanos. The Viva Kennedy clubs also acted as a catalyst to bring together regional Chicano groups as a national political force. In Texas Kennedy's win clearly resulted from the clubs' get-out-the-vote campaigns and the resultant increase in electoral participation by la raza. The Kennedy administration reciprocated this support by appointing Mexican Americans to federal positions but antagonized many raza organizational leaders by failing to make expected high-level appointments.

Kennedy's domestic program, called the New Frontier, included the extension of civil rights. However, many of his reforms, including proposed civil rights legislation, were stalled in Congress up to the time of his assassination in 1963.

FURTHER READING: Burns, James MacGregor. *John Kennedy: A Political Profile.* New York: Avon Books, 1960; Henggeler, Paul R. *The Kennedy Persuasion* Chicago: I. R. Dee, 1995; Schlesinger, Arthur M., Jr. *A Thousand Days.* Boston: Houghton Mifflin, 1965; Sidey, Hugh. *John F. Kennedy, President.* New York: Atheneum, 1963; Sorensen, Theodore C. *The Kennedy Legacy.* New York: Macmillan, 1969.

KIBBE, PAULINE R., 1909– . Born in Pueblo, Colorado, Pauline Rochester Kibbe settled in San Antonio, Texas, in 1940 after travel in Mexico. There she became involved in the Business and Professional Women's Club and in 1942 chaired its Central Planning Committee for Inter-American Understanding. When the Texas Good Neighbor Commission was created in the following year, she was named its first executive secretary. In addition to traveling the state giving talks on inter-American relations, in 1946 she wrote *Latin-Americans in Texas*, which described problems of segregation and exploitation of Mexicanos in Texas and called for a constitutional amendment to forbid discrimination, segregation, and other civil rights abuses. Kibbe's condemnation of the exploitation of Mexicano workers, especially undocumenteds, aroused Texas growers' ire, and in 1947 she was fired by the governor. Subsequently she worked for the Congress of Industrial Organizations and continued to write about Mexico and inter-American relations.

See also TEXAS GOOD NEIGHBOR COMMISSION.

FURTHER READING: Kibbe, Pauline R. *Latin-Americans in Texas*. Albuquerque: University of New Mexico Press, 1946; Kingrea, Nellie Ward. *History of the First Ten Years of the Texas Good Neighbor Commission*. Fort Worth: Texas Christian University Press, 1954.

KIT CARSON NATIONAL FOREST. In October 1966 the Kit Carson National Forest, in northwestern New Mexico, leaped into the media limelight when more than 300 members of Reies López Tijerina's Alianza Federal de Mercedes (Federal Alliance of [Land] Grants), later de Pueblos Libres (of Free Towns), took over the Echo Amphitheater campground. The aliancistas claimed a right to the land as heirs to the pueblo grant of San Joaquín del Rio Chama. Before their eviction, they "arrested" and "tried" two forest rangers for trespassing.

The temporary takeover of Echo Amphitheater resulted in the filing of federal charges against Tijerina. However, the Kit Carson confrontation also attracted young Chicano militants to the Alianza, which had previously appealed almost solely to older Nuevomexicano land grant heirs. In 1969 new confrontations with Forest Service officers at Kit Carson led to Tijerina's arrest, conviction, and three-year prison sentence.

See also ALIANZA FEDERAL DE PUEBLOS LIBRES; TIJERINA, REIES LÓPEZ.

FURTHER READING: Blawis, Patricia Bell. *Tijerina and the Land Grants*. New York: International Publishers, 1971; Meier, Matt S. " 'King Tiger': Reies López Tijerina." *Journal of the West*, 27, no. 2 (April 1988):60–68; Tijerina, Reies López. *Mi lucha por la tierra*. Mexico: Fondo de Cultura Económica, 1978; Valdez, Armando. "Insurrection in New Mexico—Land of Enchantment." *El Grito* 1, no. 1 (Fall 1967):15–24.

KNOWLTON, CLARK SHUMWAY, 1919–   . The prominent sociologist Clark Knowlton was an early specialist in arid and semi-arid land studies, the author of numerous articles and reports in professional journals and chapters in books on the topic, the recipient of grants and awards to study the social issues involved, and a member of various boards and commissions.

With a B.A. and an M.A. in sociology from Brigham Young University, Knowlton earned his doctorate in the same discipline at Vanderbilt University in 1955. After teaching at Georgia Southern College and completing a four-year stint at New Mexico Highlands University, he taught at Texas Western College (now University of Texas at El Paso, UTEP) from 1963 to 1967. His support of Reies López Tijerina created difficulties for him at UTEP, and in 1968 he left to become professor of sociology and later department chair at the University of Utah.

Deeply concerned with racial and ethnic group problems, particularly in rural areas, during the 1960s and 1970s Knowlton took an active part in numerous conferences and workshops that arose out of the Chicano movimiento. In these meetings he was an early Anglo supporter and advocate of Mexican American civil rights. As an expert on rural sociology and arid lands, he was one of the first, and few, Anglos to speak out in support of Reies López Tijerina and his Alianza.

See also ALIANZA FEDERAL DE PUEBLOS LIBRES; TIJERINA, REIES LÓPEZ.

FURTHER READING: *American Men and Women of Science: Social and Behavioral Sciences.* 13th ed. Edited by the Jacques Cattell Press. New York: R. R. Bowker, 1978; *Who's Who in the West, 1992–1993.* 23rd edition. Wilmette, Ill.: Marquis Who's Who, 1992.

L

LA FOLLETTE COMMITTEE, 1936–1940. The La Follette Civil Liberties Committee was a U.S. Senate subcommittee created to investigate the denial of American workers' civil right to organize. After studying the problem in manufacturing and mining, in 1939–1940 the committee held hearings in California agriculture, in part prodded by the 1939 publication of John Steinbeck's *Grapes of Wrath*. The committee's report, issued in 1942, found that violence and infringement of civil liberties by growers and their agents were all too common. The committee made a number of recommendations for legislation to remedy the situation, but none of them were implemented, largely because of the U.S. involvement in World War II.

See also CIVIL RIGHTS ABUSE.

FURTHER READING: Auerbach, Jerold S. "The La Follette Committee: Labor and Civil Liberties in the New Deal." *Journal of American History* 51, no. 3 (1964): 435–459; Meier, Matt S., and Feliciano Rivera. *Dictionary of Mexican American History*. Westport, Conn.: Greenwood Press, 1981.

LA RAZA UNIDA PARTY (LRUP). See RAZA UNIDA PARTY, LA.

LAND ACT OF 1851. Enacted ostensibly to clarify Californios' rights to lands granted them by Spain or Mexico by weeding out invalid titles, the 1851 Land Act created a three-man commission. The commissioners met from January 1852 to March 1856. They operated with the basic attitude that Californio claims were fraudulent until proved otherwise and that its function was to declare a maximum amount of land available to (Anglo) settlers. The decisions of the commissioners led to decades of costly litigation for Californios.

Of the 813 claims heard by the commission, 273 were declared invalid;

132 of the invalidated claims were appealed to the courts, which declared 98 of them to be valid. Of the 521 claims originally confirmed by the commission, 417 were appealed by the government, and only 5 were reversed by the courts. This gross attack on the rights guaranteed to Mexican Americans by the Treaty of Guadalupe Hidalgo was an important factor in their subsequent political disenfranchisement, loss of economic position, and further denial of civil liberties. Many historians view the Californios' loss of their land grants as the first grave violation of their civil rights.

See also LAND GRANTS.

FURTHER READING: Baker, Charles C. "Mexican Land Grants in California." *Annual Publications of the Historical Society of Southern California*. Los Angeles: California Historical Society, 1914; Ebright, Malcolm, ed. *Spanish and Mexican Land Grants and the Law*. Sunflower University Press, 1989; Gates, Paul. "The California Land Act of 1851." *California Historical Society Quarterly* 50 (December 1971):395–430; Pitt, Leonard. *The Decline of the Californios*. Berkeley: University of California Press, 1966.

LAND GRANTS. The history of Spanish-Mexican land grants in the Southwest is a story of vague boundaries, lack of records, cultural and historical differences, greed, thievery, and denial of civil rights guaranteed by treaty. From the first settlement of Mexico's northern frontier until 1846, Spain and Mexico awarded land grants in order to attract settlers to this vast, thinly populated region. Over the years three basic types of grants were made: individual, empresario, and communal or pueblo.

Individual grants existed throughout the northern frontier in California, Nuevo México, and Tejas. Pueblo grants were more common in present-day New Mexico and Colorado, whereas empresario grants were most common in Texas. The terms under which grants were made varied. Some gave the grantee complete ownership upon completion of the established requirements; some were use-only grants, principally for grazing. Most grants had their boundaries defined by natural features: rivers, hills, and trees; but some were "floating" grants (like Las Mariposas, bought by John Charles Frémont in 1847), in which a total amount of land was specified but no location or boundaries were set. Only rarely was the same area given to two grantees, but boundaries sometimes overlapped.

During the Spanish and Mexican periods California was the location of slightly over 800 grants. The New Mexico territory had a total of almost 200 grants, and Texas had about 300. The Texas Republic (1836–1845) officially declared its recognition of valid Spanish and Mexican grants; by the terms of the 1845 treaty of annexation to the United States, the state of Texas retained control over its public lands. Texas, therefore, rather than the federal government, determined the question of land grant validity in that state. The Texas legislature set up a commission that confirmed about

250 land titles in the nineteenth century. In 1923 the remaining unresolved claims became part of an agreement between the United States and Mexico, and a treaty to discharge claims of the two countries was signed in 1941, by which Mexico was to settle with the hundreds of heir-claimants. From then until the present the Mexican government has never denied its obligation to pay legitimate claims but has not actually done so.

In California soon after the Treaty of Guadalupe Hidalgo squatter pressure, which arose in large part as a result of the gold rush, led to the passage of the Land Act of 1851 by the U.S. Congress. As administered, the legislation put the onus on grantees to prove legal ownership, rather than requiring the government to prove that specific grants were invalid. Between 1852 and 1856 the land commissioners processed 813 claims, rejecting 273; 132 of the 273 were appealed, and ultimately 98 (74%) were reversed. The U.S. government appealed 417 of the original 521 confirmations by the commission and won only 5 reversals (.014%). However, even the grantees who won confirmation found themselves losing as much as a third of their grants to pay lawyers' fees, court costs, taxes, and so on. By 1870 Californio families held only about 25 percent of land parcels valued at $10,000 or more.

In New Mexico the story was somewhat different. Spared the pressures and problems that the gold rush brought to California, Nuevomexicano landowners fared somewhat better in the short run. In 1854 the U.S. Congress created the position of surveyor general for the New Mexico Territory (New Mexico, Colorado, and Arizona). Each grant having first been approved by the surveyor general (many of whom were political hacks) then had to be confirmed by Congress. Of the 205 claims filed between 1854 and 1886, 141 had been approved but only 46 confirmed by Congress.

In New Mexico the land problem was complicated by the large number of pueblo grants, vague boundary lines (in seventeenth- and eighteenth-century grants especially), and the aggressive and often successful efforts of claimants to enlarge their boundaries. For example, the famous Maxwell grant (originally Beaubien-Miranda grant) was expanded from 97,000 acres to 1,714,764. Claims were made for more land than existed in the Territory, and lawyers like Thomas Catron, who had connections with the infamous Santa Fe Ring, acquired huge tracts of land as their fees for successfully defending claims.

Because of the slowness of the confirmation process and problems arising as railroads, ranchers, and settlers began moving into the Territory, in 1891 Congress created the Court of Private Land Claims for New Mexico, Colorado, and Arizona. Nevertheless, extensive land grant litigation continued. In 1904 the court completed its work. It heard 301 petitions for a total of more than 35 million acres, rejected nearly three fourths of them, and confirmed title to about 2 million acres. Altogether about 5 million acres of private grants and 2 million acres of pueblo grants were confirmed in New Mexico. Ultimately Anglos came to control about 80 percent of the grant lands.

Faced with loss of their lands and the downward mobility that the loss engendered, Mexican Americans fought back. In New Mexico especially, they never completely accepted the loss of their lands. The Gorras Blancas at the end of the 1880s formed one crest in their resistance. During the 1960s their grievances were reawakened by Reies López Tijerina and his Alianza Federal de Mercedes ([land] grants). A deeply embedded resentment at the U.S. government's failure to abide by the spirit of Article IX of the Treaty of Guadalupe Hidalgo developed early and continues even today. The land grant problem is a civil rights issue in the Southwest that refuses to go away.

See also COURT OF PRIVATE LAND CLAIMS; GORRAS BLANCAS; LAND ACT OF 1851.

FURTHER READING: Baker, Charles C. "Mexican Land Grants in California." *Annual Publications of the Historical Society of Southern California.* Los Angeles: California Historical Society, 1914; Bannon, John Francis. *Spanish Borderlands Frontier, 1573–1821.* Albuquerque: University of New Mexico Press, 1974; Briggs, Charles L., and John R. Van Ness, eds. *Land, Water, and Culture: New Perspectives on Hispanic Land Grants.* Albuquerque: University of New Mexico Press, 1987; de la Garza, Rodolfo O., and Karl M. Schmitt. *Texas Land Grants and Chicano-Mexican Relations.* Austin: University of Texas, Institute of Latin American Studies, 1986; Ebright, Malcolm. *Land Grants and Law Suits in Northern New Mexico.* Albuquerque: University of New Mexico Press, 1994; Knowlton, Clark S. "Causes of Land Loss among Spanish Americans of Northern New Mexico." In *The Chicano*, edited by Gilberto López y Rivas. New York: Monthly Review Press, 1973; Knowlton, Clark S., ed. "Spanish and Mexican Land Grants in the Southwest: A Symposium." *The Social Science Journal* 13, no. 3 (October 1976); Weber, David. *The Mexican Frontier, 1821–1846: The American Southwest under Mexico.* Albuquerque: University of New Mexico Press, 1982.

LARRAZOLO, OCTAVIANO A., 1859–1930. After completing his formal education at St. Michael's College in Santa Fe, in the late 1870s Octaviano Larrazolo began to take a serious interest in local Democratic politics. However, after three decades of political effort he became thoroughly convinced that his failure to win elections was the result of ethnic discrimination by Democrats. Feeling that the party was distinctly inhospitable toward Nuevomexicanos, he switched his allegiance to the Republicans in 1911.

As a Republican politico, Larrazolo fought so strongly for ethnic equality in politics that some opponents accused him of dragging the race issue into every election. Winning the governorship of the recently admitted state of New Mexico in 1918, he showed himself a dedicated chief executive, deeply concerned with the many problems of Nuevomexicanos and energetically supportive of efforts to reduce their poverty. He strongly favored bilingual education as a path to improving their economic position.

In 1928 Larrazolo went to the U.S. Senate, where he employed his magnificent oratory in a continuing campaign to obtain economic equality and political access for Nuevomexicanos. He died early in 1930, after a single congressional session.

See also NEW MEXICO; POLITICAL PARTICIPATION.

FURTHER READING: Chacón, José A. "Octaviano Larrazolo: New Mexico's Greatest Governor." *La Luz* 1, no. 7 (November 1972):37–39; Córdova, Alfred C., and Charles B. Judah. *Octaviano Larrazolo: A Political Portrait*. Albuquerque: University of New Mexico, Dept. of Government, 1952; Meier, Matt S. *Mexican American Biographies: A Historical Dictionary, 1836–1987*. Westport, Conn.: Greenwood Press, 1988; Walter, Paul A. "Octaviano Ambrosio Larrazolo." *New Mexico Historical Review* 7, no. 2 (April 1932):99–104.

LAU v. NICHOLS, 1970–1974. *Lau v. Nichols* was a class-action lawsuit filed in California against the San Francisco school district alleging discrimination against one Kinney Lau because the school failed to deal with his limited comprehension of English. Reversing the unfavorable decision of the lower court, in 1974 the U.S. Supreme Court unanimously ruled that Lau must be taught in his own language. It held that the district's failure to provide a suitable program to meet his linguistic needs was a violation of his civil rights, guaranteed by both the Civil Rights Act of 1964 and the Fourteenth Amendment to the Constitution.

Lau v. Nichols was a landmark case because for the first time the court clearly held that the right of non-English-speaking students to be taught in their own language was a civil right. Only in 1980 did the state's secretary of education publish formal regulations to implement the court's ruling.

The *Lau* decision led to expansion of bilingual and bicultural education programs but also created widespread controversy. Under President Ronald Reagan (1981–1989), employment of the *Lau* remedies was reduced and their enforcement was considerably weakened. In the 1990s neoconservatives continued their attacks on *Lau*.

See also BILINGUAL EDUCATION; CIVIL RIGHTS ACT OF 1964; EDUCATION.

FURTHER READING: Weinberg, Myer. *Minority Students: A Research Appraisal*. Washington, D.C.: U.S. Department of Health, Education and Welfare, 1977; Weyr, Thomas. *Hispanic U.S.A.: Breaking the Melting Pot*. New York: Harper & Row, 1988.

LEADERSHIP. Leadership in the Mexican American rights movement has had a long but uneven history, beginning with Juan Seguín in Texas in the

1830s and Mariano Vallejo in California in the 1850s. After the U.S.–Mexican War and the Treaty of Guadalupe Hidalgo Mexican American leadership became divided between elites and social bandits.

The rapid decline of landed and political elites in the Southwest and the unfamiliarity of most Mexican Americans with the U.S. political system greatly impaired their continued leadership. Except for Nuevomexicanos, whose leaders developed political networking in the new system in order to maintain their power, the new Americans were too weak politically and economically to sustain a determined struggle for their rights. Efforts of the middle and lower classes to ameliorate their condition were largely limited to banding together in mutualista groups that provided a minimum of economic and social security and some incidental leadership experience.

In the twentieth century increased educational attainments among Mexican Americans began to provide a new base for leadership. After World War I, the initial steps in creating organizations with goals of equal opportunities and civil rights were taken by first- and second-generation Mexican Americans with better formal educations and greater awareness of their rights as citizens. However, only after the upheavals of the Great Depression and World War II did leaders begin to organize more methodically for the protection of raza rights. In part this change emphasized a less individualistic aspect of the leader's role—as an intermediary between the community and Anglo American society.

To be effective in this role the leader had to both live up to Mexican American expectations with a vigorous defense of civil rights and at the same time maintain his credentials with the Anglo establishment. A transitional figure perhaps, the new leader usually appealed strongly to the ethnic loyalty of his followers by using symbols, some from Mexican history, like Cinco de Mayo, some from religion, like the Virgin of Guadalupe.

The degree of a Chicano leader's individual success was often limited by the imperative of dual acceptance. Given the stress on achieving civil rights, the leader was often caught by the contradiction between a radical rhetoric and more limited reformist goals. The conflict in this ambiguous position may clearly be seen by considering the activities of César Chávez, José Angel Gutiérrez, Corky Gonzales, and Reies López Tijerina during the 1960s and 1970s. Additionally, the success of these four charismatic leaders was limited by the fact that none was able to develop a national organization or following. Nationwide groups like the National Association of Latino Elected and Appointed Officials and the National Council of La Raza, in contrast, seemed to lack the requisite charismatic leadership.

Personalism and a reluctance to share the leadership role have historically been seen as retarding the development of Mexican American civil rights organizations. A notable weakness of early senior leaders was their failure to recognize and encourage young politicians who might be on their way to becoming a political force. Raza leaders, often highly individualistic and competitive, sometimes found cooperation difficult, even when the common good clearly dictated it and when they were able to agree on goals. Although there has been overwhelming agreement on the need to secure civil rights, there was often little consensus on the proper way to go about achieving them.

The bitter struggle in the early 1970s between Gonzales and Gutiérrez to control La Raza Unida Party provides an outstanding example of these divisive and ultimately destructive differences. They have also undoubtedly contributed to political cynicism and a mistrust of leadership. In addition, political exclusion from and isolation within government have clearly served to hinder the development of Chicano civil rights leaders, as has their widespread reluctance, until the 1950s, to identify more closely with the Democratic and Republican parties. Among further hindrances has been a variety of political stratagems. At large elections, gerrymandered districts, poll taxes and other devices that discouraged voting, and the exclusion of potential Chicano political leaders from higher-level party positions by both Republicans and Democrats have all served to retard the development of political leaders.

Nevertheless, in all these areas of blockage Mexican Americans have made considerable advances in the past three decades. Aided by ongoing voter registration drives and rapid Latino population growth, Chicano leaders no longer quietly accept second-class citizenship. In the twenty-first century they should be able to advance from the limited successes of the past to greatly expanded frontiers of civil rights for la raza. However, at the end of the 1990s, with Chávez dead and Gonzales, Gutiérrez, and Tijerina inactive on a national level, there exists a serious problem of an individual and organizational leadership vacuum at the top.

See also individual leaders.

FURTHER READING: García, Mario T. *Mexican Americans: Leadership, Ideology, and Identity, 1930–1960*. New Haven, Conn.: Yale University Press, 1989; "Ethnic Organization and Leadership." In *The Mexican American People*. New York: Free Press, 1970; Higham, John, ed. *Ethnic Leadership in America*. Baltimore: Johns Hopkins University Press, 1978; Larralde, Carlos. *Mexican Americans: Movements and Leaders*. Los Alamitos, Calif: Hwong Publishing Co., 1976; Martínez, John R. "Leadership and Politics." In *La Raza: Forgotten Americans*, edited by Julian Samora. Notre Dame, Ind.: University of Notre Dame Press, 1966; Ortiz, Isidro D. "Latino Organizational Leadership Strategies in the Era of Reaganomics." In *Latinos and Political Coalitions*, edited by Roberto E. Villarreal and Norma G. Hernández. Westport, Conn.: Greenwood Press, 1991; Perrigo, Lynn I. *Hispanos: Historic Leaders in New Mexico*. Santa Fe, N.M.: Sunstone Press, 1985; Samora, Julian. *Minority Leadership in a Bicultural Community*. San Francisco: R & E Research Associates, 1973; Sosa, Luis R. *An Analysis of Chicano Organizations and Their Leadership*. Ph. D. diss., University Press of California, 1981; University Microfilms, 1982; Skerry, Peter. *Mexican Americans: The Ambivalent Minority*. New York: Free Press, 1993; Vigil, Maurilio. *Hispanics in American*

Politics: The Search for Political Power. Lanham, Md.: University Press of America, 1987; Woods, Frances J. *Mexican Ethnic Leadership in San Antonio, Texas*. Washington, D.C.: Catholic University of America Press, 1949. Reprint, New York: Arno Press, 1976.

LEAGUE OF UNITED LATIN AMERICAN CITIZENS (LULAC). A major Mexican American civil rights organization, LULAC was founded in 1929 at a Corpus Christi meeting of three existing rights groups: League of Latin American Citizens, Knights of America, and Order of Sons of America. Because of the increasing generational shift away from Mexico as a source of identity, the new group's models were American rather than Mexican. English was its official language. Its overwhelmingly middle class and assimilationist membership strongly opposed and denounced segregation. Its social and economic goals, to be achieved through education and hard work, stressed the rights and duties of Mexican Americans as citizens as well as the benefits.

From its inception LULAC showed a sincere concern for less fortunate members of la raza, but it was slower than some groups in developing and implementing community action programs. During World War II LULAC president George I. Sánchez used his position in the Office of Coordinator of Inter-American Affairs to advance the organization's demand for full civil rights. In the postwar era the members demanded more direct and active involvement in civil rights issues, reviving its earlier drive and putting it on the cutting edge of citizens' rights. Continuing concerns about segregation and racism in the schools led it to participate in two lawsuits: the 1946 *Méndez* case in California and the 1948 *Delgado* case in Texas, both of which were successful.

Under the presidency of Mario Obledo LULAC became even more militant in pushing civil rights issues after 1968. However, with the development of the Chicano Movement it became less indispensable to the community and therefore less effective in the political process. Nevertheless, by the beginning of the 1980s the movimiento had declined and LULAC's area of influence outside of the Southwest had grown to include Idaho, Georgia, and the Carolinas. Beset in the early 1980s by a financial crisis, followed toward the end of the decade by a series of internal scandals and leadership squabbles, it seemed unable to act decisively on issues of concern to the community.

Although it still boasts a large membership, LULAC is seen by its critics as no longer the leader in the Chicano struggle for political, social, and civil rights. This loss of position may be attributable to a combination of success, failures, weaknesses, and the considerable changes within the Mexican American community since the 1940s, to which LULAC has had some difficulty adjusting. It continues to pursue social, political, and economic goals on various fronts.

See also OBLEDO, MARIO G.; ORGANIZATIONS; SÁNCHEZ, GEORGE I.

FURTHER READING: Cárdenas, Leo. "The Bonilla Years Come to an End." *Latino* 54, no. 4 (May–June 1983):8–9, 29; García, Mario T. *Mexican Americans: Leadership, Ideology, and Identity, 1930–1960.* New Haven, Conn.: Yale University Press, 1989; Garza, Edward D. *LULAC: League of United Latin American Citizens.* San Francisco: R & E Research Associates, 1972; "History of LULAC." *La Luz* 6, no. 5 (May 1977) 15–19; Márquez, Benjamín. *LULAC: The Evolution of a Mexican American Political Organization.* Austin: University of Texas Press, 1993; Parra, Ricardo, Victor Ríos, and Armando Gutiérrez. "Chicano Organizations in the Midwest: Past, Present and Possibilities." *Aztlán,* 7, no. 2 (Summer 1976):235–253; www.lulac.org.

LEMON GROVE AFFAIR, 1931. In the tiny community of Lemon Grove near San Diego, California, a group of Mexican immigrant parents refused to accept the segregated accommodations the school board provided for their children, who had previously attended a nonsegregated school. After organizing a committee and instituting a boycott, they hired Anglo lawyers and filed suit against the school district: *Alvarez v. Lemon Grove.*

Despite the school administrators' argument that the special school was established to help the raza students learn English, the court ruled in favor of the parents. The judge pointed out that establishing a separate school for *all* Mexicano children without regard for their individual proficiency in English violated California statute law. Coming after a number of earlier, partial victories in desegregation efforts, this case became a benchmark as the first wholly successful desegregation in the ongoing struggle for the civil rights of Mexicano schoolchildren.

See also EDUCATION; SEGREGATION.

FURTHER READING: Donato, Rubén. *The Other Struggle for Equal Schools: Mexican Americans during the Civil Rights Era.* Albany: State University of New York Press, 1997; Reynolds, Annie. *The Education of Spanish-Speaking Children in Five Southwestern States.* Bulletin No. 11, Department of the Interior. Washington, D.C., 1933. Reprinted in *Education and the Mexican-American,* edited by Carlos Cortés. New York: Arno Press, 1974; San Miguel, Guadalupe, Jr. *"Let All of Them Take Heed": Mexican Americans and the Campaign for Educational Equality in Texas, 1910–1981.* Austin: University of Texas Press, 1987.

LIGA PROTECTORA MEXICANA. The league was an ephemeral organization founded in Kansas City shortly after World War I to confront the likelihood of repatriation of Mexican workers who had been recruited earlier for the U.S. war effort. A grassroots organization, during its short existence the league concerned itself not only with protecting the rights of immigrants but also with finding work for the unemployed and supplying the needy with food and clothing. The short postwar depression that fueled the threat of expulsion from the United States ended in 1921, and renewed demands for Mexican labor ended the league's raison d'être. It quickly disappeared.

See also REPATRIATION.

FURTHER READING: García, F. Chris. *La Causa Politica: A Chicano Politics Reader*. Notre Dame, Ind.: University of Notre Dame Press, 1974.

LONGORIA, FÉLIX, 1919–1945. Félix Longoria was a Mexican American soldier killed on the Philippine island of Luzon during World War II and buried there. When his widow tried to arrange for his reburial at home in 1948, the manager of the sole funeral home in the small Texas town of Three Rivers denied the use of its chapel because Longoria was Mexicano. The refusal of the mortuary to accept Longoria led to an acrimonious and emotional squabble and aroused nationwide attention and indignation over the denial of full equality to the dead veteran. Hearings about the case conducted by the state legislature resulted in a 4 to 1 vote asserting that no discrimination had occurred.

At the request of Longoria's sister-in-law, Sara Moreno, who was president of the American G.I. Forum's women's division, Dr. Héctor García intervened locally in the affair, but without success. Ultimately he asked freshman U.S. senator Lyndon Baines Johnson to use his influence. As a result of Johnson's intervention Longoria was buried in Arlington National Cemetery. The incident helped formalize the organization of the American G.I. Forum later that year by García and other civil rights activists. It also led to the establishment of the Texas Good Neighbor Commission.

See also AMERICAN G.I. FORUM; GARCÍA, HÉCTOR PÉREZ; JOHNSON, LYNDON BAINES.

FURTHER READING: Dyer, Stanford P., and Merrell A. Knighten. "Discrimination after Death: Lyndon Johnson and Félix Longoria." *Southern Studies* 17 (1978):411–426; Green, George Norris. "The Félix Longoria Affair." *Journal of Ethnic Studies* 19, no. 3 (Fall 1991):23–34; Pycior, Julie Leininger. *LBJ & Mexican Americans: The Paradox of Power*. Austin: University of Texas Press, 1997; Vigil, Maurilio. *Chicano Politics*. Washington, D.C.: University Press of America, 1978; Zelade, Richard. "Last Rites, First Rites." *Texas Monthly* (January 1986):192+.

LÓPEZ, IGNACIO L., 1908–1973. As the crusading editor of the weekly *El Espectador*, for over a quarter of a century Ignacio López gave voice to concerns of Mexican Americans rather than those of their immigrant parents. During the 1940s and the 1950s he was the preeminent southern California leader in Mexican Americans' efforts to wipe out discrimination and to gain their full civil rights. His goals were moderate: an end to injustices, complete acceptance, and integration into a pluralistic American society.

In *El Espectador*, published in San Bernardino, California, until 1961, López publicized incidents of police brutality and patent discrimination against Mexicanos. Vigilant but neither confrontational nor violent, he advocated use of the boycott and other peaceful economic weapons as well as lawsuits to achieve greater respect for their civil rights in the use of public facilities: theaters, swimming pools, and cemeteries. As a fervent disciple of American democracy he strongly stressed the need for Mexicanos to take more active and forceful steps in defense of their rights under the law.

López's activist leadership in the desegregation of public facilities was of great importance in establishing the Unity Leagues and Community Service Organization groups in the greater Los Angeles area after World War II. It was the chief ingredient in a number of victories for civil rights, including the case of *Méndez et al. v. Westminster School District* in the late 1940s. Over a decade later he was one of the organizers of the Mexican American Political Association. During the 1950s his editorials helped elect two dozen Mexican Americans to city and county offices. Considered earlier by Anglos to be radical, with the rise of militancy in the Chicano Movement during the 1960s he began to be seen for what he had always been, a determined moderate in the Mexican American struggle for civil rights. In the Nixon administration he received appointment as Spanish-speaking Coordinator in the Department of Housing and Urban Development.

See also CIVIL RIGHTS ABUSE; COMMUNITY SERVICE ORGANIZATION; MEXICAN AMERICAN POLITICAL ASSOCIATION.

FURTHER READING: García, Mario T. *Mexican Americans: Leadership, Ideology, and Identity, 1930–1960.* New Haven, Conn.: Yale University Press, 1989; McWilliams, Carey. *North from Mexico: The Spanish-Speaking People of the United States.* Updated ed. New York: Praeger Publishers, 1990.

LÓPEZ, LINO M., 1910–1978. Lino López was one of the very early leaders in the struggle for Mexican American rights. Most of his life's work centered on making greater opportunities available to raza youths, especially in education. After graduating from Loyola University in Chicago he became deeply involved in social welfare activities in the mid-1940s. He completed a long stint as director of the Pueblo, Colorado, Catholic Youth Center and in 1953 moved to Denver, where he was an educational consultant and served for a decade on the mayor's Commission on Human Relations. In 1963 he moved to San Jose, California, where he established a community service agency and continued his educational work with young Mexican Americans, helping them to organize high school clubs and pioneering in persuading schools to initiate bilingual programs. At the rise of the Chicano movimiento he accepted a position at Redlands University in southern California, where he continued his life's work of teaching and advising Chicano students. A severe auto accident followed by a stroke led to his return to Denver and a tragic death.

FURTHER READING: Valdés, Daniel. *Who's Who in Colorado*. Denver: Who's Who in Colorado, 1958.

LUCEY, ROBERT E., 1891–1977. As a forthright liberal in socioeconomic matters, archbishop of San Antonio Robert Lucey's championship of the civil rights of poor Mexicanos earned him a national reputation. A longtime advocate and supporter of greater civil and social rights for the marginalized, especially for Mexican Americans, he strongly supported the right of farmworkers to unionize and fought to bring migrant workers under the protection of federal labor legislation. In 1950 he was appointed by Harry Truman to the President's Commission on Migratory Labor. During the 1966 melon pickers' march on Austin he spoke out in their support and urged them to stand up against repression and discrimination.

Lucey was referred to by some conservatives as the "pink bishop," although he too was a conservative in many areas, even vocally supporting President Lyndon Johnson in the Vietnam War when many others were beginning to have their doubts. Nevertheless, for almost three decades he encouraged the priests of his diocese to involve themselves in civil rights issues. In 1945 he was a leader in founding the Bishops Committee for the Spanish Speaking, of which he remained executive chair for a quarter of a century, until his 1969 retirement.

See also CHURCHES; TEXAS.

FURTHER READING: Bronder, Saul. *Social Justice and Church Authority: The Public Life of Robert E. Lucey*. Philadelphia: Temple University Press. 1982; Privett, Stephen A. *The U.S. Catholic Church and Its Hispanic Members: The Pastoral Vision of Archbishop Robert E. Lucey*. San Antonio: Trinity University Press, 1988.

LUDLOW MASSACRE, 1914. At the beginning of the twentieth century the Colorado Fuel and Iron Company pursued a policy of despotic feudal control in the Trinidad coal mining district and was adamantly opposed to unionization efforts by the miners. At issue between the company and the miners, in addition to wages, were various civil rights abuses. In September 1913, after an intensive and highly successful unionization drive by the United Mine Workers, the union called a strike when the company refused to negotiate the issues raised. The strike soon erupted into violence that was brought to an end by the Colorado National Guard after 11 people had been killed.

Tensions between the miners, many of them Mexicanos, and the guardsmen and company guards persisted and increased. In April of the following year fighting broke out between the two groups. The militia used a mobile machine gun on the miners and burned down their tent city (the striking miners had been evicted from company housing), killing 66 persons, of whom 13 women and children were incinerated alive. This massacre of

April 20 was followed by open warfare and a rampage of burning and killing on the part of the enraged miners. A week later President Woodrow Wilson sent in federal troops to patrol much of southeastern Colorado. The Ludlow Massacre became a cause célèbre and in the long run served to further the struggle for workers' rights.

See also COLORADO.

FURTHER READING: Adams, Graham, Jr. *The Age of Industrial Violence, 1910–1915.* New York: Columbia University Press, 1966; Dawley, Alan. *Struggles for Justice: Social Responsibility and the Liberal State.* Cambridge, Mass.: Harvard University Press, 1991; Eastman, Max. "Class War in Colorado." In *Echoes of Revolt: The Masses, 1911–1917,* edited by William L. O'Neill. Chicago: Ivan R. Dee, 1989; Perlman, Selig, and Philip Taft. *History of Labor in the United States.* Reprint, New York: Augustus M. Kelley, 1966.

LYNCHING. All along the Mexican–U.S. border, but especially in Texas, lynching of Mexicanos, the most extreme form of civil rights violation, was common in the second half of the nineteenth century. Both the Texas Rangers and impromptu vigilance committees often took "justice" into their own hands. In California, where Mexicanos formed only a small proportion of the population (not more than 15 percent at the time), they supplied over one third of lynch mob victims between 1850 and 1895.

The 1851 Downieville lynching of "Juanita" was only the first instance in California, where lynching became fairly commonplace during the gold rush. Frequently lynching was prompted by Mexicanos' being accused of stealing gold or horses or of killing or raping Anglos. This last charge was more common in Texas, where lynching was the most extreme form of widespread violence against la raza in the second half of the 1800s. All Mexicanos were considered foreigners and therefore not entitled to any civil rights. Only rarely were protests against extralegal mob action successful in deterring vigilante violence.

The murder of Francisco Torres in southern California in 1892 is the last recorded instance of lynching on the West Coast, but it continued in Texas. The Spanish-American War in 1898 led to a temporary outburst in the persecution of Mexicanos, particularly in that state. Reports of atrocities in Mexico during the 1910–1920 revolution sometimes occasioned "retaliation" against Mexicanos north of the border.

After the turn of the century Mexicanos began to organize to defend their civil rights, and lynchings declined in number. However, from time to time economic recessions created a climate in which night-riding, terrorism, and home-burning became common forms of civil rights denial to Mexicanos. In the depression that began in the late 1920s, for example, the Ku Klux Klan actively pursued such activities, including lynching.

See also CIVIL RIGHTS ABUSE.

FURTHER READING: Acuña, Rodolfo. *Occupied America: A History of Chicanos*, 3rd ed. New York: Harper & Row, 1988; Rosales, Francisco A. *Chicano!: The History of the Mexican American Civil Rights Movement.* Houston: Arte Público Press, 1996.

M

MACHUCA, ESTHER NIETO, 1895–1980. One of the early organizers in the League of United Latin American Citizens (LULAC), Esther Machuca was a leader in the El Paso women's group, Ladies League of United Latin American Citizens, known as the Ladies LULAC. Discouraged by the lack of male support for the group, in 1936 she dissolved the two-year-old auxiliary, but then she helped reestablish it in the following year. Machuca's important contribution to LULAC was recognized by her appointment as official hostess of the 1938 national convention held in El Paso. After the convention she was appointed Ladies' Organizer General, a position she used effectively to expand the number of women's auxiliaries. She remained active in the El Paso Ladies LULAC into her early eighties. Throughout her life she believed that LULAC women should have complete equality with their male counterparts.

See also CHICANAS; LEAGUE OF UNITED LATIN AMERICAN CITIZENS.

FURTHER READING: García, Mario T. *Mexican Americans: Leadership, Ideology, and Identity, 1930–1960.* New Haven, Conn.: Yale University Press, 1989; Tyler, Ron, ed. *The New Handbook of Texas.* Vol. 4. Austin: Texas State Historical Association, 1996.

McWILLIAMS, CAREY, 1905–1980. As a young lawyer with a special interest in labor problems, Carey McWilliams became aware of the widespread denial of civil rights to minority peoples in the United States. Because of his decade-long concern about racism and repression, in 1943 he was selected by editor Louis Adamic to write a history of Mexicans in the United States for J. B. Lippincott Co. Over the next five years McWilliams researched and wrote *North from Mexico: The Spanish-Speaking People* *of the United States*, which was published in 1949 and was destined to become the primer of Mexican American history two decades later as a result of the Chicano Movement. Intensely interested in social issues, McWilliams viewed the book as a contribution to his lifelong efforts to make democracy work better in America.

However, McWilliams was not merely a chronicler of the Mexicano experience; he was also an active participant in that history. During World War II his forthright dedication to Mexican American civil rights led him to take a vigorous lead in the Sleepy Lagoon Defense Committee, which secured a reversal of the lower court's conviction of 17 Chicano youths in the sensational Los Angeles case.

After the war McWilliams was hired by the progressive journal *The Nation* to work on a special issue dealing with civil liberties. He remained as a staff member and in 1955 was named editor, a position he held until his retirement 20 years later. During a long and successful career as a journalist he was an indefatigable fighter for civil rights.

See also SLEEPY LAGOON.

FURTHER READING: California, Governor of. *Citizens Committee Report on the Zoot Suit Riots*. Sacramento, Calif.: Printing Office, 1943; Fogelson, Robert M. *The Los Angeles Riots*. New York: New York Times, 1969; McWilliams, Carey. *The Education of Carey McWilliams*. New York: Simon & Schuster, 1979; McWilliams, Carey. *North from Mexico: The Spanish-Speaking People of the United States*. New ed. New York: Praeger Publishers, 1990.

MANA: A NATIONAL LATINA ORGANIZATION. MANA, with over 4,000 members in two thirds of the states, is one of the largest Chicana organizations in the United States. It was founded in 1974 as Mexican American Women's National Association with Evangeline Elizondo of Texas as its first president. It has concerned itself with advancing the status of Chicanas and with achieving complete equality between Chicanas and Chicanos in the common struggle for their rights. Its immediate goal was to develop leadership among Chicanas in order to obtain parity with males. In order to foster self-esteem and leadership qualities among Chicanas, in 1984 it established a national academic program, the Raquel Márquez Frankel Scholarship Fund.

One of the most influential women in MANA's development was Gloria Barajas, president from 1985 to 1986. She brought her extensive experience as a community and political activist to the organization, focusing it on achieving more elective and administrative jobs in government for Chicanas as well as greater economic equality. In 1987 MANA's new president, Rita Jaramillo, initiated a review of the organization's mission and goals and also sought stronger financing for its expanded programs. MANA publishes a monthly newsletter and holds an annual convention to make Spanish-speaking women more aware of current issues affecting them. To reflect the broadened scope of its membership, in 1998 the name was changed to MANA: A National Latina Organization.

See also BARAJAS, GLORIA; CHICANAS; ORGANIZATIONS.

FURTHER READING: Crocker, Elvira Valenzuela. *MANA: One Dream, Many Voices: A History of the Mexican American Women's National Association.* Washington, D.C.: MANA, 1991; Gonzales, Sylvia Alicia. *Hispanic American Voluntary Organizations.* Westport, Conn.: Greenwood Press, 1985; Segura, Denise A., and Beatriz M. Pesquera. "Chicana Feminisms: Their Political Context and Contemporary Expressions." In *The Latino Studies Reader: Culture, Economy, and Society,* edited by Antonia Darder and Rodolfo D. Torres. Malden, Mass.: Blackwell Publishers, 1998; www.hermana.org./

MANUEL, HERSCHEL T., 1887–1976. Herschel Thurman Manuel was born, grew up, and was educated in the U.S. Midwest. After earning a doctorate from the University of Illinois, completing army service during World War I, and teaching at several universities, in 1925 he moved to the University of Texas. A 1928 research grant to explore the schooling of Spanish-speaking children led to an abiding interest in their problems and to his first book, *The Education of Mexican and Spanish-Speaking Children in Texas* (1930). His research and writing soon earned him a reputation as an outstanding educational psychologist.

Manuel continued his studies in the education of Mexicano children in Texas schools and argued strongly both for their civil right to an education and for the importance of their education to the future of Texas. He was especially noted for his interest in bilingual testing and developed a series of tests published in 1950 by the Educational Testing Service. A Hogg Foundation grant led to the publication in 1965 of his second important work, *Spanish-Speaking Children of the Southwest: Their Education and the Public Welfare.* Along with Loyd Tireman and George I. Sánchez, he was a pioneer in the study of the problems of Spanish-speaking children in an English-speaking educational environment.

See also SÁNCHEZ, GEORGE I.; TIREMAN, LOYD S.

FURTHER READING: Meier, Matt S., and Feliciano Rivera. *Dictionary of Mexican American History.* Westport, Conn.: Greenwood Press, 1981; Tyler, Ron, ed. *New Handbook of Texas.* Vol. 4. Austin: Texas State Historical Association, 1996.

MARTÍNEZ, ANTONIO JOSÉ, 1793–1867. The rights and republican privileges of Nuevomexicanos under the 1848 Treaty of Guadalupe Hidalgo and U.S. rule were a matter of great concern to Antonio José Martínez, pastor at Taos. Member of a large and politically powerful family, he was New Mexico's nineteenth-century genius and its most prominent and controversial historical personage as well as one of its first civil rights leaders.

Although opposed to the American takeover, Father Martínez, a staunch republican and patriotic citizen of recently independent Mexico, had great hopes and expectations for New Mexico and its people under the rule of the U.S. republic. In keeping with the new Anglo republican ideals and in defense of his people's liberties, he changed the curriculum in his school at Taos to include English and civil law. He also took advantage of those aspects of the new government that he viewed as favorable to Nuevomexicanos, and he himself became intensely active in governmental matters, participating in the unsuccessful statehood convention that met after the Treaty of Guadalupe Hidalgo.

During the 1850s the priest continued his fight to defend Nuevomexicano rights, served three terms in the territorial Legislative Council, and was elected its president for one term. At the time of the Civil War he supported President Abraham Lincoln's policies on the slavery issue. He also showed great concern for the plight of southwestern Indians whose rights he felt were being ignored and violated. In 1865 he sent his critical views to the congressional Doolittle Committee, asserting that under the United States the Indians had even fewer rights than under Mexico.

Father Martínez's conflict with his new French-born bishop, Jean Baptiste Lamy, began in part as an aspect of his defense of Nuevomexicano rights, including his own. It later evolved into a bitter personal quarrel between two strong-willed and headstrong men. After various public episcopal admonitions, which Martínez ignored, he was discretely excommunicated by the bishop. On July 27, 1867, he died quietly in his bed, mourned by many.

See also NEW MEXICO; POLITICAL PARTICIPATION.

FURTHER READING: Chávez, Fray Angélico. *But Time and Chance: The Story of Padre Martínez of Taos, 1793–1867.* Santa Fe, N.M.: Sunstone Press, 1981; Perrigo, Lynn I. *Hispanos: Historic Leaders in New Mexico.* Santa Fe, N.M.: Sunstone Press, 1985; Sánchez, Pedro. *Memories of Antonio José Martínez.* Santa Fe, N.M.: Rydal Press, 1978; Vigil, Maurilio E. *Los Patrones: Profiles of Hispanic Political Leaders in New Mexico History.* Washington, D.C.: University Press of America, 1980.

MARTÍNEZ, BETITA (ELIZABETH), 1925– . During her childhood in Washington, D.C., Betita Martínez became aware of discrimination and civil rights denial. In 1963 she joined the black Student Non-Violent Coordinating Committee (SNCC) as a civil rights worker in the South. During the following year she was named director of SNCC's New York office with the job of raising funds and focusing the media spotlight on civil rights abuses. A year later she was sent by SNCC to California to give a speech in solidarity with the United Farm Workers then on their march to Sacramento—her first direct contact with the reinvigorated Mexican American rights movement.

In 1968 Betita Martínez moved to Albuquerque, New Mexico, where she became active in Reies López Tijerina's Alianza Federal de Pueblos Libres, putting her experience in the black civil rights movement to use in order to advance the cause for Nuevomexicanos. Her first job in the movimiento was to develop a voice for the Alianza in its fight for lost pueblo lands. To this end she helped create and then edit a bilingual newspaper, *El Grito del Norte*. Under her editorship *El Grito* led an insistent demand for civil rights and became an important voice not only in New Mexico but throughout the entire Chicano Movement.

In addition to her invaluable civil rights work as a founder and editor of *El Grito del Norte*, Martínez is the author of five books and numerous journal articles on the Chicano experience and civil rights movement. Her most recent work is *De Colores Means All of Us: Latina Views for a Multicolored Century* (1998).

Since the mid-1970s Martínez has worked with a number of community groups and during the 1990s was active as a college professor and visiting lecturer. Convinced from her early days in the civil rights movement of the wisdom and necessity for cooperation between African Americans and Chicanos, she has emphasized this point in her talks and writing and has engaged in speaking tours with the goal of improving Latino-black relations. Her most recent project is the Institute for Multiracial Justice, a resource center for developing alliances among people of color.

See also ALIANZA FEDERAL DE PUEBLOS LIBRES; CHICANAS.

FURTHER READING: Martínez, Betita. *De Colores Means All of Us: Latina Views for a Multicolored Century*. Cambridge, Mass.: South End Press, 1998; *Las Mujeres: Mexican American/Chicana Women*. Windsor, Calif.: National Women's History Project, 1991.

MARTÍNEZ, VILMA SOCORRO, 1944– . Most of Vilma Martínez's adult life has been dominated by three important public concerns: equality before the law, elimination of discriminatory practices, and access to education. Her outstanding work at all levels of the U.S. court system in favor of civil rights and against discriminatory treatment has advanced her to the "short list" of candidates for a Supreme Court appointment.

While still in high school in San Antonio Vilma Martínez worked one summer for outstanding Texas civil rights activist Alonso Perales. He became her role model, and she decided that she too would become a lawyer in order to be of service to her people. After her political science degree from the University of Texas at Austin, in 1964 she decided to go northeast to Columbia University for her legal training because she felt discriminated against in Texas both as a Mexican American and as a woman.

Interested in using her legal education to help others, as she had witnessed Alonso Perales do, after graduating from law school in 1967 Vilma

Martínez obtained a position as a staff attorney with the National Association for the Advancement of Colored People (NAACP) in its Legal Defense Fund. While working there in 1968, she also helped create a new Chicano organization, the Mexican American Legal Defense and Educational Fund (MALDEF), and acted as liaison between the two groups. After three years with the NAACP she took a job as a counselor for the New York State Division of Human Rights, Equal Employment Opportunity Council.

A member of MALDEF since its inception, Vilma Martínez was selected in 1973 to be director of this leading Chicano civil rights organization. During the three terms of her presidency, 1973 to 1982, she sought to use legal action to secure greater Mexican American access to education, employment, and political power. Among the programs she initiated to achieve these goals were the Chicana Rights Project and an internship program to develop skilled Chicano civil rights litigators. Perhaps her greatest civil rights success was in persuading the courts to include Mexican Americans under the protection of the Voting Rights Act of 1965. She also broke new ground in *Plyler v. Doe*, which assured undocumented children the right to free public school education. By the time Martínez stepped down from MALDEF's presidency in 1982 to enter private practice, she had considerably remolded and expanded the organization.

Although Vilma Martínez joined the Los Angeles law firm of Munger, Tolles, and Olson, she continues her lifelong activism in civil rights and community public service projects. From 1980 to 1989 she served as a board member in the Southwest Voter Registration and Education Project, and at the beginning of the 1990s she returned to MALDEF's board of directors. She has also served actively on a dozen or more influential boards, commissions, and committees, including the Advisory Committee to the U.S. Commission on Civil Rights.

See also LEADERSHIP; MEXICAN AMERICAN LEGAL DEFENSE AND EDUCATIONAL FUND; PERALES, ALONSO S.; VOTING RIGHTS ACT, 1965.

FURTHER READING: Evangelista, Mario. "Advocate for La Raza." *Nuestro* 1, no. 7 (October 1977):38–40; Johnson, Dean. "Chair of the Board." *Nuestro* 9, no. 7 (September 1985):34–36; Lichtenstein, Grace. "Chicana with a Backbone of Steel." *Quest* (February-March 1980); Morey, Janet, and Wendy Dunn. *Famous Mexican Americans*. New York: E. P. Dutton, 1989; O'Connor, Karen, and Lee Epstein. "A Legal Voice for the Chicano Community." In *The Mexican American Experience*, edited by Rodolfo O. de la Garza et al. Austin: University of Texas Press, 1985; Telgen, Diane, and Jim Kamp, eds. *¡Latinas! Women of Achievement*. Detroit: Visible Ink Press, 1996.

MAVERICK, MAURY, SR., 1895–1954. Maury Maverick was a Franklin D. Roosevelt New Dealer who came from a San Antonio family active in politics for generations. A reformer and vocal defender of the poor, he strongly championed the civil rights of minorities, contrary to the common stereotype of Texas politicians. During his two terms in the U.S. House of Representatives in the 1930s he supported fair employment practices legislation and opposed bills that would have chipped away at freedom of speech. He was the only southern member in the House who supported an anti-lynching bill. Although his stand, unpopular in some quarters, lost him reelection, he was elected mayor of San Antonio, where his defense of freedom of speech for radical leftists and communists in the pecan shellers' strike of 1938 lost him further popular support. He was subsequently indicted for paying Mexicanos' poll taxes but was acquitted.

See also TENAYUCA, EMMA.

FURTHER READING: Henderson, Richard. *Maury Maverick: A Political Biography*. Austin: University of Texas Press, 1970; Pycior, Julie Leininger. *LBJ & Mexican Americans: The Paradox of Power*. Austin: University of Texas Press, 1997.

MEDINA, HAROLD R., 1888–1990. When he died at the ripe old age of 102, Judge Harold Medina, son of a Mexican father who had immigrated to the United States as a boy, left behind a legacy as one of the outstanding American jurists of the twentieth century. His deep concern for civil rights, especially free speech issues and freedom of the press, led him to become the author of a dozen books on the First Amendment and other legal matters.

After graduating from Columbia University law school in 1912, three years later Medina began a 32-year career there as a teacher. His name became a household word in the United States as the result of two trials. In the first he was the court-appointed defender of Anthony Cramer, whose acquittal on a treason charge he ultimately won on appeal to the U.S. Supreme Court. In the second he was the federal judge presiding over the highly emotional nine-month trial of 11 members of the National Committee of the U.S. Communist Party. For many Americans his patience and dignified conduct during the long trial, despite constant abuse and repeated provocation, exemplified the finest spirit of American jurisprudence.

Medina remained active as a judge, author, lecturer, and champion of the First Amendment into his early nineties. Only then did he begin to slow down. He was a role model for many young activist Chicano lawyers in the last third of the twentieth century. During his long life he was the recipient of numerous awards and honors, especially for his work in redefining court procedures and establishing legal precedents.

See also COMMUNIST PARTY; COURTS.

FURTHER READING: *Current Biography Yearbook, 1949.* New York: H. W. Wilson Co., 1950; "Harold Medina, U.S. Judge, Dies at 102." *New York Times*,

16 March 1990, B7; Hawthorne, Daniel. *Judge Medina: A Biography*. New York: W. Funk, 1952; Moore, Leonard P. "Dedication to Judge Harold R. Medina on the Occasion of His Ninetieth Birthday." *Brooklyn Law Review* 44, no. 4 (1978): xiii–xiv. *Who's Who in American Law*. 2nd ed. Chicago: Marquis Who's Who, 1979.

MEDRANO v. ALLEE. Following the 1966–1967 melon pickers' strike in Texas's Lower Rio Grande Valley, farmworker Francisco Medrano and others filed a class-action suit against the Texas Rangers and Ranger captain A. Y. Allee for interfering with their civil right to organize. The suit charged that the Rangers had deprived them of constitutional rights guaranteed under the First and Fourteenth Amendments. In 1972 the federal district court ruled in favor of the strikers and enjoined the Rangers from interfering with peaceful union activities and from intimidating strikers by making arrests without probable cause. On appeal, two years later the U.S. Supreme Court upheld the lower court's decision.

See also TEXAS RANGERS.

FURTHER READING: Samora, Julian, Joe Bernal, and Albert Peña. *Gunpowder Justice: A Reassessment of the Texas Rangers*. Notre Dame, Ind.: University of Notre Dame Press, 1979.

MÉNDEZ, CONSUELO HERRERA, 1904–1985. Austin school teacher Consuelo Méndez was an early Tejana political activist. During three critical decades, from the 1940s to the 1960s, she took an active leadership position in the state Ladies League of United Latin American Citizens and particularly in the Austin chapter. Seriously involved in local politics, she testified in a school segregation case and worked tirelessly to get Mexican American voters to the polls during elections. She even ran for the Austin city council. For her lifetime of work in education and her political activism she was honored by various groups and had a school named after her.

See also LEAGUE OF UNITED LATIN AMERICAN CITIZENS; SEGREGATION.

FURTHER READING: Tyler, Ron, ed. *The New Handbook of Texas*. Vol. 4. Austin: Texas State Historical Association, 1996.

MÉNDEZ ET AL. v. WESTMINSTER SCHOOL DISTRICT OF ORANGE COUNTY ET AL., 1946, 1947. Impelled by the revived movement for civil rights at the end of World War II, Mexican American parents in Orange County, California, filed suit in 1945 against four elementary school districts, including Westminster. They asserted that the districts placed their children in separate classes solely because of their ethnic background. Their attorneys, provided by the League of United Latin American

Citizens, pointed out that this segregation violated constitutional guarantees embodied in the Fifth and Fourteenth Amendments to the Constitution.

In February 1946 federal court judge Paul McCormick, agreeing with the complainants, ruled that such segregation violated not only the U.S. Constitution but also California statute law. Besides, he added, segregation was socially unhealthy; it fostered antagonisms and denied students the benefits of interaction with other cultures in the classroom. He ruled that separate schools, even with like technical facilities, did not provide "equal protection of the laws" and ordered the school districts to end the separation.

Unwilling to accept the court's decision and desegregate, the school districts appealed the decision, arguing that the facilities were completely equal and that the federal court had no jurisdiction. A year later the Ninth Circuit Court in San Francisco, California, upheld Judge McCormick's ruling, agreeing that the school districts were in violation of both California law and the Fourteenth Amendment to the U.S. Constitution. Despite this victory, de facto segregation continued. However, the *Méndez* case did set a precedent for the even more important *Brown v. Board of Education* victory in 1954, in which the court held that separate facilities were inherently unequal.

See also EDUCATION; LEAGUE OF UNITED LATIN AMERICAN CITIZENS; SEGREGATION.

FURTHER READING: Castro, Tony. *Chicano Power: The Emergence of Mexican America.* New York: Saturday Review Press, 1974; McWilliams, Carey. *North from Mexico: The Spanish-Speaking People of the United States.* Updated ed. Westport, Conn: Praeger Publishers, 1990; Sánchez, George I. *Concerning Segregation of Spanish-Speaking Children in the Public Schools.* Austin: University of Texas, 1951; Wollenberg, Charles. "Méndez vs. Westminster: Race, Nationality and Segregation in California Schools." *California Historical Quarterly* 53, no. 4 (Winter 1974): 317–332.

METZGER, SIDNEY M., 1902–1986. A Texan by birth, Sidney Metzger returned to San Antonio after study and ordination to the priesthood in Rome and began teaching in St. John's Seminary. In 1940 he was elevated to the bishopric and two years later became bishop of the El Paso diocese. Influenced by the late-nineteenth-century social justice teachings of Pope Leo XIII as outlined in his encyclical *Rerum Novarum*, Bishop Metzger actively supported the efforts of Texas Mexican Americans, especially farm laborers, to improve their working conditions by unionizing. In the early 1970s, despite attacks on his person, he stuck by his support for the San Antonio strikers' nationwide boycott of the Farah clothing company from 1972 to 1974 and asked other Catholic bishops to support it. Metzger retired in 1978 and died eight years later.

See also CHURCHES.

FURTHER READING: Carrillo, Emilla F. *Bishop Has Kept His Word.* New York: Carlton Press, 1966; Castro, Tony. *Chicano Power: The Emergence of Mexican America.* New York: Saturday Review Press, 1974; Coyle, Laurie, et al. *Women at Farah: An Unfinished Story.* El Paso, Tex.: Reforma, 1979.

MEXICAN AMERICAN ANTI-DEFAMATION LEAGUE. This civil rights organization, which later changed its name to the Institute for the Study of Hispanic Life and History, was concerned with the cultural as well as civil rights of Mexican Americans. As part of its effort to eliminate stereotyping and discrimination, it publicized occasions of these racist actions in order to alert the public to their existence and to eliminate them. It also sponsored conferences and seminars to achieve the same results.

FURTHER READING: Gonzales, Sylvia Alicia. *Hispanic American Voluntary Organizations.* Westport, Conn.: Greenwood Press, 1985; Meier, Matt S., and Feliciano Rivera. *Dictionary of Mexican American History.* Westport, Conn.: Greenwood Press, 1981.

MEXICAN AMERICAN LEGAL DEFENSE AND EDUCATIONAL FUND (MALDEF). Incorporated in May 1968 with a $2.2 million Ford Foundation start-up grant, MALDEF is an organization dedicated primarily to using the legal system to protect the civil rights of American citizens of Mexican descent. Its initial broad goal was to spearhead a struggle for social and economic change by an unremitting attack in the courts on racism. Over the years it has filed suits in a wide range of issues ranging from police harassment and brutality, segregation in the schools and elsewhere, exclusion from and underrepresentation on juries, intimidation of voters, at-large elections, and gerrymandering to citizen rights under Social Security and welfare legislation.

MALDEF has done yeoman's work in reducing barriers to participation by Mexican Americans in the U.S. political system and governance. It has played an important role in Mexican American gains at the ballot box, leading, for example, to election of the first-ever Mexican American congressman from Arizona in 1992. In pursuit of the protection of Chicano civil rights, it has won some of the most important suits in the areas of equality of educational opportunity and political representation.

In its creation and infancy MALDEF was under the leadership of Pete Tijerina, a lawyer and leader in the League of United Latin American Citizens, who made good use of the experience and counsel of the NAACP Legal Defense Fund (LDF). Vilma Martínez of the LDF helped prepare the MALDEF grant application and then continued to act as liaison between MALDEF and the LDF. Under Tijerina as its first executive director MALDEF established its headquarters in San Antonio, with a secondary office in Los Angeles because of that city's large Mexicano population. At the Ford Foundation's insistence on a more national image, MALDEF's headquarters were moved out of Texas in 1970 and Tijerina stepped down as director.

MALDEF's new headquarters were established in San Francisco, California, and Mario Obledo, a League of United Latin American Citizens leader who had been recruited from the Attorney General's Office, took over the directorship. Under Obledo's leadership offices in Albuquerque, Denver, and Washington, D.C., were added to those in Los Angeles and San Antonio, giving MALDEF wider scope and greater visibility nationwide. At first MALDEF's activities were largely reactive in nature, focusing on individual cases of civil rights denial and using litigation and threats of litigation. Obledo's most important contribution to MALDEF, perhaps, was his decision to take more cases to the U.S. Supreme Court on constitutional issues. After one term he turned the directorship over to Vilma Martínez in December 1973.

As director of MALDEF Vilma Martínez immediately began instituting a number of changes, including beefing up the staff by recruiting several Mexican American attorneys with extensive civil rights experience. In 1974 a Chicana Civil Rights Project was established, as were other specialized projects, followed the next year by an internship program to help train young Chicano attorneys. Most importantly, at the same time MALDEF began to be more selective in the cases it took on. By carefully choosing its test cases it whittled away at adverse precedent in areas such as politics and education. In *White v. Regester* it persuaded the U.S. Supreme Court that at-large elections were basically discriminatory, and in *Plyler v. Doe* (1982), a landmark U.S. Supreme Court ruling accepted the MALDEF contention that Texas could not exclude the children of undocumented aliens from its public schools. In that same year MALDEF filed a suit to end gross gerrymandering. In 1991 it played a significant role in the election of Gloria Molina to the Los Angeles Board of Supervisors.

See also MARTÍNEZ, VILMA; OBLEDO, MARIO; PLYLER v. DOE; TIJERINA, PETE.

FURTHER READING: Cortner, Richard. *The Supreme Court and Civil Liberties Policy.* Palo Alto, Calif.: Mayfield, 1975; Johnson, Dean. "Chair of the Board." *Nuestro* 9, no. 7 (September 1985):34–36; O'Connor, Karen, and Lee Epstein. "A Legal Voice for the Chicano Community: The Activities of the Mexican American Legal Defense and Education Fund." In *The Mexican American Experience,* edited by Rodolfo de la Garza et al. Austin: University of Texas Press, 1985; Oliveira, Annette. *MALDEF: Diez Años.* San Francisco: MALDEF, 1979; Ortega, Joe. "The Privately Funded Legal Aid Office: The MALDEF Experience." *Chicano Law Review* 1 (1972):80–84; www.maldef.org.

MEXICAN AMERICAN MOVEMENT (MAM). MAM was an early civil rights group that articulated California student discontent with the availability and quality of public higher education for Chicanos. Founded in

1938 in Los Angeles, it had its origins in the annual Older Boys Conference initiated four years earlier by the YMCA for Mexican American youths. MAM had as its goal the arousing and promoting of a civic and social consciousness in the Mexican American community through education. It persisted into the early 1950s but no longer remained strictly a youth organization, perhaps partly because of the educational benefits then available to young Chicanos through the postwar G.I. Bill. In many ways it presaged the student movement of the 1960s.

See also ORGANIZATIONS.

FURTHER READING: Gómez-Quiñones, Juan. *Mexican Students Por La Raza: The Chicano Student Movement in Southern California, 1967–1977.* Santa Barbara, Calif.: Editorial La Causa, 1978; Gómez-Quiñones, Juan. *Roots of Chicano Politics, 1600–1940.* Albuquerque: University of New Mexico Press, 1994.

MEXICAN AMERICAN POLITICAL ASSOCIATION (MAPA). MAPA was founded in 1959 by a group of California Chicano activists, including Bert Corona and Herman Gallegos, who met in Fresno to discuss ways to increase the political clout of la raza. One of the first groups to formally declare its primary interests as political, it centered its goals around Chicano issues, candidates, elections, and the vote. For example, it was instrumental in the election of Edward Roybal to the U.S. Congress in 1962 and helped secure the appointment of several Mexican American judges to state and municipal courts in California. MAPA's early success led to considerable interest throughout the Southwest in the organization as a model to be followed. Despite efforts in the late 1970s to go national, MAPA has remained largely a California organization.

MAPA's semi-autonomous chapters have defended Mexican Americans in a wide variety of civil rights situations, from police brutality to discrimination in schools and public places. It has been particularly important to isolated rural Chicanos by extending external support for their efforts to assert their civil and social rights. At the beginning of the 1980s it claimed a membership of about 5,000 in 60 California chapters. Although designated nonpartisan, MAPA has generally lent its election support to Democratic Party candidates.

See also CORONA, BERT; GALLEGOS, HERMAN; QUEVEDO, EDUARDO.

FURTHER READING: Castro, Tony. *Chicano Power: The Emergence of Mexican America.* New York: E. P. Dutton & Co., 1974; Grebler, Leo, Joan W. Moore, and Ralph C. Guzmán, eds. *The Mexican American People: The Nation's Second Largest Minority.* New York: Free Press, 1970; Santillán, Richard A. "Third Party Politics: Old Story, New Faces." *The Black Politician* 3, no. 2 (October 1971):10–18.

MEXICAN AMERICAN UNITY COUNCIL (MAUC). MAUC was a Texas economic development corporation established in 1968 as a financial resource for the Mexican American Youth Organization (MAYO). It was the brainchild chiefly of José Angel Gutiérrez, Juan Patlán, and Willie Velásquez, founders of MAYO. Under Velásquez, who became the council's first president, MAUC's basic goal was to help community people of San Antonio solve their problems.

Juan Patlán, who succeeded Velásquez, aggressively pursued funding that brought in massive aid to finance a wide variety of social service and economic development projects in San Antonio. Using Ford Foundation funding, the agency set up community programs in job training, low-cost housing, and health care. Despite strong criticism and opposition on the part of powerful U.S. representative Henry B. González of Texas, MAUC was able to work with other Chicano organizations to achieve a considerable degree of success in providing community services and fostering business development.

See also GONZÁLEZ, HENRY B.; MEXICAN AMERICAN YOUTH ORGANIZATION; PATLÁN, JUAN J.

FURTHER READING: García, Ignacio M. *United We Win: The Rise and Fall of La Raza Unida Party.* Tucson: University of Arizona, MASRC, 1989; Navarro, Armando. *Mexican American Youth Organization: Avant-Garde of the Chicano Movement in Texas.* Austin: University of Texas Press, 1995.

MEXICAN AMERICAN WOMEN'S NATIONAL ASSOCIATION (MANA). See MANA: A NATIONAL LATINA ORGANIZATION.

MEXICAN AMERICAN YOUTH ORGANIZATION (MAYO). MAYO, one of the more important student groups of the 1960s, was founded at St. Mary's College in San Antonio in 1967 by Los Cinco: José Angel Gutiérrez, Mario Compeán, Willie Velásquez, and two others. Financed originally by the Southwest Council of La Raza with Ford Foundation money, from the beginning it had a special concern for education and sought to gain control of school districts and individual schools in order to adapt curricula to Chicano student needs. But it also had as its objective to make Tejanos more aware of their civil rights and to encourage them to participate more actively in the political process. With strong grassroots ties, it was loosely structured to give its 40 local chapters latitude to experiment and improvise in solving community problems. Although MAYO had no women in leadership positions, they played an important part in its development.

MAYO rejected existing middle-class Chicano organizations as ineffectual. As its first president Gutiérrez took an aggressive stance that employed confrontation and a provocative rhetoric that stressed Chicano oppression and exploitation. MAYO combined an Alinskyite approach with a strong cultural nationalism to attract high school and college students. As the aggressive core of youthful Chicano activism in Texas, it played a leading role in various school walkouts during the late 1960s and in the elections at Crystal City.

MAYO frightened and angered the Anglo elite and stirred more conservative Mexican Americans like Congressman Henry González into active opposition. At the beginning of the 1970s MAYO was absorbed into La Raza Unida Party, which it had generated, and by 1972 only a handful of chapters continued to function. By the end of the 1970s even they had disappeared and many MAYO leaders had assumed important positions in Democratic politics, particularly through a new Tejano pressure organization, Mexican American Democrats. MAYO provided a whole generation of Tejanos with training for political leadership.

See also GUTIÉRREZ, JOSÉ ANGEL; RAZA UNIDA PARTY, LA; ROCKEFELLER FOUNDATION.

FURTHER READING: Castro, Tony. *Chicano Power: The Emergence of Mexican America.* New York: Saturday Review Press, 1974; García, F. Chris, and Rodolfo O. de la Garza. *The Chicano Political Experience: Three Perspectives.* North Scituate, Mass.: Duxbury Press, 1977; Muñoz, Carlos, Jr. *Youth, Identity, Power: The Chicano Movement.* New York: Verso, 1989; Navarro, Armando. *The Mexican American Youth Organization: Avant-Garde of the Chicano Movement in Texas.* Austin: University of Texas Press, 1995; Vigil, Maurilio. *Chicano Politics.* Washington, D.C.: University Press of America, 1978.

MIDWEST, CHICANOS IN. Mexicano agricultural workers began to develop annual migratory patterns from the Texas border region to the Midwest in the early 1900s. During World War I small groups began to overwinter in cities like Chicago, Gary, Detroit, Toledo, and St. Paul. As they settled in these places, some remained in agricultural-related work; others found better-paying jobs in packing plants, steel mills, and auto assembly factories. By the 1920s employers began actively recruiting Mexicanos in Texas for work in the Midwest's expanding industrial economy, not infrequently as unwitting strikebreakers.

Although midwestern Mexicanos tended to cluster in barrios, their long-standing patterns of ethnic isolation and cohesion began to undergo a weakening as they worked, associated, and lived with immigrant workers from various European countries. When the Great Depression descended on the country at the end of the 1920s, midwestern Mexican Americans, having been "last hired," found themselves "first fired." A decade later, reinforced by renewed migration from the Southwest, they were able to make further inroads on industrial jobs because of World War II labor demands.

As only one of a number of ethnic groups recently arrived in the industrial centers, Mexicanos encountered less firmly entrenched negative attitudes toward their civil rights than they had usually faced in the Southwest.

Like southwestern Mexican Americans in the postwar years the growing Chicano population in the Midwest began to develop organizations to protect their rights. They still looked to the Southwest as the fountainhead of Mexican American civil rights activities, and they adopted or adapted the ideas and organizations developed there. During the 1960s the Viva Kennedy movement and then the Delano grape strike had a positive impact on the further articulation of demands for greater equality.

Until the 1970s the Chicano civil rights movement in Texas continued to exert significant influence on the midwestern communities. However, this influence then declined as midwestern leaders began to develop a distinct and somewhat independent course. The establishment of the Midwest Council of La Raza in 1970 was a first milestone in their regional self-identification and separateness. As further migratory waves from the Southwest continued during the 1970s, midwestern Chicanos began a number of ambitious voter registration drives in their expanded communities. With the political clout of these new voters they were able to convince some state legislatures to create commissions that had Mexican American civil rights, problems, and goals in mind. At the same time, within labor unions Chicanos used their movement up the hierarchical ladders to develop leadership skills and to further their political influence.

See also FARM LABOR ORGANIZING COMMITTEE; LIGA PROTECTORA MEXICANA; REPATRIATION.

FURTHER READING: García, Juan R. *Mexicans in the Midwest, 1900–1932.* Tucson: University of Arizona Press, 1996; Santillán, Richard A. "Latino Political Development in the Southwest and the Midwest Regions: A Comparative Overview, 1915–1989." In *Latinos and Political Coalitions: Political Empowerment for the 1990s,* edited by Roberto E. Villarreal and Norma G. Hernández. Westport, Conn.: Greenwood Press, 1991; Valdés, Dennis Nodin. *Al norte: Agricultural Workers in the Great Lakes Region. 1917–1970.* Austin: University of Texas Press, 1991; Vargas, Zaragoza. *Proletarians of the North: A History of Mexican Industrial Workers in Detroit and the Midwest, 1917–1933.* Berkeley: University of California Press, 1993.

MOLINA, GLORIA, 1948– . Gloria Molina was born in Los Angeles and grew up in southern California. After graduating from high school she entered East Los Angeles City College, where she became politically active. She joined the Mexican American Student Association, served as a volunteer in Robert Kennedy's 1968 bid for the presidential nomination, and participated in the National Chicano Moratorium march two years later. Upon receipt of her A.B. from California State University at Los Angeles in 1970, she went to work as a job counselor for the East Los Angeles Community Union.

Strongly influenced by the Chicano Movement, after graduation Molina redoubled her interest in community affairs. She participated actively in the

Latin American Law Enforcement Association and in 1973 became the founding president of the Comisión Femenil de Los Angeles. As national president from 1974 to 1976, she was an energizing force in the commission, developing several social service programs to teach Mexican Americans how to avoid exploitation. Especially concerned about the rights of the poor and children, she was also co-founder of the Centro de Niños in Los Angeles. In addition to engaging in all these activities, she helped organize local Chicano political groups.

Molina's extensive community activities and networking became the vital base for her development into an influential political leader. She rapidly moved from California Democrat Art Torres's administrative assistant to regional director in the Department of Health, Education, and Welfare; and in 1980 she became chief deputy to Willie Brown, at that time the powerful Speaker of the California Assembly. Two years later, after an aggressive grassroots campaign and with heavy financial support from various women's groups, Molina won election to the California Assembly.

The first Chicana to be elected to the California legislature, in her freshman year at Sacramento Molina served on various committees and had 13 of her bills passed. After four years in the California Assembly, in 1987 she ran for a new Los Angeles city council position created to settle a gerrymandering suit filed by the Mexican American Legal Defense and Educational Fund (MALDEF). She won, becoming the first Chicana on the city council. In that position she continued her policy of an energetic "more open politics" approach to representing her constituents.

In 1991 with support from MALDEF and Congressman Edward Roybal, she was elected to the powerful Los Angeles Board of Supervisors, the first Mexican American in the twentieth century and the first woman ever. She promised to continue to be a grassroots activist who would shake up the board—and she has done just that as an issue-oriented, confrontational representative with a deep concern for community empowerment. She has pushed community concerns about drugs, street gangs, and affordable housing while also aggressively demanding greater accountability from county officials.

Molina has been the recipient of various awards for her community service and strong efforts in defense of civil rights. She is closely connected to the Los Angeles MALDEF, on whose board she sits. Always independent, candid, and direct, she energetically pursues liberal causes, a course that sometimes put her at odds with some of her more conservative Mexican American constituents.

See also CHICANAS; LEADERSHIP; ROYBAL, EDWARD.

FURTHER READING: Bonilla-Santiago, Gloria. *Breaking Ground and Barriers: Hispanic Women Developing Effective Leadership*. San Diego: Marín Publications, 1992; Díaz, Katherine. "Hispanic of the Year: Gloria Molina." *Caminos* 4, no. 1–2 (January-February 1983); "Galaxy of Rising Stars." *Time* 138, no. 20 (18 November 1991):73; Mills, Kay. "Gloria Molina." *Ms* 13 (January 1985):80–81, 114; Olivera, Mercedes. "The New Hispanic Woman." *Vista* 2, no. 11 (5 July 1987): 6–8; Telgen, Diane, and Jim Kamp, eds. *Notable Hispanic American Women*. Detroit: Gale Research, 1993; Tobar, Héctor. "Gloria Molina and the Politics of Anger." *Los Angeles Times Magazine*, 3 January 1993, 10–13, 32–34.

MONTALBÁN, RICARDO, 1920– . In recognition of his contributions to the social rights and economic improvement of Mexican Americans, Ricardo Montalbán was given the Golden Aztec Award by the Mexican American Opportunity Foundation in 1988.

Born in Mexico City of middle-class Spanish-immigrant parents, at 17 Montalbán followed his older brother to Los Angeles, California, where he began his acting career. A small part in Tallulah Bankhead's Broadway play *Her Cardboard Lover* enabled him to develop a film career in Mexico; and his success there led to a long-term contract with Metro-Goldwyn-Mayer (MGM) after World War II; in 1953 he was dropped by MGM, and his career began a decade of doldrums in the mid-1950s.

Influenced by the rising tide of ethnic awareness in the civil rights atmosphere of the latter 1960s, Montalbán became increasingly concerned about the way Hollywood depicted la raza as well as its continuing reluctance to hire Latino actors. Although not a social activist, early in 1969 he led some fellow Hispanic actors and businesspeople in founding Nosotros, an organization committed primarily to promoting Latino job opportunities in the film industry. He was elected Nosotros's first president. Nosotros later added the goal of improving civil rights of Latinos, and Montalbán did some commercials in Spanish for the Southwest Voter Registration Project, urging Latinos to register and to vote.

Under Montalbán's presidency Nosotros achieved some improvements for Latinos, but he felt his leadership role in the organization caused him to become the victim of a Hollywood backlash. At the end of the 1970s television came to his rescue with long-term leads in *Fantasy Island* and *Dynasty* as well as substantial roles in many other individual TV presentations during the 1980s and 1990s.

See also ORGANIZATIONS.

FURTHER READING: Duarte, Patricia. "Welcome to Ricardo's Reality." *Nosotros* 3, no. 9 (October 1979); Montalbán, Ricardo (with Bob Thomas). *Reflections: A Life in Two Worlds*. Garden City, N.Y.: Doubleday & Co., 1980; "Ricardo Montalbán." *La Luz* 1, no. 9 (January 1973):42–45.

MONTEMAYOR, ALICE DICKERSON, 1902–1989. As a charter member of the League of United Latin American Citizens (LULAC), Ladies Division, Alice Montemayor was aggressively active during the 1930s, particularly in promoting women's rights and combating attitudes of male superiority within the organization. In 1937 she was elected second national vice president, the first woman to hold a position in LULAC not specifically designated for women. She used her position to foster greater opportunities and more substantial roles for women within LULAC and to establish more women's councils. A staunch feminist, she felt that LULAC suffered severely from the egotism of its male leaders and their petty internal strife. After the 1930s she turned to other, noncivic activities.

See also LEADERSHIP; LEAGUE OF UNITED LATIN AMERICAN CITIZENS; MACHUCA, ESTHER NIETO.

FURTHER READING: *Las Mujeres: Mexican American / Chicana Women.* Windsor, Calif.: National Women's History Project, 1991; Tyler, Ron, ed. *The New Handbook of Texas.* Vol. 4. Austin: Texas State Historical Association, 1996.

MÓNTEZ, PHILIP, 1931– . Founder-president of the Association of Mexican American Educators Phil Móntez has been active as a civil rights advocate and teacher. A high school and college professor as well as a research psychologist, he also served as director of the Foundation of Mexican American Studies. As a result of his involvement in the Chicano fight for civil rights, in 1967 he was appointed director of the western field office of the U.S. Commission on Civil Rights by President Lyndon Johnson. Móntez is the author of various works on issues in biculturalism and cultural differences.

See also BILINGUALISM/BICULTURALISM.

FURTHER READING: Pycior, Julie Leininger. *LBJ & Mexican Americans: The Paradox of Power.* Austin: University of Texas Press, 1997.

MORENO, LUISA, 1907–1990. Guatemalan by birth, raised in Mexico, and educated mostly in the United States, Luisa Moreno became one of the early twentieth-century leaders in the Mexican American struggle for civil rights. As a result of personal experience working in a New York sweatshop, she began organizing raza garment workers for the American Federation of Labor (AFL) in the 1930s. Because of red-baiting in the AFL, in 1937 she joined the Congress of Industrial Organizations (CIO), helping organize workers in beets, cotton, canning, and pecan shelling. In the following year she took over a leadership role in the San Antonio pecan shellers' strike, replacing Emma Tenayuca.

After the strike Moreno began to devote more of her time and energies to the broader task of fighting discrimination and defending the civil rights of Mexican Americans. To this end, with Bert Corona and others, she helped found a new type of organization, El Congreso de los Pueblos de Habla Española, primarily concerned with achieving political power through education, voter registration, and ultimately the electoral process. However, the Congreso was short-lived, dying out during World War II because of internal conflict, the wartime climate, and Federal Bureau of Investigation harassment.

During the war Moreno also took an active part in organizing the Sleepy Lagoon Defense Committee, headed by Carey McWilliams, and helped publicize the vicious attacks by servicemen on "zoot suiters" in Los Angeles. Meanwhile, she continued her work as a labor union organizer among Chicanos, primarily in agriculture and related industries. As a vice president in the CIO and an affiliate, the radical United Cannery, Agricultural, Packinghouse, and Allied Workers of America, she spearheaded a committee investigating discriminatory practices in the workplace. In 1947 she retired from union activities, highly and widely respected for her skills in organizing and conciliating.

In the red-baiting McCarthyite years of the early 1950s Moreno's foreign birth and her earlier activity in the left-wing labor movement made her a natural target for the House Un-American Activities Committee; she was deported as an undesirable alien under the terms of the McCarran-Walter Immigration and Nationality Act of 1952. Luisa Moreno never returned to the United States. At the end of the 1950s she participated briefly in the early days of Fidel Castro's revolution in Cuba and then left for Mexico, where she lived quietly in retirement until she died a quarter of a century later.

See also CONGRESO DE LOS PUEBLOS DE HABLA ESPAÑOLA; CORONA, BERT; SLEEPY LAGOON; TENAYUCA, EMMA.

FURTHER READING: Camarillo, Albert. *Chicanos in California*. San Francisco: Boyd & Fraser, 1984; García, Mario T. *Memories of Chicano History: The Life and Narrative of Bert Corona*. Berkeley: University of California Press, 1994; Hardy, Gayle J., *American Women Civil Rights Activists*. Jefferson, N.C.: McFarland & Co., 1993; Mirandé, Alfredo, and Evangelina Enríquez. *La Chicana: The Mexican-American Woman*. Chicago: University of Chicago Press, 1979; Ruiz, Vicki L. *Cannery Women, Cannery Lives: Mexican Women, Unionization, and the California Food Processing Industry, 1930–1950*. Albuquerque: University of New Mexico Press, 1987.

MORÍN, RAÚL R., 1913–1967. After his discharge from the armed services at the end of World War II, Raúl Morín returned to Los Angeles, California, where he soon became acutely aware of the continuing discrimination against Mexican Americans. As an officer in the American G.I. Forum (and later in the Mexican American Political Association), he noted the pervasive continuance of discrimination against Chicanos and denial of their civil rights. Looking about to see how he might help remedy this situation and improve race relations, he began to write about the service and valor of Mexican Americans in World War II and Korea. He completed his account in the mid-1950s but found publishers uninterested in his book, which he titled *Among the Valiant*. In 1963 his work finally saw publication through the efforts of the American G.I. Forum.

Widely active in Chicano organizations, in veteran and civic groups, and in politics, Morín ran for the California state senate but lost. However, he was able somewhat to assuage his concerns for la raza through extensive and energetic activity on various local boards and committees. By the time of his death he had become widely known in the state for his sincere and abiding interest in defending the rights of Mexican Americans.

See also AMERICAN G.I. FORUM; DISCRIMINATION; MEXICAN AMERICAN POLITICAL ASSOCIATION.

FURTHER READING: Morín, Raúl R. *Among the Valiant: Mexican Americans in World War II and Korea*. Los Angeles: Bordon Publishing Co., 1963.

MOVIMIENTO, EL. The Chicano Movement of the 1960s and 1970s had a variety of political, economic, and social origins and goals; and it strongly stressed civil rights in all three areas. It was conceived by many as a peaceful but revolutionary move to end fundamental inequities in American society faced by Mexican Americans. Sustained at first by the expectations of Chicano veterans of World War II and the Korean conflict, during its early years it leaned heavily on the example of the black civil rights movement for strategies and tactics. For leadership it sought role models like Dr. Martin Luther King, Jr. César Chávez came closest to that model and closest to becoming the preeminent leader of the movimiento, but his low-key, nonviolent stance failed to attract many of the more aggressive youthful activists. Further, his chief concern, for rural or semi-rural Chicanos, had limited appeal for urban barrio dwellers, now an overwhelming majority among Mexican Americans.

The bulk of Movement activities took place at the community level and on high school and college campuses. A particularly notable aspect of the movimiento was the prominent role of students, most of whom felt that they were being ignored by most older Mexican American leaders as well as by Anglos. Within the Movement Chicanas asserted their equality with males and demanded an end to their inferior position and to demeaning machismo. All stressed their *chicanismo*, a vaguely defined and culturally oriented *mexicanidad* that underscored a view of themselves as a conquered people. With confrontational youthful leadership they marched and demonstrated for equality of educational opportunity, which they held as a vital civil right and the key to gaining their rightful economic and political place in the United States. Too young to be able to express their dissatisfaction through the ballot, they manifested their unhappiness through high school "blowouts," university sit-ins, direct confrontation, and civil disobedience. Their leaders dared to question the "system," the senior Mexican American political leadership, and indeed all authority. They demanded equality of treatment and opportunity through extensive reforms, particularly in education.

Disenchanted with the U.S. role in the Vietnam conflict and appalled at the high Chicano casualty rate among soldiers, younger Mexican Americans became highly politicized, worked in voter registration and get-out-the-vote drives, and ran for political office as means of achieving greater political rights. In their search for dignity and a positive identity many paradoxically both demanded equal rights as U.S. citizens and at the same time espoused degrees of political nationalism. La Raza Unida Party, which they engendered, for a few years raised hopes for the creation of an influential third force in U.S. politics.

To a degree many of their demands were met. Although the movimiento did not achieve all its goals in the areas of political rights, education, land ownership, and institutional racism, incremental gains were made. This limited success, along with internal cleavage arising from destructive power struggles among the leaders and an inability to come to an agreement on ideology, goals, and strategies, served to bring about the decline of the Movement. Its failure to expand the development of strong grassroots in the community also weakened it. As the country was swept by a tide of neoconservatism in the 1970s, many of its members turned to less oppositional organizations that focused on voter registration and election turnout, electing Chicano officials, court challenges, and political lobbying. The ballot box and the courts largely replaced confrontation and protest as ways to achieve civil rights.

During its decade of intense activity the Chicano Movement strengthened cultural pride and ethnic identity among Mexican Americans as it enhanced group consciousness. At least equally important, it initiated and nourished a heightened awareness of and concern for civil rights. That concern continues, as a legacy of the movimiento.

See also LEADERSHIP; RAZA UNIDA PARTY, LA; STUDENT ACTIVISM; STUDENT ORGANIZATIONS.

FURTHER READING: García, Ignacio M. *Chicanismo! The Forging of a Militant Ethos Among Mexican Americans.* Tucson: University of Arizona Press, 1997; García, Juan A. "The Chicano Movement: Its Legacy for Politics and Policy." In *Chicanas/Chicanos at the Crossroads: Social, Economic, and Political Change,* edited by David Maciel and Isidro D. Ortiz. Tucson: University of Arizona Press, 1996; García, Richard A. "The Chicano Movement and the Mexican American Community, 1972–1978." *Socialist Review* 40–41 (July-October 1978):117–136; Marín, Marguerite V. *Social Protest in an Urban Barrio: A Study of the Chicano Movement, 1966–1974.* Lanham, Md.: University Press of America, 1991; Muñoz, Carlos, Jr. *Youth, Identity, Power: The Chicano Movement.* New York: Verso, 1989; *El Plan de Santa Barbara.* Santa Barbara, Calif.: La Causa Publications,

1969; Rendón, Armando. *Chicano Manifesto*. 25th anniversary ed. Berkeley, Calif.: Ollin & Associates, 1996; Rosen, Gerald. "The Development of the Chicano Movement in Los Angeles from 1967–1969." *Aztlán* 4, no. 1 (Spring 1973):155–183; Ruiz, Vicki L. *From Out of the Shadows: Mexican Women in Twentieth-Century America*. New York: Oxford University Press, 1998; "The Struggle for Chicano Liberation." *International Socialist Review* 32 (November 1971):25–37.

MOVIMIENTO ESTUDIANTIL CHICANO DE AZTLÁN (MEChA). MEChA was established in 1969 at the University of California's Santa Barbara campus by combining the existing Chicano campus organizations. Groups such as the United Mexican American Students and Mexican American Youth Organization became chapters in the new umbrella organization. MEChA leaders developed and articulated the Plan de Santa Barbara, outlining the organization's philosophy and educational goals.

Leaders of the Chicano Coordinating Council on Higher Education, which hosted the three-day conference, saw MEChA as a potential spark to initiate educational and political change, both on campus and in the community. This dual goal led later to internal bickering and divisions that widened as time went on. The attitude toward Chicanas also aggravated tensions within the organization. In the 1980s MEChA turned away from community politics and began concentrating more closely on campus issues, particularly affirmative action. Internal ideological splits continued to plague the campus groups. Although MEChA had limited success outside of California and has declined since the 1970s, it remains the principal Chicano student organization.

See also PLAN DE SANTA BARBARA; STUDENT ORGANIZATIONS.

FURTHER READING: Gómez-Quiñones, Juan. *Mexican Students Por La Raza: The Chicano Student Movement in Southern California 1967–1977*. Santa Barbara, Calif.: Editorial La Causa, 1978; Muñoz, Carlos, Jr. *Youth, Identity, Power: The Chicano Movement*. New York: Verso, 1989; *El Plan de Santa Barbara*. Santa Barbara, Calif.: La Causa Publications, 1969; Valle, María Eva. "MEChA and the Transformation of Chicano Student Activism: Generational Change, Conflict, and Continuity." Ph.D. diss., University of California at San Diego, 1996.

MUÑIZ, RAMSEY, 1943– . A founding member of La Raza Unida Party (LRUP) and activist recruiter for it in north Texas, Ramsey Muñiz was a charismatic and articulate young Chicano lawyer from Waco. Within LRUP Muñiz's popularity rivaled that of José Angel Gutiérrez. After law school, in the late 1960s he became an administrative assistant in the Model Cities program, from which he resigned to run for the governorship of Texas as the LRUP candidate in 1972. He ran a poor people's campaign in the election, appealing to a grassroots Chicano yearning for social justice. Although he garnered less than 7 percent of the ballots in a three-cornered race, his 214,000 votes nearly caused the first Republican gubernatorial victory in Texas since the 1870s. For many his showing in the election indicated the potential of the electoral path to social justice and greater civil rights for Chicanos. His later conviction on drug charges seemingly ended a promising career.

See also RAZA UNIDA PARTY, LA; TEXAS.

FURTHER READING: Castro, Tony. *Chicano Power: The Emergence of Mexican America*. New York: Saturday Review Press, 1974; García, F. Chris, and Rodolfo O. de la Garza. *The Chicano Political Experience: Three Perspectives*. North Scituate, Mass.: Duxbury Press, 1977; García, Ignacio M. *United We Win: The Rise and Fall of La Raza Unida Party*. Tucson: University of Arizona, MASRC, 1989.

MURIETA, JOAQUÍN, fl. 1850s. The legendary California bandit–folk hero Joaquín Murieta was probably a composite developed by romantic writers from a number of Joaquíns and bandits. According to the legend Murieta was forced into banditry during the gold rush period as a means of avenging the rape and murder of his wife.

What is historically certain is that early in 1853 the state legislature created a temporary ranger force to capture bandits known as the Five Joaquíns. Nearing the end of their three-month authorization, the rangers encountered and shot up a small group of Mexicanos. They identified the body of one as Joaquín Murieta and preserved his head in a large jar of whiskey. A year later a pulp fiction writer, John Rollin Ridge, wrote a largely fictional account of *The Life and Adventures of Joaquín Murieta, the Celebrated California Bandit*. The success of his novel led to numerous reprints, pirated editions, and elaborations on its somewhat Robin Hood theme.

Fascination with the Murieta story in its many variations and the absence of documentation have continued down to the present. The narrative has been the basis for movies, plays, epic poems, and even a biography. In the process any vestiges of the historical Murieta have been lost, but to many Californios he had become a powerful symbol of the continuing denial of their civil liberties. Inevitably, perhaps, in the 1960s the movimiento adopted him as one of its heroes.

FURTHER READING: Jackson, Joseph Henry. *Bad Company*. New York: Harcourt, Brace and Co., 1939; Latta, Frank. *Joaquín Murieta and His Horse Gang*. Santa Cruz, Calif.: Bear State Books, 1980; Nadeau, Remi. *The Real Joaquín Murieta*. Corona del Mar, Calif.: Trans-Anglo Books, 1974; Ridge, John Rollin. *The Life and Adventures of Joaquín Murieta, the Celebrated California Bandit*. New ed. Norman: University of Oklahoma Press, 1955.

MUTUALISTAS. Mutualistas were Mexicano protective self-help social groups that evolved in the second half of the 1800s. Highly popular toward the end of the century, they developed extensively throughout the towns and villages of the Southwest. Their primary function was to provide funeral benefits and other insurance protection. Since they grew out of the Mexican cultural experience, they also became the basis for organizing popular festive occasions like Cinco de Mayo and Diez y Seis de Septiembre. Additionally, they supplied a convenient focus for socializing and a forum for the discussion of community problems. During World War I they began to take on additional tasks such as providing legal help and job referrals. Mutualistas began to decline during the 1930s and all but faded away by midcentury. Some were important in the development of labor and community organizations and local civil rights groups.

See also ORGANIZATIONS.

FURTHER READING: Hernández, José Amaro. *Mutual Aid for Survival: The Case of the Mexican American.* Malabar, Fla.: Robert A. Krieger, 1983; Rivera, José A. "Self-Help as Mutual Protection: The Development of Hispanic Fraternal Benefit Societies." *Journal of Applied Behavioral Science* 23, no. 3 (1987):387–396.

N

NATIONAL ASSOCIATION OF LATINO ELECTED AND AP-POINTED OFFICIALS (NALEO). NALEO is an issue-oriented national organization founded in 1975 to develop a clearly articulated raza lobbying voice and pressure group in the nation's capital. Fairly simple in organization, with an elected president and a secretary-treasurer as well as a national director, it was largely the brainchild of southern California congressman Edward Roybal. He envisioned it as a nationwide association of Latino government officials who would network and combine their efforts in pursuit of important objectives like civil rights, voter education and registration, educational and social welfare, and economic betterment. Although founded by Mexican American Democratic politicians, NALEO is nonpartisan.

NALEO's concern is primarily with issues, so it monitors and analyzes government policies and proposed legislative action, particularly as they affect Latinos. Financing is secured principally from dues and sponsorship fees, and to carry out its objectives both individual and corporate sponsors are solicited. Membership in NALEO is open to all appointed and elected officials, and associate membership is available to anyone interested in helping to further the organization's goals. It reports its views on issues and government policies to members via a quarterly newsletter.

See also ROYBAL, EDWARD.

FURTHER READING: Eherenhalt, Alan, ed. *Politics in America*. Washington, D.C.: Congressional Quarterly, 1983; Gonzales, Sylvia A. *Hispanic American Voluntary Organizations*. Westport, Conn.: Greenwood Press, 1985; "NALEO: Challenging and Moving Ahead." *Caminos* 5, no. 3 (March 1984):36–37; www.naleo.org.

NATIONAL CATHOLIC CONFERENCE FOR INTERRACIAL JUSTICE. The National Catholic Conference, established in 1960 to replace the Catholic Interracial Council, focuses on goals of justice and equality for minority groups in American society. Initially concerned with black-white relations and interracial dialogue, at the end of the 1980s it broadened its scope specifically to include concerns of Mexican Americans and other minorities. Today it is involved in raising sensitivity within the Anglo community to the problems of all minorities. It has advocated greater multiculturalism within the Catholic Church and lobbied for federal civil rights legislation.

FURTHER READING: *New Catholic Encyclopedia.* Vol. 10. New York: McGraw-Hill, 1967.

NATIONAL CHICANO MORATORIUM, 1970. The national Chicano moratorium arose out of an escalating concern about U.S. military involvement in Vietnam and the high level of Chicano casualties. It was also a response to widely held and deeply felt Mexican American grievances and to long-suffered rebuffs from the U.S. government. In December 1969 a Denver anti-draft conference began laying preliminary plans for the demonstration, and the following March Corky Gonzales's second Chicano Youth Conference in Denver finalized the blueprint for the Los Angeles march, which was to climax numerous earlier local demonstrations throughout the Southwest.

In August 1970 more than 25,000 Chicanos from all over the country, the largest group of Chicano demonstrators yet assembled, met in East Los Angeles to march and rally in protest against the Vietnam War. Because the war had politicized and polarized even middle-class Mexican Americans, the national moratorium march was supported by most community organizations.

The rally was closely monitored to avoid problems. However, trouble in a liquor store on the march route precipitated a massive police intrusion that immediately extended to Laguna Park, where the early marchers were enjoying a late lunch while listening to music and speakers like Corky Gonzales. Some 500 helmeted police and sheriff deputies began a sweep of the park. Tear gas canisters were fired. Panic ensued. Rock and bottle throwing in the park quickly developed into rioting, vandalizing, and looting on the Whittier Boulevard route and led to the arrest of several hundred marchers and three deaths. Among those killed was veteran journalist and news director of Los Angeles TV station KMEX Rubén Salazar. The coroner's inquest into Salazar's death turned into an attack on the moratorium march, and no indictment resulted. Many Anglos as well as Chicanos felt that Mexican American civil rights had again been brushed aside.

The moratorium was followed in the ensuing months by a number of small outbreaks of violence and incidents between demonstrators and police. These events served to strengthen ethnic nationalism and increased raza solidarity. They also helped attract Chicanos to the new Raza Unida Party, particularly in California.

See also CIVIL RIGHTS ABUSE; SALAZAR, RUBÉN.

FURTHER READING: Acuña, Rodolfo. *Occupied America: A History of Chicanos*. 3rd ed. New York: Harper & Row, 1988; Escobar, Edward J. "The Dialects of Repression: The Los Angeles Police Department and the Chicano Movement, 1968–1971." *Journal of American History* 79, no. 4 (March 1993):1483–1514; Herrera, Albert. "The National Chicano Moratorium and the Death of Rubén Salazar." In *The Chicanos: Mexican American Voices*, edited by Ed Ludwig and James Santibáñez. Baltimore: Penguin Books, 1971; Salazar, Rubén. *Border Correspondent: Selected Writings, 1955–1970*. Edited by Mario T. García. Berkeley: University of California Press, 1995; Sifuentes, Frank. "La muerte de Rubén Salazar." *Regeneración* 1, no. 6 (1970):8–9, 12.

NATIONAL CONGRESS OF HISPANIC AMERICAN CITIZENS (NCHAC). NCHAC was established in 1971 by a group of Mexican American leaders that included Polly Baca, Raúl Yzaguirre, and Paul Montemayor. Headquartered in Washington, D.C., the organization aimed to provide a highly visible lobby for Mexican American concerns before the executive, legislative, and judicial branches at both federal and state levels. The Congress was soon restructured to reflect more closely the interests of the broader U.S. Latino community. Concerned with bilingual education, housing needs, and voting rights, in its short life NCHAC provided leadership for various organizations through workshops on these issues as well as on the lobbying process itself. By the end of the 1970s the NCHAC had expired, partly as a result of internal leadership conflict. Its agenda was taken over by the Congressional Hispanic Caucus and the National Association of Latino Elected and Appointed Officials.

See also BACA, POLLY; BILINGUAL EDUCATION; YZAGUIRRE, RAÚL.

FURTHER READING: Gonzales, Sylvia A. *Hispanic American Voluntary Organizations*. Westport, Conn.: Greenwood Press, 1985.

NATIONAL COUNCIL OF LA RAZA. With a Ford Foundation grant of $630,000 the National Council was initiated in 1968 as the Southwest Council of La Raza. It was envisioned as an umbrella organization with the broad goal of ending the exclusion of Mexican Americans from the American mainstream. Its founders planned to provide a loud, persistent voice for community concerns and objectives. During its early years the National Council worked to strengthen Chicano organizations in the Southwest by providing leadership, subgrants, and other support for community empowerment. After moving from San Antonio to Washington, D.C., because of its expanded field of activity, in 1973 the name was changed to reflect its wider scope.

A nonprofit, nongovernmental group, the National Council, initially devoted most of its energies to efforts at bridging the chasm between Chicanos and Anglo society by promoting community organizations and making seed funds available to various civil rights groups including the Mexican American Legal Defense and Educational Fund (MALDEF) and the Southwest Voter Registration Educational Project. Among its successful early efforts was the creation of La Raza Investment Corporation, a Mexican American owned and operated small business investment company that provided loans and managerial assistance to barrio entrepreneurs. The agency hoped thereby both to facilitate the Mexican American move into the mainstream and to destroy denigrating stereotypes.

Under the leadership of Raúl Yzaguirre since 1972, the National Council has grown to become an institution of high credibility and great influence. Its more than 220 affiliated groups make it one of the largest Latino umbrella organizations in the country, and its civil rights network provides invaluable information to community groups. For more than two decades it has fought for greater educational opportunity and better housing for Hispanics. Through its consistent long-term support of voter registration it has helped give Latinos a stronger voice in government. Along with MALDEF, it is acknowledged by most Chicanos as a leading civil rights organization speaking for the community.

Today from its Washington headquarters the Council continues to assist in the development of various community programs with research and support. It also is concerned with job discrimination and other civil rights abuses, bilingual education, and Chicano voting patterns. Its overall emphasis continues to be on the economic, social, and health betterment of Chicanos.

See also MEXICAN AMERICAN LEGAL DEFENSE AND EDUCATIONAL FUND; ORGANIZATIONS; VOTING; YZAGUIRRE, RAÚL.

FURTHER READING: Gonzales, Sylvia A. *Hispanic American Voluntary Organizations.* Westport, Conn.: Greenwood Press, 1985; Martínez, Douglas. "Yzaguirre at the Helm." *Américas* 32, no. 6–7 (June–July 1980):49; "National Council of La Raza." *La Luz* 4, no. 5 (September-October 1975): 6A; Ortiz, Isidro D. "Latino Organizational Leadership in the Era of Reaganomics." In *Latinos and Political Coalitions: Political Empowerment for the 1990s,* edited by Roberto E. Villarreal and Norma G. Hernández. Westport, Conn.: Greenwood Press, 1991; Sierra, Christine Marie. "The Political Transformation of a Minority Organization: The Council of La Raza, 1965–1980." Ph.D. diss., Stanford University, 1983; Weise-Peredo, Martha. "An American Institution Three Decades Strong." *Agenda* 13, no. 4 (Spring 1998):1–2. Also entire spring 1998 issue of *Agenda*; www.nclr.org.

NATIONAL ORGANIZATION OF MEXICAN AMERICAN SERVICES (NOMAS). Founded in 1964 by Raúl Yzaguirre, NOMAS was one of the earlier institutions in the movimiento to articulate at the national level the concerns of Mexican Americans. Its goal was to coordinate the disparate efforts of the many local and regional Chicano groups as well as to make information about federal policies available to the community. Crippled by President Lyndon Johnson's ignoring its leadership during the 1966 Equal Employment Opportunity Commission meeting that led to the Albuquerque walkout of 50 Chicano leaders, it lingered on for a couple more years. NOMAS made three important contributions to the Mexican American civil rights movement: it provided some young Chicanos with training in organizational techniques, it opened lines to sources of private funding like the Ford Foundation, and it prepared the way for the National Council of La Raza.

See also ALBUQUERQUE WALKOUT; YZAGUIRRE, RAÚL.

FURTHER READING: Moore, Joan, and Harry Pachon. *Hispanics in the United States*. Englewood Cliffs, N.J.: Prentice-Hall, 1985.

NATURALIZATION. See CITIZENSHIP.

NEW MEXICO. As a result of Francis Drake's voyage around the world in 1579, Nuevo México was founded to forestall possible English control of the supposed Straits of Anián between the Atlantic Ocean and the Pacific Ocean. At the end of the 1500s Spanish-speaking settlers under Juan de Oñate trekked up from central Mexico, and in 1609 Santa Fe was established. During the colonial period mining potential and missionary activity among the Indians attracted settlers from central Mexico. In addition, settlement of the area was encouraged by Spain because of her continuing fear of English and then French intrusion. As a result, when the Treaty of Guadalupe Hidalgo made the region part of the United States in 1848, Nuevo México was by far the most populous area on the northern frontier, with about 60,000 Spanish-Mexican inhabitants, some 80 percent of the total northern frontier Mexicano population. Today New Mexico has a larger percentage of Hispanics than any other state—over 36 percent.

In order to avoid possible political control by the large Hispanic American population, in 1850 New Mexico was given a territorial government by the U.S. Congress rather than statehood like California. Throughout its territorial period most upper-level officials were Anglo appointees, but Nuevomexicanos managed to maintain a degree of economic and political power at middle and lower levels as is evidenced by the large number of Hispanic legislators, judges, and lesser officials.

In 1912, after more than 60 years of effort, New Mexico finally achieved statehood with a constitution that went far beyond the Treaty of Guadalupe Hidalgo in its guarantees of raza civil and cultural rights. The new constitution was influenced by New Mexico's long, unbroken Hispanic traditions and has resulted in less feeling of cultural identity loss among Nuevomexicanos.

At the same time, however, Nuevomexicanos began to see both their economic position and political influence eroding as they lost lands and as integration of the territory into the national economy began in the late 1800s, attracting eastern capital and settlers. New Mexico also attracted numerous Anglo in-migrants from other states, especially Texas, Oklahoma, and Kansas. These new New Mexicans, who settled mostly in the eastern half of the state, soon came to dominate the entire state both economically and politically.

As a result of the in-migration Nuevomexicanos had lost their numerical majority by the 1930s. This demographic shift, especially heavy after World War II, led to heightened ethnic tension because of widespread Hispano concerns about their loss of political influence and power. Although most Nuevomexicanos who ran for governor in the postwar era failed to win, in 1974 Jerry Apodaca was successful in his bid as was Toney Anaya eight years later. As governor liberal Anaya was able to put through strong affirmative action legislation.

Throughout the whole of their twentieth-century history Nuevomexicanos were elected lieutenant governors, state legislators, mayors, and lesser officers and were appointed to federal, state, and local courts, agencies, and commissions in considerable numbers. They have, at one time or another, held nearly every state elective office, have served at all levels in the state judiciary, and have won election to the U.S. Senate and House of Representatives. They have also taken important, if generally conservative, leadership roles in the state's Democratic and Republican parties. As a result, the Raza Unida Party had relatively little success in New Mexico, and problem-oriented organizations like the League of United Latin American Citizens have aroused no great enthusiasm. Reies López Tijerina, the state's most widely known contemporary citizen, found little favor with the Hispanic elites, and conservative U.S. senator Joseph Montoya publicly denounced him and his Alianza.

Though there is still room for improvement, during the past decade New Mexico experienced considerable increase in the number of Hispanic elected officials. This change has come about as a result of expanded political activism by Hispanics, a greater acceptance of Nuevomexicanos within the Democratic Party, growing political involvement on the part of Hispanic voters, and their bloc-voting.

See also ALIANZA FEDERAL DE PUEBLOS LIBRES; CHÁVEZ, DENNIS; LARRAZOLO, OCTAVIANO; POLITICAL PARTICIPATION.

FURTHER READING: Burma, John H. "The Present Status of the Spanish-Americans of New Mexico." *Social Forces* 28 (December 1949):133–138; Cortés, Carlos. *The New Mexican Hispano*. Reprint, New York: Arno Press, 1974; Cummings, Richard M. *Grito! Reies Tijerina and the New Mexico Land Grant War of*

1967. Indianapolis: Bobbs-Merrill, 1970; Fincher, Ernest B. *Spanish-Americans as a Political Factor in New Mexico. 1912–1950*. Reprint, New York: Arno Press, 1974; García, F. Chris. "New Mexico: Urban Politics in a State of Varied Political Cultures." In *Politics in the Urban Southwest*, edited by Robert D. Wrinkle. Albuquerque: University of New Mexico, Division of Government Research, 1971; Knowlton, Clark S. "Changing Spanish-American Villages in Northern New Mexico." *Sociology and Social Research* 53, no. 4 (July 1969):455–474; Ortiz, Roxanne Dunbar. *Roots of Resistance: Land Tenure in New Mexico, 1680–1980*. Chicano Studies Center, University of California at Los Angeles, 1980; Rosenbaum, Robert J. *Mexicano Versus Americano: A Study of Hispanic-American Resistance to Anglo-American Control in New Mexico Territory*. Austin: University of Texas Press, 1972; Simmons, Marc. *New Mexico: An Interpretive History*. Albuquerque: University of New Mexico Press, 1988; Vigil, Maurilio E. *The Hispanics of New Mexico: Essays on History and Culture*. Bristol, Ind.: Wyndham Hall Press, 1984; Zeleny, Carolyn. *Relations between the Spanish-Americans and Anglo-Americans in New Mexico*. Reprint, New York: Arno Press, 1974.

NEWMAN, PHILIP, 1916– . Judge Philip Newman was born in Mexico City of a Mexican mother and an American father. In the late 1920s the family moved to southern California, where his father, who became a lawyer, earned the Order of the Águila Azteca for his services to Mexican nationals. Following in his father's footsteps, Philip became a lawyer who specialized in immigration cases. He also was active in the Mexican American community, helping to establish the Community Service Organization in the Los Angeles area.

In 1964 Governor "Jerry" Brown appointed Newman a judge in the Los Angeles municipal court. In the mid-1960s he received national recognition of his expertise in Chicano civil rights concerns and problems.

See also COMMUNITY SERVICE ORGANIZATION.

FURTHER READING: Martínez, Al. *Rising Voices: Profiles of Hispano-American Lives*. New York: New American Library, 1974.

O

OBLEDO, MARIO G., 1932–   . The recipient of numerous kudos for his work in the area of civil rights, Texas-born Mario Obledo came from a poor Mexican immigrant family. He worked his way through a college education in pharmacology, interrupted by four years of service in the Korean conflict, and then studied for the law while he worked as a pharmacist.

At age 33 Obledo received appointment as an assistant attorney general for the state of Texas, and three years later, in 1969, he was elected the general counsel and second president of the Mexican American Legal Defense and Educational Fund (MALDEF), which he had helped establish. He also continued to take an active part in the Southwest Voter Registration Education Project. During his tenure in MALDEF he established the practice of taking cases of school segregation, jury exclusion, welfare rights, and job discrimination to the U.S. Supreme Court on constitutional grounds, basing arguments heavily on the Fourteenth Amendment guarantees.

In 1975 Obledo became secretary of the Department of Health and Welfare for the state of California, to which MALDEF's headquarters had moved. Seven years later he was unsuccessful in his bid to become the Democratic Party's candidate for governor, winning only 3 percent of the votes in the primary. In 1983 he was elected president of the League of United Latin American Citizens, in which he had long been active and held important positions. After his two-year term in office he stepped down to enter private law practice in Sacramento. He retains his interest in Chicano civil rights concerns.

See also LEAGUE OF UNITED LATIN AMERICAN CITIZENS; MEXICAN AMERICAN LEGAL DEFENSE AND EDUCATIONAL FUND; SOUTHWEST VOTER REGISTRATION EDUCATION PROJECT.

FURTHER READING: "A Close Look at Mario Obledo." *Latino* 54, no. 5. (August–September 1983):10; Muñoz, Carlos, Jr. *Youth, Identity, Power: The Chicano Movement.* New York: Verso, 1989; Whisler, Kirk. "Mario Obledo." *Caminos* 3, no. 4. (April 1982):18–20; *Who's Who among Hispanic Americans.* 3rd ed. Detroit: Gale Research, 1994.

OLIVÁREZ, GRACIELA, 1928–1987. A high school dropout at 16, Graciela Olivárez continued her education in a Phoenix business school. A job as Phoenix's first female disc jockey soon led to a position as women's program director for Spanish-language station KIFN, which in turn complemented her organizational work in the Chicano community. During the 1960s she became increasingly involved in the civil rights movement.

At a southwestern civil rights conference Olivárez so impressed Theodore Hesburgh, president of Notre Dame University, that he invited her to come to Notre Dame to study law. In 1970, at age 42, she became the first woman to receive a law degree from that institution. Returning to the Southwest, she continued her commitment as an activist in the civil rights movement, taught law at the University of New Mexico, and held positions of leadership in several government agencies. Because of her strong advocacy of civil rights, she was named director of the Community Services Administration by President Jimmy Carter in 1977. She left that job three years later to accept a position as senior consultant for a national service organization, United Way of America, where she continued her work fighting for the poor, powerless, and especially the elderly.

In 1982 Olivárez was named to a bipartisan board to oversee federal enforcement of legislation prohibiting discrimination based on race, ethnicity, age, sex, and religion. She also served on the boards of the American Civil Liberties Union, the University of Notre Dame Civil Rights Center, and Common Cause. From 1984 until her death she headed a consultant and public relations organization in Albuquerque. Because of a lifetime spent helping the weak and unprotected, she was the recipient of numerous honors and appointments.

See also AMERICAN CIVIL LIBERTIES UNION; CHICANAS; HESBURGH, THEODORE.

FURTHER READING: Breiter, Toni. "Dr. Oliverez [sic] Awarded Honorary Law Degree." *Agenda* 8, no. 4 (July-August 1978): 45; Hardy, Gayle J. *American Women Civil Rights Activists.* Jefferson, N.C.: McFarland & Co. 1993; "An Interview with Graciela Olivárez." *Hispanic Business* (March 1980):8–10, 12–13; O'Neill, Lois Decker, ed. *The Women's Book of World Records and Achievements.* Garden City, N.Y.: Anchor Press, 1979; Telgen, Diane, and Jim Kamp, eds. *¡Latinas! Women of Achievement.* Detroit: Visible Ink Press, 1996; Velez, Larry. "Washington's Top Advocate for the Poor." *Nuestro* 3, no. 5 (June–July 1979):33; *Who's Who in America, 1980–1981.* 41st ed. Chicago: Marquis Who's Who, 1980.

OPERATION WETBACK, 1954–1955. Operation Wetback occasioned widespread violations of Mexican American civil rights. In response to an escalating demand for cheap labor by western agribusiness and light industry along the border, the immediate post–World War II years saw a rapid increase in undocumented Mexican workers. By the early 1950s this influx led to demands for stricter enforcement of immigration laws and the expulsion of all undocumented aliens.

During the heyday of Joseph McCarthy's anti-Red witch-hunt Attorney General Herbert Brownell ordered a massive roundup and deportation of aliens without immigration papers, allegedly in order to protect the United States from communist infiltration. Using mobile forces organized on a military basis under ex-general Joseph Swing, the Immigration and Naturalization Service created a giant dragnet that rounded up and sent across the border over 1 million Mexicanos. After announcing the coming dragnet in May 1954 to encourage voluntary repatriation, the Special Mobile Force began in California, moved to Texas, and then went on to large urban centers in Illinois, Missouri, and Washington state.

Intimidation and unnecessary use of force characterized the entire operation, while civil liberties and human rights were routinely ignored. American citizens were expelled from the country, American children saw one or both parents taken from them, and undocumented husbands were separated from their Chicana wives. Despite assertions that the deportations had solved the undocumented alien problem, the results proved temporary. A decade later illegal entrance was again soaring as the bracero program was terminated in 1964 and demand for cheap labor in agriculture and industry continued.

See also CIVIL RIGHTS ABUSE; REPATRIATION.

FURTHER READING: García, Juan Ramón. *Operation Wetback: The Mass Deportation of Undocumented Workers in 1954.* Westport, Conn.: Greenwood Press, 1980; Hayes, Edward F., Richard H. Salter, Roy Plumlee, and Robert B. Lindsey. "Operation Wetback: Impact on the Border States." *Employment Security Review* 22, no. 3 (March 1955):16–21. U.S. Department of Labor.

ORENDAIN, ANTONIO, 1930–   . Born in the state of Jalisco, Mexico, Antonio Orendain came to California in 1950 because he had heard it was the land of opportunity and freedom. In the following year he met Fred Ross, Sr., and César Chávez, who were working for the Community Service Organization (CSO). From 1953 to 1962 he worked for the CSO, mostly in voter registration, under Chávez, with whom he left the CSO to help establish and organize what later became the United Farm Workers (UFW). Deeply concerned about the exploitation and mistreatment of farmworkers, Orendain became intensely involved in the Delano grape strike. For a time he headed the grape boycott in the Chicago area, from which he returned to participate in the 1966 march to Sacramento. Then he was sent by Chávez to El Paso to try to persuade Mexicanos there not to accept employment as strikebreakers in California vineyards. Despite Chávez's orders to the contrary, he also began the aggressive organizing of Texas farmworkers and was called back by Chávez.

On his return to California Orendain started a radio news program in Spanish aimed at farmworkers. After two years of success, in 1969 he was sent back to Texas by Chávez. With a small grant, he created, produced, and hosted a weekly radio program called "La Voz del Campesino," similar to his California newscast. Chávez and Orendain, both men of strongly held convictions, finally split over the issue of the opporteneness of a Texas farmworkers' strike and the latter's aggressive, publicity oriented strike tactics.

In 1975 an impatient Orendain left the UFW to create his own local organization, the Texas Farm Workers Union (TFWU). Two years later he led a march of hundreds of followers from the Rio Grande Valley to Austin (and from there to Washington, D.C.), where Governor Dolph Briscoe met them but refused to support their demand for collective bargaining legislation. The Texas offshoot of the UFW achieved no great success in spite of Orendain's dedicated leadership; he was quoted as saying that the Texas union lacked a real motivating cause. There was also an absence of liberal support; and Orendain, while charismatic in his own way, was no César Chávez. In 1982 he stepped down from his position as director of the TFWU as the labor union lost support.

During the 1980s Orendain worked as a consultant, organizer, and supervisor for various unions. In 1990 he went to work for the Hidalgo County Juvenile Probation Department as a consultant and also created a daily radio program called "Contrapunto" in which he continues to express his views about the rights of labor. He is not currently associated with any particular union. Seen by some as the grand old man of the Chicano civil rights and union organizing movement in Texas, he continues his concern about ethnic discrimination and mistreatment.

See also CHÁVEZ, CÉSAR; COMMUNITY SERVICE ORGANIZATION; TEXAS; UNITED FARM WORKERS.

FURTHER READING: Cockcroft, James D. *Outlaws in the Promised Land: Mexican Immigrant Workers.* New York: Grove Press, 1986; García, Ignacio M. "The Many Battles of Antonio Orendain." *Nuestro* (November 1979):25–29; Holly, Joe. "The Texas Farmworkers' Split." *The Texas Observer* 73, no. 8 (17 April 1981): 4–8; *Who's Who among Hispanic Americans, 1994–1995.* 3rd ed. Detroit: Gale Research, 1994.

ORGANIZATIONS. Historically Mexican Americans have created numerous multipurpose organizations, with a wide variety of goals, political, social, and economic, to defend their rights. Most of these groups began and developed at the local, grassroots level and were based on shared cultural values, language, religion, ethnic symbolism, and historical experience in the United States. Most developed in response to a crisis issue, and many therefore declined when the crisis passed.

In the second half of the nineteenth century most Mexicano organizations were mutualistas, self-help groups, often headed by immigrant leaders, which provided basic insurance and had limited goals of economic betterment. In the late 1800s groups like Las Gorras Blancas, or White Caps, were established in the Southwest to more aggressively defend economic rights, primarily to land and especially to pueblo lands, from the encroachment of railroads and speculators. Until the twentieth century brutal bigotry in the Southwest and the continuing widespread view of Mexican Americans as not really American made many civil rights objectives seem unattainably utopian.

Because la raza continued to be excluded from participation in the American mainstream, Mexican American veterans returning from World War I began to organize civic clubs to educate their fellows about their civil rights. In Texas they created the first more strictly politically oriented organizations like the Order of Sons of America, 1921, which eight years later became the heart of the League of United Latin American Citizens (LULAC). Chicanas were also active in the struggle for ethnic and racial equality. They helped establish civil rights organizations like La Sociedad Protectora Mexicana, the Mexican American Civic Council, and El Comité Mexicano Contra el Racismo. These organizations were generally moderate and middle class in their orientation, emphasizing assimilation, citizenship, and the use of English. They used the law and the courts to inch forward demands of the Chicano community for civil rights. Most of them eschewed party alignment and stressed political neutrality and restraint.

A quarter of a century later a new Mexican American generation of politicized World War II veterans created organizations that explicitly advocated direct participation in the political process as their civil right. Unwilling to accept continuing discrimination and generally rejecting accommodation politics, the veterans began to organize political groups, most of which emphasized improvement in, as well as defense of, civil rights. Another clear trend was the participation of new community leaders and youths, especially students, in the civil rights struggle. This new and usually more militant leadership intensified the struggle.

The post–World War II era saw an increase in community self-help groups and also in professional and business organizations. Nearly all had serious civil rights concerns. Among the most prominent of these organizations were the American Coordinating Council of Political Education, American G.I. Forum, Community Service Organization, Mexican American Legal Defense and Educational Fund, Mexican American Political Association, National Association of Latino Elected and Appointed Officials, Political Association of Spanish-Speaking Organizations, and a host of student groups that ultimately consolidated into the Movimiento Estudiantil Chicano de Aztlán.

In addition, during the 1950s and 1960s some earlier organizations like LULAC and the Unity Leagues, influenced in part by the strong black civil rights movement, began to devote more attention and greater resources to civil rights concerns. Numerous new local community groups such as United Neighborhood Organization and Community Organized for Public Service derived in large measure from the Chicano Movement's impulse. Except for the Southwest (later National) Council of La Raza, no truly national umbrella organization emerged from all this activity.

Between mid–1960 and 1978 the principal centers of the postwar organizational movement were Texas and California, where large-scale political organizing of unprecedented intensity took place. The resulting local and regional groups, which usually developed around charismatic leaders, were typically weak in organization and internal structure. Structural development was sometimes hindered by the notion of many younger activists that structure was inherently elitist and that spontaneity was a most desirable associational characteristic. By the mid-1970s internal personality conflicts, ideological disagreements, demeaning sexist attitudes toward Chicanas, and FBI surveillance, infiltration, and use of agents provocateurs had considerably weakened many of the smaller activist organizations. A strong nationwide neoconservative swing in the 1980s and 1990s resulted in the rejuvenation of more moderate older groups like LULAC and the American G.I. Forum.

Increasingly goals of Chicano political empowerment largely replaced earlier demands for self-determination and cultural nationalism. This trend was further propelled by the increase in the size of the raza middle class. The creation of La Raza Unida Party (LRUP) in 1970 seemed to indicate the beginning of more direct action by Mexican Americans in search of their civil rights. Although LRUP failed to fulfill its early promise, it did focus attention on the abuses of Chicanos' civil rights and did exert pressures on both the Democratic and Republican parties to be more responsive to Mexican American concerns and needs. It also led to the organizing of Mexican American Democrats (MAD), which took an increasingly important role in the party in Texas. During the late 1970s and early 1980s MAD officials began active recruitment drives at local and state levels.

See also individual organizations.

FURTHER READING: Briegel, Kaye. "The Development of Mexican American Organizations." In *The Mexican-Americans: An Awakening Minority*, edited by Manuel P. Servín. Beverly Hills, Calif.: Glencoe Press, 1970; del Castillo, Adelaida R. "Mexican Women in Organization." In *Mexican Women in the United States: Struggles Past and Present*, edited by Magdalena Mora and Adelaida R. del Castillo. Los Angeles: University of California, Chicano Studies Research Center, 1980;

Gómez-Quiñones, Juan. *Roots of Chicano Politics, 1600–1940*. Albuquerque: University of New Mexico Press, 1994; Gonzales, Sylvia A. *Hispanic American Voluntary Organizations*. Westport, Conn.: Greenwood Press, 1985; Guzmán, Ralph. "Politics and Policies of the Mexican American Community." In *California Politics and Policies*, edited by Eugene Dvorin and Arthur I. Misner. Palo Alto, Calif: Addison-Wesley, 1966; Martínez, Douglas. "Overview: Hispanic Organizations, Meeting the Challenge of the 1980s." *La Luz* 8, no. 6 (February-March 1980):8–9, 43; Ortiz, Isidro D. "Chicana/o Organizational Politics and Strategies in an Era of Retrenchment." In *Chicanas/Chicanos at the Crossroads*, edited by David R. Maciel and Isidro D. Ortiz. Tucson: University of Arizona Press, 1996; Rodríguez, Roy C. *Mexican-American Civic Organizations: Political Participation and Political Attitudes*. San Francisco: R & E Research Associates, 1978; Vigil, Maurilio E. *Chicano Politics*. Washington, D.C.: University Press of America, 1978; Vigil, Maurilio E. *Hispanics in American Politics: The Search for Political Power*. Lanham, Md.: University Press of America, 1987.

ORTIZ Y PINO DE KLEVEN, CONCHA, 1912– . As a young girl Concha Ortiz y Pino graduated from the widely famed Loretto Academy in Santa Fe and much later, after service in the state legislature, earned her B.A. degree at the University of New Mexico. Coming from a family that had been active in politics since the 1600s, she ran for the New Mexico state legislature while in her mid-twenties and was elected. She served three terms in that body and was the first woman elected to the powerful position of House majority whip.

Ahead of the times, Concha Ortiz y Pino introduced legislation to establish bilingual education (as provided for in the New Mexico constitution) and to make it possible for women to serve on juries. As an activist she encouraged greater community and political involvement and believed that women especially should take a more active role in politics. Deeply concerned for all Hispanics, she served on numerous local, state, and national commissions and boards and received various awards and honors in recognition of a lifetime of devoted service.

See also CHICANAS.

FURTHER READING: *Las Mujeres: Mexican American/Chicana Women*. Windsor, Calif.: National Women's History Project, 1991; Rebolledo, Tey Diana. *Nuestras Mujeres: Hispanas of New Mexico, Their Images and Their Lives, 1582–1992*. Albuquerque: El Norte Publications, 1992.

P

PAREDES, AMÉRICO, 1915–1999. Outstanding Mexican American folk-lorist Américo Paredes first became acutely aware of racism and discrimination as a student in the public schools of his native Brownsville. That ongoing experience led to his lifelong fight against ethnic bias and for human rights. After completing service in World War II and earning a Ph.D. in English and folklore studies from the University of Texas at Austin, he published his doctoral thesis on a Tejano folk hero and civil rights icon, Gregorio Cortez. The work achieved immediate success and brought him widespread recognition and respect, particularly in academic circles.

Paredes spent his entire academic career teaching in the University of Texas at Austin, where in the 1960s, he fought tenaciously for the development of a Chicano studies program despite anti-Mexican attitudes. Standing up to the entrenched old boy network of his Anglo colleagues, he persisted in his crusade. In 1970, with help from other Chicano faculty and graduate students, he finally succeeded in convincing the administration to authorize a center for Mexican American studies and became its first director. But his social and civil rights struggle did not end there. Again and again he had to fight against historically and institutionally ingrained Texas attitudes toward Mexicanos.

While training a whole generation of borderland folklorists, Paredes also imbued them with his strong feelings about discrimination and ethnic bias. In 1989 he received the Charles Frankel Prize from the National Endowment for the Humanities, the first Mexican American to receive this prestigious award. For his lifelong defense of human rights and work in the preservation of border culture, in the following year he was awarded the Order of the Águila Azteca, the highest honor given to a foreigner by the Mexican government.

See also CHICANO STUDIES DEPARTMENTS.

FURTHER READING: García, Kimberly. "Author Battles Racist Views." *Brownsville Herald*, 4 August 1991; Leal, Luis. "Américo Paredes and Modern Mexican American Scholarship." *Ethnic Affairs* 1 (Fall 1987): 1–11; Limón José E. "Américo Paredes, a Man from the Border." *Revista Chicano-Riqueña* 8, no. 3 (Fall 1980):1–5; *Chicano Literature: A Reference Guide*. Martínez, Julio A. and Francisco A. Lomelí, eds. Westport, Conn.: Greenwood Press, 1985; Paredes, Américo. *"With His Pistol in His Hand!" A Border Ballad and Its Hero*. Austin: University of Texas Press, 1958, 1971; Salazar, Veronica. *Dedication Rewarded: Prominent Mexican Americans*. San Antonio: Mexican American Cultural Center, 1976.

PARSONS, LUCY GONZÁLEZ, ca. 1852–1942. Lucía González was born and grew up near Fort Worth, Texas. While still in her teens she married a young socialist newspaperman, Albert Parsons, and spent the remaining years of her long life, over seven decades, in leftist labor organizing and in advocating and demonstrating for women's rights. After her husband's execution for his "part" in the Haymarket Square bombing in 1886, she continued her varied activities in support of the radical labor movement. She recruited members for the Industrial Workers of the World, wrote articles for leftist labor journals, made speaking tours, raised funds, led marches, addressed demonstrators, and was repeatedly arrested. Even in her eighties she remained an activist in support of the rights of labor and women.

See also CHICANAS.

FURTHER READING: Ashbaugh, Carolyn. *Lucy Parsons*. Chicago: Kerr Publishing Co., 1976; Mirandé, Alfredo, and Evangelina Enríquez. "Chicanas in the Struggle for Unions." In *Introduction to Chicano Studies*, 2nd ed., edited by Livie Isauro Durán and H. Russell Bernard. New York: Macmillan, 1982.

PATLÁN, JUAN J., 1939– . Juan Patlán made his principal contribution to the Chicano struggle for civil rights in the late 1960s and the 1970s. A close friend of José Angel Gutiérrez, he was one of the founders of the Mexican American Youth Organization and one of its offshoots, the Mexican American Unity Council (MAUC). In 1969 he became executive director of San Antonio–based MAUC and in that role moved it away from political activity into the field of community social services, economic development, and health care. During the mid-1970s he was elected chairman of the board of directors of the National Council of La Raza. For his contributions to improving the quality of life for San Antonio Chicanos, in 1978 he received recognition as an outstanding civic leader from the National Urban Coalition in a Washington, D.C., salute.

See also MEXICAN AMERICAN UNITY COUNCIL; MEXICAN AMERICAN YOUTH ORGANIZATION; NATIONAL COUNCIL OF LA RAZA.

FURTHER READING: *Agenda* 8, no. 2 (March/April 1978):42; Salazar, Veronica. *Dedication Rewarded: Prominent Mexican Americans*. San Antonio: Mexican American Cultural Center, 1976.

PATRÓN POLITICS. A political arrangement with deep roots in the history of the Southwest in which the patrón, Anglo or Mexican American, through his paternalistic relationship with members of the poorer classes, particularly Mexicanos, was able to assure himself of their vote at election time. In return the voters could expect minor jobs in city government, on county construction projects, and on the patrón's and his friends' ranches. In times of economic need the patrón, in old Tammany Hall fashion, might make food available to his "dependents" or provide small loans to tide them over the hard times.

In those areas where irrigated agriculture, with its migrant workers, moved in to replace the ranching economy, the patrón system declined. Obviously the patrón diminished the civil rights of the voters he controlled.

See also NEW MEXICO.

FURTHER READING: Anders, Evan. *Boss Rule in South Texas: The Progressive Era*. Austin: University of Texas Press, 1982; García, Flaviano Chris. "Manitos and Chicanos in Nuevo México Politics." *Aztlán* 5, nos. 1&2 (Spring and Fall 1974): 177–188; Pycior, Julie Leininger. *LBJ & Mexican Americans: The Paradox of Power*. Austin: University of Texas Press, 1997.

PEÑA, ALBERT A., JR., 1917–   . Albert Peña was an outstanding member of the World War II generation. Having served in the U.S. Navy from 1942 to 1946, he used the G.I. Bill to complete his college degree at St. Mary's University in San Antonio. After obtaining his law degree in 1950, he joined his father's law firm and also entered Texas politics. Six years later he began sixteen consecutive years of service as a Bexar county commissioner. He was appointed municipal court judge in San Antonio in 1977 and served on the bench until his retirement in 1992.

Peña devoted half a century of his life to the struggles of the powerless for their civil rights. As county commissioner his goals of ending discrimination against Mexican Americans in housing, education, and employment and of developing political activism caused him to be ridiculed, threatened, and even jailed briefly. In March 1966 he led the Albuquerque Walkout at the Equal Employment Opportunity Commission meeting, a decisive step in the Chicano struggle for equal rights and social justice. A self-proclaimed activist, Peña played an important role in the founding and early development of the Southwest Council of La Raza, the Mexican American Unity Council, and the Mexican American Legal Defense and Educational Fund. He also headed the Political Association of Spanish-Speaking Organizations. He participated in various liberal groups, led marches and boycotts, opposed the war in Vietnam, and forthrightly expounded his strong civil rights views in several weekly newspapers.

Although he was fully willing to work with Anglo leaders, Peña, a prominent war veteran leader in San Antonio Democratic politics, preached confrontation tactics during the Chicano Movement as a way to achieve civil rights. He quickly developed a devoted following of youthful Chicanos like Willie Velásquez and José Angel Gutiérrez who, like him, sought political and social change as well as civil rights.

See also ALBUQUERQUE WALKOUT; MEXICAN AMERICAN LEGAL DEFENSE AND EDUCATIONAL FUND; POLITICAL ASSOCIATION OF SPANISH-SPEAKING ORGANIZATIONS.

FURTHER READING: Alvarez, Frank. "UTSA Honors Judge Albert Peña, Jr." *La Prensa* (San Antonio), 17 March 1995, 1-A, 3-A; Chacón, José A. *Hispanic Notables in the United States of North America.* Albuquerque, N.M.: Saguaro Publishing Co., 1978; Pycior, Julie Leininger. *LBJ & Mexican Americans: The Paradox of Power.* Austin: University of Texas Press, 1997.

PEÑA, FEDERICO, 1947– . Best known as mayor of Denver (1983–1991), Peña was a transplanted Tejano who became a staff lawyer for the Mexican American Legal Defense and Educational Fund in Denver after working a year in an El Paso legal aid office. In 1978 he won election to the Colorado state legislature, where he soon became recognized as one of the top lawmakers and was elected minority Speaker of the House. In the legislature he supported bilingual education and co-authored a law requiring schools to offer courses in Hispanic culture; he was easily reelected to a second term. In 1983, at age 36, he was elected mayor of Denver, becoming the first raza mayor of a large city that was not heavily Latino. He served until 1991.

In 1993 Peña was appointed secretary of the Department of Transportation by President Bill Clinton, and four years later he became secretary of the U.S. Department of Energy.

See also COLORADO; POLITICAL PARTICIPATION.

FURTHER READING: Hero, Rodney. "The Election of Hispanics in City Government: An Examination of the Election of Federico Peña as Mayor of Denver." In *Land Grants, Housing, and Political Power*, edited by Antoinette Sedillo López. New York: Garland Publishing, 1995; Martínez, Chip. "Federico Peña: Denver's First Hispanic Mayor." *Nuestro* 7, no. 6 (August 1983); Novas, Himilce. *The Hispanic 100: A Ranking of the Latino Men and Women Who Have Most Influenced American Thought and Culture.* New York: Citadel Press, 1995; *Who's Who in American Politics, 1997–1998.* Vol. 16. New York: R. R. Bowker, 1998.

PERALES, ALONSO S., 1899–1960. Service in the U.S. armed forces during World War I helped to focus Alonso Perales's ideas on how to advance the economic welfare and civil rights of Mexican Americans. His discussions with other Tejanos led to founding the Order of Sons of America in 1921, and at the end of the decade he assumed the principal role in establishing the League of United Latin American Citizens (LULAC), which grew out of the Sons. Moving away from a more Mexican mutualista organizational concept to one that was more American, he played a key part in the early development of LULAC. Meanwhile, as a result of his leadership and the law degree he had achieved, he began to be called on by Washington during the late 1920s to be part of diplomatic missions to Latin America. In the 1930s he was selected by President Franklin D. Roosevelt as an advisor on Mexican American concerns.

In his first book, *El mexicano americano y la política del sur de Texas* (1931), Perales surveyed three decades of Anglo–Mexican American interaction. In 1936–1937 he published *En defensa de mi raza*, a two-volume history of the Mexican American struggle for civil rights—his driving concern. Just before American entrance into World War II, he was the chief directing force behind a racial equality bill that failed to pass in the Texas legislature.

During the war years Perales was actively involved in the Office of the Coordinator of Inter-American Affairs, along with Carlos Castañeda, George I. Sánchez, and other Mexican American intellectual leaders. In 1945 he served as legal counsel to the Nicaraguan delegation to the founding conference of the United Nations at San Francisco.

After the war Perales wrote a San Antonio newspaper column that highlighted instances of civil rights injustices and published another important work, *Are We Good Neighbors?* (1948). His answer was no, with numerous citations to substantiate his negative response. In his writing he strongly advocated both legislation and education to combat ethnic discrimination. An important highlight of Perales's career came in 1952 when he received from the government of Spain the Order of Civil Merit for his lifetime work fighting for the social equality and civil rights of Spanish-speaking Americans. He served on numerous civic committees and commissions and remained active in the Chicano civil rights struggle, especially through his leadership role in LULAC, until his death in 1960.

See also CIVIL RIGHTS ABUSE; LEAGUE OF UNITED LATIN AMERICAN CITIZENS.

FURTHER READING: *Are We Good Neighbors?* Compiled by Alonso S. Perales. San Antonio: Artes Gráficas, 1948. Reprint, New York: Arno Press, 1974; Garcia, Richard A. *Rise of the Mexican American Middle Class, San Antonio Texas, 1929–1941.* College Station: Texas A&M University Press, 1991; Perales, Alonso S. *En defensa de mi raza.* San Antonio: Artes Graficas, 1936–1937; Sloss Vento, Adela. *Alonso S. Perales: His Struggle for the Rights of Mexican-Americans.* San Antonio: Artes Gráficas, 1977.

PLAN DE SAN DIEGO, 1915. A wild, quixotic plot, allegedly originating with a Mexican national in San Diego, Texas, calling for armed revolt to overthrow U.S. rule in the Southwest, the killing of all white males over 16, and the creation of a Mexicano republic. Cloaked in secrecy and muddled by the Mexican revolution of 1910 and the increased border banditry that accompanied it, the incident seems to have been largely a reaction to turbulent border conditions, the brutal conduct of the Texas Rangers, loss of lands, and other civil rights abuses. Because of World War I, there were also allegations of a German connection. For about a year bridge destruction and raids in the border region were attributed to the plan. However, the confusion of the times and the secrecy of the plan's leaders make it difficult to ascertain the extent of the plan's involvement in these activities, if any.

See also TEXAS; TEXAS RANGERS.

FURTHER READING: Coerver, Don M., and Linda B. Hall. *Texas and the Mexican Revolution: A Study in State and National Border Policy, 1910–1920.* San Antonio: Trinity University Press, 1984; Sandos, James A. *Rebellion in the Borderlands: Anarchism and the Plan of San Diego, 1904–1923.* Norman: University of Oklahoma Press, 1992; Simmons, Ozzie G. *Anglo-Americans and Mexican-Americans in South Texas.* Reprint, New York: Arno Press, 1974.

PLAN DE SANTA BARBARA, 1969. The Plan de Santa Barbara was a cultural aspect of the Chicano civil rights movement arising out of a conference held at the University of California in Santa Barbara. The plan described the ideology, organization, and role of the Movimiento Estudiantil Chicano de Aztlán, conceived as an umbrella organization for various college and university groups. By designing college courses and programs suited to Chicano needs, the plan was expected to expand and spread knowledge of the Mexican American experience and to develop leaders in the struggle for civil rights. Although somewhat idealistic and utopian, the plan had considerable merit and some immediate success in academia. Moreover, it did help develop an aggressive young leadership that furthered the fight for Mexican American rights.

See also CHICANO STUDIES DEPARTMENTS; MOVIMIENTO ESTUDIANTIL CHICANO DE AZTLÁN.

FURTHER READING: *El Plan de Santa Barbara.* Santa Barbara, Calif.: La Causa Publications, 1969; Muñoz, Carlos, Jr. *Youth, Identity, Power: The Chicano Movement.* New York: Verso, 1989.

PLAN DEL BARRIO, 1968. The Plan del Barrio was a program outlined by Corky Gonzales in Washington, D.C., during the Poor People's March. Its "Demandas de la Raza" included better housing and greater educational opportunity, as well as bilingual education. With overtones of Chicano ethnic nationalism, it also called for the return of pueblo lands in the Southwest (wrongfully taken by the U.S. government, it contended) and for aid in developing barrio businesses owned by Mexican Americans.

See also GONZALES, CORKY.

FURTHER READING: Fager, Charles E. *Uncertain Resurrection: The Poor People's Washington Campaign.* Grand Rapids: Eerdmans, 1969; Marín, Christine. *A Spokesman for the Mexican American Movement: Rodolfo "Corky" Gonzales and the Fight for Chicano Liberation, 1966–1972.* San Francisco: R & E Research Associates, 1977.

PLAN ESPIRITUAL DE AZTLÁN, 1969. In March 1969 at the first annual Youth Liberation Conference in Denver, Corky Gonzales followed up his earlier Plan del Barrio with an elaboration he called the Plan Espiritual de Aztlán. It urged Chicanos to unite and create a new civil rights organization in order to promote Chicano self-determination and ethnic nationalism. The plan broke sharply with assimilationist goals of earlier Mexican American organizations like the G.I. Forum and the League of United Latin American Citizens. It posited a cultural homeland in the Southwest based on the Aztecs' myth of Aztlán as the place of their origin.

In the following year the plan led to the creation of the Colorado Raza Unida Party, one objective of which was to strive for the Southwest ethnic homeland. Idealist Gonzales's defeat by pragmatic José Angel Gutiérrez in the subsequent conflict within the national Raza Unida Party over leadership and direction led to his decline as a preeminent Chicano leader and spelled the end of the plan.

See also RAZA UNIDA PARTY, LA.

FURTHER READING: Marín, Christine. *A Spokesman for the Mexican American Movement; Rodolfo "Corky" Gonzales and the Fight for Chicano Liberation, 1966–1972.* San Francisco: R & E Research Associates, 1977.

PLESSY v. FERGUSON, 1896. The case of *Plessy v. Ferguson* is widely known for establishing the "separate but equal" doctrine, which reigned supreme in American education until *Brown v. Board of Education of Topeka* in 1954. In its *Plessy* decision the U.S. Supreme Court held that the Fourteenth Amendment was intended to protect only political, not social, rights. The court's ruling, which was primarily concerned with black-white relations, resulted in numerous southern state laws establishing de jure segregation, particularly in schools. In the *Brown* case, 1954–1955, more than half a century later, the Supreme Court unanimously reversed the *Plessy* doctrine, holding that separate but equal in education resulted in inherently unequal facilities, treatment, and opportunity. In the following year the court ordered the desegregation of schools "with all deliberate speed." Segregation did not end, but continued to be practiced, usually by subterfuge.

See also SEGREGATION.

FURTHER READING: Bennet, Lerone, Jr. *Confrontation: Black and White*. Baltimore, Md.: Penguin Books Inc., 1968; Logan, Rayford W. *The Betrayal of the Negro*. New York: Collier Books, 1968; Newby, I. A., ed. *The Development of Segregationist Thought*. Homewood, Illinois: Dorsey Press, 1968; Thomas, Brook, ed. *Plessy v. Ferguson: A Brief History with Documents*. Boston: Bedford Books, 1997.

PLYLER v. DOE, 1977–1982. When the state of Texas passed a law that in effect excluded undocumented children from free public education, a class-action suit was filed in the U.S. district court in the name of some of the children. The district court accepted the plaintiffs' view, argued by Mexican American Legal Defense and Educational Fund (MALDEF) lawyers, that to deny free public education to children of undocumenteds was a violation of their right to the equal protection clause of the Fourteenth Amendment and ordered the school district to enroll them. The Tyler Independent School District appealed the ruling, and in 1980 the Fifth District Court of Appeals confirmed the lower court's ruling. The state of Texas then appealed the case to the U.S. Supreme Court where MALDEF, the League of United Latin American Citizens, and the National Education Association were among groups supporting the case for the plaintiffs. The Supreme Court, in a decision written by Justice William Brennan, agreed with the lower courts, holding the Texas action to be a denial of Fourteenth Amendment guarantees and emphasizing the vital importance of education in a democratic society.

See also EDUCATION.

FURTHER READING: Biegel, Stuart. "Wisdom of Plyler v. Doe." *Chicano-Latino Law Review* 17 (1995):46–63; Carrera, John Willshire. *Immigrant Students: Their Legal Right of Access to Public Schools*. Rev. ed. Boston: National Center for Immigrant Students & National Coalition of Advocates for Students, 1992.

POLICE BRUTALITY. See CIVIL RIGHTS ABUSE.

POLITICAL ASSOCIATION OF SPANISH-SPEAKING ORGANIZATIONS (PASSO/PASO). After the success of the Viva Kennedy clubs in the 1960 elections, Tejano civil rights leaders converted these election campaign groups into a permanent organization called PASSO, which was planned as a national political pressure group. PASSO encouraged greater community involvement in politics and challenged somewhat the views of the older, more conservative Mexican American leadership. Its constitution called for a united effort in seeking political solutions to pressing social and economic community problems.

After considerable success in organizing chapters in Texas, its leaders, most of whom had developed their skills earlier in the League of United Latin American Citizens, had hopes of making it a national organization.

However, efforts to expand into nearby Arizona met with failure. Arizona Mexican Americans rejected PASSO, opting instead to create their own separate organization, the American Coordinating Council of Political Education, which they felt suited their needs better. Efforts to expand into other southwestern states encountered a similar lack of success.

Thus PASSO failed to become the coordinating umbrella organization envisioned by its founders and remained essentially a Texas group. It achieved some success in getting Chicano elected to the Crystal City town council in 1963 and worked with black groups to elect minority candidates to city offices in Texas during the second half of the 1960s. In the next decade PASSO lost much of its membership to La Raza Unida Party, which provided Texas Chicanos with a much more charismatic and aggressive leadership.

See also AMERICAN COORDINATING COUNCIL OF POLITICAL EDUCATION; KENNEDY, JOHN FITZGERALD.

FURTHER READING: Castro, Tony. *Chicano Power: The Emergence of Mexican America*. New York: Saturday Review Press, 1974; Cuellar, Robert. *A Social and Political History of the Mexican American Population of Texas, 1929–1963*. San Francisco: R & E Research Associates, 1974; Pycior, Julie Leininger. *LBJ & Mexican Americans: The Paradox of Power*. Austin: University of Texas Press, 1997; Tirado, Miguel David. "Mexican American Community Political Organization." In *La Causa Política*, edited by F. Chris García. Notre Dame, Ind.: University of Notre Dame Press, 1974.

POLITICAL PARTICIPATION. A critical aspect of the Chicano fight for civil rights is its effort to participate more fully in the American political process. Historically disadvantaged and powerless, Mexican Americans have engaged in a struggle to obtain their fair share in political power ever since the Treaty of Guadalupe Hidalgo. Except in New Mexico they soon found themselves largely excluded from politics despite civil rights guaranteed them by the treaty. Attempts at political participation were rebuffed, and as a result they developed a pattern of alienation and withdrawal. However, in the 1920s Tejanos, sparked by World War I veterans, began establishing organizations designed to enlarge the scope of their participation in politics. These groups coalesced in 1929 into the League of United Latin American Citizens, which articulated previously unspoken pragmatic goals of political accommodation.

World War II marked a decisive watershed in Mexican American participation in local and state politics. As large numbers of Chicanos moved into urban centers, more extensive community organizing became possible and greater political power resulted. In the 1950s and early 1960s Mexican American presence in politics gradually increased, but gross underrepresentation still persisted. Presidents Kennedy and Johnson both showed an openness to raza demands for greater political representation by appointing

Chicanos to federal offices, but relatively few Chicanos were successful in electoral politics.

Aware that African Americans were advancing their civil rights in the early 1960s through confrontational political tactics, Chicanos followed their example and turned to widespread activism that expressed itself in part through the Chicano Movement of the 1960s and 1970s. Post–World War II organizations like the American G.I. Forum and the Mexican American Political Association exerted pressure on the system through electoral politics to demand a fair share in political power. Their aggressive stance led to an effectiveness absent from earlier more conventional and constrained political efforts.

At the beginning of the 1970s the Nixon administration set a new record for the appointment of Mexican Americans, although privately the president expressed little faith in them. President Jimmy Carter made a further significant increase in naming Chicanos to federal offices at various levels. In 1993 President Bill Clinton appointed two Chicanos to his first cabinet, Henry Cisneros and Federico Peña, and later appointed Nuevomexicano Bill Richardson U.S. ambassador to the United Nations. In addition to cabinet-level appointments, Chicanos also gained positions at various levels in a wide range of federal agencies and departments.

Moreover, as a result of the Voting Rights Act of 1965, intense voter registration drives, and get-out-the-vote campaigns, Chicano politicians were able to attain more elective positions in the last quarter of the twentieth century. In some smaller towns in Texas and California la raza elected majorities on school boards and city councils; in two states, New Mexico and Arizona, Mexican Americans were elected to the governorship in the 1970s. These achievements were almost entirely the results of expanded participation in the political process, made possible by the Voting Rights Act and the removal of various barriers to voting such as poll taxes, literacy tests, and exclusionary residency requirements.

The first climax of widespread Chicano political participation was the creation of La Raza Unida Party (LRUP) at the beginning of the 1970s. However, this dramatic effort at participation had virtually disappeared by the late 1970s, largely because of divided leadership, bitter internal dissent, and resulting power struggles. Since then the Chicano political push has been largely within the two main parties. The names of aspiring Chicano politicians have been appearing on the ballot with increasingly greater frequency, and more of them are winning elections. According to the National Association of Latino Elected Officials, in 1985 there were 3,072 Hispanic elected officials at the city and county level, 120 at the state level, and 11 at the federal level. Texas led with 1,475 Latino officials, New Mexico was next with 584, and California was third with 460. Arizona and Colorado followed with 231 and 165 respectively. Since 1985 more have been added, and by 1992 there were 11,358 Latino municipal officials.

In 1987 Gloria Molina became the first Chicana to be elected to the city council of Los Angeles, the city with the largest Mexican American population in the United States. In 1990 Dan Morales was elected as the first Chicano attorney general in Texas history. Six years later Cruz Bustamante became the first Californio to be elected Speaker of the California Assembly and in 1998 he was elected lieutenant governor. Art Torres is the chair of the Democratic Party in California. In contrast, in 1993 José Angel Gutiérrez was unsuccessful in his Texas bid for the U.S. Senate as a Democrat.

The Mexican American community still lacks political representation commensurate with its numbers. However, in spite of slow advance and some setbacks, the political consciousness that has been aroused among Mexican Americans guarantees continuing efforts to obtain a fairer share of political power through the exercise of their civil rights.

See also MOVIMIENTO, EL; RAZA UNIDA PARTY, LA; VOTING; WORLD WAR II.

FURTHER READING: García, F. Chris, and Rodolfo O. de la Garza. *The Chicano Political Experience*. North Scituate, Mass.: Duxbury Press, 1977; de la Garza, Rudolf, Martha Menchaca, and Louis DeSapio, eds. *Barrio Ballots: Latino Politics in the 1990 Elections*. Boulder, Colo.: Westview Press, 1994; de la Garza, Rudolf O., and David Vaughn. "The Political Socialization of Chicano Elites: A Generational Approach." In *The Mexican American Experience: An Interdisciplinary Anthology*, edited by Rodolfo O. de la Garza et al. Austin: University of Texas Press, 1985; García, John A. "Political Participation: Resources and Involvement in the American Political System." In *Pursuing Power: Latinos and the Political System*, edited by F. Chris García. Notre Dame, Ind.: University of Notre Dame Press, 1997; Gómez-Quiñonez, Juan. *Roots of Chicano Politics, 1600–1948*. Albuquerque: University of New Mexico Press, 1994; Gutiérrez, David G. *Walls and Mirrors: Mexican Americans, Mexican Immigrants, and the Politics of Ethnicity*. Berkeley: University of California Press, 1995; Guzmán, Ralph C. *The Political Socialization of the Mexican American People*. Reprint, New York: Arno Press, 1976; Maciel, David R., and Isidro D. Ortiz, eds. *Chicanas/Chicanos at the Crossroads: Social, Economic, and Political Change*. Tucson: University of Arizona Press, 1996; MacManus, Susan A., and Carol A. Cassel. "Mexican-Americans in City Politics: Participation, Representation, and Policy Preferences." In *Latinos and the Political System*, edited by F. Chris García. Notre Dame, Ind.: University of Notre Dame Press, 1988; Neighbor, Howard. "Latino Participation in a Bicultural Setting." In *Latinos and Political Coalitions*, edited by Roberto E. Villarreal and Norma G. Hernández. Westport, Conn.: Greenwood Press, 1991; Santillán, Richard A. "Latino Political Development in the Southwest and Midwest Regions: A Comparative Overview, 1915–1989." In *Latinos and Political Coalitions*, edited by Roberto E. Villarreal and Norma G. Hernández. Westport, Conn.: Greenwood Press, 1991; Vigil, Mauricio. *Chicano Politics*. Washington, D.C.: University Press of America, 1977; Welch, Susan, and John R. Hibbing. "Hispanic Representation in the U.S. Congress." In *The Mexican American Experience: An Interdisciplinary Anthology*, edited by Rodolfo O. de la Garza et al. Austin: University of Texas Press, 1985; Yzaguirre, Raúl. "Keys to Hispanic Empowerment." In *Latinos and Political Co-*

alitions: Political Empowerment for the 1990s, edited by Roberto E. Villarreal and Norma G. Hernández. Westport, Conn.: Greenwood Press, 1991.

POLL TAX. A poll tax is a payment required in order to vote. Poll taxes were enacted in many southern states in the aftermath of the Civil War to deter the recently freed slaves from voting. For decades the tax was criticized by many as unfair to the poor, both black and white, whom it effectively disenfranchised.

In 1964 during the surge of the civil rights movement the U.S. Congress passed the Twenty-fourth Amendment to the Constitution, which outlawed state poll tax requirements as a prerequisite in federal elections. Two years later the U.S. Supreme Court extended the prohibition to all elections, local and state as well as national. The end of poll taxes as a deterrent to voting led to intensified voter registration drives among Mexican Americans in the Southwest, to greater participation in elections, and to heightened demands for full civil rights.

See also VOTING RIGHTS ACT, 1965.

FURTHER READING: Bardolph, Richard. *The Civil Rights Record.* New York: Thomas Y. Crowell Co., 1970; Graham, Hugh Davis. *The Civil Rights Era, 1960–1972.* New York: Oxford University Press, 1990.

POOR PEOPLE'S MARCH, 1968. Early in 1968 Martin Luther King, Jr., and Ralph Abernathy of the Southern Christian Leadership Conference began to organize a march on Washington, D.C., in order to air grievances and to demand of an indifferent, if not hostile, Congress greater compliance with existing civil rights legislation and directives. King selected Reies López Tijerina to organize a Mexican American delegation from the Southwest. During the march Tijerina proved an independent and somewhat contentious subordinate to Abernathy (who had taken over the leadership after King's assassination), whom he accused of slighting the role of the Chicano contingent. With his co-leader, Corky Gonzales, he tried to convert the march into an important vehicle for Chicano civil rights demands.

In Washington Tijerina used the march to stage a confrontation with officials in the Department of State, arguing vociferously that the loss of lands guaranteed by the Treaty of Guadalupe Hidalgo was a denial of basic rights. He also tried, unsuccessfully, to involve the Mexican ambassador in his dispute with the Department of State. Corky Gonzales took the opportunity of the march to launch a call for Chicano cultural nationalism in his Plan del Barrio, which also demanded bilingual education and better housing for Chicanos as well as land reforms. All the leaders, black, brown, and white, called for increased access to jobs, improved housing, and greater educational opportunities.

See also GONZALES, CORKY; TIJERINA, REIES LÓPEZ.

FURTHER READING: Fager, Charles E. *Uncertain Resurrection: The Poor People's Washington Campaign*. Grand Rapids: Eerdmans, 1969; Fulks, Bryan. *Black Struggle: A History of the Negro in America*. New York: Dell Publishing Co., 1969; Tijerina, Reies López. *Mi lucha por la tierra*. Mexico: Fondo de Cultura Económica, 1978.

PRECIADO DE BURCIAGA, CECILIA, 1945–   . A widely respected voice in the field of educational rights, Cecilia Preciado began her professional life as a high school Spanish teacher in Chino, California. A subsequent brief and unsatisfying experience in the U.S. foreign service led to a staff job in the Inter-Agency Committee for Mexican American Affairs (IAC-MAA) on which she had been volunteering. From the IACMAA it was only a short step to the U.S. Commission on Civil Rights, where she worked as a research analyst on the status of Mexican Americans in education. Her experiences on the commission led to a lifelong commitment to opening wider the door to educational opportunities for U.S. Latinos.

When Cecilia accepted a position as provost for Chicano affairs and assistant to the president offered her by Stanford University, she and her husband, José Antonio Burciaga, returned to California in 1974. At Stanford her job was to increase the number of Mexican Americans in the student body, on the faculty, and in staff positions. She did so well that three years later she was promoted to the position of assistant provost for faculty affairs, where her principal effort was concentrated on bringing more minority and women faculty members to Stanford.

In the second half of the 1980s Burciaga was promoted to associate dean of graduate studies, whose job was to recruit larger numbers of women and minorities for Stanford's various doctoral programs. She was also the director of the Office of Chicano Affairs and for a time affirmative action officer as well. In 1991 she was again promoted, this time to associate dean and director of development. In April 1994, after 20 years at Stanford, Burciaga was fired by the university's new president, Gerhard Casper, in what was described as part of a campuswide budget-cutting necessary to keep Stanford "one of the world's great universities." Her firing caused widespread criticism and protest by both students and faculty.

By her quiet, steady work to advance the rights of women and minorities, Preciado de Burciaga has given outstanding service to the cause of civil rights. Her dedication to human rights was honored by the Eleanor D. Roosevelt Humanitarian Award from the San Francisco United Nations Association as well as by appointments to various California and national boards and commissions.

See also CHICANAS; EDUCATION.

FURTHER READING: "Cecilia Preciado de Burciaga." *La Luz* 6, no. 11 (November 1977); Johnson, Lynn. "Cecilia Burciaga Encourages Political Involvement." *Aurora* (March 1979); Telgen, Diane, and Jim Kamp, eds. *Notable Hispanic American Women*. Detroit: Gale Research, 1993.

PRIMER CONGRESO MEXICANISTA, EL, 1911. The Primer Congreso Mexicanista, held at Laredo, Texas, in 1911, was one of the very early efforts at a wider organization of Mexican Americans in militant defense of their civil and social rights. It was prompted, in part, by the extraordinarily vicious abuse suffered by border Mexicanos at the turn of the century. Largely the brainchild of journalist and Mexicano rights leader Nicasio Idar, it took the first firm step away from the mutualista concept. It encompassed several hundred delegates from various state Tejano groups who discussed, among other grievances, what might be done about discrimination in the schools and official toleration of Anglos lynching Mexicanos. A growing awareness of the potential effectiveness of group action convinced the leaders that only by uniting, by organizing widely, could they be successful in asserting their rights as Americans and in obtaining redress of their grievances. The slogan they adopted for the congress was Por la raza y para la raza.

Notable aspects of the Congreso were its special invitation to Mexicanas to participate and the role they played in the conference discussions, led by Jovita Idar, Nicasio's daughter. Although secondary to the male leadership, their active participation led to the establishment of a women's auxiliary, La Liga Femenil Mexicanista, with goals of fighting "in the name of la raza and for la raza." The auxiliary was presided over by Jovita Idar.

To center continuing attention on the many problems faced daily by Mexicanos in Texas, the delegates created a statewide organization made up of local chapters and titled it La Gran Liga Mexicanista de Beneficencia y Protección. In addition to their concerns about civil rights the leaders, many of them immigrants, showed a degree of cultural nationalism by supporting language retention and rejecting total assimilation. In the early years of the twentieth century they led an organization that was protectively militant, nonsexist, and culturally nationalist. Not until the civil rights movement of the 1960s did there appear a broad, organized movement with the spectrum of goals enumerated by the Congreso.

See also CHICANAS; IDAR, NICASIO; ORGANIZATIONS.

FURTHER READING: "Form New Organization: Congreso Mexicanista Is Brought into Existence." *San Antonio Express*, 16 September 1911, 9; Limón, José E. "El Primer Congreso Mexicanista de 1911: A Precursor to Contemporary Chicanismo." *Aztlán 5*, nos. 1&2 (Spring and Fall 1974):85–117; " 'Por la raza y para la raza': Congreso Mexicanista, 1911." In *Foreigners in Their Native Land: Historical Roots of the Mexican American*, edited by David J. Weber. Albuquerque: University of New Mexico Press, 1973.

PROPOSITION 187, 1994. Passed by California voters in the 1994 elections, Proposition 187 made undocumented aliens ineligible for public school education, social services, and health care (except in emergencies). It also required various governmental agencies to report suspected undocumented aliens to the state's attorney general and to the U.S. Immigration and Naturalization Service.

FURTHER READING: Acuña, Rodolfo F. *Sometimes There Is No Other Side: Chicanos and the Myth of Equality*. Notre Dame, Ind.: University of Notre Dame Press, 1998; Alarcón, Rafael. *Proposition 187: An Effective Measure to Deter Undocumented Migration to California?* San Francisco: Multicultural Education, Training and Advocacy, 1994; García, Rubén J. "The Racial Politics of Proposition 187." In *The Latino/a Condition: A Critical Reader*, edited by Richard Delgado and Jean Stefancic. New York: New York University Press, 1998.

PROPOSITION 209, 1996. Proposition 209, titled the California Civil Rights Initiative and passed by California voters in November 1996, amended the state constitution to prohibit preferential treatment and discrimination by state or other public entities in employment, education, and contracting. With its declared intent of "leveling the playing field" it prohibits the use of preferences, quotas, and set-asides based on ethnicity, gender, color, race, or national origin. Preferences based on other criteria remained unaffected. Critics argued that it would unfavorably affect efforts to redress past inequities. During the 1996 elections a great deal of heated discussion was generated on both sides of the issue.

Immediately upon approval of the proposition by the voters, it was challenged in the courts by its opponents, who contended that the new law would effectively dismantle federal affirmative action programs and would be devastating to women and minority citizens in areas of American society where they have historically been excluded, grossly underrepresented, or discriminated against. Judge Thelton Henderson found for the plaintiffs and enjoined implementation or enforcement of the proposition. However, heavy voter support of the proposition has had a chilling effect on all affirmative action programs in the state.

See also AFFIRMATIVE ACTION.

FURTHER READING: Acuña, Rodolfo F. *Sometimes There Is No Other Side: Chicanos and the Myth of Equality*. Notre Dame, Ind.: University of Notre Dame Press, 1998; Chávez, Lydia. *The Color Bind: California's Battle to End Affirmative Action*. Berkeley: University of California Press, 1998.

PROPOSITION 227, 1998. Titled the English Language in the Public Schools Initiative, Proposition 227 was passed by California voters in June 1998. It changed the regulations concerning the teaching of students with limited English-speaking ability. The new legislation essentially prohibits the teaching of public school classes (except foreign-language classes) in any language other than English. Although the law allows some exceptions, it marks a drive toward a severe retreat from bilingual education practices in the state.

Proposition 227 was largely financed by wealthy Silicon Valley businessman Ron Unz and was strongly supported by the conservative Center for Equal Opportunity founded by Linda Chávez, former head of U.S. English, an organization with goals of ending bilingual education and establishing English as the official language of the United States by law. The new legislation was immediately taken to the courts, with both the American Civil Liberties Union and the Mexican American Legal Defense and Educational Fund filing for a restraining order. In their view the proposition violates the federal Equal Opportunities Act of 1974 as well as the Fourteenth Amendment.

See also BILINGUAL EDUCATION; CHÁVEZ, LINDA.

FURTHER READING: Cornejo, Ricardo J. "Bilingual Education: Some Reflections on Proposition 227." *Hispanic Outlook in Higher Education* (9 October 1998):27–32.

Q

QUEVEDO, EDUARDO, 1903–1968. Los Angeles civic leader Eduardo Quevedo was deeply involved all his life in defending the civil rights of Chicanos. In the late 1930s he was one of the important principals in founding the Congreso de Los Pueblos de Habla Española along with Josefina Fierro de Bright. During World War II he was the chair of the Coordinating Council for Latin American Youth. In late 1942 he started a club to provide teenage Chicanos with an outlet for their energies, and eight months later he protested the actions of the Los Angeles police department and sheriff's office in the Zoot Suit rioting. Later that year he participated energetically in the Sleepy Lagoon Defense Committee. His activities there caused him to be singled out for intense federal scrutiny.

After the war years Quevedo continued to be involved in the community as a successful organizer. In 1959 he had an important role, along with Bert Corona, in calling the meeting that led to the founding of the Mexican American Political Association. He then became the first president of this new politically oriented group, giving it successful guidance in its formative years. Quevedo also served on various state commissions and boards as a result of his civil rights interests.

See also CONGRESO DE LOS PUEBLOS DE HABLA ESPAÑOLA; MEXICAN AMERICAN POLITICAL ASSOCIATION; SLEEPY LAGOON.

FURTHER READING: "Zoot Suit War." *Time*, 21 June 1943.

R

RACISM. A conglomeration of habits, attitudes, actions, and policies based on the false assumption that there are innate differences in the three races (Negroid, Mongoloid, Caucasoid). Racism is usually expressed by policies and acts of prejudice, domination, discrimination, segregation, and persecution—in short, denial of civil rights. Whether expressed by individual acts or in institutional practices, racism commonly serves to justify one group's domination over another.

Racism, discrimination, and economic exploitation have had an important part in shaping the Mexicano experience in the United States. Most Mexican Americans are of mixed Native American and European descent, and historically many have been denied upward mobility and excluded from superior economic, social, and political positions on the basis of their Indian ancestry. Further, widespread discrimination based on race and ethnicity has often denied them even their basic civil rights as U.S. citizens.

The postponement of statehood for New Mexico for over half a century because of its Hispano population majority is a glaring historical example of racism in politics at the local and national levels. Not until the black civil rights movement during the John F. Kennedy and Lyndon B. Johnson administrations did leaders in the government begin to seem receptive to Mexican American demands for equal rights.

See also DISCRIMINATION; SEGREGATION.

FURTHER READING: Daniels, Roger, and Harry Kitano. *American Racism*. Englewood Cliffs, N.J., Prentice-Hall, 1970; McWilliams, Carey. *North from Mexico: The Spanish-Speaking People of the United States*. New ed. Westport, Conn.: Praeger Publishers, 1990; Martínez, Thomas M. "Advertising and Racism: The Case of the Mexican-American." *El Grito* 2, no. 4 (Summer 1969):3–13; Montejano, David. *Anglos and Mexicans in the Making of Texas, 1836–1986*. Austin: University of Texas Press, 1987; Rose, Arnold, ed. *Race Prejudice and Discrimi-*

nation: Readings in Intergroup Relations in the United States. New York: Alfred A. Knopf, 1951; Schorr, Daniel L. "Reconverting Mexican Americans." *New Republic* 115, no. 13 (September 1946):412–413.

RAMÍREZ, BLANDINA CÁRDENAS, 1944–   . In 1983 Blandina Ramírez became a central figure in a civil rights wrangle with the president of the United States. With an undergraduate degree in journalism from the University of Texas at Austin in 1967 and a doctorate in education from the University of Massachusetts seven years later, Ramírez was able to secure political appointments in Washington, D.C. During the second half of the 1970s she served on the Texas Advisory Committee to the federal Commission on Civil Rights. She was also a member of the Mexican American Legal Defense and Educational Fund's board of directors.

Blandina Ramírez was appointed a commissioner to the U.S. Civil Rights Commission by President Jimmy Carter in the last year of his term, 1980. Service on the commission caused her to realize the need to look at civil rights abuses in a historical context of institutional discriminatory practices. Apparently because of her vocal criticism of President Ronald Reagan's (1981–1989) lack of enthusiasm for civil rights, she and two other commissioners were fired in mid-1983 and three new, more amenable commissioners were appointed by the president to take their places. When the legislation authorizing the commission expired in November 1983, the Democratically controlled Congress reorganized the commission with eight members, four to be appointed by the president and four by the Congress. Then Congress appointed its four new commissioners, one of whom was Blandina Ramírez.

See also CIVIL RIGHTS COMMISSION.

FURTHER READING: Bonilla-Santiago, Gloria. *Breaking Grounds and Barriers: Hispanic Women Developing Effective Leadership.* San Diego: Marín Publications, 1992; Cerrudo, Margaret. "Blandina Cárdenas Ramírez: On the Forefront of Civil Rights and Education." *Intercambios Femeniles,* 4, no. 1 (Summer 1988):20; "MALDEF Fights for Rights Commission." *MALDEF* 13, no. 2 (Fall/Winter 1983): 1–2; Telgen, Diane, and Jim Camp, eds. *Notable Hispanic American Women.* Detroit: Gale Research, 1993.

RAMÍREZ, HENRY M., 1929–   . After studying for the priesthood, in the mid-1950s Henry Ramírez left the seminary to enter the teaching profession. By the second half of the 1960s he had achieved a national reputation as a result of his innovative ideas involving the community in the education of Mexican American students. In 1968, largely because of the New Horizons program he had developed to reduce high school dropouts among Chicano students, he was named director of the Mexican American Studies Division of the U.S. Commission on Civil Rights by President Lyndon B. Johnson.

In 1971 Ramírez was appointed to a cabinet-level position as chair of the Council on Opportunities for Spanish-Speaking People by President Richard M. Nixon, who was seeking the Latino vote as he prepared to run for a second term. A strong believer in civic participation, in that position Ramírez encouraged greater Latino involvement in community organizational development and in politics. He also made a sustained effort to secure policy-making government appointments for qualified Chicanos. When the council's mandate expired in 1975, Ramírez retired to private life as an educational consultant.

See also JOHNSON, LYNDON BAINES.

FURTHER READING: Martínez, Al. *Rising Voices: Profiles of Hispano-American Lives*. New York: New American Library, 1974; Newlon, Clarke. *Famous Mexican Americans*. New York: Dodd, Mead & Co., 1972.

RAMÍREZ, SARA ESTELA, 1881–1910. Sara Ramírez was born and educated in Mexico but then moved to Laredo, Texas, where she became deeply involved at the beginning of the twentieth century in the struggle for the rights of la raza on both sides of the border. She was a staunch liberal in Mexican politics and became Ricardo Flores Magón's official representative in Texas. Moreover, she applied her liberal principles to a Texas career as a border poet, journalist, teacher, labor organizer, and human rights advocate. In her writings she advocated a new society free of racial, class, and gender discrimination.

A precursor in Chicana feminism, in all her activities Ramírez constantly concerned herself with the liberation of women, whom she urged to take a more active part in the direction of their lives and in their self-realization. When this early leader in defending the rights of la raza died at the age of 29, she was eulogized in the border press as the most knowledgeable Mexicana in Texas.

See also CHICANAS.

FURTHER READING: Mirandé, Alfredo, and Evangelina Enríquez. *La Chicana: The Mexican-American Woman*. Chicago: University of Chicago Press, 1979; Tovar, Inés Hernández. "Sara Estela Ramírez: The Early Twentieth Century Texas-Mexican Poet." Ph.D. diss., University of Houston, 1984; Zamora, Emilio. "Sara Estela Ramírez: Una rosa roja en el movimiento." In *Mexican Women in the United States: Struggles Past and Present*, edited by Magdalena Mora and Adelaida R. Del Castillo. Los Angeles: University of California, Chicano Studies Research Center, 1980.

RANGEL, IRMA, 1931– . In 1982 Irma Rangel became the first Tejana elected to the state legislature. Born to parents who had moved from migrant farm labor to middle-class business entrepreneurship, as a young woman she first studied to become a school teacher. After a decade and a half in the classroom she returned to her earlier dream of studying law. She graduated from St. Mary's Law School in San Antonio in 1969 and subsequently was employed in several legal positions, in which she encountered firsthand the problems of la raza. Her newfound awareness led her to enter politics and eventually to seek and win election to the Texas legislature.

As a lawmaker Irma Rangel has been especially concerned about equal educational opportunity, particularly for women, which she sees as an important key to achieving a successful life. As a legislator she has also emphasized equal access to jobs, fair employment practices, and voting rights for Mexican Americans. She continues to push for equality of educational opportunity.

See also CHICANAS; POLITICAL PARTICIPATION.

FURTHER READING: Munson, Sammye. *Our Tejano Heroes: Outstanding Mexican-Americans in Texas.* Austin: Panda Books, 1989; Phaup, James D. "Ms. Rangel Goes to Austin: The Education of a Legislator." In *Texas Politics Today*, edited by William Earl Maxwell and Ernest Crain. St. Paul: West Publishing Co., 1978; *Who's Who among Hispanic Americans, 1994–1995.* Detroit: Gale Research, 1994.

RAZA UNIDA PARTY, LA (LRUP). Arising out of the Mexican American Youth Organization (MAYO) and the second Crystal City electoral revolt in 1969, the Raza Unida Party was formally established in January 1970 at a meeting of Texas Chicano leaders headed by José Angel Gutiérrez. Several months later Corky Gonzales announced the creation of a Colorado Raza Unida Party.

The concept *La Raza Unida* was not new, dating from the nineteenth century, when the term was first used by Juan N. Cortina in 1848; the phrase was also used by El Paso student activists who formulated a Plan de la Raza Unida in 1967.

The new organization, which quickly replaced MAYO, was conceived not as a single unified organization but, rather, as an umbrella structure that would include a variety of organizations. It soon spread from Texas to the entire Southwest and even to the Midwest, with chapters formed in Illinois, Michigan, Ohio, and Indiana.

Generally LRUP hoped to bring Chicano concerns forcefully to the attention of American society. Its immediate goals were to register Chicanos and organize them into a united independent voting bloc. Where Mexican American voters formed a majority, this bloc could elect candidates to local and state offices; where they were not a majority, they might act as a balance of power, or swing vote, between major party candidates. LRUP's results were mixed.

LRUP victories in local Texas elections in 1970 and 1971 greatly heartened and animated Chicanos. With these successes under its belt LRUP was persuaded by the arguments of Corky Gonzales and his followers to form a nationwide third party. At a convention held in El Paso in September 1972, a national LRUP was established, but there followed a bitter and divisive struggle between Gonzales and Gutiérrez for leadership. The latter, a pragmatic politico heading a largely rural and semi-rural constituency that stressed local issues and generally opposed fielding national candidates, was elected the first national LRUP president. However, Gonzales's more urban organizational viewpoints prevailed.

In the November elections the LRUP candidate for the Texas governorship, Ramsey Muñiz, received over 6 percent of the votes cast, resulting in the first election of a governor by a less-than-majority vote. Elsewhere LRUP candidates were successful in school district and other local elections; some were even elected to minor statewide offices. However, LRUP was unable to develop grassroots support outside of Texas and failed to qualify for the statewide ballot in California and Arizona. This failure was a major political setback.

Although LRUP won local political victories in the mid-1970s, the bloc was no longer solid. Between 1972 and 1974 the LRUP vote dropped by about 50 percent. During the latter year Gonzales took the Colorado LRUP out of the national party. In 1976 the founding of the Mexican American Democrats organization by liberal and activist Chicanos in south Texas cut further into LRUP strength. Two years later Mario Compeán, running for governor of Texas on the LRUP ticket, suffered a humiliating defeat, obtaining less than 2 percent of the vote. His failure to win the minimum vote resulted in LRUP's being dropped from future ballots. Power struggles and personality conflicts within LRUP further weakened the organization, and by the end of the decade it was moribund. The arrest of Muñiz on drug charges gave the party the coup de grace.

Although less than a long-term success as a third party, LRUP did have a substantial role in advancing the civil rights and political empowerment of Chicanos. The ideas it put forward continue to have a real impact on the community's concept of ethnic politics. Further, it forced the Democratic and Republican parties to a more serious recognition of raza concerns and to accept more Chicanos within the party structure, fielding them as candidates at local and state levels. Also, it caused many Mexican Americans to look more critically and with deeper interest at the local, state, and national political scene.

See also CRYSTAL CITY; GONZALES, CORKY; GUTIÉRREZ, JOSÉ ANGEL; MEXICAN AMERICAN YOUTH ORGANIZATION; MUÑIZ, RAMSEY; POLITICAL PARTICIPATION.

FURTHER READING: Compeán, Mario, and José Angel Gutiérrez. *La Raza Unida Party in Texas*. New York: Pathfinder Press, 1970; Foley, Douglas F., Clarice Mota, Donald E. Tost, and Ignacio Lozano. *From Peones to Politicos: Ethnic Relations in a South Texas Town, 1900–1987*. Rev. ed. Austin: University of Texas, Center for Mexican American Studies, 1988; García, Ignacio M. *United We Win: The Rise and Fall of La Raza Unida Party*. Tucson: University of Arizona, MASRC,

1989; Gutiérrez, José Angel. *La Raza and Revolution*. San Francisco: R & E Research Associates, 1972; Muñoz, Carlos, Jr., and María Barrera. "La Raza Unida Party and the Chicano Student Movement in California." In *Latinos and the Political System*, edited by F. Chris García. Notre Dame, Ind.: University of Notre Dame Press, 1988; Navarro, Armando. *The Cristal Experiment: A Chicano Struggle for Community Control*. Madison: University of Wisconsin Press, 1997; Pendas, Miguel, and Harry Ring. *Toward Chicano Power: Building La Raza Unida Party*. New York: Pathfinder Press, 1974; Santillán, Richard A. *Chicano Politics: La Raza Unida*. Los Angeles: Tlaquilo Publications, 1973; Santillán, Richard A. "Viva La Raza Unida." *The Black Politician* 3, no. 3 (January 1972):2–5, 36–38; Shockley, John S. *Chicano Revolt in a Texas Town*. Notre Dame, Ind.: University of Notre Dame Press, 1974.

REPATRIATION. Although the term is usually used to refer specifically to the massive movements of the early 1930s and the mid-1950s, repatriation has been an ongoing process, beginning immediately after the Treaty of Guadalupe Hidalgo when Mexicans who wanted to remain under Mexico rule were assisted by the Mexican government in moving southward across the new border. In the mid-1850s and again in the 1870s Mexico offered various incentives to encourage repatriation but had little response. In all, less than 2 percent of the Mexicano population repatriated in the nineteenth century.

There was a heavy repatriation surge in 1921 when the post–World War I recession sent more than 200,000 unemployed Mexicans back across the border, at which point the government of Mexico then spent $2.5 million to transport them to their hometowns and villages. The long Great Depression that began at the end of the 1920s caused the next surge in repatriation.

Statistics on the volume of this depression-instigated movement are mostly educated guesses, but an idea of the numbers can be obtained from census figures. Between 1930 and 1940 the number of Mexicanos living in the United States but born in Mexico dropped from approximately 640,000 to 377,000, a decline of 263,000. Some recent estimates suggest that as many as half a million Mexican nationals and, in many cases, their American-born children and wives were pushed across the border in the early 1930s, some by deportation and some by fear of deportation.

As nativism and xenophobia swept the country, this repatriation involved widespread ignoring of human and civil rights and their gross violation. Very few deportees were able to obtain a court hearing; and of those that did, many received merely a summary hearing that lasted only a few minutes. The civil rights aspects of this drastic population reduction caused by the Great Depression unquestionably spurred Chicano interest in political empowerment.

The next extensive repatriation drive was Operation Wetback in the mid-1950s. As in the 1930s, this mass roundup and deportation of undocumented Mexicans was heralded by a publicity campaign aimed at encouraging voluntary return to Mexico. Between 1950 and 1955 about 3.7 million deportations occurred; only 63,500 were preceded by formal hearings. President Eisenhower's appointee as attorney general, Herbert Brownell, cited communist infiltration as the chief reason for the mass roundups and deportation of undocumenteds. That rationalization meant that less-than-gentle methods were sometimes used and civil rights were often ignored. Behind the "Red scare" excuse nativism and xenophobia clearly lurked.

See also CIVIL RIGHTS ABUSE; OPERATION WETBACK.

FURTHER READING: Acuña, Rodolfo. *Occupied America: A History of Chicanos.* 3rd ed. New York: Harper & Row, 1988; Balderrama, Francisco E. *Decade of Betrayal: Mexican Repatriation in the 1930s.* Albuquerque: University of New Mexico Press, 1995; García, Juan Ramón. *Operation Wetback: The Mass Deportation of Undocumented Workers in 1954.* Westport, Conn.: Greenwood Press, 1980; Hoffman, Abraham. "Stimulus to Repatriation." In *The Chicano,* edited by Norris Hundley. Santa Barbara, Calif.: Clio Press, 1975; Hoffman, Abraham. *Unwanted Mexican Americans in the Great Depression: Repatriation Pressures, 1929–1939.* Tucson: University of Arizona Press, 1974; Kiser, George C., and David Silverman. "Mexican Repatriation during the Great Depression." *Journal of Mexican American History* 3 (1973):139–164.

REYNOSO, CRUZ, 1931– . With his law degree from Boalt Hall at the University of California, Cruz Reynoso became an important early leader in the California Rural Legal Assistance (CRLA) program. After serving as assistant chief in California's Division of Fair Employment Practices, in 1967 he was appointed general counsel in the federal Equal Employment Opportunity Commission in Washington. He then returned to California to accept the position of deputy director of CRLA; soon he assumed the directorship. He stepped down from that position in 1972 to teach law at the University of New Mexico. Four years later he was appointed an associate justice in the California Court of Appeals, and in 1982 he became the first Mexican American appointed to the California Supreme Court. When he failed to receive voter reconfirmation in the 1986 election as the result of a well-financed conservative attack on his liberal views, he retired to private law practice in Los Angeles.

Reynoso's importance in the Mexican American civil rights struggle is attested to by appointment to various federal and state commissions and to the United Nations Commission on Human Rights.

See also CALIFORNIA RURAL LEGAL ASSISTANCE; COURTS.

FURTHER READING: "Cruz Reynoso, a Distinguished Career," *Caminos* 5, no. 2 (February 1984):36; *Who's Who in America, 1984–1985.* Chicago: Marquis Who's Who, 1984.

RÍOS, ANTHONY P., 1914–1999. One of the founders and developers of the Community Service Organization (CSO), Tony Ríos was a staunch believer in using the ballot to develop what he called "barrio power" in order to achieve raza rights. Ríos was born in Calexico but moved to Los Angeles in the 1930s where he began a career as labor activist while still a teenager, representing his fellow lemon pickers in negotiations with the growers. During a decade of working for various unions he helped organize Los Angeles steel workers as well as agricultural workers, but his most important contribution to la raza's betterment was in community organizing long before such activity became accepted or widespread.

Ríos was one of the principal leaders in a move to "get out" the Mexican American vote that elected Edward Roybal to a Los Angeles city council seat in 1949. To mobilize that vote he helped create and direct the CSO. Throughout his lifelong commitment to the CSO he continued to strongly advocate and be deeply involved in voter registration drives and citizenship classes. Over the years he also helped found and was an officer in various other Mexican American organizations. Because of his extensive involvement in community action he found himself appointed to numerous committees and commissions dealing with civil rights and other community concerns.

When the Chicano Movement blossomed in the late 1960s, the veteran activist was proud of its youthful leaders' demands and efforts for civil rights but felt that the more confrontational militants among them failed to appreciate the long and torturous process of building barrio power. He remained single-mindedly devoted to CSO's goals of overall improvement of la raza's condition until his death from pneumonia in May 1999.

FURTHER READING: Woo, Elaine. "Anthony Rios Dies: Helped Latinos Find Their Political Voice." *Los Angeles Times* (22 May 1999): A17r.

ROCKEFELLER FOUNDATION. The Rockefeller Foundation was established in 1909 by oil magnate John D. Rockefeller with an initial grant of $50 million in Standard Oil of New Jersey stock. Chartered to advance "the wellbeing of mankind throughout the world," it promoted a wide variety of programs aimed at helping the economically deprived. Initially it concentrated in the fields of public health and medicine. One of its achievements in its early years was the eradication of hookworm, an intestinal parasite that plagued the rural poor, particularly in the American South. Today among its principal objectives are equality of opportunity, educational advancement, and various cultural concerns.

Always seeking to advance its goals in contemporary terms, in the late 1960s the Rockefeller Foundation began to provide invaluable start-up funds to such important Chicano civil rights organizations as the Mexican American Legal Defense and Educational Fund in San Antonio and the

Southwest (now National) Council of La Raza in Phoenix. Its financial support of these and other Mexican American groups was crucial to the development of the Chicano civil rights struggle in the 1960s.

See also MEXICAN AMERICAN LEGAL DEFENSE AND EDUCATIONAL FUND; NATIONAL COUNCIL OF LA RAZA.

FURTHER READING: Fosdick, Raymond B. *The Story of the Rockefeller Foundation*. Reprint, New Brunswick, N.J.: Transaction Publishers, 1989; Nielsen, Waldemar A. *The Big Foundations*. New York: Columbia University Press, 1972; Shaplen, Robert. *Toward the Well-being of Mankind: Fifty Years of the Rockefeller Foundation*. Garden City, N.Y.: Doubleday, 1974.

RODRÍGUEZ, RICHARD, 1944– . Richard Rodríguez's first published work, *Hunger of Memory: The Education of Richard Rodríguez, an Autobiography* (1981), made him an instant celebrity as well as the center of considerable controversy. His defense of civil rights in the book won for him the Anisfield-Wolf Award for Race Relations from the Cleveland Foundation in 1982, and his criticism of affirmative action and bilingual education caused many Chicanos to accuse him of betraying la raza.

Rodríguez objected to affirmative action mainly because he felt it benefited principally Mexican American middle-class members like himself, who were no longer deeply disadvantaged, rather than barrio youths who most needed remedial assistance. Class, not ethnicity, he argued, should be the basis of affirmative action. A literature specialist, he personally rejected the help of affirmative action by turning down several job offers from prestigious universities.

Rodríguez's second book, *Days of Obligation: An Argument with My Mexican Father* (1993), although less controversial, reiterated his firm belief in English as the "public language." At the same time he lamented the loss of ethnic cultures in the United States and worldwide. He believes that everyone should learn the "public language" and that most bilingual and bicultural programs were and are ill-conceived. He continues to express his views with candor and clarity in the media, particularly on radio and in the press.

See also AFFIRMATIVE ACTION; BILINGUAL EDUCATION.

FURTHER READING: Holt, Patricia. "Richard Rodríguez." *Publishers Weekly*, (26 March 1982): 6–8; Rodríguez, Richard. *Hunger of Memory: The Education of Richard Rodríguez, an Autobiography*. Boston: David R. Godine, 1981; Tardiff, Joseph C., and L. Mpho Mabunda, eds. *Dictionary of Hispanic Biography*. Detroit: Gale Research, 1996; Zweig, Paul. "The Child of Two Cultures." *New York Times Book Review* (28 February 1982).

ROMANO-V., OCTAVIO I., 1932– . As a speaker, writer, editor, and publisher Octavio Romano was one of the important early activists in the

Chicano movement for greater civil rights. A social anthropology professor at the University of California, Berkeley, he spoke out against demeaning stereotypes of Mexican Americans in the many talks that he gave in the late 1960s and early 1970s.

In addition to giving speeches, mostly at colleges and universities, Octavio Romano's important contribution to the Mexican American struggle for rights was in helping to found Quinto Sol Publications in 1967 and in editing *El Grito: A Journal of Contemporary Mexican-American Thought*, of which he was also one of the founders. Quinto Sol provided a publisher for Chicano authors at a time when Anglo literary experts widely denied that there was such a thing as Chicano literature. *El Grito* served as a forum for essays defending Chicanos' social and civil rights at a time when forums in which such discussion could take place were extremely limited.

See also CHICANO LITERATURE; STEREOTYPING.

FURTHER READING: Martínez, Julio A. *Chicano Scholars and Writers: A Bio-Bibliographical Directory*. Metuchen, N.J.: Scarecrow Press, 1979; Meier, Matt S. *Mexican American Biographies: A Historical Dictionary, 1836–1987*. Westport, Conn.: Greenwood Press, 1988.

ROSS, FRED, SR., 1910–1992. When he graduated from the University of Southern California in 1936, Fred Ross was unable to get a teaching position as he had hoped. Instead, he went to work for the California State Relief Agency and in the late 1930s managed a migrant workers' camp for the U.S. Farm Security Administration. After an administrative position in an internment camp for Japanese Americans during World War II, he returned to southern California, where he went to work organizing Unity Leagues for the American Council on Race Relations. Making the acquaintance of Saul Alinsky led to his involvement in developing Community Service Organization (CSO) groups to demonstrate to barrio residents how they might protect and advance their civil rights.

Through his CSO organizing Ross made the acquaintance of César Chávez, whom he persuaded Alinsky to hire as a CSO organizer in 1954. When Chávez left the CSO nearly a decade later to begin developing his union among harvest agricultural workers, he prevailed upon Ross to join in the effort. Throughout the Delano grape strike (1965–1970) and beyond into the mid-1970s, Ross was responsible for training recruiters and organizers for the UFW union in its struggle for farmworkers' rights. After a life dedicated to defending and advancing the rights of the poor and powerless, he died in 1992.

See also COMMUNITY SERVICE ORGANIZATION; UNITED FARM WORKERS; UNITY LEAGUES.

FURTHER READING: Rodríguez, Roberto. "Fred Ross: Unsung Hero." *Caminos*

5, no. 8 (September-October 1985):40; Ross, Fred W. (Sr.) *Community Organization in Mexican-American Communities*. Los Angeles: American Council on Race Relations, 1947; Ross, Fred W. (Sr.) *Conquering Goliath: César Chávez at the Beginning*. Keene, Calif.: UFW, 1989.

ROYBAL, EDWARD R. 1916– . Edward Roybal's life has been devoted to service, from volunteer work testing school children for tuberculosis to 30 years in the U.S. House of Representatives advancing the cause of civil rights.

Born February 10, 1916, in Albuquerque, New Mexico, Roybal grew up in Boyle Heights, a Mexicano barrio of Los Angeles, and attended public school there. After graduating in 1933 from Roosevelt High and completing a stint in the Civilian Conservation Corps, he entered the University of California at Los Angeles, from which he earned an undergraduate degree in accounting.

While working for 20th Century Fox Studios after graduation, he first became aware of the high incidence of tuberculosis among Mexican Americans and the importance of testing for the disease among children. His volunteer work testing school children led to a position as a public health educator for the Los Angeles County Tuberculosis and Health Association. Roybal's career with the association was interrupted by World War II. Upon his discharge from the U.S. Army he resumed his career in public health as director of health education for the tuberculosis association. In his new position he quickly perceived the politics of public health service and decided to file for political office.

After running unsuccessfully in 1947 for a seat on the Los Angeles City Council, he was able to win two years later with the support of the Community Service Organization. The first Mexican American to serve on the city council in the twentieth century, he subsequently won reelection regularly. As a councillor, he emphasized community rights to health care.

After 13 years on the council, in 1962 Roybal ran for the U.S. House of Representatives and took his place in Washington, D.C. For the next thirty years he was easily reelected every two years. In Congress he continued to demonstrate his concern for human rights, health care, and social reform. Roybal strongly supported bilingual education and advanced civil rights for Chicanos by introducing and shepherding through Congress a bill to create the cabinet-level Committee on Opportunities for Spanish Speaking People. During a half century of public service he constantly advocated greater citizen participation in the political process.

To further the cause of civil rights, in 1975 Edward Roybal conceived and helped create the National Association of Latino Elected and Appointed Officials, and two years later was instrumental in establishing the Hispanic Congressional Caucus. In addition to his vigorous participation in these groups and his service on congressional committees, he was also active in a variety of nongovernmental organizations with broad human rights goals.

A moderate, nonconfrontational, and energetic activist, Congressman Roybal retired from politics in January 1993 after a lifetime of service to his fellow Americans. In retirement he has continued to champion the rights of all Americans to health care.

See also LEADERSHIP; NATIONAL ASSOCIATION OF LATINO ELECTED AND APPOINTED OFFICIALS; POLITICAL PARTICIPATION.

FURTHER READING: Cantú, Héctor. "Roybal: A Long-Distance Runner Who Made a Difference." *Hispanic Business* 14, no. 5 (May 1992):50, 52; Díaz, Katherine A. "Congressman Edward Roybal: Los Angeles before the 1960s." *Caminos* 4, no. 7 (July–August 1983):15–17, 38; Ehrenhalt, Alan, ed. *Politics in America.* Washington, D.C.: Congressional Quarterly, 1983; Griffith, Beatrice W. "Viva Roybal—Viva America." *Common Ground* 10 (Autumn 1949):61–70; Rodríguez, Roberto. "Congressman Edward Roybal: Elder Statesman." *Américas 2001* 1, no. 1 (June–July 1987):23–25; Roybal, Edward R. "Hispanics: A Political Perspective." *Social Education* 43 (February 1979):101–103; Vigil, Maurilio E. *Hispanics in Congress: A Historical and Political Survey.* Lanham, Md.: University Press of America, 1996.

S

SACRAMENTO MARCH, 1966. By early 1966 the first bloom of the Delano grape strike was beginning to fade. Strikebreakers had been brought into the vineyards; financial support for the strikers had yet to be developed. Recognizing the need for a dramatic project to raise the strikers' lagging spirits as well as the importance of a vehicle for publicity and recruiting, César Chávez announced a march from Delano to the capitol steps to demand help from the governor of California in the battle for farmworker rights.

Based loosely on the concept of a pilgrimage to a shrine—called a *peregrinación* by the marchers—the march was heralded by large banners of the image of the Virgin of Guadalupe. However, it attracted Protestants, Jews, agnostics, and atheists as well as Catholics. The 300-mile, 25-day march began in Delano with some 60 marchers, grew at times to as many as 1,000, and swept into Sacramento on Easter Sunday only to find that Governor "Pat" Brown had opted to visit his friend Frank Sinatra in Palm Springs rather than meet the farmworkers.

To offset this disappointment, at Sacramento Chávez was able to announce the welcome news that the Schenley liquor company, which owned several vineyards in California's central valley, had agreed to negotiate with the union. The march served its purposes extremely well and was later imitated by striking farmworkers in Texas.

See also CHÁVEZ, CÉSAR.

FURTHER READING: "From Delano to Sacramento." *America* 114 (April 1966): 430; "March of the Migrants." *Life* 60, no. 17 (April 1966):94–95; Matthiesen, Peter. *Sal si puedes: César Chávez and the New American Revolution.* New York: Random House, 1969.

SÁENZ, JOSÉ DE LA LUZ, 1888–1953. Although he remains a little-known figure in the Mexican American civil rights struggle, José de la Luz

Sáenz played an important part in its early development. The first male Mexican American graduate of the Alice, Texas, public high school, he enjoyed a long career as a teacher and south Texas community leader with an abiding interest in education.

Returning from service in World War I and strongly believing that Mexican Americans' contributions in the war should assure all Mexicans of all citizen rights, Sáenz continued his prewar efforts to advance the cause of equal treatment and full civil rights for Mexican Americans. He was active in the formation of the League of United Latin American Citizens (LULAC) in the late 1920s, playing an important part in developing its first constitution. From 1930 to 1932 he served on its board of trustees, and throughout the 1930s and 1940s he promoted and refined LULAC's point of view through numerous articles in south Texas English- and Spanish-language newspapers. A strong belief in the democratic ideal sustained him in his long fight for equality of treatment for Mexicanos. When he died in 1953, he was buried in the National Cemetery at Fort Sam Houston in San Antonio.

See also LEAGUE OF UNITED LATIN AMERICAN CITIZENS.

FURTHER READING: Zamora, Emilio. "Fighting on Two Fronts: The World War I Diary of José de la Luz Sáenz and the Language of the Mexican American Civil Rights Movement." Paper presented at the Fifth Conference of Recovering the U.S. Hispanic Literary Heritage, Houston, Tex., 4–5 December 1998.

SAGER, MANUELA SOLÍS, 1912–1996. Although primarily a labor organizer, Manuela Solís spent a long lifetime in support of civil rights and human dignity. While still a teenager she began organizing workers to demand their rights. Her early leadership in the cause of Chicano laborers in Texas made a valuable contribution to their struggle for social and civil rights. Her vigorous efforts in developing unions among agricultural and garment workers during the early 1930s led to appointment, with her husband James Sager, as official organizers in the Rio Grande Valley by the South Texas Agricultural Workers Union when it was founded in 1935. Three years later she and her husband were among the leaders of the San Antonio pecan shellers' strike.

A member of the Communist Party for 60 years, Sager was aggressively involved in all the major struggles against racist discrimination and for civil rights that took place during her lifetime. She played an energetic role in defending immigrants' rights, advocating electoral politics, promoting the early feminist movement in Texas, promoting the Chicano movimiento, and supporting various other liberal and leftist causes. At the beginning of the 1970s she spoke out forcefully for the Raza Unida Party as part of her long fight for Mexicano civil rights.

Manuela Solís Sager died in California while visiting her son.

See also TENAYUCA, EMMA.

FURTHER READING: Calderón, Roberto R., and Emilio Zamora. "Manuela Solis Sager and Emma Tenayuca: A Tribute." In *Between Borders: Essays in Mexicana/Chicana History*, edited by Adelaida R. Del Castillo. Encino, Calif.: Floricanto Press, 1990; *Las Mujeres: Mexican American/Chicana Women*. Windsor, Calif.: National Women's History Project, 1991.

SALAZAR, RUBÉN, 1928–1970. Print and television journalist Rubén Salazar was, without dispute, the most prominent casualty in the twentieth century Chicano struggle for civil rights. A journalism graduate of the University of Texas at El Paso, Salazar got his early newspaper experience as a reporter on the El Paso *Herald Post*, the *Press Democrat* in Santa Rosa, California, and the *San Francisco News*. In 1959 he became a member of the staff of the *Los Angeles Times*. During his years in the city room he wrote a column in which he gave voice to the civil rights concerns and other matters of interest to Chicanos in East Los Angeles. His series of articles on the Los Angeles Latino community earned him a reputation for conscientious and objective reporting as well as an award.

In 1965 Salazar was sent to Vietnam to cover the rapidly escalating American involvement there and two years later was named *Los Angeles Times* bureau chief in Mexico City. Back in Los Angeles at the end of 1968, Salazar was given the assignment of covering the Mexican American community in which the Chicano Movement was getting under way.

In late 1969 Salazar accepted a position as news director of station KMEX-TV but continued to write a weekly *Times* column interpreting the Chicano community. A political moderate, he wrote in a responsible, professional manner condemning racism, segregation, and denial of civil rights. Abuses by the police became his area of special concern, and as a result he soon became the target of local police investigation and federal surveillance.

In late August 1970 Rubén Salazar covered the National Chicano Moratorium march in Los Angeles, organized to protest U.S. involvement in Vietnam. Toward the end of the march he was relaxing with friends in the Silver Dollar Cafe when he was killed instantly by a tear gas projectile that hit him in the head. The subsequent televised 16-day coroner's inquest did not indict the deputy sheriff who fired the projectile. Many, both Anglos and Chicanos, felt that the inquest was seriously botched.

The tragic and never adequately explained killing of the prominent and popular Salazar transformed him into an instant martyr of the Chicano Movement. His unfortunate death and the coroner's flawed decision made him a symbol of police abuse and the failure of the American justice system to uphold the civil rights of Mexican Americans.

See also CIVIL RIGHTS ABUSE; NATIONAL CHICANO MORATORIUM.

FURTHER READING: "Death in the Barrio." *Newsweek*, 14 September 1970; Gómez, David F. "Killing of Rubén Salazar: Nothing Has Really Changed in the Barrio." *Christian Century* 88 (January 1971):49–52; Gómez, David F. "The Story of Rubén Salazar." In *Introduction to Chicano Studies*, edited by Livie I. Durán and H. Russell Bernard. 2nd ed. New York: Macmillan, 1982; Salazar, Rubén. *Border Correspondent: Selected Writings, 1955–1970*. Edited by Mario T. García. Berkeley: University of California Press, 1995; Salazar, Sally. "Rubén Salazar: The Man Not the Myth." *The Press Democrat*, Santa Rosa, Calif. (29 August 1980).

SALVATIERRA v. DEL RIO INDEPENDENT SCHOOL DISTRICT,

1930. *Salvatierra v. Del Rio* was a class-action suit filed in the Texas courts by Mexican American parents against school officials of the border town of Del Rio. In this early legal challenge to ethnic segregation in Texas public schools, the parents, with help from the recently formed League of United Latin American Citizens, argued that placing their children in a separate facility because of their ethnicity violated the U.S. Constitution. The issue was neither the content nor the quality of the education, only the placing of their children in a building separate from the other students because they were Mexicano. The school superintendent countered that language problems, plus late enrollment and irregular attendance of migrant workers' children, were the basis for the separation and denied that the school was discriminating on the basis of ethnicity or race.

In a decision disheartening to the parents, the court held that there was no evidence of intent to discriminate and that the school district policies were based on legitimate educational practices. In other words, it said that while racial discrimination was illegal, segregation based on educational grounds was permissible and did not violate the Constitution. This decision formed the basis for judicial responses to Mexican American challenges to school segregation in Texas until the *Delgado* case in 1948.

See also DISCRIMINATION; SEGREGATION.

FURTHER READING: San Miguel, Guadalupe, Jr., *"Let All of Them Take Heed": Mexican Americans and the Campaign for Educational Equality in Texas, 1910–1981*. Austin: University of Texas Press, 1987; Tyler, Ron, ed. *The New Handbook of Texas*. Vol. 5. Austin: Texas State Historical Association, 1996.

SAMORA, JULIAN, 1921–1996.

Growing up, Julian Samora frequently encountered pervasive discrimination and prejudice against Mexican Americans, an experience that spurred him to a lifelong commitment as an educator to fight for civil and societal rights. His 1953 doctoral degree from Washington University led to a pioneering role as a university professor in Chicano sociology.

A leader in the first generation of Mexican American scholars, Samora spent almost all of his 28-year academic career at Notre Dame University, which, as head of the sociology department, he made into a leading center of research and publishing about the Chicano experience. He also attracted numerous graduate students who formed a "school" of followers. Moreover, he found time to research and write; he was the author or co-author of numerous works, the best known of which were *La Raza: Forgotten Americans* (1966) and *Gunpowder Justice* (1979), a critical history of the Texas Rangers.

In addition to his academic leadership and his research and publishing, Samora was an activist who helped found the Southwest Council of La Raza and the Mexican American Legal Defense and Educational Fund, two outstanding advocacy organizations for Chicano rights. He also modestly accepted some credit for the Chicano Movement that began in the mid-1960s. He worked tirelessly to persuade government agencies to implement and enforce policies aimed at helping Mexican Americans achieve their civil rights. His important role as a leading Mexican American scholar and an energetic civil rights activist was acknowledged by a presidential Hispanic Heritage Award as well as by the Mexican government's giving him the Order of the Águila Azteca, its highest award to a foreigner.

See also MEXICAN AMERICAN LEGAL DEFENSE AND EDUCATIONAL FUND; MOVIMIENTO, EL.

FURTHER READING: Rodríguez, Roberto. "Chicano Studies Pioneer Praised." *Black Issues in Higher Education* 12 (October 1995):34–37; Thomas, Robert M., Jr. "Julian Samora, 75, a Pioneering Sociologist." *New York Times*, 6 February 1996, B11.

SÁNCHEZ, GEORGE I., 1906–1972. George I. Sánchez, grand old man of the Mexican American civil rights struggle, spent a lifetime as an activist persistently advocating greater social justice for la raza. Both as an individual and as a professional he was constantly concerned with the interests and rights of Chicanos, particularly with educational rights. He was an early champion of bilingual education as a way of improving educational opportunity for Spanish-speaking children. He viewed education as the key to effecting social change and wider enjoyment of civil rights by Mexican Americans.

Jorge Isidro Sánchez y Sánchez, son of a miner, received his early education in Jerome, Arizona, graduated from Albuquerque (New Mexico) High School at 16, and began teaching in a one-room school. By the end of the 1920s he had earned his A.B. degree at the University of New Mexico. With a Rockefeller Foundation fellowship he was able to continue his studies at the University of Texas at Austin, under Herschel T. Manuel. In 1934 he completed the requirements for a doctorate in education at the University of California, Berkeley. His doctoral dissertation was titled "The Education of Bilinguals in a State School System."

After three years spent surveying rural schools in the Southwest, the

American South, and northern Mexico for the Julius Rosenwald Fund and
one year in Venezuela as director of the National Teaching Institute, Sánchez returned to the Southwest as associate professor at the University of
New Mexico. In 1940 he moved to the University of Texas at Austin, which
remained his academic base for the rest of his life. From it he sallied forth
frequently to share his sociological and educational expertise with occu-
pants of the White House and with various government agencies.

During World War II Sánchez took a leave of absence from academia to
work in the Office of Coordinator of Inter-American Affairs. An outstanding expert on the scholastic and social needs of Spanish-speaking children,
he returned to the university after the war and spent a quarter of a century
constantly and deeply involved with their education. In 1951 he was the
driving force in founding and directing the American Council for Spanish-
Speaking People, which focused attention on issues of school segregation
and discrimination. In addition, he continued to carry a full teaching load
at the university.

Outside the university Sánchez remained active in Mexican American
organizations with civil rights objectives. He served as director of education
in the League of United Latin American Citizens for several years and was
its president in 1941–1942. During the 1960s he strongly supported the
Chicano Movement, which he saw as an important step in righting historical wrongs suffered by la raza. Nevertheless, some young activists criticized
him for not supporting Chicano nationalism and for being, in their view,
insufficiently militant. On the other hand, his outspoken and clearly articulated views in support of the movement may have hurt him professionally
and financially.

Author of over 100 journal articles, reports, and bulletins as well as a
number of important books, George I. Sánchez remains best known for his
1940 seminal work *Forgotten People: A Study of New Mexicans.* An outstanding scholar, he served as spokesman for la raza for more than 40
years, condemning educational and social segregation and demanding
greater equality of opportunity for all Americans.

See also BILINGUAL EDUCATION; EDUCATION; MOVIMIENTO,
EL; SEGREGATION.

FURTHER READING: García, Mario T. *Mexican Americans: Leadership, Ideol-
ogy, and Identity, 1930–1960.* New Haven, Conn.: Yale University Press, 1989;
Getz, Lynne Marie. *Schools of Their Own: The Education of Hispanos in New
Mexico, 1850–1940.* Albuquerque: University of New Mexico Press, 1994; Leff,
Gladys R. "George I. Sánchez: Don Quixote of the Southwest," Master's thesis,
North Texas State University at Denton, 1976; Paredes, Américo, ed. *Humanidad:
Essays in Honor of George I. Sánchez.* Los Angeles: University of California, Chi-
cano Studies Center, 1977; Romo, Ricardo. "George I Sánchez and the Civil
Rights Movement: 1940–1960." *La Raza Law Journal* 1, no. 3 (Fall 1986):342–
362; Welsh, Michael. "A Prophet without Honor: George I. Sánchez and Bilin-

gualism in New Mexico." *New Mexico Historical Review* 69, no. 1 (January 1994):19–34.

SCHECHTER, HOPE MENDOZA, 1921– . When Esperanza Mendoza dropped out of high school at age 17, she went to work in the Los Angeles garment industry, and after World War II she returned to help organize garment workers to defend their rights. During the late 1940s and early 1950s she began to interest herself in community affairs and was one of the southern California founders of the Community Service Organization, on the board of which she served for seven years.

After her marriage to Harvey Schechter in 1955, she turned increasingly to Democratic politics but continued her deep concern for the raza community. Her continuing devotion to Mexican American problems and her expanding political activities in the Democratic Party led her to accept positions on the board of directors in the Mexican American Youth Opportunities Foundation and in the Council of Mexican American Affairs. She also served on various councils and groups associated with the Democratic Party. Throughout her career the concerns and rights of her fellow working-class Mexican Americans gave shape to the driving forces in her life.

See also COMMUNITY SERVICE ORGANIZATION.

FURTHER READING: "Hope Mendoza Schechter: Activist in the Labor Movement, the Democratic Party, and the Mexican-American Community." Berkeley: Regional Oral History Office, Bancroft Library, University of California, 1980.

SECRETARIAT FOR THE SPANISH SPEAKING. The Bishops Committee for the Spanish Speaking, which evolved into the Secretariat for the Spanish Speaking, was created in 1945 under the leadership of San Antonio archbishop Robert E. Lucey. It aimed to develop social as well as spiritual programs for improving the lives of Mexican Americans. With a serious concern for community self-help development, it also provided a variety of social services, including citizenship classes, voter registration, youth programs, and leadership training.

In 1975, as the Secretariat, it became an agency of the National Conference of Catholic Bishops. From its headquarters in Washington, D.C., the secretariat acts as a concept and planning center and as an organizing tool for programs in areas as disparate as health, employment, housing, education, and civil rights—in addition to various pastoral concerns. The secretariat played a vital role in bringing the Delano grape strike to a successful conclusion in 1970.

See also CHURCHES; LUCEY, ROBERT E.

FURTHER READING: Curran, Charles E. *Directions of Catholic Social Ethics.* Notre Dame, Ind.: University of Notre Dame Press, 1985; Dolan, Jay P., and Gilberto M. Hinojosa, eds. *Mexican Americans and the Catholic Church, 1900–1965.* Notre Dame, Ind.: University of Notre Dame Press, 1994; Privett, Stephen A. "Planting Seeds: National Committees for the Spanish Speaking." *Living Light* 31 (Winter 1994):3–16; Privett, Stephen A. *The U.S. Catholic Church and Its Hispanic Members: The Pastoral Vision of Archbishop Robert E. Lucey.* San Antonio: Trinity University Press, 1988; Walsh, Albeus. "Work of the Catholic Bishops Committee for the Spanish Speaking in the U.S." Master's thesis, University of Texas at Austin, 1952.

SEGREGATION. Segregation is the isolation of ethnic or racial groups by law or custom resulting in discrimination in favor of one group over another. Segregation may be de facto (without a legal basis) or de jure (based on legislation). With some widespread exception in education, most of the segregation suffered by Mexicanos has been de facto. Although de jure segregation has been declared illegal, de facto segregation of Mexican Americans continues to exist.

Mexican Americans have been subjected to segregation in three areas: schools, housing, and public and semi-public facilities. In the last category they have been refused service in restaurants, restricted in use of swimming pools, forced to sit in certain seats in theaters, denied rooms in hotels, and refused personal services. The campaigns against such customary practices by southern Californian Ignacio López in his paper *El Espectador*, by the American G.I. Forum in Texas, and by the Alianza Hispano-Americana in Arizona have had considerable success. This discrimination, once commonplace in areas of heavy Mexicano population, has greatly attenuated since the 1960s.

Although conditions have improved in recent decades, in housing Mexican Americans have historically been forced to live in barrios, separate sections apart from mainstream townspeople. This segregation is partly the result of income levels, but real estate firms' policies of ethnic discrimination and racism, embodied in restrictive housing covenants, also account for the isolation. These widely practiced exclusionary usages have often forced Mexican Americans to accept inferior housing. Nearly all such practices have their basis in custom, not in law. In the matter of school segregation, in contrast, law has had a paramount role.

As a result of school board policies, segregation in the schools was widespread until the past few decades, with separate schools or classrooms often justified on the basis of a language problem. Education codes fixed separation of Mexican American children in the fabric of school systems. Only at the end of the 1920s did Chicano parents begin fighting school districts' segregation policies and demanding better educational opportunities for their children. In the 1930 case of *Salvatierra v. Del Rio Independent School District* (Texas), the court, finding that Mexicano children were being indiscriminatingly segregated without regard for individual language ability, held that separate classes could be used only for legitimate educational goals. In the *Méndez*, or Westminster, California, case 15 years later, a federal court ruled that the school board's policy of segregation violated the Fourteenth Amendment to the U.S. Constitution, which guaranteed equal protection of the law. The school district resisted this decision, but the court's opinion was upheld on appeal. The League of United Latin American Citizens (LULAC) supplied the attorneys who fought this important case. LULAC's long and outstanding leadership in fighting school segregation since the 1930s has been notable.

See also EDUCATION; HOUSING; LEAGUE OF UNITED LATIN AMERICAN CITIZENS.

FURTHER READING: Donato, Rubén. *The Other Struggle for Equal Schools: Mexican Americans during the Civil Rights Era*. Albany: State University of New York Press, 1997; González, Gilbert G. "The Rise and Fall of De Jure Segregation in the Southwest." In *Chicano Education in the Era of Segregation*. Philadelphia: Balch Institute Press, 1990; Guzmán, Ralph. "The Hand of Esau: Words Change, Practices Remain in Racial Covenants." *Frontier* 7, no. 8 (June 1956):7, 16; Montejano, David. "The Demise of Jim Crow." In *Land Grants, Housing, and Political Power*, edited by Antoinette Sedillo López. New York: Garland Publishing, 1995; Moore, Joan W., and Frank Mittelbach. *Residential Segregation in the Urban Southwest*. Los Angeles: Mexican American Study Project University of California, 1966; Rangel, Jorge C., and Carlos C. Alcalá. "Project Report: De Jure Segregation of Chicanos in Texas Schools." *Harvard Civil Rights–Civil Liberties Law Review* 7 (March 1972):307–391; "Residential Segregation." In *The Mexican American People: The Nation's Second Largest Minority*, edited by Leo Grebler, Joan W. Moore, and Ralph C. Guzmán. New York: Free Press, 1970; Sánchez, George I. *Concerning Segregation of Spanish-Speaking Children in the Public Schools*. Austin: University of Texas Press, 1951; Wollenberg, Charles. *All Deliberate Speed: Segregation and Exclusion in California Schools, 1855–1975*. Berkeley: University of California Press, 1976.

SEGUÍN, JUAN NEPOMUCENO, 1806–1889. Juan Seguín served his native Texas faithfully and well as a soldier and officer during the Texas revolt against Mexican centralism in 1836 and then as a Texas senator and mayor of San Antonio. One of the leading Tejano officials of the nineteenth century, as mayor he staunchly defended Tejano rights and was repaid with the bitter enmity of Anglo adventurers who descended on Texas after her independence. Their intense, unremitting hatred and harrying followed him for the rest of his life.

Seguín was born in San Antonio, son of a prominent civic leader. Given his father's political and economic prominence, Juan naturally entered the political arena at an early age. As a Tejano political leader he became a close friend of the Anglo impresario land grantee Stephen F. Austin, with whom he served in the fight for Texas independence. After the struggle had been won, he was unjustly accused of traitorous sentiments and of being too favorably disposed toward the Mexican army when it later invaded in attempts to reconquer Texas.

Repeated threats to his life and mounting danger to his family finally forced Seguín to move his family out of Texas. Across the border he was jailed by local military officials and, on President Antonio López de Santa Anna's direct orders, given the choice of army service or imprisonment. With a large family to provide for, the impoverished Seguín felt he had little choice. After the 1848 Treaty of Guadalupe Hidalgo he was allowed to return to his native Texas with his family, despite strong vocal opposition.

During the 1850s and 1860s Seguín continued his interest in Texas politics, living quietly on a family ranch near San Antonio and writing his memoirs, in which he defended his conduct and described the hounding by his enemies. In the 1870s Seguín once again crossed the Rio Grande, and in 1889 he died at the home of one of his sons in the Mexican border state of Nuevo León.

See also TEXAS.

FURTHER READING: Seguín, Juan. *Personal Memoirs of John N. Seguín from 1834 to . . . 1842.* San Antonio: Ledger Book and Job Office, 1858; Seguín, Juan. *A Revolution Remembered: The Memoirs and Selected Correspondence of Juan N. Seguín,* edited by Jesús F. de la Teja. Austin: State House Press, 1991; Vernon, Ida S. "Activities of the Seguins in Early Texas History." *West Texas Historical Association Year Book* 25 (October 1949):11–38.

SERRANO v. PRIEST, 1968–1976. In 1968 John Serrano filed a suit against the California state treasurer arguing that his son's receiving an inferior education was the result of property tax–financed schools. He held that this was a violation of his son's civil rights. The California courts, up to and including the California Supreme Court, held for Serrano, opining that financing through property taxes failed to give equal protection under the law. In 1976 the U.S. Supreme Court upheld the decision of the California courts but limited its finding to that state, basing its decision on the California constitution. The decision was an important step in shifting school financing away from a property tax base.

See also EDUCATION.

FURTHER READING: Acuña, Rodolfo. *Occupied America: A History of Chicanos.* 3rd ed. New York: Harper & Row, 1988; Kanellos, Nicolás. *Chronology of Hispanic American History.* New York: Gale Research, 1995.

SILEX, HUMBERTO, 1903–? Nicaraguan immigrant Humberto Silex spent his life as a labor organizer along the Mexico–U.S. border, particularly in the Southwest copper industry. After brief service in the U.S. Army toward the end of World War I, he worked at various jobs in the Midwest and Southwest. Early in the 1930s he settled in El Paso, where he soon went to work for American Smelting and Refining Company (ASARCO). By 1937 he became seriously involved in union organizing for the Congress of Industrial Organizations (CIO). In 1940 he was fired and blacklisted for his organizing activity. However, he regained his job through the 1935 Wagner-Connery Labor Relations Act and resumed his union activity.

Silex strongly supported and recruited for the International Union of Mine, Mill, and Smelter Workers, CIO, which opposed all discrimination. As president of Local 509 Silex was instrumental in obtaining a ruling to end discriminatory practices at ASARCO. After World War II he was one of the leaders in a successful four-month-long 1946 strike of 1,100 workers, mostly Mexicanos, against ASARCO and Dodge-Phelps. While the strike was in progress, the Immigration and Naturalization Service initiated what was to be a years-long effort to deport Silex, despite his completely legal status. His blacklisting was to last even longer, forcing him to be in constant search for work.

See also CIVIL RIGHTS ABUSE.

FURTHER READING: Acuña, Rodolfo. *Occupied America: A History of Chicanos.* 3rd ed. New York: Harper & Row, 1988; Arnold, Frank. "Humberto Silex: CIO Organizer from Nicaragua." *Southwest Economy and Society* (Fall 1978):3–18.

SLEEPY LAGOON, 1942–1944. Sleepy Lagoon was the name given by the press to an important murder case in late 1942. In the death by beating of one José Díaz on the outskirts of Los Angeles, 24 members of a Chicano street gang were indicted by the grand jury. After a lengthy trial in which no direct evidence was brought forward to link the accused to Díaz's death and in which anti-Mexican bias was rampant, 17 of the indicted youths were found guilty of murder or assault.

A Sleepy Lagoon Defense Committee, organized by Josefina Fierro de Bright and headed by Carey McWilliams, led a campaign to appeal the court's decision. In October 1944 the California District Court of Appeals by unanimous vote voided the verdicts of the lower court for lack of evidence; it also criticized the judge, Charles W. Fricke, and the prosecutor for their biased and racist conduct of the trial.

The flagrant and systematic violation of the accused youths' civil rights in the Sleepy Lagoon affair aroused widespread indignation that led to limited and temporary amelioration of civil rights abuses in the Los Angeles area.

See also COURTS; FIERRO DE BRIGHT, JOSEFINA; MCWILLIAMS, CAREY.

FURTHER READING: Barrett, Edward L., Jr. *The Tenny Committee.* Ithaca, N.Y.: Cornell University Press, 1951; Cortez, Rubén. "Sleepy Lagoon and the 'Mexican Crime Campaign.' " *Probe* 2, no. 4 (April 1969):4, 10. Endore, S. Guy. *The*

Sleepy Lagoon Mystery. Los Angeles: Sleepy Lagoon Defense Committee, 1944. Reprint, San Francisco: R & E Research Associates, 1972; Eulau, Heinz H. "Sleepy Lagoon Case." *New Republic* 111 (December 1944):795–796; McWilliams, Carey. *North from Mexico: The Spanish-Speaking People of the United States.* Revised ed. New York: Praeger Publishers, 1990; *The Sleepy Lagoon Case.* Los Angeles: Sleepy Lagoon Defense Committee, 1943. Reprinted in *The Mexican American and the Law.* New York: Arno Press, 1974.

SOCIAL RIGHTS. The term *social rights* perhaps should be limited to those rights or privileges in social intercourse that are not guaranteed by constitutional provisions or statute legislation and for the violation of which there is no recourse in law. Like human rights, social rights may become civil rights through the passage of appropriate legislation.

FURTHER READING: Pole, J. R. *The Pursuit of Equality in American History.* Berkeley: University of California Press, 1979.

SOUTHWEST VOTER REGISTRATION EDUCATION PROJECT (SVREP). Modeled on the Voter Education Project initiated by African Americans in the 1960s, the SVREP was founded in 1974 by Willie Velásquez in San Antonio with the help of a small grant. It aimed to work with existing agencies and has been closely allied with the Mexican American Legal Defense and Educational Fund and other Chicano organizations and community groups with objectives similar to its own. Relying on a small staff and a large volunteer network, it centers its activities on voter registration drives and also files suits over voting restrictions suffered by Chicanos. It has also conducted studies and issued reports on political matters of concern to the Mexican American community.

Aided by the 1975 and 1982 changes in the 1965 Voting Rights Act, the SVREP registered over half a million new Mexican American voters in the Midwest and Southwest during the decade between the mid-1970s and 1985. With the help of dedicated volunteers and sophisticated research tools, its activities in elections and in the courts have been a significant factor in the larger number of Chicanos elected to public office in recent years. Although less successful in the Midwest and the rest of the Southwest than in Texas, the SVREP has clearly been the number one agency in putting Mexican Americans on the election rolls, electing more Mexican American officials, and obtaining greater political rewards for la raza from Anglo-dominated political organizations.

See also POLITICAL PARTICIPATION; VELÁSQUEZ, WILLIE.

FURTHER READING: Pycior, Julie Leininger. *LBJ and Mexican Americans: The Paradox of Power.* Austin: University of Texas Press, 1997; Skerry, Peter. *Mexican Americans: The Ambivalent Minority.* New York: Free Press, 1993; Weyr, Thomas. *Hispanic U.S.A.: Breaking the Melting Pot.* New York: Harper & Row, 1988; www.wcvi.org.

STEREOTYPING. Stereotyping is the ascribing to all persons of a group a single, identical pattern of characteristics, attitudes, or abilities. Over the decades Mexican Americans have suffered from two somewhat contradictory stereotypes: the indolent ignorant peasant and the knife-wielding violent criminal. There are also the somewhat contradictory stereotypes of Mexican immigrants as taking jobs from American citizens and of coming to the United States just to get on relief rolls. Denigrating epithets like "greaser," "beaner," and "wetback" have added negative implications of uncleanliness and inferior status.

During the early post–World War II era the nationally popular Judy Canova radio program featured a lazy, stupid character named Pedro who spoke poor English with a heavy accent, and in the early 1970s a potato chip company used a comic bandit stereotype, Frito Bandito, to advertise its product. Complaints by Chicanos ended these two offensive infringements of their social rights but, of course, not all stereotyping itself.

See also TÍO TACO.

FURTHER READING: Limón, José E. "Stereotyping and the Chicano Resistance: An Historical Dimension." *Aztlán* 4, no. 2 (Fall 1973):257–270; Martínez, Thomas M. "Advertising and Racism: The Case of the Mexican American." *El Grito* 2, no. 4 (Summer 1969):3–13; Pettit, Arthur G. *Images of the Mexican American in Fiction and Film.* College Station: Texas A & M University Press, 1980.

STUDENT ACTIVISM. Chicano student activism was an integral expression of the worldwide youth rebellion of the 1960s. The greatly enlarged Mexican American classroom population, widespread educational stereotyping, and denial of rights combined in the post–World War II era to unleash a powerful student protest movement. Turning away from the passive role assigned to young people by Mexican culture, these predominantly working-class youths began to create militant organizations that aggressively sought reforms at high school, college, and university levels. Walkouts and boycotting of classes by high school students were paralleled at colleges and universities by sit-ins, teach-ins, demonstrations, and demands for Chicano professors and courses in Chicano history and culture, development of Chicano studies programs, and admission of more Chicano students. At all levels student activists demanded to be heard in the entire academic process.

Student activism developed first in California and Texas, particularly in southern California and south Texas, probably because of their large urban Chicano populations. In 1968 Chicano students walked out of five East Los Angeles high schools when their earlier demands for educational equality with Anglo students were ignored. Inspired by this example, student protests quickly spread to New Mexico, Colorado, and the rest of the Southwest. In spite of considerable harassment by school authorities and police and a degree of apathy on the part of many elders in the Chicano community, the protesters persisted in their demands. Slowly overcoming the initial completely negative reaction of school administrators, they were eventually able to achieve many of their goals. Along the way they created numerous student organizations, thereby providing a degree of institutional continuity to the movement.

The lessons learned on college and university campuses also taught students the potential of active participation in community affairs and the political arena. However, weakened by its partial success and beset by internal differences, student activism declined by the mid-1970s. The movement itself became less aggressive as Chicano professors and students moved toward the mainstream. That the battle for equality in education has not been completely won is indicated by the small number of Chicanos attending colleges and universities, prevailing high dropout rates in high school, attacks on affirmative action programs, and continuing outbursts of student dissatisfaction from time to time in the 1980s and 1990s.

See also STUDENT ORGANIZATIONS; CASTRO, SAL; GONZALES, CORKY.

FURTHER READING: Acuña, Rodolfo. *Occupied America: A History of Chicanos.* 3rd ed. New York: Harper & Row, 1988; Briegel, Kaye. "Chicano Student Militancy: The Los Angeles High School Strike of 1968." In *An Awakened Minority: The Mexican-Americans,* edited by Manuel P. Servín. 2nd ed., Beverly Hills, Calif.: Glencoe Press, 1974; Frisbie, Parker. "Militancy among Mexican American High School Students." *Social Science Quarterly* 53, no. 4 (March 1973): 865–883; Gómez-Quiñones, Juan. *Mexican Students Por La Raza: The Chicano Student Movement in Southern California 1967–1977.* Santa Barbara, Calif.: Editorial La Causa, 1978; Hammerback, John, Richard J. Jensen, and José Angel Gutiérrez. *A War of Words: Chicano Protest in the 1960s and 1970s.* Westport, CT: Greenwood Press, 1985; Muñoz, Carlos, Jr. *Youth, Identity, Power: The Chicano Movement.* New York: Verso, 1989; San Miguel, Guadalupe, Jr. "Actors Not Victims: Chicanas/os and the Struggle for Educational Equality." In *Chicanas/Chicanos at the Crossroads,* edited by David R. Maciel and Isidro D. Ortiz. Tucson: University of Arizona Press, 1996; San Miguel, Guadalupe, Jr. *"Let All of Them Take Heed." Mexican Americans and the Campaign for Educational Equality in Texas, 1910–1981.* Austin: University of Texas Press, 1987; Vidal, Mirta. *Chicano Liberation and Revolutionary Youth.* New York: Pathfinder Press, 1971.

STUDENT ORGANIZATIONS. In the second half of the 1960s across the Southwest student activists and community leaders created organizations to give support and continuity to the Chicano Movement. The primary concentration of these organizations was on the quality of education and other student concerns, but civil rights on campus, in the community, and in the political sphere also became major issues for them.

By the mid-1960s student activists, many with training in organizing gained through federal War on Poverty programs, were seriously concerned with the formation of Chicano campus groups. In the second half of the decade a large number of student organizations were established from California to Texas, the two states in the forefront of the movement because of their large Chicano student populations. In southern California the Mexican American Student Association (MASA) was organized at the East Los Angeles Community College in 1966 and was quickly followed by the United Mexican American Students (UMAS), which developed from a meeting at Loyola University in Los Angeles and soon incorporated MASA groups as chapters. UMAS supplied much of the leadership and organization during the Los Angeles student walkouts of 1968. By the end of the following year UMAS had spread over the entire Southwest and even showed up in Indiana at Notre Dame University.

In the northern California area Chicano students at San Jose State College (now University) started the organizing movement in 1964 with a group they called Student Initiative, which was more political and less community oriented than its southern counterparts. This was later reorganized as the Mexican American Student Confederation. Nearly all these groups at first stressed advancement through education and looked forward to a new generation of Chicano professionals. Later they became more politically committed to broader civil rights goals.

At the same time in Texas José Angel Gutiérrez and other student leaders at St. Mary's University organized the Mexican American Youth Organization (MAYO) with the aid of an $8,000 Ford Foundation grant in 1968. From its beginnings MAYO was aggressively political in putting forward student and community concerns. It quickly spread to other college and high school campuses in Texas.

In New Mexico, Hispanic college and high school students seemed less actively engaged. New Mexico Highlands University students formed the Spanish American Students Organization, only later replacing *Spanish American* with the word *Chicano*. In Albuquerque, high school students soon followed suit, creating the Chicano Youth Association.

In California the explosion of Chicano student groups led in 1969 to a unifying conference at the University of California in Santa Barbara. For the name of the new umbrella organization the conferees chose Movimiento Estudiantil Chicano de Aztlán (MEChA) and then drew up a detailed plan for developing college programs. This they later issued as the Plan de Santa Barbara. Most of the earlier organizations, particularly in California, ultimately became MEChA chapters.

By the beginning of the 1970s student protest had brought about a degree of reform in education. Although discrimination continued to exist, student organizational protests forced teachers and professors to become more sensitive to ethnic slurs, to add Mexican cultural materials to their courses, and to develop new courses in the history, sociology, art, and culture of the Mexican American. School administrations hired more Chicano teachers, counselors, and even administrators and provided new or better school buildings and other facilities. In addition, the student groups had boosted community spirit and pride, helping lead to more active political participation by their elders.

The decline of the Chicano Movement from the late 1970s onward led to some atrophying and decline of student organizations.

See also EDUCATION; MOVIMIENTO ESTUDIANTIL CHICANO DE AZTLÁN; ORGANIZATIONS.

FURTHER READING: *Chicano Organizations.* Compiled by Patricia Durán, Betty Flores, and Isabel Romo. Los Angeles: Chicano Studies Center, University of California, 1971, García, F. Chris, and Rodolfo O. de la Garza. *The Chicano Political Experience: Three Perspectives.* North Scituate, Mass.: Duxbury Press, 1977; Gómez-Quiñones, Juan. *Mexican Students Por La Raza: The Chicano Student Movement in Southern California, 1967–1977.* Santa Barbara, Calif.: Editorial La Causa, 1978; Meier, Matt S., and Feliciano Rivera. *Mexican Americans/American Mexicans: From Conquistadors to Chicanos.* New York: Hill & Wang, 1993; Muñoz, Carlos, Jr. *Youth, Identity, Power: The Chicano Movement.* New York: Verso, 1989; Navarro, Armando. *Mexican American Youth Organization: Avant-Garde of the Chicano Movement in Texas.* Austin: University of Texas Press, 1995.

STUDENT WALKOUTS, 1968–1969. Influenced in part by a worldwide climate of youthful unrest and protest, by the leadership of the Brown Berets, and particularly by teacher Sal Castro, thousands of Chicano students walked out of East Los Angeles high schools in March 1968, asserting that they were being ignored and their educational rights abused. The walkouts set in motion a chain of similar protests in urban centers all over the West and Midwest, but especially in Texas, Colorado, Arizona, and New Mexico as well as elsewhere in California. The students protested overcrowding, poor educational facilities, racist and poorly trained teachers, an inadequate curriculum, and a dropout rate of over 50 percent. They demanded more Chicano teachers, counselors, and administrators as well as courses in the Mexican American experience and Mexican culture.

The high school "blowouts" led to comparable actions by Chicano college and university students who, by demonstrations, sit-ins, and abstention from graduation ceremonies, emphasized their demands for Chicano faculty, courses, departments, and administrators as well as for the admission of more Chicano students. The reasonableness of their demands combined with unthinking oppressive reaction from school officials and considerable police brutality to rally most Chicano community organizations behind the students and their leaders. Later a dozen of the militant leaders of the Los Angeles walkouts were arrested for criminal conspiracy; on appeal the charge was held unconstitutional and then dropped.

Although Chicano efforts for educational change were diffused because of differences over goals and absence of a central organization, by 1970 the student walkouts had achieved a degree of success. They were less successful in Arizona and least successful in New Mexico. The student walkouts formed the opening act in the Chicano Movement. Since the early 1970s the walkout technique has been used sporadically by Chicano students to push school administrators toward greater awareness of their cavalier disregard of the students' educational rights and to persuade them to give serious consideration to the students' educational grievances.

See also CASTRO, SAL; EDUCATION.

FURTHER READING: Acuña, Rodolfo. *A Community under Siege: A Chronicle of Chicanos East of the Los Angeles River, 1945–1975.* Los Angeles: Chicano Studies Research Center, University of California, 1984; Carter, Thomas P. *Mexican Americans in School: A History of Educational Neglect.* New York: College Entrance Examinations Board, 1970; Fields, Rona Marcia. "The Brown Berets: A Participant Observation Study of Social Action in the Schools of Los Angeles." Ph.D. diss., University of Southern California, 1970; Frisbie, Parker. "Militancy among Mexican American High School Students." *Social Science Quarterly* 53, no. 4 (March 1973):865–883; Muñoz, Carlos, Jr. *Youth, Identity, Power: The Chicano Movement.* New York: Verso, 1990; Salazar, Rubén. *Border Correspondent: Selected Writings, 1955–1970,* edited by Mario T. García. Berkeley: University of California Press, 1995; Vigil, Maurilio. *Chicano Politics.* Washington, D.C.: University Press of America, 1978.

T

TAYLOR, PAUL SHUSTER, 1895–1984. Dr. Paul S. Taylor was one of the very early researchers in the field of Mexicano rights. With an undergraduate degree in labor economics from the University of Wisconsin and a doctorate in economics from the University of California, Berkeley (UCB), he spent the rest of his academic life at Berkeley, teaching, counseling, researching, and writing. Ultimately he published 13 volumes on the conditions of Mexicano labor in the United States, in addition to other works, numerous journal articles, and conference presentations.

In 1927 Taylor began his studies of Mexican labor and immigration—which were to engross him for the remainder of his long life. At the end of the 1930s when the LaFollette Civil Liberties Committee undertook its investigation of denial of civil liberties in California agriculture, Taylor was both its star witness and its source of research on the issue. Along with pictures by his famed photographer wife, Dorothea Lange, his statistics, charts, and graphs served to shape the committee's report. From the late 1920s onward, Taylor served on various government agencies as a member, consultant, or advisor. He retired from UCB in 1962 but kept his office there and continued his research and writing. Despite his advanced years he took an important part in many early Chicano Movement conferences and was widely revered as the grand old man in the farmworkers' struggle for their civil right to form unions without interference from growers.

See also LA FOLLETTE COMMITTEE; MOVIMIENTO, EL.

FURTHER READING: Street, Richard. "The Economist as Humanist—the Career of Paul S. Taylor." *California History* 58, no. 4 (Winter 1979–1980):350–361.

TELLES, RAYMOND L., 1915– . The 1957 election of Raymond Telles as the first Mexican American mayor of El Paso in the twentieth century was an important step in the raza struggle for political rights. A major advance in itself, the election also stimulated further and broader participation in Texas politics by Chicanos and engendered among them a renewed sense of self-confidence.

Born in El Paso into a politically active family, Telles graduated from high school into a Works Progress Administration job that enabled him to obtain a business school education. He was drafted into the army in World War II and returned to El Paso with the rank of major in the U.S. Air Force. Persuaded to run for El Paso county clerk in 1948, he won that election and subsequent reelections. His nine years of model administration as county clerk helped expand the involvement and success of Tejanos in local and state politics. His success also convinced El Paso's raza leaders that Telles, who was the best-known border political leader at the time, would be an ideal candidate for the mayoralty. Tired of being treated as second-class citizens, Mexican Americans voted in record numbers to elect Telles in 1957.

Telles was reelected mayor of El Paso in 1959. Not a social crusader, he advanced the Chicano struggle for justice and equality of opportunity, but he neither sought nor produced revolutionary socioeconomic changes. His temperate approach to innovation enabled him to pursue a moderately successful reform program and still mollify the Anglo establishment. He addressed problems of the community in a bit-by-bit, incremental approach. During his administration city services were extended to the barrio, some barrio tenements were condemned and replaced with low-cost housing, and Chicanos were enabled to get a toehold in the police and fire departments. They began to enjoy greater equality of opportunity because of these changes, which could never be undone.

In 1961 Telles was appointed ambassador to Costa Rica by President John F. Kennedy, the first Mexican American ambassador. During the Lyndon Johnson administration he became an appointee to the new U.S.–Mexican Border Commission, a position he lost in 1969 when Richard M. Nixon took over the presidency. His subsequent run for the U.S. Congress ended in ignominious defeat, possibly in part because the new Chicano militants viewed him as passé. After serving on the Equal Employment Opportunity Commission in Washington during the Nixon administration, he left government service for the private sector.

Telles had a dual importance in the Mexican American civil rights struggle. First, his election as mayor of El Paso was a symbolic first climax to the World War II generation's fight for political participation. Second, his excellent administration removed obstructions in the path of opportunity for the following generations of Chicanos.

See also KENNEDY, JOHN FITZGERALD; POLITICAL PARTICIPATION; TEXAS.

FURTHER READING: García, Mario T. *The Making of a Mexican American Mayor: Raymond L. Telles of El Paso.* El Paso: Texas Western Press, 1998; García, Mario T. *Mexican Americans: Leadership, Ideology, and Identity, 1930–1960.* New Haven, Conn.: Yale University Press, 1989.

TENAYUCA, EMMA, 1917–1999. Exposed from early youth to a wide spectrum of economic and political ideas and discussion by her father and maternal grandfather, Emma Tenayuca became a social activist before she left high school. An inquisitive and serious student, she spent hours reading Charles Darwin, Thomas Paine, and later Karl Marx. Her reading gradually led her from a theoretical reformist position to a more active radical stance.

At the beginning of the 1930s Tenayuca began speaking out publicly for raza civil rights. In 1931, while a high school freshman, she helped organize and lead a march of depression-unemployed workers on the capitol in Austin. At age 17 she was an observer at the Finck Cigar Company strike in San Antonio and was jailed with the strikers. After graduation from high school she spent much of her free time distributing civil rights pamphlets and helping organize Mexican American workers in a radical union called the Workers Alliance, sponsored by the communist-dominated Trade Union Unity League. She also helped organize a San Antonio chapter of the International Ladies Garment Workers Union.

By the mid-1930s Emma Tenayuca had become convinced that confrontational tactics were essential to bring about real political and economic change. Because she felt that only the Communist Party was concerned about Mexican American rights, she joined it. In 1937 she led a sit-in of unemployed Mexican Americans at the San Antonio city hall to protest discrimination in relief programs and to demand jobs for the unemployed. Her strong activist role inevitably led to arrests. Frequently jailed, she emerged from her brief incarcerations only more determined to continue demanding social justice and civil rights for the poor.

In late 1937 Tenayuca married Homer Brooks, a Communist Party organizer. She remained a party member until the Soviet-German rapprochement 18 months later, in 1939. She and her husband continued to demand an end to all economic, political, and social discrimination against Mexicanos.

Her enthusiasm, energy, and convictions made Tenayuca an effective organizer and a dynamic leader. When several thousand San Antonio pecan shellers struck in late January 1938 for higher pay and better working conditions, she took a leading role and soon became the strike's symbol. Her communist affiliation caused Tenayuca to be replaced as strike leader, but the strikers declared their faith in her by naming her their honorary representative. The strike was later settled by arbitration, and her career as a political activist and labor organizer in Texas came to an end.

Blacklisted by the House Un-American Activities Committee, Tenayuca found she was unable to obtain employment in San Antonio. She soon left for Los Angeles, where she went to work for the American Federation of Labor as a recruiter, but she was never able to find her place in the California Mexican American labor movement.

Subsequently Tenayuca enrolled in college, obtained A.B. and M.A. degrees, and then returned to Texas, where she taught quietly in a San Antonio elementary school until her retirement in 1982. She also participated in the local activities of Citizens Organized for Public Service.

See also COMMUNIST PARTY; ORGANIZATIONS.

FURTHER READING: Calderón, Roberto, and Emilio Zamora. "Manuela Solís Sager and Emma Tenayuca: A Tribute." In *Chicana Voices: Intersection of Class, Race, and Gender*, edited by Teresa Córdova et al. Austin: Center for Mexican American Studies, University of Texas, 1986; Hardy, Gayle J. *American Women Civil Rights Activists*. Jefferson, N.C.: McFarland & Co., 1993; Larralde, Carlos. *Mexican American Movements and Leaders*. Los Alamitos, Calif.: Hwong Publishing Co., 1976; Rips, Geoffrey, and Emma Tenayuca. "Living History: Emma Tenayuca Tells Her Story." *Texas Observer*, 28 October 1983, 7–15. Zophy, Angela H., ed. *Handbook of American Women's History*. New York: Garland Publishing, 1990.

TEXAS. The state of Texas has had a reproachful history in the matter of civil rights for Mexican Americans. As a result of a large influx of immigrants from the slave states of the old South, when Texas became part of the United States in 1845 it had some 30,000 Anglos and about 4,000 Tejanos (a ratio of 7.5 to 1). Anti-Mexican feelings ran high. By 1860 the numbers had changed to 600,000 Anglos and 12,000 Mexicanos (a 50 to 1 ratio). The arrival of ever larger numbers of Anglos in the 1870s and 1880s resulted in a further increase in the population imbalance, heightened anti-Mexican feeling, and aggravated violence along the border. Greatly outnumbered in the new society, Tejanos were routinely denied basic civil rights guaranteed them by the Treaty of Guadalupe Hidalgo and the U.S. Constitution.

During the years of the Texas Republic (1836–1846), Tejano elites sought to participate in the new political system, which many of them had helped bring about, rather than abandon their properties and cross the border into Mexico. However, even before the U.S.–Mexican War, Mexicanos as a group were treated as a conquered people without rights. After the war many of the Anglo veterans who settled in Texas took the view that Spanish-speakers had been the enemy and therefore deserved ill-treatment. This attitude, based on racist and nativist rationalizations, in their minds justified the mistreatment of all Mexicanos. Land ownership quickly shifted from Tejanos to Anglos. Through loss of their lands many of the Tejano elite began to suffer, often becoming victims of racism and sinking in economic and social status. The poorer classes endured typical frontier violence, in which Mexicano-bashing was widely acceptable among Anglos. Laws as well as southern traditions frequently denied Mexican Americans their rights. In the Cart War of 1857 some Mexicano freighters suffered the ultimate denial of their civil rights—death at the hands of Anglo competitors.

Repeated denial of liberties guaranteed by the Treaty of Guadalupe Hidalgo often led to social banditry and occasionally to more widespread uprisings. The so-called El Paso Salt War of 1877, for example, was largely a response to denial of traditional rights enjoyed by Mexicanos. Further, the negative experiences of Juan N. Cortina and Gregorio Cortez with American justice were unexceptional. The Texas Rangers' extreme violence and complete denial of civil liberties to rural Mexicanos were justified through racial stereotyping. Efforts were made to deny Mexican immigrants their right to naturalization because of Native American ancestry. Using nativist arguments, an 1890s movement to disenfranchise all Mexican Americans found considerable support in south Texas politics. Lynching of Mexicanos was common in the second half of the nineteenth century, but urban Mexicanos along the border suffered less and continued to participate in local politics. In San Antonio a local organization, La Agrupación Protectora Mexicana, protested the lynchings, fought against police brutality, and defended the civil rights of Mexicanos in the first decades of the 1900s.

During World War I a "brown" scare, brought on in part by heavy immigration to provide a wartime workforce, led to large numbers, hundreds, perhaps over a thousand, of Mexicanos in Texas being hunted down and murdered by vigilantes and Rangers. In 1915 the Plan de San Diego became a convenient excuse for heightened repression of Mexicanos by the Texas Rangers.

Over time the older paternalistic relations of Anglos and Mexicanos in a ranching culture became less personal, and the "factories in the fields" of the Winter Garden area more and more made use of migratory workers, who found conditions ever more oppressive. As Mexicanos became increasingly urbanized, relations between the two groups underwent further changes.

During the Great Depression of the early 1930s thousands of Mexicans, and some Mexican Americans, were "repatriated" with little regard for civil and human rights. World War II served to arouse Texas Mexicanos to greater awareness of their rights; but often, as the cases of Félix Longoria and Macario García showed, these were denied them, even in death in the Longoria case. However, Chicano leaders did come forward, and organizations to fight for civil rights were created. By the 1960s a panoply of civil and political rights organizations had developed and many political, social, and educational rights seemed on the road to achievement. Political participation by Chicanos greatly increased as the postwar generation of Mexican Americans provided leadership for the movimiento.

Nevertheless, repression of civil rights, especially of farmworkers, has continued, often with support from local sheriffs and the Texas Rangers. Although conditions in Texas have improved over the years and new goals for Chicanos seem attainable, police brutality and violent denial of civil rights have by no means completely disappeared. Moreover, Tejano social and economic problems are often ascribed to cultural and ethnic inferiority. Mexicanos often continue to be blamed for poor economic conditions as well as for high levels of unemployment. The stereotype of the lazy, dirty, not-too-bright Mexicano taking a siesta in the sun is still with us.

See also LONGORIA, FÉLIX; PLAN DE SAN DIEGO; SEGUÍN, JUAN N.; TEXAS RANGERS.

FURTHER READING: Clinchy, Everett Ross, Jr. *Equality of Opportunity for Latin-Americans in Texas*. Reprint, New York: Arno Press, 1974; Cortés, Carlos, ed. *The Mexican Experience in Texas*. New York: Arno Press, 1976; de León, Arnoldo. *They Called Them Greasers: Anglo Attitudes towards Mexicans in Texas, 1821–1900*. Austin: University of Texas Press, 1983; de León, Arnoldo. *Mexican Americans in Texas: A Brief History*. Arlington Heights, Ill.: H. Davidson, 1993; Fehrenbach, T. R. *Lone Star: A History of Texas and Texans*. New York: Macmillan, 1968; Foley, Neil. *White Scourge: Mexicans, Blacks, and Poor Whites in Texas Cotton Culture*. Berkeley: University of California Press, 1997; Kibbe, Pauline R. *Latin-Americans in Texas*. Albuquerque: University of New Mexico Press, 1946. Reprint, New York: Arno Press, 1974; Montejano, David. *Anglos and Mexicans in the Making of Texas, 1836–1986*. Austin: University of Texas Press, 1987; Perales, Alonso S. *Are We Good Neighbors?* San Antonio: Artes Gráficas, 1948. Reprint, New York: Arno Press, 1974; Perales, Alonso S. *El Mexicano Americano y la política del sur de Texas*. San Antonio: Artes Gráficas, 1931; Rubel, Arthur J. *Across the Tracks: Mexican Americans in a Texas City*. Austin: University of Texas Press, 1966; San Miguel, Guadalupe. Jr. *"Let All of Them Take Heed": Mexican Americans and the Campaign for Educational Equality in Texas, 1910–1981*. Austin: University of Texas Press, 1987; Shelton, Edgar. *Political Conditions among Texas Mexicans*. San Francisco: R & E Research Associates, 1974; Shockley, John S. *Chicano Revolt in a Texas Town*. Notre Dame, Ind.: University of Notre Dame Press, 1974; Simmons, Ozzie G. *Anglo-Americans and Mexican-Americans in South Texas*. Reprint, New York: Arno Press, 1974; Stewart, Kenneth L., and Arnoldo de León. *Not Room Enough: Mexicans, Anglos and Socioeconomic Change in Texas, 1650–1900*. Albuquerque: University of New Mexico Press, 1993; Taylor, Paul. *An American-Mexican Frontier: Nueces County*. Chapel Hill: University of North Carolina Press, 1934; Tyler, Ron, ed. *New Handbook of Texas*. 6 Vols. Austin: Texas State Historical Association, 1996.

TEXAS GOOD NEIGHBOR COMMISSION. Established in 1943, the commission arose out of an attempt to placate the Mexican government when it refused to send braceros to Texas during World War II because of extreme discrimination and exploitation there. In 1947 it was made a permanent state agency.

An association sanctioned and funded by the Texas government but made up mostly of volunteers, the commission's objective was to promote good will, understanding, and mutual respect among both Anglos and Mexicans. To these ends it advocated measures to reduce discrimination and interethnic conflict and fostered cultural and educational exchanges. However, when Pauline Kibbe, its first head, was critical of Texas farm labor conditions, she was fired by Governor Beauford Jester.

Viewed from its inception by many Texas politicians as a public relations gimmick, the commission later concerned itself primarily with border diplomacy at the visiting dignitary level rather than with the rights of Mexicano workers. Its effectiveness in achieving its limited goals, particularly in the area of civil rights, was questioned by some critics; but it had a useful role in opening and maintaining unofficial channels of communication along the border. The commission was abolished in 1987.

See also KIBBE, PAULINE.

FURTHER READING: Kibbe, Pauline R. *Latin-Americans in Texas*. Albuquerque: University of New Mexico Press, 1946; Kingrea, Nellie Ward. *History of the First Ten Years of the Texas Good Neighbor Commission*. Fort Worth: Texas Christian University Press, 1954; Perales, Alonso S. *Are We Good Neighbors?* San Antonio: Artes Gráficas, 1948; Reprint, New York: Arno Press 1974; Stevenson, Coke R., and Ezequiel Padilla. *The Good Neighbor Policy and Mexicans in Texas*. Mexico City, 1943. Reprinted in *The Mexican American and the Law*. New York: Arno Press, 1974.

TEXAS RANGERS. To Mexican Americans in Texas the Rangers from their inception have been seen as being on the other side, as being the enemy. Originally a mounted militia created by Stephen F. Austin in 1823 because of frontier conditions, during and after the 1836 Texas revolt from Mexico the Rangers became a paramilitary force whose purpose was to deter marauders on the southern border and northwestern frontier of Texas. During the U.S.–Mexican War an enlarged Ranger force fought in Mexico under generals Zachary Taylor and Winfield Scott. After the war the Rangers resumed their earlier tasks of policing border bandits, cattle rustlers, and Indians. Like the larger society of the Southwest, the Rangers considered Mexicanos and Indians as hindrances to Anglo frontier expansion and development and therefore "natural" enemies.

During the post–Civil War reconstruction of the South the Rangers were replaced with a state police force, but in 1874 they were reestablished by the Texas legislature. The new Texas Rangers concerned themselves with rustling, border banditry, and cattlemen's feuds. Many felt themselves little constrained by ideas of law or civil rights, despite their "law and order" mentality. Holding that violence was the way to pacify the Texas frontier, they adopted an attitude described as "shoot first and ask questions later." The civil rights of many innocent Mexicanos suffered as a result, often fatally.

In the twentieth century the highly controversial Texas Rangers became largely an Anglo landowners' force, enforcing pass systems, vagrancy legislation, and other restraints on Mexicano liberties, particularly in rural areas. First used to enforce virtual serfdom in rural Texas, it was then used to hold back the tide of agricultural unionism and Mexican American participation in politics. During World War I the agency, expanded to about 1,000, terrorized Mexicanos in the border region and was responsible for numerous Mexicano deaths along the border. As the result of widespread complaints, in 1919 state legislator José T. Canales introduced and secured passage of legislation that reduced the force to fewer than 100 men. In 1935 Ranger embroilment in state politics caused the agency to be brought under a newly created Department of Public Safety.

During the Chicano Movement the Rangers continued in the tradition of their nineteenth-century patterns. At the time of the 1963 Crystal City elections, for example, Captain Alfred Y. Allee used the Rangers to actively harass Mexican American candidates. Three years later in the Rio Grande Valley melon strike the use of verbal abuse, harassment, threats, and mass arrests were among Ranger techniques criticized by civil rights activists, the press, and ordinary citizens. In 1974 the U.S. Supreme Court ruled against the Rangers in *Medrano v. Allee*, a lawsuit arising out of the 1966–1967 melon strike.

See also CANALES, JOSÉ TOMÁS; CIVIL RIGHTS ABUSE; TEXAS.

FURTHER READING: Coles, Robert. "Our Hands Belong to the Valley: Texas Americans." *Atlantic* 235 (March 1975):72–78; Proctor, Ben H. "The Modern Texas Rangers: A Law Enforcement Dilemma in the Rio Grande Valley." In *The Mexican Americans: An Awakening Minority*, edited by Manuel P. Servín. Beverly Hills: Glencoe Press, 1970; Samora, Julian, Joe Bernal, and Albert Peña. *Gunpowder Justice: A Reassessment of the Texas Rangers*. Notre Dame, Ind.: University of Notre Dame Press, 1979; Williams, Doran. "The Starr County Strike." *Social Progress* 59, no. 5 (May–June 1969):25–29; Webb, Walter Prescott. *The Texas Rangers: A Century of Frontier Defense*. Boston: Houghton Mifflin, 1935.

THE EAST LOS ANGELES COMMUNITY UNION (TELACU). See EAST LOS ANGELES COMMUNITY UNION, THE (TELACU).

TIERRA AMARILLA, 1967. Tierra Amarilla, a small village in Rio Arriba County in northwestern New Mexico, made the front pages of the nation's newspapers in mid-1967. In June Reies López Tijerina and members of his Alianza Federal de Pueblos Libres, in an ongoing conflict with the district attorney, Alfonso Sánchez, descended on the courthouse to make a citizens' arrest. A confrontation ensued, followed by gun-play between law officers and Alianza members. The aliancistas fled, only to be subsequently hunted down by helicopters, airplanes, and even tanks. The event attracted national media coverage and many Americans, Anglo and Chicano, believed or feared that the Tierra Amarilla incident signaled the beginning of a revolutionary movement or at least of a guerrilla action.

Tijerina was soon apprehended and charged with various crimes in state and federal courts, but he was released on bail and continued his disturbing confrontational activities. By the end of the year he was acquitted of three federal charges arising out of the courthouse shootout. However, in 1970, while already serving a three-year federal prison term for his activities in the second Kit Carson National Forest confrontation, he was convicted in New Mexico courts on state complaints based on the Tierra Amarilla incident.

See also ALIANZA FEDERAL DE PUEBLOS LIBRES; TIJERINA, REIES LÓPEZ.

FURTHER READING: Knowlton, Clark S. "Tijerina, Hero of the Militants." In *An Awakened Minority: The Mexican-Americans*, edited by Manuel P. Servín. 2nd ed. Beverly Hills: Glencoe Press, 1974; Meier, Matt S. " 'King Tiger': Reies López Tijerina." *Journal of the West* 27, no. 2 (April 1988):60–68; Nabokov, Peter. *Tijerina and the Courthouse Raid*. 2nd ed. Berkeley, Calif.: Ramparts Press, 1970.

TIJERINA, PETE, 1922–   . Even before he studied law at St. Mary's University in 1951, San Antonio attorney and judge Pete Tijerina became involved in the Mexican American struggle for civil rights as a leader in the League of United Latin American Citizens (LULAC). As state civil rights chair of LULAC Council No. 2 he fought civil rights abuses through his "traveling squad" of LULAC members who were available to move around the state to investigate and take action to correct injustices. The continued exclusion of Chicanos from juries in Texas, despite the U.S. Supreme Court's ruling in *Hernández v. The State of Texas*, induced him to mount a major battle to end this discrimination.

Another of Tijerina's important contributions to the fight for Mexican American civil rights was his leading role in founding the Mexican American Legal Defense and Educational Fund (MALDEF). In 1967 he made application to the Ford Foundation for a grant to create a Texas organization to monitor court rulings on Mexican Americans' civil rights. He was successful beyond his fondest dreams, obtaining a five-year $2.2 million grant for a MALDEF that would blanket the entire Southwest. He established headquarters in San Antonio in the following year. As the agency's first executive director he was responsible for organizing committees in California, Arizona, Colorado, and New Mexico, as well as Texas. Tijerina resigned as director when MALDEF's headquarters were moved to San Francisco, California, in 1970, at the Ford Foundation's insistence, in order to create a more national image and organization. Having a special interest in equality of educational opportunity, he remained active in LULAC, serving for years as national civil rights chair. Currently he is in private practice in San Antonio.

Pete Tijerina took a leading role in several important lawsuits over civil rights. In *Rodríguez v. Brown* he successfully challenged the exclusion of Mexican Americans in Bexar County's jury selection process, although the practice continued. He was also successful in increasing Mexicanos' rights to economic equality by winning a suit against the San Antonio Public Service Board for discrimination in hiring.

See also HERNÁNDEZ v. THE STATE OF TEXAS; LEAGUE OF UNITED LATIN AMERICAN CITIZENS; MEXICAN AMERICAN LEGAL DEFENSE AND EDUCATIONAL FUND.

FURTHER READING: Oliviera, Annette. *MALDEF: Diez Años.* San Francisco: MALDEF, 1978; Pycior, Julie Leininger. *LBJ and Mexican Americans: The Paradox of Power.* Austin: University of Texas Press, 1997; Salazar, Veronica. *Dedication Rewarded: Prominent Mexican Americans.* San Antonio: Mexican American Cultural Center, 1976; San Miguel, Guadalupe, Jr. *"Let All of Them Take Heed": Mexican Americans and the Campaign for Educational Equality in Texas, 1910–1981.* Austin: University of Texas Press, 1987.

TIJERINA, REIES LÓPEZ, 1926– . Reies López Tijerina occupies a unique position in the Mexican American civil rights experience. During the 1960s he seemed to have the answer to Mexican American demands for vigorous action to recover lost land grants and to obtain civil rights. Supported by both conservative rural Nuevomexicanos and radical young Chicanos, he never wavered in his strong commitment to equality for all Mexican Americans.

After sporadic formal education in Texas schools, Reies Tijerina's reading of the Bible first led him to the life of an itinerant nondenominational preacher along the Mexican border. Meanwhile, he gradually developed a pragmatic concern for social justice. After an unfortunate experience leading an Arizona utopian community, followed by travel in Mexico and California, he finally settled in northern New Mexico, where the complex history of Spanish and Mexican land grants soon became his obsession. To work for restoration of land rights he organized the Alianza Federal de Mercedes (Federal Alliance of [Land] Grants) in 1963 and began to recruit supporters.

Tijerina and his followers drew attention to their demands for civil rights by a variety of aggressive actions. They filed lawsuits against the government, they marched on the state capitol at Santa Fe, they laid claim to part of the Kit Carson National Forest. A confrontation there with forest rangers and the later raid on the Tierra Amarilla courthouse resulted in criminal charges. Freed on bail, Tijerina continued to promote the goals of the retitled Alianza Federal de Pueblos Libres (Federal Alliance of Free Towns) by a series of activities to publicize his demands, including strident leadership in the Poor People's March in mid-1968.

Tijerina was eventually convicted on state and federal indictments and jailed; in mid-1971 he was released on parole. His civil rights leadership appeared greatly diminished by his conviction and absence from the public forum. At the end of his five-year parole he resumed the presidency of a much-diminished Alianza. As the Chicano Movement declined in the late 1970s, he assumed a less confrontational stance in the struggle for Chicano rights but remained in the fray in the role of elder statesman. A 1987 interview in Mexico City quoted him as vowing to continue his fight against discrimination. However, his sphere of influence had clearly been dramatically reduced from the national to the local, principally the Tierra Amarilla region.

Tijerina voiced widespread and deep, but diffuse and unarticulated feelings of outrage by Nuevomexicanos at loss of their lands and of mistrust in government. His civil rights leadership derived primarily from his visceral appeal to people who were deeply conscious of their lack of political power. The nexus of his power is seen in his 1969 letter from prison, in which he assured his followers, "For the land, culture, and inheritance of my people I am ready not only to suffer imprisonment, but I would, with pleasure and pride, sacrifice my life to bring about the justice which is so much deserved by my people—the Spanish American people."

See also ALIANZA FEDERAL DE PUEBLOS LIBRES; KIT CARSON NATIONAL FOREST; TIERRA AMARILLA.

FURTHER READING: Blawis, Patricia Bell. *Tijerina and the Land Grants*. New York: International Publishers, 1971; Knowlton, Clark S. "Tijerina, Hero of the Militants." In *An Awakened Minority: The Mexican-Americans*, edited by Manuel P. Servín. 2nd ed., Beverly Hills, Calif.: Glencoe Press, 1974; Meier, Matt S. " 'King Tiger': Reies López Tijerina." *Journal of the West* 27, no. 2 (April 1988):60–68; Tijerina, Reies López. "From Prison." In *The Chicanos: Mexican American Voices*, edited by Edward W. Ludwig and James Santibáñez. Baltimore: Penguin Books, 1971; Tijerina, Reies López. *Mi lucha por la tierra*. Mexico: Fondo de Cultura Económica, 1978.

TÍO TACO. Tío Taco is a phrase, equivalent to Uncle Tom among blacks, used to describe a Mexican American who denies his ethnicity and tries to assimilate to the extent of rejecting his cultural heritage. The pejorative term was widely used during the Chicano Movement by militants to label and demean their conservative antagonists within the Mexican American community. For example, Texas congressman Henry B. González was frequently denounced as a Tío Taco by youthful Chicano activists during the movimiento. Related expressions are coconut (brown on the outside but white inside) and the more vehement *vendido* (sellout).

See also MOVIMIENTO, EL.

FURTHER READING: Martínez, Thomas M. "Advertising and Racism: The Case of the Mexican American." *El Grito* 2, no. 4 (Summer 1969):3–13; Steiner, Stan. *La Raza: The Mexican American.* New York: Harper & Row, 1969; Thornton, Richard V. "Tío Taco Is Dead." *Newsweek*, 29 June 1970, 22–28.

TIREMAN, LOYD S., 1896–1959. One of the pioneers in researching the educational disadvantages suffered by Mexicano children, Loyd Tireman was a complex and sometimes difficult man who often failed to recognize his own cultural biases. Although he was animated by good intentions, his search for ways to improve the schooling of Spanish-speaking children was marred by his underlying assumption that the Hispanic culture of the Southwest was inherently inferior to Anglo culture. He was an early advocate of bilingual education, but he saw it almost solely as a way to improve the students' English-language facility, thereby Anglicizing them.

As founder of the experimental San José Training School Tireman matched the best and most innovative teachers in New Mexico with the latest pedagogical techniques. Perhaps his most important contribution to improving the education of Mexicano children was his awareness and understanding that parental and community involvement in their children's schooling was the key to students' success.

See also BILINGUAL EDUCATION; MANUEL, HERSCHEL T.; SÁNCHEZ, GEORGE I.

FURTHER READING: Bachelor, Davis L. *Educational Reform in New Mexico: Tireman, San José, and Nambe.* Albuquerque: University of New Mexico Press, 1991; Getz, Lynne Marie. *Schools of Their Own: The Education of Hispanos in New Mexico, 1850–1940.* Albuquerque: University of New Mexico Press, 1992.

U

UNDERREPRESENTATION. One of the persistent complaints of Mexican American civil rights leaders is that la raza has been underrepresented in all aspects of U.S. social, economic, and political life—underrepresented by gerrymandering, underrepresented in the decennial census counts, underrepresented on juries, underrepresented in the professions and in college graduates, underrepresented in political parties and in elective and appointive governmental positions. La raza forms only over 3 percent of all full-time state and federal employees, although it forms over three times that percentage of the total population. Overrepresented in the armed services, la raza bulked large in the casualty lists from Korea and Vietnam.

See also GERRYMANDERING; POLITICAL PARTICIPATION.

FURTHER READING: Santillán, Richard A. "Political Reapportionment and Hispanic Communities." *Agenda: A Journal of Hispanic Issues* 11, no. 2 (March–April 1981):18–19, 42.

UNITED FARM WORKERS (UFW). Originally organized in 1962 by César Chávez as the Farm Workers Association, the organization changed its name to the United Farm Workers (UFW) 10 years later when it became a full-fledged AFL-CIO union. From its beginnings more than just a labor union, it aimed at achieving social justice and human dignity. In its push for greater equality for Mexican Americans, the UFW quickly developed into a cooperative that included a credit union, clinic, pharmacy, grocery, gas station, and other service entities.

In 1965 Chávez took the association out on its first strike, by rose grafters, and later that year followed with the famous Delano grape strike, which concluded successfully after a five-year struggle. Following a policy of strict nonviolence prescribed by Chávez, the strikers, aided by other unions and widespread support from college students, various members of the clergy, and finally the Catholic Bishops Committee, were able to hold out until victory was won. The long conflict was punctuated by a number of dramatic events: the 1966 march to Sacramento, the intrusion of the Teamsters' union, Chávez's 25-day fast in 1967, the national boycott of table grapes in the next year, and in 1969 the extension of the boycott to Europe.

After its Delano success the UFW moved its main unionizing activity to the Salinas Valley lettuce fields. Here a long, drawn-out conflict developed and full success eluded the union. Meanwhile, it lost most of the grape contracts when they expired in 1973 and growers failed to renew, alleging failure of the UFW to supply the needed workers at peak times and other administrative weaknesses in the union.

In 1975 the California Agricultural Labor Relations Act seemed to favor the union by mandating secret-ballot union elections. UFW membership, which had dropped from its 1970 high of nearly 80,000 to a low of 5,000 in 1973, now rebounded to 45,000. However, the state legislature and the appointed agricultural labor board emasculated the law by failing to provide the necessary funding and enforcement. Membership dropped to about 21,000.

Acquiescing to the failure of the legislative approach, in the 1980s the union reverted to the boycott technique, but now with a modern twist: computers, mailing lists, a printing press, and TV spots. Meanwhile, the UFW was weakened further by internal dissent and personality clashes, an anti-union trend in the country, and the urbanization of Mexicanos. Chávez's personal and absolute control of the union had earlier caused a number of co-workers to leave and it continued to be criticized and to weaken the UFW's struggle. In an effort to recapture the early dream, in the 1980s the UFW lessened its emphasis on field organizing and emphasized broader social goals like the reduction of pesticide use.

By the 1990s the union claimed only about 26,000 workers, nearly all in California. The boycotts had become so institutionalized that few consumers seemed aware of them; however, the UFW remained the symbolic leader in the fight for farm labor rights. Despite the long struggle, most farmworkers continued to live below the poverty level.

After César Chávez died in 1993, his son-in-law, Arturo Rodríguez, became head of the union.

See also CHÁVEZ, CÉSAR; HUERTA, DOLORES; SACRAMENTO MARCH; VIZZARD, JAMES.

FURTHER READING: Ferriss, Susan, and Ricardo Sandoval. *The Fight in the Fields: César Chávez and the Farmworkers Movement*. New York: Harcourt Brace, 1997; Fuller, Varden. "A New Era for Farm Labor." *Industrial Relations* 6, no. 3 (May 1967):285–302; Fusco, Paul, and George Horwitz. *La Causa: The California Grape Strike*. New York: Macmillan, 1970; Jenkins, J. Craig. *The Politics of In-*

surgency: The Farm Worker Movement in the 1960s. New York: Columbia University Press, 1985; Levy, Jacques E. *César Chávez: Autobiography of La Causa.* New York: W. W. Norton, 1974; www.ufw.org.

UNITED NEIGHBORHOOD ORGANIZATION (UNO). UNO was established in 1975 with the help of Juan Arzube, auxiliary bishop of Los Angeles, California, after a visit he made to San Antonio, Texas, where he witnessed the civil rights work being done by Communities Organized for Public Service (COPS). Although UNO was based on the San Antonio organizational model and its early leaders received the benefit of advice and training from Ernesto Cortés himself, UNO was unable to repeat the COPS success story. It concentrated on economic issues in the community rather than on a political approach. This difference in approach may have been a response to the large nonvotable undocumented population and other differences in Los Angeles. At any event, UNO has concerned itself primarily with housing, segregation, insurance rates, and nongovernmental services. Lack of support from Cardinal James Francis McIntyre of Los Angeles and limited help from his successor, Cardinal Timothy Manning, undercut the early successes of UNO, and by the latter 1980s it had become moribund.

See also CHURCHES, CORTÉS, ERNIE.

FURTHER READING: Acuña, Rodolfo. *Occupied America: A History of Chicanos.* 3rd ed. New York: Harper & Row, 1988; Skerry, Peter. *Mexican Americans: The Ambivalent Minority.* New York: Free Press, 1993.

UNITY LEAGUES. In the post–World War II era Chicano activists organized a variety of civil rights groups appealing to various sectors of la raza. Unlike prewar middle-class Mexican American organizations, the Unity Leagues recruited membership largely from poorer Mexicanos. In 1947 Ignacio López, crusading editor of the San Bernardino weekly *El Espectador*, was the prime mover in initiating the Unity Leagues in the Los Angeles area. Fred Ross, Sr., a Saul Alinsky disciple and representative of the Industrial Areas Foundation as well as the local American Council on Race Relations, also played an important organizing role.

Using a variety of approaches, the Unity Leagues hoped to bring an end to discrimination against Mexican Americans. To rally and unite the community the leagues widely publicized incidents of flagrant racism, filed suits in the courts, and engaged in voter registration and get-out-the-vote campaigns. Skillfully guided by López and using both community organizations and political pressure, the leagues had some success in the late 1940s and the 1950s. They won several segregation lawsuits, elected some local officials, and in 1949 had a part in Edward Roybal's winning a Los Angeles city council seat, thereby initiating his long and honorable career in politics.

See also LÓPEZ, IGNACIO; ROSS, FRED, SR.

FURTHER READING: García, F. Chris. *La Causa Política: A Chicano Political Reader.* Notre Dame, Ind.: University of Notre Dame Press, 1974; McWilliams, Carey. *North from Mexico: The Spanish-Speaking People of the United States.* New ed. Westport, Conn.: Praeger Publishers, 1990; Ross, Fred W. (Sr.) *Community Organization in Mexican-American Communities.* Los Angeles: American Council on Race Relations 1947; Tuck, Ruth. "Sprinkling the Grass Roots." *Common Ground* 7 (Spring 1947):80–83.

V

VALDEZ, LUIS, 1940– . Although not centrally involved in the Mexican American civil rights movement, Luis Valdez played an important role in the struggle to improve the economic and political position of la raza. In the first year of the Delano grape strike he brought his theatrical skills to the support of César Chávez's fight for human dignity and civil rights. Between 1965 and 1967 he created a series of one-act plays that educated the strikers and the general public about the problems of la raza and the goals of La Causa. By the combined use of stinging satire and broad comedy he entertained while he taught.

Having expanded his operation after 1967, Valdez called national attention to the denial of civil rights to 23 Chicano youths during World War II in his very successful play *Zoot Suit*, which he later also made into a film. His even more successful film *La Bamba*, based on the short life of Ritchie Valens, served to further educate the American public about the social problems of Mexican Americans. In addition to his own direct contributions as the founder of the Teatro Campesino and as a theatrical director, Valdez has been the inspiration behind the creation throughout the United States of more than 100 theatrical groups. These organizations and the Teatro Campesino have served to advance the cause of Mexican American civil rights.

See also SLEEPY LAGOON; UNITED FARM WORKERS; ZOOT SUIT RIOTS.

FURTHER READING: *Dictionary of Literary Biography. Vol. 122: Chicano Writers, Second Series*. Detroit: Gale Research, 1992; Elam, Harry J., Jr. *Taking It to the Streets: The Social Protest Theater of Luis Valdez and Amiri Baraka*. Ann Arbor: University of Michigan Press, 1997; Hurwitt, Robert. "The Evolutionary/Revolutionary Luis Valdez." *Image*, 5 January 1986.

VALLEJO, MARIANO GUADALUPE, 1808–1890. Commander of the San Francisco presidio in Mexican California at age 23, two years later Vallejo became military commander of all northern California. As a prominent member of the Vallejo clan he was also an outstanding political and civic leader. Although he was mildly favorable to a takeover of California by the Americans, he was imprisoned by them at Sutter's Fort during the Bear Flag revolt of 1846.

When California prepared to become a state three years later, he was a leading figure among the eight Californios who participated in writing its first constitution. By speaking out for raza concerns and by active participation in committee work, he and his seven compatriots were able to obtain some protection for the rights guaranteed the former Mexicans by the Treaty of Guadalupe Hidalgo. To give Californios some protection against discriminatory taxes on their landholdings, they got the local election of tax assessors. They also succeeded in providing for the printing of laws in Spanish and public school instruction in Spanish—both ended by the mid-1850s. Their signal failure was in the matter of the franchise; this first California constitution limited the vote to white males, despite treaty guarantees.

Vallejo spent his declining years as a patriarchal figure engaged in orchardist concerns, in writing his memoirs, and in enjoying his family and friends.

See also CALIFORNIA.

FURTHER READING: Hunt, Rockwell D. *California's Stately Hall of Fame.* Caldwell, Ida.: Caxton Publishers, 1950; McKittrick, Myrtle M. *Vallejo, Son of California.* Portland, Ore.: Binfords & Mort, 1944; Rosenus, Alan. *General M. G. Vallejo and the Advent of the Americans: A Biography.* Albuquerque: University of New Mexico Press, 1995.

VARELA, MARÍA, 1940–   . From 1963 to 1967 María Varela was a civil rights field worker in the Student Non-Violent Coordinating Committee with the job of developing voter registration materials. Later after her experience organizing among African Americans in Mississippi, she joined Reies López Tijerina's staff in Albuquerque, where she put the skills she had learned in the black civil rights movement to work for her fellow Mexican Americans. Turning her attention to the economic survival and amelioration of Tierra Amarilla dwellers, in 1973 she helped organize a farm cooperative in that part of northwestern New Mexico. Next came a clinic and an Oficina de Ley, with the objectives of improving the health and defending the rights of poor Hispanos. There soon followed Ganados del Valle, a wool-growing and weaving cooperative, which has proved very successful.

At the end of the 1970s Varela worked in Albuquerque to develop a political coalition between the black and Chicano communities to fight for the civil rights of both groups. Primarily because of her work in community economic development, she was honored in 1990 with a MacArthur Foundation fellowship, the "genius award," from which she received a $305,000 stipend. Also an outstanding photographer, she has documented both the black and Chicano civil rights movements with her camera; her photographs have been exhibited at the Smithsonian Institution and at the New York Public Library.

See also BLACK CIVIL RIGHTS INFLUENCE; TIJERINA, REIES LÓPEZ.

FURTHER READING: Chu, Dan, and Leslie Linthicum. "McArthur Grant Winner María Varela . . ." *People*, 14 January 1991, 115; "María Varela." *New America* 4, no. 3 (1982):111–113; *Las Mujeres: Mexican American/Chicana Women.* Windsor, Calif.: National Women's History Project, 1991; Ryan, Michael. "The Village That Came Back to Life." *Parade Magazine*, 3 May 1992, 8, 11.

VÁSQUEZ, TIBURCIO, 1835–1875. Tiburcio Vásquez belongs to that group of Mexicanos, sometimes referred to as social bandits, who were pushed into a life outside the law. To avoid being lynched in the death of an Anglo constable during a Monterey dance hall fracas in 1852, he was forced into a life of brigandage. At a time when Californios were feeling deeply the loss of their lands and rights as well as a decline in their economic and social position, he soon began to be viewed by many as an avenger of their wrongs.

Arrested and jailed several times on horse-stealing and cattle-rustling charges, upon his release from San Quentin in 1870 Vásquez formed a small outlaw band that became proficient at daring payroll holdups and stage robberies. In 1874 a posted reward of $6,000 dead and $8,000 alive brought on an intensive hunt that eventually landed Tiburcio in the hands of the law. While awaiting trial he justified his actions to news reporters as a defense of Mexicano rights in the face of great Anglo injustice. On March 19, 1875, he was executed in San Jose, California, by hanging.

See also CALIFORNIA; CIVIL RIGHTS ABUSE.

FURTHER READING: *The California Outlaw: Tiburcio Vásquez.* Compiled by Robert Greenwood. Reprint, New York: Arno Press, 1974; Castillo, Pedro, and Alberto Camarillo, eds. *Furia y muerte: los bandidos chicanos.* Los Angeles: Chicano Studies Center, University of California, 1973; Hoyle, Millard F., comp. *Crimes and Career of Tiburcio Vásquez.* Hollister, Calif.: Evening Free Lance, 1927; Sawyer, Eugene T. *The Life and Career of Tiburcio Vásquez.* Reprint, Oakland, Calif.: Biobooks, 1944.

VELÁSQUEZ, BALDEMAR, 1947– . Although primarily a labor organizer, Texas-born Baldemar Velásquez has devoted his entire adult life to the broader goal of bettering the lives of midwestern farmworkers. His goals and approaches to them were greatly influenced by the civil rights ideas of Mohandas K. Gandhi and Martin Luther King, Jr., as well as of César Chávez.

From a migrant farmworker family himself, Velásquez developed civil rights concerns that came naturally from early experiences with racial slurs and maltreatment from field supervisors and growers. Volunteer work with the Congress of Racial Equality while he was a college student gave him further valuable insight into working-class problems. His experiences resulted in deep convictions about social justice and agricultural workers' rights. These convictions led him to begin organizing, with the help of his father and several other farmworkers, the Farm Labor Organizing Committee (FLOC) when he was only 20 years old. As longtime president of FLOC Velásquez has pursued goals of social justice and decent treatment for farm laborers and has also committed FLOC to alliances and public stands supporting various civil rights organizations. Under his leadership FLOC has focused on farmworker education and the establishment of law clinics.

Among the many honors recognizing his accomplishments, Velásquez was named a fellow of the prestigious McArthur Foundation in 1990 and in the following year received the Hispanic Leadership Award from the National Council of La Raza. In 1994 he was honored with the Águila Azteca, Mexico's highest award to a foreigner.

See also FARM LABOR ORGANIZING COMMITTEE; MIDWEST, CHICANOS IN.

FURTHER READING: Barger, W. K., and Ernesto M. Reza. *The Farm Labor Movement in the Midwest.* Austin: University of Texas Press, 1994.

VELÁSQUEZ, WILLIE, 1944–1988. Greatly influenced by leaders in the black community as well as by Chicanos, especially Reies López Tijerina, Tejano Willie Velásquez was one of Los Cinco who created the Mexican American Youth Organization (MAYO) in 1967. In the following year he developed an important source of MAYO financing by obtaining funding for an economic development organization, the Mexican American Unity Council. As the result of his views on the importance of voting, he also wrote a proposal for funding the Southwest Council of La Raza and founded the Southwest Voter Registration Education Project (SVREP).

During the latter years of the movimiento Velásquez viewed organizations and legislation as the principal routes to the achievement of greater civil and political rights. Although he was one of the founders of MAYO, in 1969 he resigned from the organization because of internal bickering, increasing militancy, and especially the Raza Unida third-party concept. He argued that the wise course of action was to work through the Democratic Party in the two-party system.

Velásquez's most important contribution to the Mexican American civil rights struggle was, almost certainly, his 1974 creation of the SVREP, of which he remained director until his death. A veteran of south Texas politics, for over a decade during the last years of his life he traveled extensively throughout the Southwest, particularly in Texas, persuading Mexican Americans that the route to civil rights was to register and vote, and then encouraging them to do so. He is widely recognized as one of the most important organizers of Chicanos in their struggle for political representation and civil rights. In 1995 he was posthumously awarded the nation's highest civilian honor, the Presidential Medal of Freedom, by President Bill Clinton.

See also BLACK CIVIL RIGHTS INFLUENCE; MEXICAN AMERICAN YOUTH ORGANIZATION; RAZA UNIDA PARTY, LA; SOUTHWEST VOTER REGISTRATION EDUCATION PROJECT.

FURTHER READING: Navarro, Armando. *Mexican American Youth Organization: Avant-Garde of the Chicano Movement in Texas.* Austin: University of Texas Press, 1995; Pycior, Julie Leininger. *LBJ and Mexican Americans: The Paradox of Power.* Austin: University of Texas Press, 1997; Rosales, Francisco A. *Chicano!: The History of the Mexican American Civil Rights Movement.* Houston: Arte Público Press, 1996; Weyr, Thomas. *Hispanic U.S.A.: Breaking the Melting Pot.* New York: Harper & Row, 1988.

VIGILANTISM. Vigilantism is the taking over of governmental, especially judicial and law enforcement, functions by an extra-legal group, often a posse or self-appointed committee. During the second half of the 1800s vigilante activity was widespread in the American West, and Mexican Americans were often its victims. From the gold fields of California to the cattle ranches of Texas, because of their race Mexicanos were first stereotyped as guilty of crimes and then subjected to vigilante "justice," which often meant being hanged from the nearest tree. Vigilantism in the West, while theoretically invoked to create law and order in an area where there was no judicial system or where it was too weak to be effective, was often merely a lynch law for Mexicanos.

See also CIVIL RIGHTS ABUSE.

FURTHER READING: Blew, Robert W. "Vigilantism in Los Angeles, 1835–1874." *Southern California Quarterly* 54, no. 1 (Spring 1972):11–30; Caughy, John W. *Their Majesties, the Mob.* Chicago: University of Chicago Press, 1960; Hollon, W. Eugene. *Frontier Violence.* New York: Oxford University Press, 1974.

VIZZARD, JAMES L., 1916–1988. James Vizzard was a student and disciple of Paul S. Taylor, the early authority on Mexican immigration and Mexicano labor, and a friend of Chicago-based rights activist Saul Alinsky. Vizzard became a Jesuit priest in 1946 and for the rest of his life was a vocal and ardent defender of the rights of farmworkers. After graduate studies in agricultural economics at several universities, in 1955 he began a 13-year involvement in the National Catholic Rural Life Conference, during which time he became acquainted with and a close friend of César Chávez. Poor health forced Vizzard to resign, but he was soon appointed director of the Jesuit social apostolate in California.

At Chávez's urging, in 1972 Vizzard agreed to become the Washington, D.C., legislative representative and spokesperson for the United Farm Workers. In that position he engaged in intensive lobbying that resulted in the Farm Labor Contractor Registration Act Amendment of 1974 and the Child Labor Law Amendment of the same year. Three years later he had to resign because of seriously deteriorating health; he spent the remainder of his life at Santa Clara University. Throughout his life he fought for the rights of the poor, particularly of Mexicano farm laborers. Over the years he testified before numerous congressional committees as an expert witness on agricultural economics and the rights of labor. He was the author of over 200 articles related to those topics.

See also CHURCHES; UNITED FARM WORKERS.

FURTHER READING: Meier, Matt S., and Feliciano Rivera. *Dictionary of Mexican American History*. Westport, Conn.: Greenwood Press, 1981; Vizzard, James L. "The Extraordinary César Chávez." *Progressive* 30 (July 1966):16–20.

VOTING. Low levels of voter registration and voter turnout are obvious weaknesses in the Mexican American struggle for political power. Longtime discriminatory practices have clearly continued to affect political participation among Mexican Americans today. Historically, taking part in the political process was severely discouraged and hindered by a variety of factors, principally legal or de facto disenfranchisement and constant and venomous discouragement.

California's first constitution excluded many dark-skinned Californios from the ballot box by limiting the vote to white males, despite the guarantees of the Treaty of Guadalupe Hidalgo. In Texas intimidation, threats, and physical abuse as well as the grandfather clause were widely used for over a century to discourage Mexican Americans from registering to vote and from going to the polls. In some states interpretation of English-language passages and literacy tests, which could easily be applied selectively, were extensively used to exclude Mexican Americans from the ballot box. The almost complete domination of politics by Anglos, with the partial exception of New Mexico and to a lesser extent south Texas, has clearly helped discourage Mexican American participation in politics, as have a variety of stratagems.

For example, gerrymandering and at-large elections were frequently employed to dilute the Mexican American vote. To make the situation worse, until fairly recently poll taxes were used in many states to further discourage voting. In some states a requirement of annual re-registration to retain eligibility was one more technique to deter Mexican American voting. For years limited and inconvenient access to registration as well as residency requirements kept many migrant workers from being able to participate in the political process. Further, onerous filing fees have helped discourage Chicano candidacy for elective political positions.

There has also been a cultural factor involved, especially among immigrant citizens, many of whom may have felt somewhat cynical about elections and government in general from past experience in both Mexico and the United States. Lastly, poverty and low levels of education are widely accepted as having a negative effect on registration and voting. Some political scientists believe that the individual's level of education is the single, most important factor in registration and election turnout.

After the mid-twentieth century, court suits challenging gerrymandering and at-large election practices helped turn the tide, and in the 1960s a series of civil rights acts, aimed primarily at blacks, for the first time made it more possible for many Mexican Americans to take part in the electoral process. The Voting Rights Act of 1965 and the amendments of 1975 and 1982 led to voter registration drives, spurred by the Southwest Voter Registration Education Project (SVREP) and other similar groups. Between 1976 and 1980 the number of Mexican Americans registered to vote increased by 25 percent and the number who voted was up by 20 percent. During the 1980s continuing registration drives led to further increases in raza registrations; however, the number actually voting remained unsatisfactorily low. In the presidential election year 1992 only 35 percent of eligible Latinos were registered to vote, and only about one third of those registered actually voted.

In 1996 the SVREP, the Midwest Voter Registration Education Project, and the Hispanic Education and Legal Fund joined forces to form Latino Vote USA '96, which registered over 1 million new raza voters in Texas and California. Despite low socioeconomic status and inferior education, an increased ethnic consciousness has stimulated Chicano registration and electoral participation. In the 1996 elections 6.6 million Latinos were registered and 5 million voted. In Texas 1.4 million Latinos voted—an impressive 60 percent increase over 1992. In California nearly 70 percent of the newly registered voters actually cast their ballots in 1996, a rate much higher than that of any other group.

Impelled by anti-immigrant propositions on the ballot, in the 1996 election for the first time more than a million California Latinos went to the polls. After lagging badly in the past two decades, when only 25–30 percent of those registered actually voted, in the 1996 presidential election about 50 percent cast their ballots. In November 1998 a California newspaper headline proclaimed, "Latinos Prove Powerful at Polls." Latinos had won their first statewide office in over 100 years, electing Cruz Bustamante as lieutenant governor. They also won their first big-city mayoralty race with Ron Gonzales in San Jose, and six more seats in the legislature at Sacramento. Mexican Americans even elected their first California Republican legislator, Rod Pacheco, who was named minority Assembly leader. In New Mexico's 1998 political contests voters elected four Mexican Americans to state offices: secretary of state, attorney general, treasurer, and auditor. In Colorado Denver attorney Ken Salazar became the state's first Mexican American attorney general.

Today Mexican American voters have come of age and their voting record is highly respectable. Further, electoral statistics and population projections clearly indicate the potential political power available to them through the ballot in the new millennium.

See also CIVIL RIGHTS ABUSE; GERRYMANDERING; SOUTHWEST VOTER REGISTRATION EDUCATION PROJECT; VOTING RIGHTS ACT, 1965.

FURTHER READING: Buehler, Marilyn H. "Voter Turnout and Political Efficacy among Mexican-Americans in Michigan." *Sociological Quarterly* 18 (1977):504–517; Camarillo, Lydia. "Counting Our Election Returns." *Hispanic* (January/February 1997):108; DeSipio, Louis. *Counting on the Latino Vote: Latinos as a New Electorate.* Charlottesville: University Press of Virginia, 1996; *Documents of the Chicano Struggle.* New York: Pathfinder Press, 1971; García, F. Chris, and Rodolfo O. de la Garza. *The Chicano Political Experience: Three Perspectives.* North Scituate, Mass.: Duxbury Press, 1977; García, John A. "Political Participation: Resources and Involvement among Latinos in the American Political System." In *Pursuing Power: Latinos and the Political System,* edited by F. Chris García. Notre Dame, Ind.: University of Notre Dame Press, 1997; Gonzales, Raymond J. "Why Chicanos Don't Vote." *California Journal* 6, no. 7 (July 1975):245–246; Guerra, Sandra. "Voting Rights and the Constitution: The Disenfranchisement of Non-English Speaking Citizens." In *Land Grants, Housing, and Political Power,* edited by Antoinette Sedillo López. New York: Garland Publishing, 1995; Vigil, Maurilio E. "The Hispanic Vote." *Hispanics in American Politics.* Lanham, Md.: University Press of America, 1987.

VOTING RIGHTS ACT, 1965. Initially advanced by President Lyndon Johnson to protect the civil rights of black Americans, the Voting Rights Act, also known as the Civil Rights Act of 1965, for the first time made the Fourteenth and Fifteenth Amendments enforceable. It provided for direct federal intervention, where necessary, to enable citizens to register and vote. The law included a limited prohibition against the use of literacy tests to disqualify citizens from voting and specifically rejected the inability of some citizens to speak English as a basis for denying them the franchise. Although the act was basically a response to the denial of the vote to African Americans in the South and to the voting rights campaign they initiated, it served also to pave the way for accelerated voter registration and get-out-the-vote drives among Chicanos. It proved, therefore, to be an important step in the Mexican American civil rights movement.

In 1970 the Voting Rights Act was extended for five more years with an added provision to prevent the erection of new barriers to political participation. In 1975 the act was again extended with important additions for Mexican Americans. The national ban on literacy tests was made permanent. New provisions included a requirement for bilingual ballots in certain language-dominated areas and provisions allowing individuals to file suit against local jurisdictions for denial of their voting rights. Seven years later the act was extended to the year 2007 and included an absolute abolition of all discriminatory practices such as at-large elections.

Although in 1965 and 1970 Congress was primarily concerned with black Americans, the 1975 and 1982 acts specifically aimed at language-minority groups like Mexican Americans. Despite some continuing obstacles to more effective use of the ballot by Chicanos, the success of the voting rights acts for Mexican Americans is attested to by the increased size of their vote and the growing number elected to public office.

See also VOTING.

FURTHER READING: Bardolph, Richard, ed. *The Civil Rights Record*. New York: Thomas Y. Crowell Co., 1970; de la Garza, Rodolfo O., and Louis DeSipio. "Save the Baby, Change the Bathwater, and Scrub the Tub: Latino Electoral Participation after Twenty Years of Voting Rights Act Coverage." In *Pursuing Power: Latinos and the Political System*, edited by F. Chris García. Notre Dame, Ind.: University of Notre Dame Press, 1997; García, John A. "The Voting Rights Act and Hispanic Political Representation in the Southwest." In *Land Grants, Housing, and Political Power*, edited by Antoinette Sedillo López. New York: Garland Publishing, 1995; Graham, Hugh Davis. *The Civil Rights Era, 1960–1972*. New York: Oxford University Press, 1990; Polinard, J. L., Robert D. Wrinkle, Tomás Longoria, and Norman B. Binder. *Electoral Structure and Urban Policy: The Impact on Mexican American Communities*. Armonk, N.Y.: M. E. Sharpe, 1994.

W

WASHINGTON MARCH, 1996. A rally of Latino civil rights advocates and other activists, estimated at between 20,000 and 30,000, descended on Washington, D.C., to voice their demands for equality of treatment in the United States. This impressive Hispanic march came in response to the mounting attacks on affirmative action and to other Chicano concerns.

Called a new beginning for Latino civil rights by the organizers, who were spearheaded by Los Angeles activist Juan José Gutiérrez, the march rallied at the Ellipse, where the participants listened to various speakers. The leaders described the centerpiece of the march, a platform listing seven demands focused on human and constitutional rights for all and including a streamlined citizenship process. The festive crowd was notable for the large number of grassroots community workers and the scarcity of invited high-profile Latino politicians and celebrities.

FURTHER READING: *Hispanic Link Weekly Report*, 23 September 1996, 1; Ramos, George. "Thousands of Latinos March in Washington." *Los Angeles Times*, 13 October 1996, A1, A39.

WORLD WAR I, 1914–1919. After U.S. entrance into World War I in 1917, thousands of Mexican Americans, proportionately more than members of any other ethnic group, voluntarily enlisted in the armed services. Although they continued to experience much of the discrimination they had encountered in civilian life, as a result of their service they had their horizons broadened and their levels of expectation raised. Many Chicano enlistees had distinguished records, and most developed a greater consciousness of themselves as U.S. citizens. Experiences in the military lessened their longstanding southwestern isolation, pushed them farther into the American mainstream, and provided leadership training. These newly acquired leadership skills were quite valuable to the Chicano organizational development that followed in the 1920s.

See also LEADERSHIP; ORGANIZATIONS.

FURTHER READING: Acuña, Rodolfo. *Occupied America: A History of Chicanos.* 3rd ed. New York: Harper & Row, 1988; Christian, Carole. "Joining the American Mainstream: Texas Mexican Americans during World War I." *Southwestern Historical Quarterly* 92, no. 4 (April 1989):555–595; Meier, Matt S., and Feliciano Rivera. *Dictionary of Mexican American History.* Westport, Conn.: Greenwood Press, 1981; Sáenz, J. Luz. *Los México-americanos en la gran guerra: y su contigente en pro de la democracia, la humanidad y la justicia.* San Antonio: Artes Gráficas, 1933.

WORLD WAR II, 1939–1945. World War II became a watershed in the experience of Mexican Americans by providing the more than 300,000 who served in the armed forces a variety of opportunities to improve the quality of life and their position in American society. Through the G.I. Bill it enabled many veterans to obtain university educations. It gave many their first exposure to possibilities outside the confines of the barrio or the rural Southwest. It nurtured new aspirations and helped create a feeling of self-confidence that in turn led to the founding of a host of civil rights organizations in the postwar period. The war led to a political consciousness that fueled vigorous protests against discriminatory practices.

During the war the growth of the military-industrial complex in the Southwest helped create a large, urbanized raza population, whose members then had better educational opportunities than their parents. Mexicano workers became more aggressive in demanding equality in employment, and the government used the Fair Employment Practices Committee to enforce the prohibition against discrimination in wartime industries with government contracts. The committee's investigations of discriminatory labor practices, particularly in the Southwest, both righted some patent wrongs and enabled Mexican Americans to speak out more freely in defense of their rights.

World War II also illuminated the social as well as the economic plight of Mexican Americans. As a result, state and federal agencies moved to alleviate prejudice against them. Public schools inaugurated programs to reduce segregation and to engender appreciation of Mexican and Latino culture. Teacher-training institutes and workshops were held to implement these objectives and to develop more accepting attitudes toward Mexicano children and their civil rights. Although only partially successful, these efforts at least created awareness that there was an "Anglo problem."

The World War II Chicano generation replaced the Mexican Dream of its immigrant parents or grandparents with its own American Dream. Wartime experience helped lead to the creation of the American G.I. Forum, Community Service Organization, Mexican American Political Association,

Political Association of Spanish-Speaking Organizations, American Coordinating Council on Political Education, and other regional and national groups whose leaders vigorously took up the gauntlet for civil rights. These groups were all explicitly political in their objectives, challenged discriminatory practices, and demanded full civil rights for all Chicanos. In addition, older organizations like the Alianza Hispano-Americana and the League of United Latin American Citizens, now having an expanded membership of veterans, moved with the changing times and strongly emphasized civil rights issues in their agendas.

The veterans of World War II, overwhelmingly native-born, had a deepened sense of citizenship, which reinvigorated the long Mexican American struggle for civil rights. Now using political pressure organizations and the ballot box, they renewed and expanded the fight against discrimination and racism. Their postwar children, brought up in this heady atmosphere, went farther, creating a string of student groups, the Chicano Movement, and finally La Raza Unida Party—all in the defense and promotion of raza rights. In summation, the war led to greater Chicano participation in all aspects of American life.

See also LEADERSHIP; MOVIMIENTO, EL; ORGANIZATIONS.

FURTHER READING: García, F. Chris, and Rodolfo O. de la Garza. *The Chicano Political Experience: Three Perspectives*. North Scituate, Mass.: Duxbury Press, 1977; McWilliams, Carey. *North from Mexico: The Spanish-Speaking People of the United States*. New ed. New York: Praeger Publishers, 1990; Meier, Matt S., and Feliciano Rivera. *Mexican Americans/American Mexicans: From Conquistadors to Chicanos*. New York: Hill & Wang, 1993; Morín, Raúl. *Among the Valiant: Mexican Americans in World War II and Korea*. Los Angeles: Borden Publishing Co., 1963; Weinberger, Casper W. "A Heritage of Valor—Hispanics in America's Defense." *Nuestro* (November 1983):18.

X

XIMENES, VICENTE T., 1919– . In 1967 Vicente Ximenes, an attorney with a graduate degree in economics, was named by President Lyndon B. Johnson to a four-year term on the Equal Employment Opportunity Commission (EEOC) and then was selected to head the newly created Inter-Agency Committee on Mexican American Affairs (IACMAA). Commissioner Ximenes, who had previously served in the Agency for International Development and had earlier been involved in organizing workers, doing research, and teaching economics, was also an active participant in various activities of the American G.I. Forum.

A member of the U.S. Civil Rights Commission, Ximenes used his EEOC position to further advance the struggle for the rights of disadvantaged minorities, adopting a new tactic, affirmative action. In order to secure the support of business in the elimination of discrimination in private-sector employment, he organized EEOC hearings and conferences in several southwestern cities. In fall 1967 he programmed the first National Conference on Mexican American Affairs, held in El Paso, Texas. During his tenure as chair of the IACMMA, some 4,000 Mexican Americans were able to obtain federal positions. In 1982 he returned to Albuquerque, where he then founded a human rights group. His moderate efforts to secure justice for the disadvantaged had measurable success, resulting later in his being singled out by the United Nations for its human rights award.

See also CIVIL RIGHTS COMMISSION; EQUAL EMPLOYMENT OPPORTUNITY ACT; JOHNSON, LYNDON BAINES.

FURTHER READING: Alford, Harold J. *The Proud Peoples.* New York: David McKay Co., 1972; Chacón, José A. *Hispanic Notables in the United States of North America.* Albuquerque, N.M.: Saguaro Press, 1978; Pycior, Julie Leininger. *LBJ and Mexican Americans: Paradox of Power.* Austin: University of Texas Press, 1997.

Y

YZAGUIRRE, RAÚL, 1939– . Raúl Yzaguirre began his civil rights career early. While still in high school he became concerned with improving educational opportunities for Mexican American students. To this end he organized youth chapters of the American G.I. Forum. After service in the U.S. Air Force, he entered the university, where he was instrumental in creating a Chicano umbrella organization he called the National Organization for Mexican American Services (NOMAS). Upon graduation from George Washington University he went to work in the Migrant Division of the Office of Economic Opportunity (OEO). In 1969 he left the OEO to organize Interstate Research Associates, a Mexican American research and consulting firm for whose services he saw a great need.

Five years later Yzaguirre agreed to take over the helm of the National Council of La Raza (NCLR), which had recently moved from Texas to Washington, D.C. As executive director of the now nationwide organization, formerly the Southwest Council of La Raza, he was primarily responsible for making the council an effective Chicano umbrella organization that mediated between the community and large corporations. Under his leadership the NCLR became a truly national organization, with an annual budget of over $5 million. In 1979 Yzaguirre became the first Mexican American to receive the Rockefeller Public Service Award.

See also NATIONAL COUNCIL OF LA RAZA; NATIONAL ORGANIZATION OF MEXICAN AMERICAN SERVICES.

FURTHER READING: Gonzales, Sylvia A. *Hispanic American Voluntary Organizations*. Westport, Conn.: Greenwood Press, 1985; "Interview with Raúl Yzaguirre." *La Luz* 1, no. 11 (March 1973):26–28, 30; Martínez, Douglas. "Yzaguirre at the Helm." *Américas* 32, no. 6–7 (June–July 1980):49; "The Movement's Organization Man." *Nuestro* 6, no. 2 (March 1982).

Z

ZAPATA, CARMEN, 1927– . Singer-dancer Carmen Zapata was born in New York City, where for two decades she appeared in Broadway musicals like *Oklahoma*. In 1967, after her marriage failed and her mother died, she moved to southern California, where she developed an extensive and highly successful movie and television career despite the stereotyping she often encountered. In 1969 she was one of the co-founders, along with Ricardo Montalbán, of Nosotros, the Latino actors' rights organization. In the following year she began what was to become the renowned Bilingual Foundation of the Arts, dedicated to bringing Spanish-language theater both to Latinos and, in translation, to Anglos. In 1993 she retired from the foundation.

Always an unflagging activist, Zapata has served on the boards of various groups, including the Mexican American Opportunities Foundation, the California Arts Council Ethnic Advisory Minority Panel, and the National Conference of Christians and Jews. For her tireless efforts she has been the recipient of numerous local, national, and international awards.

See also CHICANAS.

FURTHER READING: "Carmen Zapata." *Nuestro* 2, no. 7 (July 1978):13–14; Hadley-García, George. *Hispanic Hollywood*. New York: Carol Publishing Group, 1990; Ragua, David. *Who's Who in Hollywood, 1900–1976*. New Rochelle, N.Y.: Arlington House, 1976; Telgen, Diane, and Jim Kamp, eds. *¡Latinas! Women of Achievement*. Detroit: Visible Ink Press, 1996.

ZOOT SUIT RIOTS, 1943. One of the most highly publicized and extensive violations of Mexican Americans' civil rights was the so-called Zoot Suit riots that occurred during World War II. By that time Los Angeles had a large second-generation Mexican American population, many of whose teenage members had adopted the zoot suit outfit then popular among youths.

In the early spring of 1943, in the wake of the Sleepy Lagoon convictions, tensions remained high in the city and a number of small altercations occurred in which armed forces personnel tore pants off zoot suiters. When Chicano youths retaliated, they were subjected to harsh treatment and arrest by the authorities. At the beginning of June there occurred serious clashes in which restive sailors and soldiers attacked zoot-suited Chicano youths on the streets of Los Angeles. Zoot suiters were dragged off streetcars and out of buses and theaters; many were assaulted and had their clothes ripped off and their longish hair cut. A virtual undeclared war on Chicano youths rapidly ensued.

What had begun as a series of street brawls became a full-scale race riot, fueled by a sensationalist press. Police and sheriff's deputies followed the action, ignoring the armed services aggressors and arresting the victims for disturbing the peace. The violence in Los Angeles triggered similar racial attacks on Mexican Americans in a number of cities with sizable Chicano populations. Finally, as a result of pressure from Washington, the military police cracked down and military leaves were canceled. By mid-June the attacks tapered off and order was restored.

A citizens' committee was appointed by Governor Earl Warren to investigate the causes of the Zoot Suit rioting and to make recommendations. Its damning report and serious concerns about denial of civil liberties led to a few programs to improve communications between Los Angeles officials and the Mexican American community. There was also some ameliorative action, for example, the creation of the Los Angeles Commission on Human Relations. Overall, however, little was actually achieved in improving civil rights enforcement or conditions in the barrio. In the Los Angeles Chicano community this outrageous attack on civil liberties left a residue of great bitterness against the authorities. This feeling was strongly renewed and reinforced a quarter of a century later by the killing of Rubén Salazar during the Chicano Moratorium.

See also CIVIL RIGHTS ABUSE; SLEEPY LAGOON; WORLD WAR II.

FURTHER READING: Acuña, Rodolfo. *Occupied America: A History of Chicanos.* 3rd ed. New York: Harper & Row, 1988; California, Governor. *Citizens Committee Report on the Zoot Suit Riots.* Sacramento, Calif.: State Printing Office, 1943; McWilliams, Carey. *North from Mexico: The Spanish-Speaking People of the United States.* Updated ed. Westport, Conn.: Praeger Publishers, 1990; McWilliams, Carey. "Zoot Suit Riots." *New Republic* 108 (June 1943):818–820; Sánchez, George I. "Pachucos in the Making." *Common Ground.* 4, no. 1 (Fall 1943): 13–20; Tuck, Ruth. "Behind the Zoot Suit Riots." *Survey Graphic* 32 (August 1943):313–316, 335–336.

APPENDIX A

Mexican American Civil Rights Chronology

1836	Texas gained de facto independence from Mexico
1845	Texas was annexed to the United States
1848	Guadalupe Hidalgo Treaty ended the two-year U.S.–Mexican War
1850	California's Foreign Miners' License Tax, aimed at Mexicanos
1850s	Mexican American land rights violated; squatter litigation ensued
1851	Land Act of, passed by U.S. Congress for California only
1853–54	Gadsden Purchase Treaty adjusted Mexican–U.S. border
1855–59	*El Clamor Público*, published in Los Angeles, defended Chicano rights
1857	Cart War in Texas, a denial of basic civil rights
1859	Juan Cortina border uprising against Anglo mistreatment of Mexicanos
1866	Civil Rights Act of
1868	Fourteenth Amendment to the Constitution ratified
1870	Civil Rights Enforcement Act of
1875	Civil Rights Act of
	Romualdo Pacheco became first, and only, Mexican American governor of California
1877	Salt War at El Paso, caused by nonacceptance of Mexicano rights
1880	Census: Mexican-descent population of about 230,000
1880s	Gorras Blancas (White Caps) resistance in New Mexico
	Mutualista organizations begin to develop widely in the Southwest

1891   Court of Private Land Claims, created by U.S. Congress for New Mexico Territory

1894   Alianza Hispano-Americana founded in Tucson, Arizona

1897   *In Re Ricardo Rodríguez*

1901   Gregorio Cortez began his famous ride in Texas

1903   Mexican American role in defending Arizona copper miners' rights

1907–08 Repatriation of Mexican workers because of economic decline

1911   El Primer Congreso Mexicanista, first civil rights convention

1914   Ludlow Massacre, of Colorado coal miners

1915   Plan de San Diego (Texas) arose from civil rights abuses and prompted more severe repression

1916   Ezequiel Cabeza de Baca, first Mexican American elected governor of New Mexico, a strong advocate of Hispanic civil rights

1917   Immigration Act, imposed a head tax and literacy requirements, which were waived because of World War I

        Bisbee, Arizona, "deportations"

1918   Octaviano A. Larrazolo elected governor of New Mexico, supported bilingual education

1920   Census: 486,000 Mexican-born; 252,000 U.S.-born

1921   La Orden de Hijos de América founded in San Antonio

        Pan American Round Table, an anti-discrimination group, established in San Antonio

        Comisiones honoríficas mexicanas developed to help Mexican immigrants defend their civil rights

        Anti-Mexican feeling intensification because of postwar depression

1925   Border Patrol created by U.S. Congress

1926   La Sociedad de Madres Mexicanas, early civil rights group, organized by Chicanas in Los Angeles

1929   League of United Latin American Citizens (LULAC) founded in Texas

1930   Census: 1,509,000 Mexican-descent population; more than half U.S.-born

        Salvatierra v. Del Rio Independent School District, an early step in the struggle to end school segregation in Texas

1930–34	Thousands of Mexicanos repatriated without due process
1931	Lemon Grove (California), a benchmark ruling in school segregation
1933	Major strikes in California agriculture, initiated by Mexicanos
1934	La Liga Obrera de Habla Española founded in Gallup, New Mexico
1935	Gallup, New Mexico, incident; miners' eviction from homes led to riots
1938	Mexican American Movement (MAM), early Chicano youth civil rights group in southern California, stressed education
	Pecan shellers' strike in San Antonio; Emma Tenayuca's leadership
	El Congreso de Pueblos de Habla Española established in California as a national civil rights group
1940	Census: 1,571,000 Mexican-descent population
	Unity Leagues in California, fought discrimination and segregation
1941	Fair Employment Practices Committee established by executive order
1942–44	Spanish-Speaking People's Division established as part of the Office of Inter-American Affairs
1942	Sleepy Lagoon murder trial; violation of civil rights of the accused
1943	Zoot Suit race riots in Los Angeles, San Diego, and Oakland
1944	Fair Employment Practices bill (which failed to pass) authored by Senator Dennis Chávez of New Mexico
1945	Bishops Committee for the Spanish Speaking created
1945–47	*Méndez et al. v. Westminster School District* case, the first serious blow to school segregation
1947	Community Service Organization (CSO) established, modeled on earlier Unity Leagues; Fred Ross's role
	Félix Longoria case in Three Rivers, Texas, aroused national response
	American G.I. Forum founded in Corpus Christi; Héctor P. García
1948	*Delgado et al. v. Bastrop Independent School District* segregation case in Texas
1950	Census: about 2,282,000 Mexican-descent population
1951	*Gonzales et al. v. Sheely et al.*
	Bloody Christmas
1952	McCarran-Walter Act passed; later used to deport Mexican labor leaders

1953   Mexican activists deported as a result of McCarthyism

            Council of Mexican American Affairs founded in Los Angeles

1954   Operation Wetback, a massive repatriation effort, began in June; over
            1 million Mexicanos deported, nearly all without due process

1955   *Hernández v. The State of Texas* decision recognizing Chicanos as a
            distinct white ethnic group

            Brown v. Board of Education decision declaring that public schools
            could not segregate students by race

1957   *Hernández v. Driscoll Consolidated Independent School District*

            Civil Rights Act of, first civil rights legislation in twentieth century

            Civil Rights Division created in Justice Department

            Raymond Telles elected mayor of El Paso, first Chicano in twentieth
            century

1959   Mexican American Political Association (MAPA) began in California

1960   Civil Rights Act of

            Census: Mexican American population of 3,465,000

            Viva Kennedy election clubs established throughout the Southwest

            Extensive Chicano voter registration drives by various groups

            Henry B. González, first Mexican American elected to U.S. House of
            Representatives

            Political Association of Spanish Speaking Organizations (PASO/
            PASSO) founded in Texas

1962   Precursor to United Farm Workers union founded by César Chávez

1963   Equal Pay Act of

            Crystal City, Texas, first Chicano political revolt in

            Reies López Tijerina founded the Alianza Federal de Mercedes

1964   Civil Rights Act of, a comprehensive revision

            Poll tax in federal elections outlawed by Twenty-fourth Amendment

            Head Start program created

            Equal Employment Opportunity Commission established

            War on Poverty programs increased Chicano political awareness

1965   Voting Rights Act of

Chicano students civil rights organizing, which led to UMAS, MASC, MEChA, MAYO, Brown Berets, and El Frente

Delano grape strike by César Chávez

1966   California Rural Legal Assistance organization established

Albuquerque walkout, led by Albert Peña

Sacramento march from Delano, led by César Chávez

Santa Fe march from Albuquerque, led by Tijerina's Alianza

Austin march, led by Antonio Orendain

Mexican American Student Association founded in East Los Angeles

Crusade for Justice in Denver, organized by Rodolfo "Corky" Gonzales

Chicana Ernie Evans became first woman elected secretary of state of New Mexico

1967   Mexican American Youth Organization (MAYO) founded in San Antonio by José Angel Gutiérrez and other activists

United Mexican American Students (UMAS) founded in Los Angeles

El Plan de Santa Barbara emerged from a conference held in that city

Age Discrimination in Employment Act

Vicente Ximenes named head of Equal Employment Opportunity

Commission by President Lyndon Johnson

Héctor Pérez García became first Mexican American appointed to the U.S. Civil Rights Commission

Inter-Agency Committee on Mexican American Affairs created by President Lyndon Johnson; Vicente Ximenes its first chairperson

Raza Unida founded in Texas, precursor to La Raza Unida Party

Brown Berets founded in Los Angeles by David Sánchez

Tierra Amarilla, New Mexico, courthouse gun battle by Tijerina's Alianza group

1968   Civil Rights Act of

Fair Housing Act of

Bilingual Education Act passed by U.S. Congress

Students walked out of Los Angeles high schools, demanding rights

Mexican American Legal Defense and Educational Fund, landmark civil rights organization, founded in Texas

Plan del Barrio formulated

Congress of Mexican American Unity founded in Los Angeles

Centro de Acción Social Autónoma (CASA) founded in southern California; Bert Corona's role

Poor People's March on Washington, D.C.

1969   Movimiento Estudantil Chicano de Aztlán (MEChA) organized at Santa Barbara, California, out of earlier student groups

First Chicano Youth Conference in Denver led to the Plan Espiritual de Aztlán

Colorado La Raza Unida Party founded by Corky Gonzales

Nosotros, an equal opportunity organization for Latino actors, formed by Ricardo Montalbán and others

Office of Minority Business Enterprise established

1970   Census: approximately 6,000,000 Mexican Americans

Rev. Patrick Flores, strong civil rights supporter, became first Mexican American appointed bishop (and in 1979 archbishop) in the Catholic Church

La Raza Unida Party (LRUP) formed in Texas out of MAYO by José Angel Gutiérrez

National Chicano Moratorium protest in Los Angeles against Vietnam War

Rubén Salazar killed during East Los Angeles moratorium march

1971   Crystal City, Texas, victory of La Raza Unida Party

First Chicana Conference brought 600 to Houston, Texas

Serrano v. Priest led to equalized financial base for school districts

El Centro de Acción Social Autónoma (CASA) organized, Bert Corona

Farah strike on Texas border; 4,000 workers, two-year struggle

1972   Local Fiscal Assistance Act

Equal Employment Opportunities Act amended 1964 Civil Rights Act, creating the Equal Employment Opportunities Commission

La Raza Unida Party national convention, September, in El Paso

Medrano v. Allee, in which U.S. Supreme Court ruled against Texas Rangers

1974   Southwest Voter Registration Education Project (SVREP) established in Texas, Willie Velásquez its creator and director

MANA founded, as Mexican American Women's National Association

Communities Organized for Public Service founded in San Antonio by Ernie Cortés and others

Raúl H. Castro became first Mexican American governor of Arizona

Equal Educational Opportunity Act passed by Congress

Lau v. Nichols decision laid basis for expanded bilingual education

1975   National Association of Latino Elected Officials (NALEO) founded
        Age Discrimination Act passed by Congress

        Congress expanded the 1965 Voting Rights Act to include Chicanos

        Jerry Apodaca became first Mexican American elected governor of New Mexico in over 50 years

1976   Vilma Martínez became first Mexican American to receive the Jefferson Award, for her civil rights work

1977   Congressional Hispanic Caucus resulted from Representative Edward Roybal's initiatives

        Plyler v. Doe case, re denial of public education by Texas to children of undocumented immigrants

1978   *Bakke* case decision upheld by U.S. Supreme Court

1979   Access to public education for children of undocumented aliens became a widely discussed issue

        Raúl Yzaguirre became first Mexican American to receive the Rockefeller Public Service Award

        Joan Báez founded and headed Humanitas International organization, in order to promote human rights

1980   Census: approximately 9,000,000 Mexican-descent Americans

1981   Henry Cisneros became first Mexican American mayor of San Antonio since Juan Seguín in the early 1840s

1982   1965 Voting Rights Act renewed

        Gloria Molina became first Chicana elected to the California Assembly

        Plyler v. Doe; U.S. Supreme Court decision favored complainant

1984   Associate Justice of the Texas Supreme Court Raúl A. González, first Tejano elected to statewide office

        Héctor Pérez García became first Mexican American honored with the U.S. Medal of Freedom

        Ernie Cortés became first Chicano awarded a MacArthur (genius) fellowship

1986   Immigration Reform and Control Act, included curbs on employer abuses of workers' rights

1987   Gloria Molina became first Chicana elected to Los Angeles city council

              U.S. v. Paradise et al., in which U.S. Supreme Court restricted race-based promotions

1988   Lauro Cavazos became secretary of education; first Mexican American named to a presidential cabinet

1990   Census: 13,496,000 Mexican Americans out of 22,354,000 Hispanics, who comprise 9 percent of U.S. population

              Civil Rights Bill of, vetoed by President George Bush

              Dan Morales elected Texas's first Chicano attorney general

1991   Civil Rights Act of, passed

              Gloria Molina became first woman and first Mexican American in the twentieth century elected to Los Angeles Board of Supervisors

1992   *Freeman et al. v. Pitts et al.* in which U.S. Supreme Court ruled school segregation based on residential pattern not unconstitutional

              Voters Assistance Act made possible bilingual voting information

              Roybal-Allard became first Chicana elected to the U.S. House of Representatives

1992–96   *Hopwood v. State of Texas*

1993   Henry Cisneros appointed secretary of housing and urban development by President Bill Clinton

              Federico Peña appointed secretary of transportation

              Racially based congressional apportionment boundaries held unconstitutional by U.S. Supreme Court

1994   Proposition 187, anti–illegal alien legislation, passed by California voters

1995   Willie Velásquez posthumously awarded the Presidential Medal of Freedom, America's highest civilian honor

1996   Estimated Hispanic population: 28,269,000

              Cruz Bustamante became first Mexican American elected Speaker of the California Assembly

              California Proposition 209 passed

              Latino March for Justice brings thousands to Washington, D.C.

1998   Proposition 227, approved by California voters, ordered end to bilingual education classes not taught in English

Antonio Villaraigosa second Mexican American elected Speaker of the California Assembly

Louis Caldera became first Mexican American secretary of the army

Cruz Bustamante elected lieutenant governor of California

1999   Bustamante sworn in as lieutenant governor, the first Mexican American to hold that office since Romualdo Pacheco in 1871

APPENDIX B

Bill of Rights: The First Ten Amendments to the U.S. Constitution

The framers of the Constitution and most of their contemporaries held the opinion that individual rights could best be defended by inaction. In an era of great fear of centralized power, they added to the Constitution the first ten amendments, the Bill of Rights, directed against possible abuses of common law rights and civil liberties by their new federal government. They viewed the individual states as the principal protectors of their own citizens and ultimately rejected James Madison's concern about possible violation of rights by state and local governments. As a result of the foregoing, early concern about civil rights was generally limited to protecting citizens from abuse by the federal government.

With the exception of a flurry of constitutional amendments and federal legislation at the end of the Civil War, this essentially negative view of civil rights legislation held sway until the twentieth century. Only then did many Americans come to see that their rights could be protected and might be advanced by positive action on the part of government. This shift from minimal prohibitive legislation to affirmative government intervention in the advancement of civil rights continues today and is accompanied by increasing concern about denial of civil liberties by nongovernmental groups and individuals.

ARTICLE 1

Congress shall make no law respecting an establishment of religion, or prohibiting the free exercise thereof; or abridging the freedom of speech, or of the press; or the right of the people peaceably to assemble, and to petition the government for a redress of grievances.

ARTICLE II

A well regulated militia, being necessary to the security of a free State, the right of the people to keep and bear arms, shall not be infringed.

ARTICLE III

No soldier shall, in time of peace be quartered in any house, without the consent of the owner, nor in time of war, but in a manner to be prescribed by law.

ARTICLE IV

The right of the people to be secure in their persons, houses, papers, and effects, against unreasonable searches and seizures, shall not be violated, and no warrants shall issue, but upon probable cause, supported by oath or affirmation, and particularly describing the place to be searched, and the persons or things to be seized.

ARTICLE V

No person shall be held to answer for a capital, or otherwise infamous crime, unless on a presentment or indictment of a grand jury, except in cases arising in the land or naval forces, or in the militia, when in actual service in time of war or public danger; nor shall any person be subject for the same offense to be twice put in jeopardy of life or limb; nor shall be compelled in any criminal case to be a witness against himself, nor be deprived of life, liberty, or property, without due process of law; nor shall private property be taken for public use without just compensation.

ARTICLE VI

In all criminal prosecutions, the accused shall enjoy the right to a speedy and public trial, by an impartial jury of the State and district wherein the crime shall have been committed, which district shall have been previously ascertained by law, and to be informed of the nature and cause of the accusation; to be confronted with the witnesses against him; to have compulsory process for obtaining witnesses in his favor, and to have the assistance of counsel for his defense.

ARTICLE VII

In suits at common law, where the value in controversy shall exceed twenty dollars, the right of trial by jury shall be preserved, and no fact tried by a jury shall be otherwise reexamined in any court of the United States, than according to the rules of the common law.

ARTICLE VIII

Excessive bail shall not be required, nor excessive fines imposed, nor cruel and unusual punishment inflicted.

ARTICLE IX

The enumeration in the Constitution of certain rights shall not be construed to deny or disparage others retained by the people.

ARTICLE X

The powers not delegated to the United States by the Constitution, nor prohibited by it to the States, are reserved to the States respectively, or to the people.

The first ten amendments to the Constitution were submitted by Congress September 25, 1789, and were ratified by three fourths of the states by December 15, 1791.

APPENDIX C

Fourteenth Amendment: Section 1

All persons born or naturalized in the United States, and subject to the jurisdiction thereof, are citizens of the United States and the States wherein they reside. No state shall make or enforce any law which shall abridge the privileges or immunities of citizens of the United States; nor shall any State deprive any person of life, liberty, or property, without due process of law; nor deny to any person within its jurisdiction the equal protection of the laws.

The Fourteenth Amendment was drawn up in 1866, ratified in late June 1868, and went into effect the following month.

APPENDIX D

Treaty of Guadalupe Hidalgo

The civil rights guaranteed by the treaty as signed by the United States and Mexico reads as follows:

ARTICLE IX

The Mexicans who, in the territories aforesaid, shall not preserve the character of citizens of the Mexican Republic, conformably with what is stipulated in the preceding article [this refers to their right to remain Mexican citizens or become U.S. nationals], shall be incorporated into the Union of the United States and be admitted at the proper time (to be judged by the Congress of the United States) to the enjoyment of all the rights of citizens of the United States according to the principles of the Constitution; and in the mean time shall be maintained and protected in the free enjoyment of their liberty and property, and secured in the free exercise of their religion without restriction.

The article as originally written read as follows:

ARTICLE IX

The Mexicans who, in the territories aforesaid [territories previously belonging to Mexico], shall not preserve the character of citizens of the Mexican Republic, conformably with what is stated in the preceding Article, shall be incorporated into the Union of the United States, and admitted as soon as possible, according to the principles of the Federal Constitution, to the enjoyment of all the rights of citizens of the United States. In the mean time, they shall be maintained and protected in the enjoyment of their liberty, their property, and the civil rights now vested in them according to the Mexican laws. With respect to political rights, their condition shall be on an equality with that of the inhabitants of the other territories of the United States; and at least equally good as that of the inhabitants of Louisiana and the Floridas, when these provinces, by transfer from the French Republic and the Crown of Spain, became territories of the United States.

The rest of the article as originally written dealt with the Roman Catholic Church, its property, and its personnel.

APPENDIX E

Acronyms

ACCPE, American Coordinating Council of Political Education
ACLU, American Civil Liberties Union
ADA, Americans for Democratic Action
AFL-CIO, American Federation of Labor–Congress of Industrial Organizations
AFT, American Federation of Teachers
AGIF, American G.I. Forum
AHA, Alianza Hispano-Americana
AID, Agency for International Development
ANMA, Asociación Nacional México-Americana
ASARCO, American Smelting and Refining Company
AWOC, Agricultural Workers Organizing Committee
BFA, Bilingual Foundation of the Arts
CAP, Community Action Patrol
CASA, Centro de Acción Social Autónoma
CASAC, Citizenship Association Serving All Citizens
CAWIU, Cannery and Agricultural Workers Industrial Union
CCC, Civilian Conservation Corps
CCOSSP, Cabinet Committee on Opportunities for Spanish Speaking People
CFIC, Colorado Fuel and Iron Company
CHC, Congressional Hispanic Caucus
CIO, Congress of Industrial Organizations
CMAA, Council of Mexican American Affairs
CMAU, Congress of Mexican American Unity
CNN, Cable News Network
COPS, Communities Organized for Public Service

CPLC, Chicanos por La Causa

CRLA, California Rural Legal Assistance

CSO, Community Service Organization

EEOC, Equal Employment Opportunity Commission

FAIR, Federation for American Immigration Reform

FBI, Federal Bureau of Investigation

FEPC, Fair Employment Practices Committee

FHA, Federal Housing Administration

FLOC, Farm Labor Organizing Committee

HEW, Department of Health, Education, and Welfare

HUD, Department of Housing and Urban Development

IA-CMAA, Inter-Agency Committee for Mexican American Affairs

IAF, Industrial Areas Foundation

ILGWU, International Ladies Garment Workers Union

IMAGE, Incorporated Mexican American Government Employees

IMAGE, Involvement of Mexican Americans in Gainful Endeavors

INS, Immigration and Naturalization Service

IRCA, Immigration Reform and Control Act of 1986

LACL, Latin American Citizens League

LAFTA, Latin American Free Trade Association

LRUP, La Raza Unida Party

LULAC, League of United Latin American Citizens

MACC, Mexican American Cultural Center

MAD, Mexican American Democrats of Texas

MALC, Mexican American Liberation Committee

MALCS, Mujeres Activas en Letras y Cambio Social

MALDEF, Mexican American Legal Defense and Educational Fund

MAM, Mexican American Movement

MANA, Mexican American Women's National Association

MAPA, Mexican American Political Association (California)

MAPA, Mexican Americans for Political Action (Texas)

MASA, Mexican American Student Association

MASC, Mexican American Student Confederation

MAUC, Mexican American Unity Council

MAYO, Mexican American Youth Organization

MEChA, Movimiento Estudiantil Chicano de Aztlán

NAACP, National Association for the Advancement of Colored People

NALEO, National Association of Latino Elected and Appointed Officials

NCCHE, National Chicano Council on Higher Education

NCHAC, National Congress of Hispanic American Citizens

NCLR, National Council of La Raza

NCRLC, National Catholic Rural Life Conference

NDEA, National Defense Education Act

NEA, National Education Association

NFWA, National Farm Workers Association

NLRB, National Labor Relations Board

NMU, National Miners Union

NOMAS, National Organization of Mexican American Services

OEO, Office of Economic Opportunity

PADRES, Padres Asociados para Derechos Religiosos, Educativos, y Sociales

PASSO/PASO, Political Association of Spanish-Speaking Organizations

PAU, Pan American Union

SNCC, Student Non-Violent Coordinating Committee

SVREP, Southwest Voter Registration Education Project

TELACU, The East Los Angeles Community Union

TFWU, Texas Farm Workers Union

TUUL, Trade Union Unity League

UCAPAWA, United Cannery, Agricultural, Packing, and Allied Workers of America

UCB, University of California, Berkeley

UCLA, University of California, Los Angeles

UFW, United Farm Workers

UMAS, United Mexican American Students

UNESCO, United Nations Educational, Scientific, and Cultural Organization

UNICEF, United Nations International Children's Emergency Fund

UNO, United Neighborhood Organization

USC, University of Southern California

USSR, Union of Soviet Socialist Republics

VA, Veterans Administration

WPA, Works Progress Administration

YMCA, Young Men's Christian Association

APPENDIX F

Notes on Spanish Pronunciation

A	as in f*a*ther: paso, arte, alma
E	as in m*e*sa: peso, estilo
I and Y	as in mach*i*ne and org*y*: piso, Díos, Ynez
O	as in s*o* and n*o*te: pozo, olmo; OO (rare) is pronounced long O
U	like oo in m*oo*n and m*oo*t: puso, unido (NEVER like U in mute) Between G and E or I not pronounced, as in guest, guide, guerrilla
C (+A, O U or + a con- sonant)	as in *c*at and *c*lear: cama, como, cura, cual, clamor, acción
C (+ E or I)	as in *c*ertain: centro, cero, hacer, decir
Ch	as in *ch*urch: chocolate, leche, churro (Ch is no longer considered a separate letter in Spanish)
G (+A, O, U or a conso- nant)	as in *g*ate: Garcia, golfo, gusano, amigo, gracias The G in the GUA combination is pronounced so softly by some that it sounds almost like wa: Guadalupe, guayabera
G (+E or I)	like hard H in *h*ag, *h*og, *h*ug: gente, ingeniero, gitano, agitar
H	not pronounced, as in *h*eir: hijo, hotel, herencia, humano
J	like hard H in *h*ot, *h*ag: José, Guadalajara
LL	like LLI in mi*lli*on but with low stress on the L part of the sound: calle, llano

Ñ	like NI in *oni*on and NY in ca*ny*on: cañon, España, tamaño, ñame
QU	like K in *k*ite [or the QU in quay (këy)]: querida, quetzal, Quito
S	like SS in mi*ss*: mesa, Jesús, rosa, asistir
X	before a consonant like English S: extraño; intervocally like X in e*x*it: éxito
Z	like SS in ki*ss*: zona, zapata, mestizo

The remaining consonants are pronounced approximately as in English.
As for stress, in general:

Words ending in a vowel, N, or S are stressed on the next-to-last syllable.

Words ending in all other letters are stressed on the last syllable.

Words that do not follow these two rules carry written accent marks.

Capital letters are often not marked with a written accent.

Index

Page numbers set in **boldface** indicate the location of a main entry.

About the Authors

MATT S. MEIER is Patrick A. Donohoe, S. J. Professor Emeritus at Santa Clara University. A pioneer in researching and teaching the history of Mexican Americans, his earlier books include *Notable Latino Americans: A Biographical Dictionary* (Greenwood, 1997), *Mexican American Biographies* (Greenwood, 1988), the update of Carey McWilliams's *North from Mexico* (1990), *Dictionary of Mexican American History* (Greenwood, 1981), and *The Chicanos* (1972).

MARGO GUTIÉRREZ is Mexican American and Latino Studies librarian and bibliographer at the Nettie Lee Benson Latin American Collection, University of Texas, Austin. She is the coauthor of *The Border Guide* (1992).